PURE

U C135 PD=
OLUMBIA SOCAR
PR 19 236P
TTORNEY THURGOOD MARSHALL NAACP=

317P

Rcd. APR 19 1948
Rfd. to
Ack.

D.O.

=CONGRATULATIONS FOR YOUR OUTSTANDIN
ICTORY IN OPENING THE DEMOCRATIC PRIMARIES TO NEGROES IN S
CAROLINA IT IS THE NEW EMANCIPATION TO THOUSANDS OF NEGROE
CAROLINA RAISING THEM TO FIRST CLASS CITIZENSHIP=

UNEXAMPLED COURAGE

UNEXAMPLED COURAGE

THE BLINDING OF SGT. ISAAC WOODARD

AND THE AWAKENING OF

PRESIDENT HARRY S. TRUMAN AND

JUDGE J. WATIES WARING

RICHARD GERGEL

SARAH CRICHTON BOOKS
Farrar, Straus and Giroux
New York

Sarah Crichton Books
Farrar, Straus and Giroux
175 Varick Street, New York 10014

Library of Congress Cataloging-in-Publication Data
Names: Gergel, Richard, author.
Title: Unexampled courage : the blinding of Sgt. Isaac Woodard and the awakening of
    President Harry S. Truman and Judge J. Waties Waring / Richard Gergel.
Description: First edition. | New York : Sarah Crichton Books ; Farrar, Straus and
    Giroux, 2019. | Includes bibliographical references and index.
Identifiers: LCCN 2018021690 | ISBN 9780374107895 (hardcover : alk. paper)
Subjects: LCSH: Waring, Julius Waties, 1880–1968. | Woodard, Isaac, 1919–1992—
    Trials, litigation, etc. | African Americans—Civil rights—United States—History—
    20th century. | African Americans—Violence against—South Carolina—History—
    20th century.
Classification: LCC E185.61 .G377 2019 | DDC 323.1196/073—dc23
LC record available at https://lccn.loc.gov/2018021690

Designed by Richard Oriolo

Our books may be purchased in bulk for promotional, educational, or
business use. Please contact your local bookseller or the Macmillan
Corporate and Premium Sales Department at 1-800-221-7945, extension
5442, or by e-mail at MacmillanSpecialMarkets@macmillan.com.

www.fsgbooks.com
www.twitter.com/fsgbooks · www.facebook.com/fsgbooks

1   3   5   7   9   10   8   6   4   2

ENDPAPER PHOTOGRAPHS: (*Clockwise, from top left*) *Briggs v. Elliott* plaintiffs: Alex M. Rivera
Collection, J. E. Shepard Memorial Library, NCCU Archives, Records and History Center;
Isaac and Sarah Woodard: Special Collections and Archives, Georgia State University Library;
Thurgood Marshall: Cecil J. Williams; Truman meets Walter White: Courtesy of the
South Caroliniana Library, University of South Carolina, Columbia, S.C.; voter registration:
Alex M. Rivera Collection, J. E. Shepard Memorial Library, NCCU Archives, Records
and History Center; telegram: Library of Congress, NAACP Collection, *Elmore v. Rice* File;
Isaac Woodard: J. DeBisse, Library of Congress, Prints & Photographs Division,
Visual Materials from the NAACP Records (LC-USZ62-128327); Charleston federal
courthouse: Alex M. Rivera Collection, J. E. Shepard Memorial Library,
NCCU Archives, Records and History Center; J. Waties Waring:
Courtesy of the South Caroliniana Library, University of South Carolina, Columbia, S.C.

TO BELINDA

CONTENTS

Introduction: A Collision of Two Worlds   3

PART I: THE BLINDING

1. A Tragic Detour   9
2. A Wave of Terror   24
3. "The Place Was Batesburg"   38
4. The Bystander Government   48

PART II: THE AWAKENING

5. "My God . . . We Have Got to Do Something"   63
6. The Isaac Woodard Road Show   84
7. The Gradualist   93
8. A "Baptism in Racial Prejudice"   114

PART III: THE CALL TO ACTION

9. "I Shall Fight to End Evil Like This"   135
10. "We Know the Way. We Need Only the Will."   160
11. Confronting the American Dilemma   171
12. There Will Be No Fines   189
13. Fighting the "Battle Royal"   200
14. Driving the "Last Nail in the Coffin of Segregation"   221

Conclusion: Unexampled Courage   249

APPENDIX: A FORENSIC ANALYSIS OF THE BLINDING OF ISAAC WOODARD   271

NOTES   275

ACKNOWLEDGMENTS   305

INDEX   309

UNEXAMPLED COURAGE

INTRODUCTION:
A COLLISION OF TWO WORLDS

THE UNITED STATES emerged from World War II in ascendency, having conquered Nazi Germany and imperial Japan. Looking over a war-ravaged world, American leaders sought to remake foreign governments in America's own image, as democracies committed to individual liberty and human rights. But beneath the veneer of America's grand self-image was a stark reality: African Americans residing in the old Confederacy lived in a twilight world between slavery and freedom. They no longer had masters, but they did not enjoy the rights of a free people. Black southerners were routinely denied the right to vote, segregated physically from the dominant white society as a matter of law, and relegated to the margins of American prosperity.

African Americans living in other regions of the country faced their own racial challenges. This gaping chasm between the ideal world envisioned by white Americans and the real world experienced by black Americans represented, as the Swedish economist and social scientist Gunnar Myrdal put it, "a moral lag in the development of the nation" and "a problem in the heart of America."[1]

Seen from today's perspective, the American triumph over Jim Crow segregation and disenfranchisement might seem to have been inevitable, the collapse of morally indefensible practices wholly inconsistent with the U.S. Constitution. But in 1945, with southern state governments resolutely committed to the racial status quo and the federal government largely a passive bystander, there was no obvious path to resolving this great American dilemma. Something had to be done, but what, and by whom?

On February 12, 1946, Sergeant Isaac Woodard, a decorated African American soldier, was beaten and blinded in Batesburg, South Carolina, by the town's police chief on the day of his discharge from the U.S. Army and while still in uniform. The brutality and injustice of Woodard's treatment encapsulated the angst and outrage of the nation's 900,000 returning black veterans, who felt their service in defense of American liberty was not appreciated. Soon, protests and mass meetings in response to the Woodard incident were held in black communities across America. Civil rights leaders demanded federal action to hold the police officer accountable for Woodard's brutal treatment and to protect the rights of the nation's black citizens from racial violence. Demands for action soon reached the doorstep of the new president, Harry S. Truman, and placed him in the crosswinds of Roosevelt's disparate New Deal coalition, which included southern segregationists and newly emerging black voters in critical swing states outside the South. Although counseled by his staff and political allies to stay away from divisive civil rights issues, Truman responded to the Woodard blinding by directing his excessively cautious Department of Justice to act. Within days, the department charged Lynwood Shull, the police chief of Batesburg, with criminal civil rights violations and began the process of establishing the first presidential committee on civil rights, to address the widespread reports of violence against returning black veterans. Truman's civil rights committee would, within the year, issue a report recommending a bold civil rights agenda, culminating in Truman's historic executive order in July 1948 ending segregation in the armed forces of the United States.

The Justice Department's prosecution of Shull before an all-white jury in the federal district court in Columbia, South Carolina, resulted in the police chief's quick acquittal. But the jury's failure to hold the obviously culpable police officer accountable profoundly troubled the presiding judge, J. Waties Waring, and sent him on a personal journey of study and reflection on race and justice in America. Within months following the Shull trial, Waring began issuing landmark civil rights decisions, then unprecedented for a federal district judge in the South. Despite blistering public denunciations, death threats, and attacks on his home, Waring persisted in upholding the rule of law in his Charleston, South Carolina, courtroom, including his 1951 dissent in a school desegregation case, *Briggs v. Elliott*, in which he declared government-mandated segregation a per se violation of the Fourteenth Amendment. Three years later, a unanimous U.S. Supreme Court would adopt Waring's reasoning and language in *Brown v. Board of Education*, destroying the legal foundation of Jim Crow segregation.

While conducting research for this book, I came across a statement attributed to the legendary civil rights leader Julian Bond in which he asserted that the Isaac Woodard incident ignited the modern civil rights movement. Intrigued, I contacted Bond in September 2014 to hear his explanation of that statement. I shared with him the connection of the Woodard incident to the racial awakening of President Truman and Judge Waring and asked if that was the basis of his statement. Bond explained that while my research tended to confirm his statement, he had meant to express the belief that the tragic circumstances of Woodard's blinding had inspired a generation of African Americans to action. He then recalled from memory the story of Woodard's blinding and described a photograph he remembered from his childhood. As Bond described the image, he began to weep openly over the telephone. Composing himself, he apologized for his tears but stated that after all these years "I still weep for this blinded soldier."[2]

The power of the Isaac Woodard story moved people of goodwill to act in the postwar era and still had the force to move Julian Bond to tears nearly seventy years later. In the end, Woodard's blinding would open the eyes of many Americans, black and white. This is a story that deserves to be told, with all its pathos, its brutality, and its redemption of the American system of justice.

THE BLINDING

1.

A TRAGIC DETOUR

A S THE CLOCK struck 7:00 p.m. on August 14, 1945, President Harry S. Truman assembled the White House press corps in the Oval Office. The ebullient president, standing behind his desk, informed the reporters that earlier that afternoon the Japanese government had unconditionally surrendered, bringing an end to World War II. The reporters spontaneously burst into applause and then raced for the door, to share this historic announcement with the rest of the nation. Thousands gathered in Lafayette Square across from the White House to celebrate, and soon there were calls of "We want Truman! We want Truman!" The president came onto the North Portico of the White House to make a few remarks. "This is a great day," Truman declared, "the day we've been waiting for. This is the day for free governments in the world. This is the day that fascism and police government ceases in the world. The great task ahead [is] to restore peace and bring free government to the world."[1]

Over the ensuing months, millions of American soldiers returned home. Among them were nearly 900,000 African Americans who believed that their service and sacrifices in the defense of American liberty might provide them with their rightful place in America's "free government." While black soldiers had been assigned to segregated units and frequently given the most menial tasks, their wartime service afforded them opportunities for education, leadership, and recognition. Many of those serving in Europe had experienced respectful treatment from local citizens and realized the possibility of living in a world where skin color was not the defining characteristic of one's life. And many returning black soldiers, regardless of where they had served, were resolved to no longer acquiesce in the indignities of racial segregation and disenfranchisement that had characterized their prewar lives.

However, the stark reality was that three-fourths of the black veterans were coming home to communities in the old Confederacy. This was the world of Jim Crow, where black citizens were relegated to the margins of American democracy and expected to be the bootblacks and mudsills of the nation's economy.

Beginning in the 1890s, southern state and local governments started adopting a vast number of what came to be known as Jim Crow laws mandating segregation in almost every aspect of civic life. These statutes and ordinances were validated by the U.S. Supreme Court's 1896 decision in *Plessy v. Ferguson*, which upheld a Louisiana law *requiring* racially segregated railway cars. In the years following *Plessy*, laws were adopted requiring racial separation in factories, parks, public transportation, hospitals, restaurants, and even cemeteries. The clear message was that black citizens were not fit to be in the presence of white people except as maids, laborers, and yardmen.

The widespread adoption of these Jim Crow laws followed the election of a new generation of racial demagogues across the South, a generation bent on defeating the old planter class that had long controlled southern politics and promising the complete subjugation of black citizens. Once they were in power, state legislatures under their control moved swiftly to adopt a vast array of laws to prevent African Americans from voting. Black disenfranchisement was accomplished through an endless variety of tricks and devices denying access to the ballot, including "grandfather clauses," poll taxes, "understanding clauses," literacy requirements, all-white party primaries, and old-fashioned terror and intimidation. Despite the protection of the Fifteenth Amendment of the U.S. Constitution guaranteeing that the "right of citizens of the United States to vote shall not be denied or abridged . . . on account of race, color, or previous condition of servitude," the U.S. Supreme Court in the 1898 decision of *Williams v. Mississippi* upheld various Mississippi state constitutional provisions that effectively disenfranchised all black voters in the state.[2]

The clash between the expectations and demands of returning black veterans and the unforgiving racial practices of the Jim Crow South would soon produce widespread conflicts.[3] Although the Jim Crow system sought to maintain the separation of the races, encounters between blacks and whites were a daily reality of southern life. Public transportation, including buses, trains, and trolleys, was shared, but strict rules governed where blacks could sit and when they must relinquish their seats to white customers. Many black servicemen and recently demobilized soldiers resented and resisted these Jim Crow practices, and public transportation became a flash point for racial tensions.

In July 1944, Booker T. Spicely, an African American private on leave from Camp Butner, was shot and killed in the nearby town of Durham, North Carolina, by a bus driver after he refused to relinquish his seat to a white passenger. That same month, Second Lieutenant Jack Roosevelt Robinson had a confrontation with a civilian bus driver in Killeen, Texas, near Camp Hood, when he refused an order to move to the back of the bus. Lieutenant Robinson faced a general court-martial over the incident but was acquitted after a full trial. Americans would come to know the young lieutenant three years later by his nickname, Jackie Robinson, when he broke the color line of Major League Baseball.

As African American soldiers in large numbers returned stateside in early 1946, reports of racial incidents on public transportation increased. One soldier stationed at Fort Jackson in Columbia, South Carolina, refused in February 1946 to sit at the back of the bus as directed by the driver. When the driver ordered him off the bus, the soldier cursed the driver. Several white passengers followed the black serviceman off the bus, attacked him, and broke his jaw. In another incident that year, an African American corporal, Marguerite Nicholson, was arrested in Hamlet, North Carolina, after she refused to move to a segregated car once her train crossed into the segregated South. She was beaten by the local police chief in the course of her arrest, spent two days in jail, and was fined $25. A black airman stationed at a base near Florence, South Carolina, was arrested because he sat next to a white woman on a bus.[4]

———

On the cool winter night of February 12, 1946, Isaac Woodard Jr. climbed aboard a Greyhound bus in Augusta, Georgia, on his last leg home to Winnsboro, South Carolina, from a journey that had begun in the Philippines several weeks before. Woodard, who was twenty-six years old, had just completed an arduous three-year tour in the U.S. Army, where he served in the Pacific theater, earned a battle star for unloading ships under enemy fire during the New Guinea campaign, and won promotions, ultimately to the rank of sergeant. One of nine children of Sarah and Isaac Woodard Sr., he was born on March 8, 1919, on a farm in Fairfield County, South Carolina. The county was an impoverished, majority-black community in the central part of the state. The Woodard family, as landless sharecroppers, was on the lowest rung of what was essentially a feudal society. The family struggled to subsist, and the Woodard children frequently worked in the fields rather than attend school. Isaac junior quit school at age eleven, after completing the fifth grade, and left home at fifteen in search of relief from the family's crushing poverty. His mother would later observe that Fairfield County whites, who owned virtually all of the land and wealth of the community, did not "think of a Negro as they do a dog. Looks as if all they want is our work."

Woodard worked in North Carolina for a number of his early adult years, doing $2-a-day construction jobs, laying railroad tracks, delivering milk for a local dairy, and serving in the Civilian Conservation Corps. As World War II approached and it appeared likely he would be inducted into the armed forces, he returned to Fairfield County and briefly took a job at a local sawmill, Doolittle's Lumber, while he awaited his induction notice. He worked as a "log turner," a backbreaking and dangerous job that earned him but $10 a week. Because they faced such dismal employment options, it is not surprising that despite the perils of service in the armed forces, Woodard and many other African Americans residing in the rural South viewed military service as a promising alternative.[5]

Woodard entered service at Fort Jackson, South Carolina, on October 14, 1942, as a private and did his basic training in Bainbridge, Georgia. He was a member of the 429th Port Battalion, which shipped out in October 1944 for New Guinea, where he served as a longshoreman, loading and unloading military ships in the Pacific. The New Guinea campaign was a multiyear battle by the Allies, mostly Australians and Americans, to recapture New Guinea Island from a deeply entrenched Japanese army. The campaign involved some of the most arduous and intense fighting of the war, and all armies suffered significant casualties. The Allies ultimately prevailed through a series of dramatic water landings devised by General Douglas MacArthur.

Isaac Woodard was part of a segregated support unit during the major New Guinea maritime landing operations, and his unit took intense enemy fire and casualties as they performed critical operations. He showed solid leadership and won promotions to technician fifth grade, equivalent to the rank of corporal, and later technician fourth grade, equivalent to the rank of sergeant. He received the American Campaign Medal, the Asiatic-Pacific Campaign Medal, and the World War II Victory

Medal. As the army demobilized, Woodard was given an honorable discharge notice and traveled from Manila to the United States by troopship, arriving in New York on January 15, 1946. After transport by troop train to Camp Gordon, Georgia, he was discharged nearly a month later, on February 12.[6]

Now, a little more than three years after joining the army, Woodard was returning home with sergeant stripes on his sleeve and battle medals on his chest. Although at five feet eight inches and 143 pounds he was not a large and imposing man, his military service as a longshoreman had left him in top physical condition. Upon discharge, he was taking the Greyhound bus from Augusta, Georgia, to Columbia, South Carolina, and ultimately to Winnsboro, the seat of Fairfield County. There he was to be reunited with his wife, Rosa Scruggs Woodard, after several years of separation.

⸻

The Greyhound bus on which Woodard traveled was mostly filled with recently demobilized soldiers still in uniform who had been discharged only hours earlier from Camp Gordon. They were in a jovial mood as the bus progressed in the darkness through the small towns on its route— first to Aiken and then to the even smaller communities of Edgefield, Johnston, Ridge Spring, and Batesburg—with black and white soldiers mixing and socializing on the bus in a manner that likely made the few white civilian passengers and the white bus driver uncomfortable. The events that would transpire that fateful evening, both on and off the bus, would later be the subject of great dispute, but what is clear is that Sergeant Woodard displayed a degree of assertiveness and self-confidence that most southern whites were not accustomed to nor prepared to accept.

According to Woodard's later account, his troubles that evening began with an angry exchange of words with the bus driver, Alton Blackwell. Woodard stated that he approached the driver during what was to be a brief stop to ask if he could step off the bus to relieve himself. Buses during this era did not have restroom facilities, and Greyhound drivers were instructed that any request by a passenger to step off the bus should be accommodated. According to Woodard, Blackwell responded, "Hell, no. God damn it, go back and sit down. I ain't got time to wait." Woodard stated that he responded to the driver, "God damn it, talk to me like I am talking to you. I am a man just like you." He stated that Blackwell then reluctantly told him to "go ahead then and hurry back." Woodard stepped off the bus and quickly returned without further words with the driver.[7]

Blackwell later described a distinctly different set of events in his encounter with Woodard. He claimed that his disagreement with Woodard arose initially from the soldier's repeated requests to leave the bus to relieve himself during what were scheduled to be brief stops in various small communities. According to Blackwell, these frequent exits by Woodard put the bus behind schedule for its arrival in Columbia, where many of the passengers were making connections. Blackwell would later claim that he detected the odor of alcohol on Woodard and observed him drinking from a bottle of whiskey and then passing the bottle to a white soldier sitting next to him. As the evening progressed, Blackwell asserted that Woodard became increasingly intoxicated, profane, and disruptive. He claimed that after a white civilian passenger complained to him about Woodard's conduct, he resolved to have the soldier removed from his bus at the next stop, which was in Batesburg, South Carolina. Apparently then unconcerned about staying on schedule, he exited the bus in search of a police officer to have Woodard removed.[8]

Subsequent investigative interviews and sworn testimony of other passengers on the Augusta-to-Columbia bus offered conflicting accounts regarding Woodard's behavior on the bus. Two soldiers, one black and one white, gave FBI agents sworn statements that they saw Woodard (and other soldiers) drinking on the bus, but both denied that Woodard was in any way disruptive. One civilian witness, a white woman, later stated that Woodard and a white soldier were sitting together, drinking, and "using language not becoming to a gentleman [that] should not be used in the presence of a lady." No witness ever corroborated the bus driver's claim that Woodard left the bus at every stop.[9]

Batesburg was a small town of several thousand people, approximately half black and half white, nestled in the western portion of Lexington County, about thirty miles from Columbia, the state capital. It was an oddly situated town immediately adjacent to another small town and rival, Leesville, with their town business districts only approximately a hundred yards apart. As in most small southern rural communities of that era, whites controlled essentially all aspects of economic and political life, and blacks, disenfranchised and mostly impoverished, lived marginal existences and sought to avoid any conflict with the ruling white establishment.

Batesburg's two-man police force was headed by Lynwood Shull, then forty years old, who had served as the department's chief for nearly eight years. Unlike two of his brothers, Shull did not serve in the military during World War II. He was five feet nine inches tall, with blue eyes and gray-streaked brown hair. He tipped the scales at well over two hundred pounds and was sliding into middle-age obesity. He wore his police uniform essentially all the time, changing into a suit only for Sunday morning services at the local Methodist church. The Shull family was politically connected: Lynwood's father had at one time served in a patronage position as supervisor of a local prison farm. Later, when an investigator from the National Association for the Advancement of Colored People (NAACP) began looking into the Woodard incident, local African Americans privately expressed fear of the Shull family, citing incidents of excessive force by Chief Shull against black citizens and abusive actions by his father while running the prison farm.[10]

Blackwell found Chief Shull with a younger officer, Elliot Long, sitting nearby in the town's one patrol car. He reported that he had two soldiers, one black and one white, who were drunk and disorderly and he wanted them off his bus. The driver then climbed back onto his bus and informed Woodard he had someone who wanted to speak to him. Woodard complied, and as he exited the bus, the driver told Chief Shull that "this soldier has been making a disturbance on the bus." As Woodard later recounted, he tried to explain to Shull his exchange with the bus driver, in which he was cursed by the driver and told to return to his seat when he asked for the opportunity to relieve himself. Before he could complete his explanation, Woodard stated, Shull removed a baton from a side pocket, struck him across his head, and told him to "shut up." A black soldier sitting on the bus, Lincoln Miller, later gave the FBI an affidavit stating that he observed an officer "pull a black jack out of his pocket and hit Woodard over the head with it." A white soldier, Jennings Stroud, told the FBI he saw a policeman "hit the colored fellow a fairly good lick which did not knock him down, but seemed to show the colored fellow [his] authority."[11]

Shull's statements and testimony about when he first struck Woodard with his blackjack were inconsistent and would become a focus of attention at later criminal and civil trials. In Shull's initial interview with FBI agents, he stated he first struck Woodard with his police-issued blackjack after walking a considerable distance from the bus stop and in response to the soldier's allegedly refusing to continue walking with him to the city jail. Later, he changed his story and admitted that he "may have" struck Woodard with his blackjack at or near the bus stop, as observed by the two soldiers interviewed by the FBI.[12]

Law-enforcement officers during this era routinely carried blackjacks, which were baton-type weapons, generally leather, with shotgun pellets or other metal packed into the head and with a coiled-spring handle. These devices were so common that most police uniforms came with a "blackjack pocket" along the pants leg. A leather strap at the base of the blackjack allowed an officer to secure the device to his wrist. The coiled-spring handle produced tremendous energy and a whipping force in the head of the device, which from time to time resulted in devastating injuries or death when an officer struck a citizen in the face or head. In an early 1990s federal appellate court decision, the court quoted expert testimony indicating that a blow from a blackjack to the head was "potentially lethal and . . . universally prohibited."[13] Shull's blackjack strike to Woodard's head near the bus stop that February evening—variously described as a "tap," a "punch," and a "good lick"—immediately quieted Woodard's efforts to explain himself.

After striking Woodard in the head, Shull placed the sergeant under arrest and began escorting him to the town jail several blocks away. To secure him, Shull twisted Woodard's arm behind his back and pushed him down one of Batesburg's main streets, Railroad Avenue, and then right onto Granite Street to the jail. Shull left his other officer, Elliot Long, to question the supposedly drunk and disorderly white passenger, whom the driver was never able to reliably identify.

As the police chief and the soldier proceeded toward the town jail and out of sight, Woodard reported that Shull asked him whether he was discharged from the army. Woodard said that when he replied "yes," Shull immediately struck him again on the head with the blackjack. The correct answer, Shull informed the soldier, was "yes, sir." Woodard responded by grabbing the blackjack from Shull and wrenching it away. At that moment, in Woodard's telling, Officer Long appeared with his gun drawn. Drop your weapon, he told Woodard—or "I will drop you."

Woodard reported that when he complied with Long's directive and allowed the blackjack to fall to the ground, Shull retrieved it and began to angrily beat him in the head and face. Woodard stated that he lost consciousness and lay on the ground for an unknown period of time. When he came to, Shull instructed him to stand up. As Woodard struggled to his feet, he reported, Shull struck him violently and repeatedly in one eye, and then the other, with the end of the blackjack, driving the baton "into my eyeballs." The force used by Shull was so great that it broke his blackjack. Woodard stated he was then dragged into the town jail and placed in a cell, where he was the only prisoner present. Shortly thereafter, Shull and Long left for the evening, with Woodard in a semiconscious haze.[14]

In his various statements and trial testimony, Shull denied beating Woodard repeatedly with his blackjack or driving the end of the weapon into his eyes but offered varied accounts regarding the number of times he struck him, the location where the strikes occurred, and the circumstances leading to the use of the blackjack. When first confronted about the incident by an Associated Press reporter, Shull stated that the soldier attempted to take his blackjack and he "cracked him across the head." In his initial FBI interview, Shull claimed that he "bumped" Woodard with the baton after he refused to continue walking to the city jail. He claimed that after this "bump" with the blackjack, Woodard tried to wrench the weapon from his hand and, in self-defense, he struck Woodard a single time in the face with the blackjack. Later, Shull stated that while they were walking to the jail, Woodard "suddenly grabbed" the blackjack without any provocation, and he struck Woodard with the weapon once in self-defense. When confronted with these inconsistencies under cross-examination, Shull admitted he might have struck Woodard with his blackjack on three occasions: at the bus stop, while walking to the jail, and when Woodard attempted to take the blackjack from him.[15]

Shull denied that he beat Woodard into unconsciousness and left him dazed in the town jail overnight. Instead, he claimed that after striking Woodard with his blackjack one time outside the jail, he was able to move the soldier into a cell without further incident. He stated that Woodard voiced no complaints that evening about his eyes and was in good health when Shull left the jail. He also denied that Officer Long was present for any of his altercation with Woodard, which Long affirmed.[16]

When Woodard woke the next morning, he could not see. He had been awakened by Shull, who informed him he was due in city court that morning. This presented several practical problems. Woodard reported he was unable to see and needed assistance to move from one place to another. Further, the brutal beating of the night before had left his face covered with dried blood, which he could not see or remove without help. Shull led Woodard to the sink and cleaned him up for his court appearance. Then, said Woodard, Shull guided him to the city court to face a charge of drunk and disorderly conduct.

Woodard's case was called by the Batesburg town judge, H. E. Quarles, who also served as the town's mayor. Woodard attempted to explain to the judge the circumstances that had led to his conflict with the bus driver and with Chief Shull. Shull stepped in to inform Quarles that Woodard had attempted to take his blackjack on the way to the jail. Quarles responded by stating that "we don't have that kind of stuff down here" and promptly found Woodard guilty. Woodard was given a fine of $50.00 or "30 days hard labor on the road." He attempted to locate the money to pay the fine but had only $44.00 in cash and a check from the army for mustering-out pay of $694.73. According to Woodard, he wanted to endorse the check to pay the fine but was incapable of doing so because "I had never tried to sign my name without seeing." The judge ultimately agreed to suspend the balance of the fine and accept payment of $44.00.[17]

Shull's account of the morning differed. He denied that Woodard said he could not see, although one eye appeared "swelled practically shut" and the other was "puffed." He claimed Woodard was able to negotiate himself over to the city court without assistance and could see sufficiently to count out the money in his pocket. According to Shull, when his case was called, Woodard stated he was guilty and "guessed he had too much to drink." Judge Quarles would later testify that Woodard was able to see while in the city court that morning and that he pleaded guilty to the charge of drunk and disorderly conduct. Later medical evaluations of Woodard's eye injuries made Shull's and Quarles's claims that Woodard could see that morning implausible if not medically impossible.[18]

With his court hearing completed and having paid the fine, Woodard was free to go. But according to Woodard, he was blind and incapable of navigating independently. He returned to the jail to lie down on a cot, telling Shull he felt ill. Shull attempted to locate the town physician, W. W. King, to see Woodard but was told the doctor was on a house call. Confronted with a prisoner who claimed he could not see as a result of traumatic injuries, and unable to obtain the assistance of a physician, Shull seemed at a loss for what to do next. One account had him repeatedly pouring water on Woodard's eyes and asking after each application, "Can you see yet?" Shull testified he went to the town pharmacist for advice and was told to apply eyewash and warm towels until King arrived. He followed this advice, but Woodard did not improve.[19]

King showed up later that afternoon. He found both of Woodard's eyes "badly swollen," and when he opened the lids, "there was an escape

of bloody fluid." Although he prepared no medical record of his examination, he later testified that Woodard's injuries were confined exclusively
to his eyes, with swelling only over the eyelids and nose. He concluded
that Woodard "had serious damage to both eyes" and "was badly in
need of a specialist." He recommended that Shull immediately transport
Woodard to the Veterans Administration Hospital in Columbia, some
thirty miles away. In compliance with King's instructions, Shull loaded
Woodard into the town's police vehicle and drove him to the VA Hospital,
telling the on-call physician that evening that Woodard had suffered his injuries as a result of an encounter with a police officer after being arrested
for drunk and disorderly conduct.[20]

Woodard was initially evaluated by the medical officer on duty,
Major Albert Eaddy, who had trained as a psychiatrist. Eaddy immediately
appreciated that Woodard's condition was wholly beyond his expertise.
Because the VA Hospital had no eye specialist, he summoned the ear,
nose, and throat specialist, Captain Arthur Clancy, to Woodard's bedside.
Clancy observed that both of Woodard's eyelids were black and blue and
swollen, and there was massive hemorrhaging inside each eye. He was
then able to determine that Woodard's right cornea was lacerated. He did
not note any other injuries that were visible in that initial examination.
He would later diagnose Woodard with a rupture of his right globe and
massive intraocular hemorrhaging to both eyes. He also indicated that
Woodard's remaining vision was "nil" and that there was no available
treatment for his condition.[21]

Woodard was seen the following morning, February 14, by Dr. Mortimer Burger, an internist, who conducted a full physical examination.
Burger documented a history of Woodard's having been beaten on the head
by a police officer and knocked unconscious. He noted that Woodard's
eyelids were moderately swollen and tender, with a thick coat of pus and
bloody material. When he pulled back the soldier's eyelids, he observed
hemorrhaging of the eyeballs. He also documented the presence of dried
blood over Woodard's right ear and swelling on the forehead and on the
upper portions of his cheek. He noted that there was swelling over the

nose but no gross deformities; a skull X-ray confirmed the absence of any fracture to the nose. Thus, Burger's initial examination suggested that Woodard had suffered facial and head trauma greater than would be expected from a single strike by a blackjack. Because Woodard had bilateral blindness and lacked any fracture of the facial or nasal bones, a fair question was how Woodard could have been blinded in both eyes from a single strike of a blackjack.[22]

Woodard remained at the VA Hospital for the next two months and was treated with antibiotics and other medications related to the traumatic injuries to his eyes. There was no treatment offered or recommended that would restore his vision. Upon his discharge on April 13, Woodard was diagnosed with bilateral phthisis bulbi "secondary to trauma," which meant he had two shrunken, nonfunctioning eyes as a result of his encounter in Batesburg. The VA physicians determined that he was totally and permanently blind, unable to discern light sufficiently to tell when a 60-watt bulb was on or off. Woodard's discharging doctors offered him no hope for future treatment and could only recommend that he attend a school for the blind.[23]

While Woodard was hospitalized, VA staff applied for VA disability benefits on his behalf. But there was a major complication: Woodard had been discharged around 5:00 p.m. from Camp Gordon, Georgia, approximately five hours before suffering his disabling injury. Although he was still in uniform and had not yet reached home, VA rules at the time disqualified him from full benefits and limited him to partial disability benefits of $50 per month. (This denial of full pension benefits would later become highly controversial but would not be rectified for more than fifteen years, when Congress finally amended the law to allow full service-related disability for a soldier who suffered a disabling injury while traveling home after discharge from the military.)[24]

As Woodard convalesced in the VA Hospital, his wife, Rosa, then living in Winnsboro, showed little interest in continuing their relationship. According to a Woodard family member, Rosa did not look forward to a future life with a disabled husband. Like many southern black families,

Woodard's parents and siblings had moved north during the war in search of greater economic opportunities, and the entire family now resided together in New York City. When Woodard was finally discharged from the hospital, two of his sisters traveled to South Carolina to gather up their blinded brother and bring him to the new family home at 1100 Franklin Avenue in the Bronx.[25]

Life was a struggle for Woodard. He complained to his mother, "My head feels like it's going to burst [and] my eyes ache." He fumbled around the home, having no training for independent living as a blind person. His mother prayed nightly for some relief for her son, lamenting that a loss of a leg or arm would have been less devastating than the loss of sight.[26]

The Woodard family resolved to seek specialized evaluation and treatment in the newly emerging field of ophthalmology to determine if there was any potential treatment for Isaac. Dr. Chester Chinn, America's first African American ophthalmologist, examined Woodard in his Manhattan office on April 25, 1946. He determined that the structural injuries to Woodard's eyes were more extensive than diagnosed by the VA physicians, finding that Woodard had suffered traumatic ruptures of both globes. This made any prospect for recovery essentially nonexistent. Chinn also diagnosed Woodard with "bilateral phthisis bulbi of traumatic origin" and rated his prognosis "hopeless." For Sergeant Isaac Woodard, now twenty-seven, blinded, unemployed, abandoned by his wife, and limited to a VA pension below subsistence level, "hopeless" might have seemed an apt prognosis of his life ahead.[27]

2.

A WAVE OF TERROR

ORLD WAR II was a transformative moment in American history,
when the nation shed its isolationist instincts and emerged as the
unquestioned leader of the free world. The defeat of Nazism and fascism
did not bring about the hoped-for world of international collaboration
and peace. Instead, a new and threatening cold war developed between
the United States and the Soviet Union. Out of the vacuum of a war-
torn Europe and Asia, Stalinist Russia sought to promote itself as the
champion of emerging nations against colonialism and capitalism. The
United States advocated the exportation of American democracy and
human rights, hoping to create a new world order in its own image.

But the American self-image as the champion of human dignity and
equality confronted the reality of this nation's treatment of its black citi-

zens. Each lynching or other incident of racial violence was widely reported on the world stage as America's adversaries pointed to the glaring
gap between this nation's declared values and the realities of Jim Crow
and black disenfranchisement. As Dean Acheson, then undersecretary of
state, observed in May 1946, "The existence of discrimination against minority groups in the United States is a handicap to our relations with
other countries."[1]

During the war, African American newspapers and civic organizations aggressively promoted a link between racial progress at home and
military victory abroad. In February 1942, *The Pittsburgh Courier*, the
largest-circulation black-owned newspaper in the United States, began
the "Double V" campaign, which advocated the twin victories of an end
to discrimination at home and military conquest overseas. Week after
week, the *Courier* featured stories that advocated making "democracy
real" by ending Jim Crow practices and reported widespread endorsement of the campaign by various national organizations and local "Double V" clubs. A "Double V" logo was produced and widely distributed to
the paper's subscribers. This campaign sought to avoid the disappointment experienced by black veterans after World War I, when many soldiers returned from military service to confront widespread racial
violence and overt hostility from their white neighbors.[2]

As the war ended, civil rights leaders recognized that some recent
progress had been made and sought to build upon these successes. Roosevelt's New Deal programs, while segregated, were racially inclusive, an
important departure from the practice in southern states of directing
government resources and programs primarily to white citizens. As the
South Carolina civil rights activist Modjeska Simkins observed, Roosevelt "took the jug by the handle. He tried to give the people who were
down and had nothing something . . . It was a shot in the arm for the
Negroes."

Although many black leaders appreciated President Roosevelt's in-
clusion of African Americans in New Deal programs, and admired the
public and private actions of Eleanor Roosevelt, they understood that

there were certain lines FDR would not cross. This reflected Franklin Roosevelt's delicate dance to maintain his disparate New Deal coalition, which included black leaders committed to equal rights and southern elected officials determined to maintain the racial status quo. NAACP leaders were particularly frustrated with Roosevelt's unwillingness in the 1930s to lend a hand in breaking Senate filibusters over anti-lynching legislation, which Roosevelt concluded would be defeated regardless of his public position and might jeopardize his otherwise strong support from southern legislators for the New Deal. Roosevelt did issue an important executive order in 1941 creating the Fair Employment Practices Committee to combat discrimination in the defense industry, which avoided a threatened march on Washington led by the civil rights leader A. Philip Randolph. With Roosevelt's death, on April 12, 1945, and the assumption of the presidency by Vice President Harry Truman, civil rights leaders hoped that the new leader might be more willing to publicly embrace their cause.[3]

Truman was not a newcomer to the issue of civil rights. As a U.S. senator from Missouri, he had voted for the creation of a permanent federal employment practices commission, signed a petition in 1938 to stop a filibuster attempting to defeat anti-lynching legislation, and supported legislation to ban the poll tax. His consistent support for civil rights legislation was a natural consequence of his political origins as an ally of Tom Pendergast, the Kansas City political boss whose machine relied on loyal support from the city's black wards. In explaining his vote for anti-lynching legislation, Truman told a southern colleague that "the Negro vote in Kansas City and St. Louis is too important" to vote otherwise.

Truman's progressive civil rights record stood in some contrast with his personal prejudices. He differentiated between "political equality," by which he meant the government's duty to treat all citizens equally regardless of race, and "social equality," which were code words for racial integration. Thus, Truman was able to reconcile in his own mind a passionate support for fair and equal treatment for all citizens while continuing to harbor some racial views more typical of those held at the time by his neighbors in southern Missouri.[4]

Shortly after assuming office, Truman scheduled a meeting in the Oval Office with the NAACP's executive secretary, Walter White, sending a subtle but unmistakable message to the civil rights community. White was then the preeminent civil rights leader in America, and his career was already the stuff of legend. He went to work for the NAACP in 1918 and soon made a name for himself with his detailed reports from the field on lynchings and other incidents of racial violence. White's fair complexion, blond hair, and blue eyes allowed him to pass as Caucasian. He frequently interviewed witnesses and participants in lynchings, with his subjects volunteering information to the presumed white reporter. When the NAACP's executive secretary, James Weldon Johnson, retired in 1929, White succeeded him. By the time Truman assumed the presidency in 1945, White had become a critical link between the national Democratic Party leadership and the civil rights community.[5]

Early in his first year in office, Truman and his advisers determined that the emerging African American presence in major cities outside the South made black voters potentially important players in the 1946 congressional elections and in the 1948 presidential election. Many northeastern Republican elected officials, including Governor Thomas Dewey of New York, also appreciated the importance of black urban voters and had positive civil rights records. Truman's advisers understood that while black voters had broadly supported Roosevelt in the past three elections, there was no guarantee that his Democratic Party successor would enjoy such loyalty. Moreover, they recognized that any major slippage in the support of black voters could be fatal to the Democratic Party's efforts to maintain control of Congress and the presidency.[6]

NAACP leaders were also encouraged by their victory in an important 1944 voting rights decision, *Smith v. Allwright*. By an 8–1 vote, the Supreme Court had declared unconstitutional the Texas Democratic Party's all-white primary. This was no small win, because the only election that then mattered in the South was the Democratic primary. Because blacks were excluded from the primary, on the premise that the Democratic Party was a "private club" that could deny membership to anyone it wished, the few blacks allowed to register and vote in the South were relegated to meaningless participation in the general election. Beyond the importance of the specific holding in *Smith v. Allwright*, the willingness of an overwhelming majority of the U.S. Supreme Court justices to strike a state law limiting black voting rights suggested that a new, more sympathetic attitude now prevailed in the highest court of the land. This stood in stark contrast to Supreme Court decisions of an earlier era that had given southern states the green light to adopt laws mandating segregation and disenfranchisement.

The association's impressive victory in *Smith v. Allwright* brought added attention and prestige to the thirty-five-year-old chief counsel of the NAACP's Legal Defense Fund, Thurgood Marshall. He had joined the NAACP's legal staff soon after his 1933 graduation from Howard University Law School, where he had been number one in his class. He was mentored by Charles Hamilton Houston, the NAACP's brilliant chief counsel and the dean at Howard Law School. Marshall proved to be a natural leader, revered by local NAACP counsel for having a "mind like a machine gun," deep knowledge of emerging legal trends and developments, and an uncanny talent as a storyteller. When Houston relinquished the chief counsel position in 1940, Marshall was his obvious successor. Marshall adopted Houston's highly disciplined and successful practice of careful case selection, meticulous development of the factual record, and strategic building of one case precedent on top of another. This approach would produce a run of major Supreme Court victories for the Legal Defense Fund, culminating in the unanimous decision in *Brown v. Board of Education* in 1954.[7]

Soon after the *Smith* decision, Truman's attorney general, Tom Clark, personally lobbied southern political leaders to voluntarily comply with the Supreme Court's order by allowing blacks to vote in the Democratic primary. With the exception of Georgia and South Carolina, all southern states agreed, at least officially, to allow black voters to participate. This avoided what would have been a highly divisive and politically damaging legal battle across the South to enforce the Supreme Court's decision in *Smith*. A federal district court in Georgia, following the clear mandate of *Smith v. Allwright*, ordered the Georgia Democratic Party to allow black voters to participate in the 1946 Democratic primary. With only South Carolina holding out on the white primary issue, progress on the voting front, even in the Deep South, seemed finally to be made.[8]

Beyond these positive developments, there was an unmistakable resolve among many returning black veterans to chart a new path on civil rights. The war experience had produced a dynamic for change that could not be suppressed by the conventional methods of intimidation and violence. This new spirit of activism was reflected in the exponential growth of NAACP membership—from a prewar level of fifty thousand to more than half a million members by 1945.[9]

As black veterans returned to their home communities, they began to encounter open hostility to any signs of resistance to long-standing racial practices. Reports of incidents of racial violence and even murder began coming into the NAACP's national offices and the U.S. Department of Justice, and the volume grew in the early months of 1946, surprising and alarming both civil rights advocates and members of the Truman administration. It quickly became clear that southern resistance to changes in the racial status quo was unaffected by the war experience and the service of African American soldiers. Local and state governments in the South did not pursue criminal prosecutions in this new wave of racial violence, and civil rights groups urged the Truman administration to take immediate action to protect the constitutional rights of black Americans victimized by mob violence.

A number of the racial attacks drew national attention and became the focus of mass meetings and letter-writing campaigns demanding government action and protection. The first of these attacks was the blinding of Isaac Woodard, which occurred on February 12, 1946. However, the

Woodard blinding did not promptly come to the attention of the NAACP, because there were initially no reports from local leaders or the press about the incident.

Nearly two weeks after the Woodard incident, on February 25, 1946, racial violence erupted in Columbia, Tennessee, when a black veteran, James Stephenson, complained about shoddy work performed by a local business in repairing his mother's radio. A white employee did not like Stephenson's attitude and struck him. Stephenson, a former member of the U.S. Navy boxing team, responded with a series of blows, sending the white employee through the store's plate-glass window. Matters quickly escalated as local ruffians pronounced Stephenson's actions a threat to local order and plans were made to lynch him. Stephenson and his family were secreted out of town as a white mob, led by local law-enforcement officers, entered the town's black community in an effort to seize Stephenson. Black residents responded with a volley of gunfire, striking at least four police officers. Hours later, a large contingent of Tennessee state highway patrolmen, led by what a Justice Department official later described as "a thoroughly brutal character," entered the area with machine guns, "shooting wildly" into homes and businesses. The state police ransacked black-owned businesses, stole jewelry and cash, and wrote "KKK" on coffins in a black-owned funeral home. One patrolman shouted, "You black sons of bitches had [your] way last night, but we are going to have ours this morning." Dozens of black men were arrested, and two were shot and killed while in police custody.

Controversy over the Columbia, Tennessee, incident swirled across the nation. Black leaders described the event as a "white riot" and sought federal government protection and intervention. Local white politicians asserted that the state law-enforcement response was justified because of the attack and the injuries to white officers. Thurgood Marshall appeared on the scene to represent the black defendants and described the police conduct as "true storm trooper fashion." The Truman administration sent in FBI agents and Justice Department lawyers to pursue civil rights claims against the state police officers and members of the white mob who had ransacked black homes and businesses, but they were unable to persuade an all-white federal grand jury to indict any white person involved in the incident. Walter White denounced the grand jury's failure to act and warned that federal inaction had sent a signal to Klan members across the South that they could "terrorize the Negro community . . . without fear of federal interference."[10]

As the Tennessee story broke in the national press, local civil rights activists in South Carolina received a report that there was a black soldier at the Columbia VA Hospital who had had his eyes "beaten out" by a police officer. John McCray, who edited the local black newspaper, *The Lighthouse and Informer*, and often did double duty as an investigator for the NAACP, was dispatched to follow up. McCray reported that a soldier by the name of Isaac Woodard Jr. had been pulled off a Greyhound bus while still in uniform, arrested, and beaten by a police officer with a black-jack until he was unconscious and blinded. Woodard told McCray, mistakenly, that the incident occurred in Aiken, South Carolina. McCray's written report was relayed to the national NAACP office and eventually landed on the desk of Walter White.

The McCray report lacked a number of critical details. Woodard did not know the name of his assailant, and his account of the assault was somewhat complicated. McCray reported that Woodard would soon be discharged from the VA Hospital and would be heading to the Bronx to join his family. The NAACP arranged to have Woodard come into the national office for an interview with its legal staff when he arrived in New York.

On April 23, 1946, ten days after his discharge from the VA Hospital, Isaac Woodard walked into the NAACP's national office for an in-depth interview. He met with Franklin Williams, a recently hired NAACP attorney who had graduated from Fordham Law School less than a year earlier. After conducting the interview, Williams drafted an affidavit setting forth the details of the sergeant's removal from the bus, assault, and blinding. The affidavit stated that Woodard had departed by bus from Atlanta after his discharge from Camp Gordon and that the assault had occurred about an hour and a half later in Aiken, South Carolina. Williams, a native of Queens, New York, and Woodard, formerly a resident of Fairfield County, South Carolina, apparently did not realize that Atlanta was not particularly close to Camp Gordon and that Aiken was farther from Atlanta than suggested in Woodard's affidavit. Woodard's confusion about the town he had departed from (which was Augusta, Georgia, not Atlanta) and the location of his assault (which was Batesburg, South Carolina, not Aiken) would later be a source of controversy as the story emerged in the national media.[11]

As the Woodard affidavit circulated in the NAACP's national office, it became clear that the incident might generate significant national attention. The image of a returning uniformed and decorated African American sergeant being beaten and blinded on his day of discharge from military service seemed to capture in one incident the gravity and injustice associated with this new wave of violence. The primary difficulties in promoting the story were that Woodard could not identify his attacker by name and that initial inquiries by national staff to local NAACP leadership in Aiken did not produce any evidence to support Woodard's account.

The NAACP's national staff appreciated that the organization's recent surge in membership, particularly from returning veterans, demanded an activist voice in defense of the victims of mob violence. The Woodard story, if it could be verified, was potentially a powerful weapon to educate the public and to promote federal action to protect the civil rights of returning black veterans. Robert Carter, the top assistant to Thurgood Marshall, urged the South Carolina NAACP president, James Hinton, to pursue the story vigorously. Marshall personally followed up with a letter to Hinton on April 30, 1946, stating that the association needed a "full report re Isaac Woodard, Jr. case . . . at earliest date." The NAACP's plan was, in Marshall's words, to "blast the whole story out into the open" as soon as sufficient facts were developed.[12]

Walter White wrote to Robert Patterson, secretary of war, on May 6, 1946, informing him of the Woodard incident. White provided the secretary with a copy of the Woodard affidavit and referred to the incident as "one of the most vicious cases of mistreatment of a veteran we have come across." White asked Secretary Patterson to conduct a full departmental investigation into the matter and requested that the investigators be "chosen with care to assure that the full facts will be developed." Patterson responded to White's letter six weeks later, on June 17, declaring that the War Department had no jurisdiction over the matter because Woodard was "a civilian at the time of the incident."[13]

After receiving a brush-off from the secretary of war, and with South Carolina officials showing not the slightest inclination to investigate the incident, the NAACP began a major public relations campaign around Woodard's blinding. The association issued a formal press release on July 17, 1946, demanding a full investigation by the Justice Department and the prosecution of the person responsible for Woodard's injuries. What's more, a $1,000 reward was offered for the arrest and conviction of the policeman who "brutally beat and blinded" Woodard. Friendly reporters were provided with the Woodard affidavit and given other background information. Soon provocative headlines such as "Negro Vet Tells How Dixie Cops Gouged Out Both Eyes with Club" and "Veteran's Eyes Gouged Out by Hate Crazed Dixie Police" were carried in major black and liberal northern newspapers.[14]

The initial press reports of the Woodard incident prompted numerous letters of outrage and anguish to the White House, the Department of Justice, the War Department, and the NAACP. Many of the letters were from distressed black veterans. One wrote to President Truman expressing his alarm that a returning veteran "is not permitted to travel in his own native country . . . without being beaten unmercifully and deprived of his eyes. I could hardly keep from shedding tears as I read this report." One of the black vets wrote that he "didn't go overseas to fight the Japs and Germans" to be treated "so unjust and cruel" at home. A letter to the editor of *The Washington Post* expressed shock that "the most terrible of all wars has taught some people absolutely nothing."[15]

The outpouring of public support for Woodard exceeded the NAACP's expectations. After some articles referenced his home address, strangers showed up unannounced offering support to the blinded veteran, creating a chaotic situation around the Woodard household.[16] The NAACP convened a meeting of various labor, veterans', and civil rights organizations on July 24, 1946, to rally support for full pension benefits for Woodard. Meanwhile, Walter White sent a letter to all NAACP branch presidents across the country urging them to organize mass meetings, print placards, and write to President Truman and various other government officials seeking a full investigation and pension benefits for Woodard.[17]

As the Woodard story began to capture attention in the national press, reports of vicious race-baiting emerged in the Georgia gubernatorial campaign pitting the former governor Eugene Talmadge against a racially moderate ally of the outgoing governor, Ellis Arnall. Talmadge promised, if elected, to restore the party's all-white primary and warned black voters not to attempt to vote in the upcoming Democratic primary. Talmadge won the July 17, 1946, primary election despite losing the popular vote to the more moderate candidate because Georgia's county unit voting system required the winning candidate to carry a majority of the state's counties.

The day after the Georgia primary, a black veteran, Maceo Snipes, had unexpected white visitors to his home. The previous day Snipes had reportedly been the only black man who dared to vote in Taylor County, Georgia, a rural community ninety miles south of Atlanta. Snipes believed that as an American veteran who had fought for his country, he was entitled to vote. He was shot at the front door of his home and died several days later. Terrorized by the incident, his relatives buried his body in an unmarked grave, and many family members then fled the county in fear of further retribution. Although Snipes's death certificate indicated his death was a homicide, no one was ever prosecuted.[18]

Just days after the Snipes shooting, an even more violent racial incident occurred in rural Georgia. The saga began when a black farmhand, Roger Malcolm, got into a dispute with his white employer, allegedly because of sexual advances the man had made toward Malcolm's pregnant wife. In the midst of what became a physical altercation, Malcolm stabbed the white employer with a knife. Malcolm was arrested and placed in the local jail in Monroe, Georgia. He was soon released from jail, likely orchestrated by individuals seeking to inflict their own version of private justice on him. Malcolm sought refuge at the home of a prominent white farmer for himself, his wife, and his sister-in-law and her husband, George Dorsey, a recently discharged veteran. A large white mob, which included local law-enforcement officers, intercepted the two couples at an isolated rural bridge known as Moore's Ford. Roger Malcolm and George Dorsey were removed from the vehicle in which they were traveling and marched into the woods for execution. The two women reacted hysterically, and one of them called out the name of a white member of the mob, begging for mercy for the men. Apparently realizing that they were leaving witnesses behind, the mob took the two women with their husbands. The four were taken into the woods and shot sixty-six times. The victims were virtually unrecognizable, and Roger Malcolm was castrated. One of the ringleaders later explained that the execution of George Dorsey was necessary because "until George went into the army, he was a good nigger. But when he came out, they thought they were as good as any white people."

There was widespread outrage as the story of the Moore's Ford massacre was reported across the national media in the late summer of 1946. President Truman and Attorney General Clark promised a thorough investigation, and Governor Arnall offered a $10,000 reward for information leading to the conviction of the perpetrators. Local ministers denounced the massacre as "an outrage against humanity." Two local assistant U.S. attorneys were promptly dispatched to the scene. They reported that the sheriff stated he had no idea who had committed these crimes. Based on this less than thorough investigation, the government lawyers indicated they could not see how any federal laws had been violated.

President Truman was furious about this inept federal response and ordered a full FBI investigation into the incident. Despite the presence of a dozen FBI agents, numerous witness interviews, and the offer of a large cash reward for information, not one local white person cooperated with the efforts to prosecute the perpetrators of the Moore's Ford murders. An all-white federal grand jury issued no indictments, although the names of many of the members of the mob were known to law enforcement and civil rights groups. As Attorney General Clark stated, "We just couldn't get any citizens there to give us information, although we know they have it." Walter White harshly criticized the federal investigation and observed that the Moore's Ford murders were the "inevitable result of Talmadge's and the Ku Klux Klan's advocacy of violation of the laws of the federal government and human decency."[19]

Shortly after the Moore's Ford massacre, in August 1946, yet another incident of racial violence was reported, this time from Minden, Louisiana. Two black men, John C. Jones, an army veteran, and his seventeen-year-old cousin, Albert Harris, were arrested for allegedly prowling in the backyard of a white woman and placed in the local jail. Jones had previously been identified by some whites as "an uppity nigger," apparently because he had spoken out against what he believed to be an unfair land transaction involving his grandfather. After several days of being held without charges, Harris and Jones were released on August 8. A white mob was waiting as they departed the jail. The two men were dragged into waiting cars and beaten. Harris was pistol-whipped and thrown out of the vehicle on the side of the road, apparently thought to be dead. Jones was struck repeatedly with a meat cleaver and burned with a blowtorch, then left to die. Harris awoke from his beating just in time to hear his older cousin cry out in pain from the torture and managed to get himself home. His family spirited him out of the state, and he eventually agreed to cooperate with federal law-enforcement officials in the prosecution of those who had murdered Jones. Despite Harris's eyewitness identification of the culprits, who included two local law-enforcement officers, the men were acquitted by an all-white Louisiana federal jury.[20]

The level of rage and violence involved in these widely reported incidents, and the failure to obtain a single conviction holding the perpetrators accountable, brought passionate demands that the federal government take a stand to protect the lives and safety of its black citizens. In each of these incidents, a wall of silence existed in the communities, with essentially no white person willing to step forward. In the midst of this emotional debate about the lack of accountability for the perpetrators of racial violence, the story of Isaac Woodard's blinding fully emerged in the national press. Surely, civil rights leaders argued, the federal government could hunt down and prosecute the single police officer who had beaten and blinded this returning uniformed American veteran on the day of his discharge. But Woodard had been beaten and blinded by a white police officer in the Jim Crow South, and it soon became clear that nothing about vindicating the rights of a victim of racial violence in 1946 would be simple or easy.

3.

"THE PLACE WAS BATESBURG"

THE SURGE OF VIOLENCE against returning black veterans and the absence of any meaningful response by southern state and local prosecutors made it clear to the national leadership of the NAACP that any real progress in the area of civil rights in the South would require the active engagement of the federal government. Disenfranchisement rendered the sizable African American population in the South politically impotent, and southern elected officials, almost to a person, were resolutely committed to rigidly maintaining the racial status quo.

NAACP leaders understood that the federal government was not a monolith under the control of a single person. The legislative branch was under the sway of long-serving southern legislators, who used their seniority and the filibuster to bottle up the Congress, even when there was widespread public support for such measures as anti-lynching legislation. While the judicial branch was beginning to show the first signs of receptiveness to civil rights issues, any significant progress in the courts was a long-term project. But with Harry Truman as president, civil rights leaders, most notably Walter White, were convinced that the right application of pressure and political support might persuade Truman to act to advance the cause of civil rights.

In the postwar world, the NAACP needed to create a more robust communications operation to spread its message, publicize incidents of racial injustice, and galvanize its membership into action. Because most Americans were now receiving their news and entertainment over the radio, it was essential that the NAACP increase its presence on the airwaves, through both national radio programs and local radio stations.

As the NAACP staffed up its operations, Walter White persuaded Oliver "Ollie" Harrington to leave his position with *The Pittsburgh Courier* to head the association's newly created public relations department. Harrington attended the Yale School of Art and became renowned as the creator of a popular cartoon series in the black press, known as *Bootsie*. During World War II, he served as a war correspondent for *The Pittsburgh Courier* in Europe and North Africa and garnered considerable recognition and stature for his frontline reports. Although Harrington would work for the NAACP for only a year, he was able to modernize its public relations operations and devoted most of his efforts to publicizing the story of the blinding of Isaac Woodard.[1]

The initial efforts to promote the Woodard story in the black press and with liberal northern newspapers were successful to a point, but White and Harrington searched for ways to make it a major national story. They turned their attention to a new weekly program broadcast on ABC Radio featuring the legendary radio and movie personality Orson Welles. Welles became a national sensation in 1938 when he produced and starred in a national radio broadcast of H. G. Wells's *War of the Worlds*. Although the broadcast repeatedly stated that it was fictional, the Welles presentation was so compelling that there was widespread hysteria that America was being invaded by Martians. Welles was then only twenty-three years old. Three years later, in 1941, he co-wrote, directed, and starred in *Citizen Kane*, which was nominated for nine Academy Awards. Walter White was personally acquainted with Welles and viewed him as an ally and advocate of the civil rights movement.

Welles's new radio program, *Orson Welles Commentary*, focused on contemporary political and social issues. Despite its high-sounding name and its creator's acclaim, the program lacked focus and direction. Welles was in dire need of topics and issues that might provoke controversy and create a national audience for his show.

On July 24, 1946, Orson Welles received a hand-delivered letter from Walter White detailing the blinding of Isaac Woodard. While the NAACP "had many horrible cases pass through this office," White wrote, there was "never one worse than this," and he enclosed in the letter an affidavit signed by Woodard describing his beating and blinding. White further informed Welles he sought his assistance "to publicize and get action on this case."[2]

Welles instantly recognized the drama associated with Woodard's blinding as well as the whodunit quality of the story, because Woodard's attacker had not yet been identified. He invited Walter White and Ollie Harrington to meet him the following day at the Adelphi Theatre in New York, where he was then producing the musical version of *Around the World in Eighty Days*. Welles told White and Harrington he was ready to "begin the fight immediately." He declared it his mission to identify the unknown law-enforcement officer who had blinded Woodard and to bring him to justice.[3]

Just three days after meeting with White and Harrington, and apparently without any independent corroboration of the information provided by the NAACP, Welles led off his July 28, 1946, national radio program quoting from Woodard's affidavit. Delivered with Welles's remarkable talent for dramatic inflection and tone, the narrative was both compelling and tragic. The details of Woodard's beating and blinding were shared in devastating detail. Welles assumed the role of crusader and avenger, addressing his comments to Woodard's unknown attacker, whom he dubbed "Officer X": "We invite you to luxuriate in secrecy, it will be brief. Go on. Suckle your anonymous moment while it lasts. You're going to be uncovered! We will blast out your name! We'll give the world your given name, Officer X . . . We're going to make it public with the public scandal you dictated but failed to sign."[4]

The Woodard affidavit contained, however, errors of geography, and those errors were repeated by Welles in his broadcast. Woodard was under the impression that the town where he was assaulted was Aiken, South Carolina, a small resort town near the Georgia–South Carolina state line. But in fact, he had been beaten and arrested in Batesburg, South Carolina, some twenty-eight miles away. Welles's broadcast identified Aiken as the city of Woodard's attack, comparing it to the Nazi concentration camp at Dachau, and he declared that Woodard's assertion of freedom in Aiken "cost a man his eyes."[5]

The response to the national radio broadcast was electric. The NAACP and various federal government agencies were flooded with messages of concern and protest from black citizens, many of them veterans. The power of the public airwaves, particularly when the story was delivered by an unparalleled talent like Orson Welles, galvanized the civil rights community across the country and brought widespread demands that Woodard's attacker be identified and prosecuted for his actions.

Things became complicated when the city fathers of Aiken vigorously denied that Woodard had been attacked in their town and demanded that Welles retract his story. Aiken's mayor, Odell Weeks, wrote to Welles, telling him that a careful search of town records failed to reveal any evidence of an attack on Woodard. Mayor Weeks observed that it was "indeed unfortunate that you did not fully verify this story before you broadcast it." The police chief of Aiken, J. M. Sprawls, ordered the local theater to cease showing a Welles movie then running, and police officers burned posters promoting the movie. Town leaders also discussed suing Welles for defamation.[6]

The NAACP received reports shortly after Welles's first broadcast that questioned the accuracy of Woodard's statement that he had been beaten in Aiken. Lincoln Miller, who had earlier been interviewed by the FBI as a witness to Woodard's arrest, sent a letter to the national office of the NAACP on July 30, 1946, stating that he had been on the bus with Woodard and had observed a police officer strike the sergeant with a blackjack. Miller stated that the town where the attack took place was Batesburg, not Aiken. Shortly thereafter, on August 8, Miller was interviewed by the South Carolina NAACP's general counsel, Harold Boulware, and confirmed in a sworn statement that Woodard was taken off the bus in Batesburg. The national NAACP office also received letters from local association members in Aiken casting further doubt on Aiken as the location of Woodard's attack.[7]

In his next weekly radio broadcast, on August 4, Welles acknowledged the complaints of Aiken's mayor and noted he had conflicting information from town leaders and Woodard. He indicated he had sent investigators to South Carolina to sort out the issue and recognized it was possible that Woodard was mistaken about the location of his attack. Welles stated that it was possible the "soldier might easily have made a mistake, but there's a man in a policeman's uniform who made a worse mistake." Never short on bravado, Welles invited the mayor to "join with me in a manhunt," if for no other reason than to clear the good name of his town.[8]

Behind the public display of self-confidence, both Welles and the NAACP were intensely embarrassed about the error. Robert Carter, Thurgood Marshall's top assistant, was deeply involved in the efforts to locate the town where Woodard had actually been beaten. In one communication with Harold Boulware, Carter explained, "Frankly, Boulware, we are over the barrel about this whole Woodard incident, and it is necessary that we get more definite information on where it occurred or else we will be placed in a very unhappy situation as well as those people who went out on a limb with us."[9]

While controversy swirled over the location of Woodard's blinding, Welles's broadcasts drew the attention of a more ominous opponent,

Congressman John E. Rankin of Mississippi, the chairman of the House Committee on Un-American Activities and an outspoken segregationist. On August 7, Rankin wrote to J. Edgar Hoover complaining that Welles's broadcasts were "highly inflammatory and extremely dangerous." Rankin urged Hoover to "secure a copy" of the July 28 broadcast and "look it over." Hoover responded in a letter, dated August 12, 1946, informing Rankin he had referred the congressman's letter to Assistant Attorney General Theron Lamar Caudle "in order that the Criminal Division of the Department of Justice may review and give consideration to the substance of the broadcast."[10]

Just when it looked as if the Woodard story was about to be discredited, the investigative efforts of the NAACP and Welles's staff began to pay off. On August 14, Ollie Harrington sent Welles a telegram informing him that "our investigators find evidence pointing to Batesburg, S.C. as the place where Woodard attack occurred" and that the FBI privately confirmed this information. On August 17, an Associated Press reporter, likely tipped off by the NAACP, confronted Batesburg's police chief, Lynwood Shull, and asked if he had been involved in the Woodard attack. Shull acknowledged that he had, admitting, "I hit him across the front of his head" and "cracked him across the head" when Woodard attempted to grab his blackjack. A day later, on August 18, Welles referred to these breaking developments during his weekly broadcast and promised to address the story fully the next week.[11]

The following Sunday, August 25, an exuberant Welles opened his radio broadcast with these dramatic words: "This is Orson Welles speaking. The place was Batesburg. Isaac Woodard thought it happened in Aiken. He was wrong . . . The blame belongs . . . in Batesburg. Batesburg, South Carolina." Welles then described the work of his investigators in locating a minister and several workmen who had observed the police chief of Batesburg and a highway patrolman pouring "buckets of water over the head and body of a soldier." Welles reported the officers were "washing away" blood and between each pouring asking the soldier, "Can you see yet?" According to Welles, he simply responded no. That soldier was Isaac Woodard.

But Welles was not finished. He explained that when he brought the Woodard story to national attention, "the name of the guilty policeman was unknown and it looked as though it always would be. I promised to get that name, I have it now." Welles then dramatically disclosed to his national audience the name of Woodard's attacker:

> All clues led to Mr. L. L. Shull, chief of police in Batesburg, South
> Carolina. Now we have him. We won't let him go. I promised I'd
> hunt him down. I have. I gave my word I'd see him unmasked.
> I've unmasked him. I'm going to haunt Police Chief Shull for all
> the rest of his natural life. Mr. Shull is not going to forget me. And
> what's important, I'm not going to let you forget Mr. Shull.[12]

The public disclosure of Shull's identity by Orson Welles on national radio generated widespread demands that Shull face criminal prosecution under federal civil rights laws. Welles received thousands of letters about the broadcasts and hundreds of requests for copies of his transcripts. Welles's biographer Simon Callow described the Woodard radio broadcasts as the "single most effective political action of [Welles's] life."[13]

The importance of identifying the officer responsible for Woodard's beating and blinding is hard to overstate. In all other prominently reported incidents of racial violence then under investigation, a wall of silence was erected that made the prosecution of the perpetrators difficult. In the Woodard incident, the perpetrator was identified, and civil rights activists across the country demanded justice for the blinded veteran. The absence of any federal enforcement action in the other widely publicized racial crimes gave special force to the demand for action in the Woodard case.

As the Woodard incident emerged as a major national story, various organizations spontaneously stepped forward to promote and support the blinded veteran. Some groups undertook independent fund-raising efforts, and others invited Woodard to public meetings to share his story. The NAACP struggled to manage the situation, viewing Woodard and his story as under the organization's exclusive control. But by this point, it was like trying to put lightning in a bottle as Woodard emerged as a living martyr for the cause of equal justice.

The most notable of the independent efforts was undertaken by the *Amsterdam News*, a black-owned, New York–based weekly newspaper with a circulation exceeding 100,000. The paper's publisher, Dr. C. B. Powell, had trained as a physician but turned his considerable talents to business in the 1930s. By the mid-1940s, Powell was one of the most successful black entrepreneurs in the nation and was devoted to the cause of civil rights. He used his newspaper as a bully pulpit and was moved by the plight of Isaac Woodard.

Powell took personal charge of a benefit concert on Woodard's behalf, which he hoped would financially assist the blinded veteran and raise public consciousness about the incidents of mob violence being reported across the South. Powell's organizational skills and high standing in the black community were soon on public display as he announced the newspaper's plan for the benefit concert. Co-chairs of the event included the world heavyweight champion Joe Louis and New York's mayor, William O'Dwyer. The lineup of performers included Cab Calloway, Carol Brice, and Nat King Cole. In an August 9, 1946, press conference promoting the concert, Joe Louis stated, "This is the kind of thing I like to be involved in because I am always in my people's corner." Not thinking small, the newspaper announced that it had arranged to use the city-owned Lewisohn Stadium in Harlem for the benefit concert.

The public response was extraordinary. The entire twenty-three-thousand-seat stadium was sold out, and an estimated ten thousand people were turned away. The crowd roared approval as W. C. Handy's orchestra performed "St. Louis Blues" and Cab Calloway performed "Hi-De-Ho." In an original song, "The Blinding of Isaac Woodard," Woody Guthrie sang, "I thought I fought on the islands to get rid of their kind, but I see the fight a lot plainer now that I am blind." The audience response, Guthrie would later say, was the greatest he ever received as an entertainer.

But the loudest applause of the evening was reserved for Woodard, who spoke to the crowd in a "faltering voice," expressing his deep appreciation for the outpouring of support on his behalf. Woodard told the hushed audience that he wanted to see "that justice is done" regarding the police officer who had blinded him. Although not a skilled orator, he was a powerful, living symbol of racial injustice, a man who had devotedly served his country in wartime only to be blinded in the rural South because of the color of his skin. As one reporter observed, Woodard's "simple speech . . . caused many to cry—people who have long been hardened to the ways of life, and the injustices heaped on a persecuted minority."[14]

The Woodard benefit concert was a resounding financial and community success. Over $10,000 was raised (approximately $130,000 in today's dollars) for the blinded veteran, which allowed him to purchase a home. The benefit concert was trumpeted by the *Amsterdam News* as a "racial milestone" because the "entire affair was conceived, promoted and executed by Negroes" and reflected a united effort by the black community to "stop talking and do something." In a column likely written by Powell, the community was urged to bring "the same singleness of treatment as characterized the effort to help Woodard" to attack the "torment and torture of lynching and violence in the South."[15]

The efforts of the NAACP, the *Amsterdam News*, Orson Welles, and others to promote Woodard's story were clearly part of a larger effort to address the numerous incidents of racial violence reported across the South in 1946. With the heightened public attention and outrage over these incidents, the NAACP convened a meeting of forty civil rights, religious, and labor organizations to "plan joint action" on the "wave of terror" and "rising tide of mob violence . . . in South Carolina, Georgia, Mississippi and other states." The organizations participating included the American Federation of Labor (AFL), the Congress of Industrial Organizations (CIO), the American Civil Liberties Union, the American Jewish Congress, the Federal Council of Churches, and the National Urban League. The groups resolved to organize an umbrella organization known as the National Emergency Committee Against Mob Violence, whose primary purpose would be to persuade the "full force of the federal government to bring the lynchers before the bar of justice."[16]

The new organization established a smaller executive committee of major civil rights leaders with the objective of immediately setting up meetings with President Truman and Attorney General Clark to reengage the federal government as a protector of the rights of its African American citizens. In this effort, the National Emergency Committee sought nothing less than the reversal of the federal government's role as a passive bystander to the denial of the constitutional rights of the nation's black citizens. Although their efforts in the short term would meet with limited success, the civil rights leaders were about to trigger a series of actions and events, some anticipated and some not, that would forever transform American history.

4.

THE BYSTANDER
GOVERNMENT

THE **WIDESPREAD REPORTS** of racial violence in the postwar period placed the Truman administration in dangerous political crosscurrents that threatened to tear apart Roosevelt's New Deal coalition. Civil rights groups, which had strong influence with black voters in key swing states, demanded decisive action by the federal government, including criminal prosecutions by the Justice Department against law-enforcement officers and members of white mobs involved in incidents of racial violence. Southern Democratic Party leaders, among the most reliable members of the New Deal coalition, expressed outrage and alarm at any suggestion that the federal government might initiate criminal proceedings in local civil rights cases, regardless of the degree of violence and rage inflicted on black victims. With the public disclosure of the identity of the police officer who had beaten and blinded Isaac Woodard, the Truman administration was whipsawed between demands from civil rights groups for the federal criminal prosecution of Lynwood Shull and insistence by local political leaders that the federal government had no role to play in this purely local matter.

The call for a firm and aggressive federal response in the Woodard incident raised the larger question of the federal government's proper role, if any, in protecting the civil rights of its black citizens. From the founding of the national government, the country was divided over the legal status of its black residents, most of whom had arrived as enslaved persons. In the nearly 160 years since the inception of the United States, each generation of political leaders struggled with this issue, with profound regional differences. With the new wave of racially inspired mob violence in 1946, it was now Harry Truman's turn to confront what seemed to be this unresolvable American dilemma.

When members of the Constitutional Convention met in Philadelphia in the summer of 1787 to draft a new constitution, they realized that a stronger and more robust central government was essential. One issue—slavery—was the critical obstacle to the creation of a new central government. Southern states would not join any national government that had the power to end slavery. To secure southern acceptance of the new constitution, northern delegates agreed to provisions that gave disproportional representation to the southern states. Most notable of these was the Three-Fifths Compromise, which allowed the slaveholding states to count their slaves as three-fifths of a person for purposes of determining congressional representation and votes in the Electoral College while otherwise treating them as chattel. These provisions, for all practical purposes, enabled white southerners to block the abolition of slavery through normal democratic processes, regardless of the wishes of a majority of the American people. The deal struck at the Constitutional Convention left the legal status of enslaved persons to the states; slavery was not to be the business of the national government.[1]

Over the ensuing years, sectional tensions became exacerbated whenever southerners perceived that possible congressional action might threaten the future of slavery. The admission of newly created states was often a lightning rod for controversy because the status of those states as free or slaveholding might upset the delicate national balance on the issue of slavery. Congress often found itself lurching from one sectional dispute to another, the controversies surrounding the Missouri Compromise (1820) and the Kansas-Nebraska Act (1854) being among the most notable. The success of southern congressmen in facilitating the adoption of the Fugitive Slave Act in 1850 resulted in bounty hunters acting on behalf of southern slave owners seizing runaway slaves in free states. Ugly scenes of bounty hunters capturing and seizing runaway slaves incited popular resistance to slavery in the North and the Midwest and contributed to the formation of the antislavery Republican Party. When an outspoken critic of slavery, Abraham Lincoln, was elected president in November 1860, a number of southern states, led by South Carolina, seceded from the Union even before Lincoln took office.[2]

Once president, Lincoln battled to preserve the Union, making it clear that if "I could save the Union without freeing any slave I would do it." As the war progressed, he came to appreciate the political, diplomatic, and military benefits of a declaration freeing enslaved persons in the states in rebellion. On September 22, 1862, Lincoln announced the Emancipation Proclamation, declaring that on January 1, 1863, all enslaved persons in the Confederate states were "thenceforward and forever free." Only after this announcement and the recruitment of black troops for service to the Union army did the Civil War clearly become a war to end slavery. With this new mission, the national government for the first time acted on behalf of the millions of black men and women then living in bondage.[3]

As the Civil War ended in the spring of 1865, a number of prominent abolitionists urged the federal government to adopt a plan for national reconstruction that recognized and protected the rights of the newly liberated black citizens. Lincoln's death, on April 15, 1865, just days after General Robert E. Lee's surrender at Appomattox, elevated an ill-prepared vice president, Andrew Johnson, to office. President Johnson favored the immediate restoration of civilian state governments in the former Confederate states to be headed by native-born unionists, southerners who had opposed secession. Southern unionists tended to favor a generous restoration of civil rights to the former Confederates and adoption of state laws that placed severe restrictions on the legal rights of the newly freed slaves. These newly adopted "Black Codes" restricted the freedmen's right to negotiate the terms of their labor and to exercise freedom of movement and appeared to reinstate slavery under a different name. Public reaction in the North was swift and angry, leading to a broad sweep of the 1866 congressional elections by the Republican Party. The new Congress was now prepared to impose a punitive "reconstruction" on what appeared to be an unreconstructed South.

These remarkable circumstances—the ending of a bitter and bloody civil war, the assassination of a beloved president, and the efforts of southern leaders to keep the recently freed slaves in a new form of servitude— gave rise to Radical Reconstruction. The first of the Reconstruction Acts, adopted in March 1867, divided the South into five military districts and placed the formerly rebellious states under military rule. The states could return to civilian rule by adopting the Fourteenth Amendment, which guaranteed equal protection of the laws. By 1868, most of the former states of the Confederacy had complied with the requirements of the Reconstruction Acts and regained representation in Congress. A year later, Congress passed the Fifteenth Amendment, guaranteeing universal male suffrage, and sent it to the states for ratification. By 1870, all of the former states of the Confederacy had returned to the Union, and two of them, Mississippi and South Carolina, had black-majority electorates and congressional delegations.[4]

However, Republican control of the southern state governments eroded quickly as former Confederates signed loyalty oaths and were allowed to vote and to return to public life. In states with black majorities, Mississippi and South Carolina, white militia groups actively undermined the Republican governments and suppressed black political participation through a systematic campaign of terror. In 1875, white militias implemented a plan of violence, voter intimidation, and election fraud in Mississippi to orchestrate a takeover of the state government by the white minority. A year later, South Carolina militiamen, calling themselves "Red Shirts," implemented a similar campaign of terror and ballot box stuffing that appeared to narrowly defeat the incumbent Republican governor, Daniel Chamberlain. The election results were challenged because three Democratic-controlled counties reported substantially more votes than the number of people who lived there.[5]

But there was still a bigger election result under contest: the presidency of the United States. The Democratic candidate, Samuel Tilden, had won the popular vote and was one electoral vote short of victory. Election results were contested in three southern states: South Carolina, Louisiana, and Florida. Credible claims of election fraud were made in each of these states, with the outcome of the national election hanging in the balance. A special election commission was appointed to adjudicate the disputed elections, with an apparent advantage to the Republicans. In the midst of this controversy, southern Democrats privately went to supporters of the Republican nominee, Rutherford B. Hayes, with a proposition. The southern Democrats would deliver their electoral votes for Hayes in return for a withdrawal of federal troops from the South and an agreement that the southern states (and not the federal government) would determine the legal rights and status of their black citizens. The Republicans agreed, and shortly thereafter Hayes was declared the newly elected president. Following his assumption of office, federal troops left South Carolina and the other southern states, bringing an end to Reconstruction.[6]

Following what would become known as the Compromise of 1877, the federal government abandoned its briefly assumed role as protector of the rights of black Americans and left their fate in the hands of southern state governments. Over the ensuing years, black political participation in the former Confederate states disappeared under the pressure of voter intimidation and election law changes. By the late nineteenth century, meaningful black political participation in the southern states ceased to exist.

In the face of this methodical movement to subjugate and disenfranchise the South's black citizens, the federal government stood by as a silent witness to this destruction of constitutionally protected rights. This federal retreat on civil rights was sanctioned by the U.S. Supreme Court in a long line of late nineteenth-century decisions, culminating in rulings upholding government-mandated racial segregation in *Plessy v. Ferguson* (1896) and black disenfranchisement in *Williams v. Mississippi* (1898). The Thirteenth, Fourteenth, and Fifteenth Amendments, known as the Civil War Amendments, were hollowed out into meaningless provisions by the combination of hostile U.S. Supreme Court justices, an indifferent federal government, and a determined and uncompromising white South.[7]

In the years prior to World War II, civil rights advocates pressed Congress in vain to protect black citizens from mob violence. Their focus was a seemingly modest proposal: the declaration of lynching as a federal crime. From the 1880s forward, literally thousands of black men and women were lynched, mostly in rural southern communities. In its most common form, a white vigilante group would form on the report of some alleged outrage by a black person. Frequently, local law-enforcement officials were participants or complicitous in the mob activity. No other issue seemed to divide Americans more regionally than the subject of lynching. Most Americans outside the South viewed lynching as a barbaric activity, while many white southern elected officials defended the practice as necessary to the maintenance of social order.

Numerous proposals were presented to Congress to address the scourge of lynching. Beginning in 1918, and continuing every few years into the 1930s, one or both houses of Congress debated anti-lynching legislation. Dramatic filibusters and emotional debate were regular features of this long-running fight. But each year, despite strong public sentiment in support of anti-lynching measures, the legislation faltered.[8]

As World War II ended, civil rights leaders turned their attention to the Truman administration as the most promising path for the engagement of the federal government in the fight for equal rights. Their persistent call for federal engagement was understandable, because it was hard to imagine any meaningful progress against the harsh realities of Jim Crow laws and black disenfranchisement without concerted action from the national government. Indeed, the only period in which real progress had been made in civil rights was during Reconstruction with a federal occupying force. Even if civil rights leaders were successful in persuading the Truman administration to initiate criminal prosecutions against perpetrators of racial mob violence, there remained formidable obstacles to effective federal action under civil rights statutes adopted during Reconstruction. For starters, the federal criminal statute that provided the most significant punishment for civil rights violations contained very broad language, which the Supreme Court had held raised significant due process issues because of statutory vagueness. Another federal civil rights statute that did not have statutory vagueness problems had its own weaknesses, most notably that it applied only to governmental employees, making it ineffective in the prosecution of private citizens involved in lynchings and other incidents of mob violence. Further, the violation of the statute was only a misdemeanor, with punishment limited to one year in prison.[9]

Beyond these significant weaknesses in federal civil rights statutes, the Justice Department had a wholly inadequate staff to process and investigate the fifteen hundred to two thousand civil rights complaints received annually. The Civil Rights Section, which was part of the Criminal Division of the Justice Department, had only seven full-time attorneys and no independent investigative staff. Consequently, the Department of Justice in the 1930s and 1940s brought fewer than two dozen prosecutions per year, mostly peonage cases involving black workers forced to labor with essentially no compensation. The Civil Rights Section's staff was viewed by activists as inept and timid, with a tendency to "collapse" in the face of any serious opposition.[10]

The absence of any investigative staff within the Civil Rights Section required the office to depend on the FBI to conduct its investigations. This was no small problem. Local FBI agents in the South were, for the most part, native southerners who maintained close ties to local law-enforcement officers. This was a natural affinity because most FBI investigations were conducted at the request of local police agencies, and mutual trust and confidence between local law enforcement and FBI agents were essential to the FBI's local support mission. Civil rights investigations, particularly those into incidents of mob violence, often involved allegations of direct or indirect participation by local law-enforcement officers. Thus, a federal civil rights investigation often required FBI agents to conduct criminal investigations of officers whom they knew and relied on in other criminal investigations. Moreover, as white southerners, most FBI agents had little sympathy for civil rights protesters and generally identified with the accused local police officers. It was also an open secret that the FBI director, J. Edgar Hoover, had little interest in pursuing civil rights investigations and tended to view most civil rights activities as communist inspired or influenced.[11]

In those rare circumstances in which the Civil Rights Section sought to initiate a criminal prosecution in the South, it confronted the reality of all-white grand juries and trial juries. Because federal juries were drawn from voter lists, and blacks were for the most part excluded from voting in southern states, Justice Department prosecutors found their jurors in southern states to be profoundly unsympathetic if not hostile to federal civil rights prosecutions.

On top of all these formidable obstacles, Justice Department prosecutors often faced resistance from local U.S. attorneys when they sought to pursue criminal civil rights cases in their districts. Under normal federal practice, local U.S. attorneys have broad discretion in determining which cases to prosecute. Civil rights prosecutions, when they occurred, were generally initiated and run out of Washington. Most U.S. attorneys received appointments because of close political ties to their U.S. senators, who were almost universally hostile to any federal civil rights prosecution.

Thus, Justice Department prosecutors in civil rights cases often found themselves fighting not just defense counsel but rearguard actions by the local U.S. attorney. It is hardly surprising that under these very adverse circumstances, convictions for civil rights violations in mob violence and excessive force cases were exceedingly rare.[12]

As civil rights complaints poured into the Justice Department in the spring and summer of 1946, key members of the White House staff and high-ranking members of the department appreciated the need to identify meritorious federal civil rights cases for prosecution. Attorney General Tom Clark and Theron Lamar Caudle, the assistant attorney general in charge of the Criminal Division, closely monitored FBI reports and news articles in search of potential cases to prosecute. As reports of incidents of mob or racially inspired violence were received, FBI agents were dispatched to investigate.

When the first press reports appeared about the blinding of Isaac Woodard, Assistant Attorney General Caudle wrote to J. Edgar Hoover on July 17, 1946, directing that a preliminary investigation be opened on the matter. Caudle reported in his memorandum to Hoover the allegation that Woodard had been blinded in Aiken, South Carolina, as a result of being "beaten in the head with a billy club by a policeman, knocked down on the floor and hit in the eyes while in a prone position." He suggested the agents' interviews include Woodard, then residing in New York City, and the police officer "who arrested the complainant."[13]

Hoover's initial report back to Caudle was not encouraging. He reported that his agents based in Atlanta and Savannah had no information concerning the matter and that the chief of police in Aiken was unaware of any confrontation between one of his officers and a black soldier. Hoover did note a report of a victim of a police assault arriving at the VA Hospital in Columbia and indicated that this was now being pursued. As letters of inquiry and concern from prominent African Americans arrived at the White House and the Justice Department during this period,

Attorney General Clark and presidential staff members reported that the FBI was in the field investigating the matter. As the FBI investigation was progressing in late July 1946, the first press reports of the mass murders at Moore's Ford began to circulate, further heightening the pressure on the Truman administration to take some decisive action on civil rights.[14]

Hoover received his first substantive report on the Woodard investigation on July 30, 1946, in the form of an "urgent" telex from the special agent in charge of the Savannah FBI office, D. K. Brown. Although acknowledging that the investigation was "incomplete," the investigating agents made no effort to disguise their skepticism regarding Woodard's claims. Agent Brown informed Hoover that it appeared Woodard "boarded bus in intoxicated condition and had arguments with bus driver in route from Augusta, Ga. to Batesburg, S.C. concerning victim's desire to stop the bus in order that he could go to the restroom." Agent Brown further reported that "physician reports reflect victim probably struck in both eyes with blackjack but condition of eyes does not justify conclusion that eyes were gouged with pistol butts, night sticks or other instruments."[15]

The FBI field agents provided Hoover with a detailed report on August 5, 1946, that included summaries of interviews with Woodard's VA treating physicians. Dr. Arthur Clancy, the ear, nose, and throat physician who was Woodard's principal treating doctor at the VA, expressed skepticism at the claim that the sergeant's bilateral blindness was the result of a single strike with a blackjack. He explained to the agents that the bone structure of the eyes would make it "rather difficult to strike both eyeballs at one time with one blow." Woodard's other VA treating physician, Dr. Mortimer Burger, detailed to the agents multiple injuries he observed on Woodard's eyelids, eyes, upper cheek, right ear, and nose bridge, which were more extensive than would be expected from a single strike of a blackjack.

The August 5 field report also summarized the results of interviews with three soldiers who had been on the Greyhound bus with Woodard that evening. Although there was some inconsistency among them about whether Woodard was drinking on the bus, none observed any boisterousness or evidence of drunkenness. Two of the soldiers, Lincoln Miller and Jennings Stroud, confirmed Woodard's statement that he was initially struck by Shull when he stepped off the bus in Batesburg without any apparent provocation. This conflicted with Shull's statement to the FBI that he struck Woodard only once with the blackjack and that this was near the town jail when Woodard attempted to take the blackjack from him.[16]

A fundamental issue in evaluating the conflicting accounts centered on whether Shull had struck the sergeant a single time and only in self-defense, as he claimed, or multiple times, resulting in Woodard's being rendered unconscious and ultimately blinded. Common sense suggested that blinding a man in both eyes with a single strike of a blackjack was not a likely occurrence, and the observations by the VA doctors certainly raised questions about Shull's account of events. The interviews with soldiers on the bus further challenged Shull's veracity regarding when he first struck Woodard. However, as the investigation proceeded, the FBI documented no further inquiries regarding the number and location of strikes received by Woodard from Shull's blackjack and did not pursue any independent assessments by specialists in ophthalmology or forensic medicine to address this critical issue. Instead, the field agents focused their efforts on determining whether Woodard had been drinking on the bus.

The FBI's field report was reviewed within the Civil Rights Section by William J. Holloran. In a memorandum to the section chief, Turner L. Smith, Holloran stated that the evidence was "contradictory in important respects" and there was no "clear violation" of federal criminal civil rights statutes. Holloran observed that because of the "great public interest in the case" and the "severe physical injury suffered by the victim," it was probably better that the case not be closed "without exploring every fruitful lead to determine the actual facts." Holloran noted that the "medical evidence indicates that Woodard's blindness was caused by one . . . or probably more blows directly to the eyes." As a follow-up to Holloran's memorandum, Assistant Attorney General Caudle wrote to Hoover the same day, suggesting some further lines of investigation for the bureau, but there was no recommendation at that time that the FBI further investigate whether Woodard's devastating injuries came from a single blow or from multiple blows of Shull's blackjack.[17]

Hoover was sent a memo from his assistant director, D. M. Ladd, on September 3, 1946, summarizing the findings from the Woodard investigation. Ladd stated that "it appeared that Woodard was drinking on the bus in violation of state law" and "frequently demanded that the bus be stopped for convenience." He further observed that en route to the town's police station Woodard "resisted arrest, attempted to take the Chief's blackjack away from him, and as a result . . . [the chief] struck the victim over the head with the blackjack." Ladd stated that Shull contended he struck Woodard only once and the medical reports "did not indicate that Woodard had been severely beaten." When Woodard complained of pain the next day, Ladd reported he was taken to the VA Hospital in Columbia, where he remained for two months, and was "released as hopelessly blind in both eyes."[18]

Even though Hoover was well known to have little sympathy for victims in civil rights investigations, the obvious deficiencies in the bureau's findings and conclusions in the Woodard investigation were too much for him. Underlining Ladd's statement about Woodard's hospitalization and permanent blindness, Hoover handwrote, "This does seem like a flagrant case & must be vigorously pressed." There is no indication in the investigative file that Hoover's comments were relayed down the line to the FBI field agents handling the matter, who continued to be dismissive of Woodard's claims of civil rights violations against Shull.[19]

Officials in the Civil Rights Section shared the view of the FBI field agents regarding Woodard's civil rights claims but were reluctant at that time to close the file because of the case's widespread notoriety. Indeed, by late August 1946, all of the federal government officials directly involved in the investigation and potential prosecution arising out of the blinding of Isaac Woodard were convinced that Shull had done nothing wrong and that the file would soon be closed as a no-action case. As they would soon learn, they could not have been more wrong.

THE AWAKENING

5.

"MY GOD . . . WE HAVE GOT
TO DO SOMETHING"

HARRY S. TRUMAN was a man often underestimated. Perhaps this was because of his short stature, his high-pitched voice, or his lack of refined social graces. But people who worked closely with him in civilian life, or under his command during World War I, knew his capabilities. They grew to admire him for his integrity, coolness under fire, and basic decency. He was dogged in pursuit of any mission he undertook and spoke in a straightforward manner that inspired confidence and mutual respect. From his first race for elective office in Jackson County, Missouri, in 1922, to his uphill battle for reelection as Missouri's U.S. senator in 1940 against the better-financed sitting governor, to his 1948 presidential campaign when virtually every pollster and political reporter predicted his political demise, Truman proved to have an uncanny ability to speak to the common man and to exceed everyone's expectations. His pugnacious spirit and willingness to confront his political opponents with everything he had communicated to laborers, farmers, and black voters that Harry Truman was on their side.

Truman was born in 1884 in a portion of Missouri highly sympathetic with the Confederate cause. Both of his grandfathers were slaveholders. His mother, Martha Ellen "Mattie" Truman, was a die-hard unreconstructed southern sympathizer who abhorred Abraham Lincoln and considered John Wilkes Booth a hero.

Family finances prevented Truman from attending college, and after working for several years in the back offices of a bank, he returned home to help his father on the family farm. His likely lifetime work as a farmer was interrupted by World War I, in which he eventually rose to the rank of captain of a local National Guard unit and commanded a battery of mostly working-class Irish Catholics. Truman whipped the men under his command into shape, and his battery went from being among the worst to the best in his regiment. When his battery confronted enemy fire for the first time, near the small French village of Saulxures, some of the men ran for their lives, only to see their captain standing tall and cursing them with everything he had. Truman's men came to revere him for his leadership and his courage and would affectionately refer to him as "Captain Harry." In turn, Truman was passionately devoted to the men in his battery, and later, as commander in chief, to all men in uniform.[1]

As World War I ended, Truman and an army buddy, Eddie Jacobson, decided to go into business together in a haberdashery. Truman's father had passed away, and Harry sold his share of the farm to provide the capital for his new business. But an economic downturn after World War I crushed the fledgling business and left Truman and Jacobson hopelessly in debt. Truman's declining business fortunes coincided with a growing interest in electoral politics. A friend from the army, Jimmy Pendergast, whose family commanded one of the great political machines in the country from its base in Kansas City, persuaded the Pendergast organization to support Truman for judge of the Eastern District of Jackson

County. The Pendergasts' "family business," headed by the legendary boss Tom Pendergast, included not just political control of Jackson County but also saloons, wholesale liquor, prostitution, and gambling. With his distinguished war record and solid family background, Truman's candidacy offered much-needed respectability to the Pendergast organization.

The position Truman sought, despite its name, had no judicial function and was akin to a county supervisor. He won a highly contested four-way race for the position in 1922 but lost his reelection bid two years later, when the Republicans swept the election. In 1926, again with the support of the Pendergast organization, Truman was elected presiding judge of Jackson County, which gave him, for the first time, real administrative responsibilities, a living wage, and political power. He held the presiding judge position for eight years and by all accounts handled his duties with efficiency and integrity.[2]

Truman held Tom Pendergast in high esteem and always claimed that the boss never asked him to do anything immoral or illegal. For his part, Tom Pendergast appreciated Truman's competency and did not seek to entangle Truman in the more sordid aspects of his political and business empire. When in later years a number of Pendergast-associated public officials were prosecuted for taking kickbacks and participating in other forms of corruption, Truman observed to his wife, Bess, that it "looks like everybody got rich in Jackson County but me." He also learned a thing or two about retail politics from Tom Pendergast, particularly the need to provide first-rate constituent services.[3]

Harry Truman sought to expand his horizons beyond Kansas City and, as an ardent Roosevelt supporter, longed to go to Washington and be part of the New Deal. His initial efforts to obtain the endorsement of the Pendergast organization for a congressional and a Senate seat were unsuccessful. Finally, in 1934, Truman was summoned by Tom Pendergast and informed he was the organization's candidate for an open seat in the U.S. Senate. This race would certainly not be a cakewalk for Truman or the Pendergast organization. His opponents included two sitting congressmen, and political pundits did not take Truman's candidacy seriously. He was ridiculed by opponents as Tom Pendergast's "bellhop," but Truman amazed political observers with his tenacity, appeal to farmers, and "devastating fire" in his counterattacks against opponents. When the dust settled and the votes were counted, Truman prevailed, with half his total vote being delivered by the Pendergast machine from Jackson County. His victory was viewed by many as a triumph for Tom Pendergast rather than for the newly elected senator. When Truman arrived in Washington, he found that his reputation as a machine lackey preceded him. Some dismissed him as "the Senator from Pendergast."[4]

Truman devoted himself to his new duties, arriving at his office so early every morning that he was provided with his own passkey to the Senate office building, reportedly the first senator ever given one. He rarely missed a committee meeting and worked hard on constituent services. He voted faithfully with Roosevelt, including support for the president's reviled court-packing proposal. But the Roosevelt people paid little attention to Truman, and the cloud over him as a machine hack persisted. As Truman began to hit his stride in his senatorial duties, a new threat to his political survival emerged. Federal officials launched a major criminal investigation of Tom Pendergast and his organization. In April 1939, a little over a year before Truman's reelection for the U.S. Senate, Tom Pendergast was indicted by a federal grand jury for income tax evasion. A month later, Pendergast pleaded guilty and was sent to federal prison, leaving his political machine in shambles.

But Truman's reelection difficulties were just beginning. Governor Lloyd Stark, previously a close Truman ally who had won the governorship with the support of the Pendergast organization, filed to run against Truman and pronounced himself an anti-machine political reformer. Stark was widely popular, and word in political circles, from Washington to back home in Missouri, was that Truman would surely be defeated. Ignoring the pundits, Truman pursued his reelection campaign with tireless optimism and a ferociousness that exceeded even his successful 1934 Senate campaign.

Truman was not without friends in his reelection effort. Labor unions strongly supported his reelection, as did Missouri's other sitting senator, Bennett Clark. Because of his solid civil rights voting record, he received strong black support. He was not bashful about his views on racial issues. In one campaign stop before a virtually all-white audience, Truman stated that he believed in the "brotherhood of man; not merely the brotherhood of white men, but the brotherhood of all men before the law." Referencing segregation and the persistent exploitation of black citizens, he stated that "surely, as freemen, they are entitled to something better than this."

Even with a weakened Pendergast organization, Truman managed to carry Jackson County by a large margin, and with solid support from rural counties he narrowly defeated Governor Stark by six thousand votes. His reelection was one of the biggest political surprises in the country that year and amazed his Senate colleagues. Upon his return to Washington, Truman was treated in the Senate chamber as a conquering hero, and it seemed, finally, that the stain of Pendergast had been removed.[5]

In his second term, Truman emerged as a real player in the Senate. He proposed and then chaired an important select committee on defense contracts, bringing to light significant fraud and inefficiencies in federal defense contracting. Although the committee was officially titled the Senate Special Committee to Investigate the National Defense Program, it became known as the Truman Committee. It would eventually issue twenty-one reports and was credited with saving the government $250 million. No longer an obscure backbench senator from Missouri, Truman was now known nationwide for his work fighting fraud in the defense industry. He was featured on the cover of *Time* in March 1943 as "Investigator Truman" and was described as a "watchdog" for the country and "scrupulously honest."[6]

As the 1944 presidential election approached and Roosevelt announced his intention to seek an unprecedented fourth term, a number of prominent

Democrats began voicing concern that Vice President Henry Wallace was a drag on the ticket. The truth was that few insiders expected Roosevelt to survive his fourth term, placing heightened significance on the vice president. A number of major Democratic operatives, including big-city bosses and southern congressmen, viewed Wallace as too liberal and too independent to suit them.

As momentum built in the Democratic Party establishment to dump Wallace, word soon spread that Roosevelt viewed James F. Byrnes of South Carolina as an acceptable vice presidential candidate. This prospect particularly excited southern congressmen, who understood that no southerner could likely win the presidency outright, but Byrnes might assume the office should Roosevelt not survive his fourth term.

On paper, Jimmy Byrnes looked like an ideal vice presidential candidate, having served in all three branches of government, including a brief tenure on the U.S. Supreme Court. But Byrnes had real political liabilities. He had actively opposed federal labor legislation, and powerful union leaders, key members of the Roosevelt coalition, made it clear he was not an acceptable choice. Black leaders voiced vehement opposition to Byrnes, noting that he had an abysmal civil rights record dating back two decades and had ridiculed Walter White during Senate debate on anti-lynching legislation while the NAACP leader was sitting in the gallery. Big-city bosses, who were mostly Irish Catholic, also resented the fact that Byrnes had converted from Catholicism as an adult, which they perceived to be an act of political expediency.

Henry Wallace showed no intention of stepping aside as Roosevelt's running mate, and the situation was complicated by Roosevelt's telling both Wallace and Byrnes he wanted them with him on the ticket. As the Democratic convention delegates arrived in Chicago on July 19, 1944, to renominate Roosevelt, the only drama remaining was who would be Roosevelt's running mate. Roosevelt further confused the situation by giving a key party activist a handwritten note indicating that Harry Truman was his preference for vice president. Truman, who had planned to place Byrnes's name in nomination at the convention, was shocked by the report that he was Roosevelt's choice for vice president. He had never been close with Roosevelt and had not spoken with him in more than a year. When Roosevelt confirmed his preference for Truman, Byrnes immediately withdrew from the race, but Wallace insisted on a convention vote. Truman won the vice presidential nomination in a close floor vote, with his selection dubbed the "Missouri Compromise." Southerners generally supported Truman against Wallace, confident that his background as a farmer from southern Missouri would make him naturally sympathetic to their efforts to preserve the racial status quo.[7]

Truman lunched with Roosevelt at the White House shortly after his nomination and was distressed by the president's physical condition. Although mentally sharp, Roosevelt looked haggard, and his hands shook so badly he was unable to pour cream into his coffee. Truman wrote to Bess after the lunch that Roosevelt was physically "going to pieces." Roosevelt was reelected in November 1944, and he and Truman were sworn in on January 20, 1945.

Truman would serve only eighty-two days as vice president. He and Bess continued to live in the same $120-per-month five-room apartment that he had occupied since his earliest Senate days. Truman, like most vice presidents of that era, was given few duties by the White House and had only two private meetings with Roosevelt. He spent most of his time in his Capitol Hill office or presiding over the Senate.

On the afternoon of April 12, 1945, Truman was having a drink with Speaker of the House Sam Rayburn in the Speaker's hideaway office when an anxious White House aide called and told him to come "quickly and quietly to the White House." A few minutes later, Truman was ushered into the private quarters of the White House to speak to Mrs. Roosevelt. The First Lady said, "Harry, the President is dead." Truman, momentarily speechless, responded, "Is there anything I can do for you?" Mrs. Roosevelt replied, "Is there anything *we* can do for *you*. For you are the one in trouble now."[8]

Truman entered the presidency at an extraordinary moment in American history. The war in Europe had been won, but the U.S. armed forces were in the final stages of planning the invasion of Japan. The new president was briefed about a massive, secret project to design and build an atomic weapon. No one was sure if it would work, but if it did, there was little doubt the bomb would cause massive death and destruction at a level previously unknown. Believing that the new weapon would save tens of thousands of American lives that would be lost in a land invasion of Japan, Truman authorized its use.

Truman traveled to San Francisco in June 1945 and participated in the signing of the United Nations Charter. A month later, he met with Winston Churchill and Joseph Stalin in Potsdam to negotiate final details relating to the end of the war in Europe. On August 6, 1945, during his return by ship to the United States after Potsdam, he was informed by his military command that the atomic bomb had been dropped on Hiroshima earlier that day and was a "clear cut success in all respects." On August 9, 1945, a second bomb was dropped on the port city of Nagasaki. Five days after the bombing of Nagasaki, on August 14, 1945, Japan surrendered unconditionally.[9]

Shortly after assuming office, Truman wanted to send a message to civil rights leaders that they had a friend in the White House. On May 5, 1945, just twenty-three days after he became president, Truman met privately in the Oval Office with Walter White. A month later, he wrote a letter to the chairman of the House Rules Committee, where a proposed Fair Employment Practices Committee bill was languishing, to ask that the bill be acted on favorably. Truman described employment discrimination on the basis of race as "un-American" and declared that fair employment practices "should be established permanently as part of our national law." A number of southern congressmen privately began expressing angst about whether Harry Truman was really on their side. One reporter observed that the "orange blossoms and magnolias which symbolized the honeymoon" between Truman and southern congressional leaders "are about to wither."[10]

Truman hoped to walk a political tightrope on the civil rights issue, making some positive moves to earn the support of black voters without alienating the Democratic Party's white voter base in the South. He and his senior White House staff were initially confident that meaningful civil rights progress could be made in a way that would not alienate the party's southern political base.[11]

But extraordinary events soon overtook the Truman administration's efforts to finesse the civil rights issue. First came the events in Columbia, Tennessee, in February 1946, which were viewed by white southerners as uncontrolled lawlessness by blacks, and by civil rights leaders as a "white riot" in which African Americans had been victimized. Walter White sent a telegram to Truman urging a full investigation of the events, and Attorney General Clark, under pressure from an aggressive NAACP publicity campaign, announced on March 7, 1946, that he would impanel a federal grand jury. Tennessee officials denounced the federal government's involvement.

Meanwhile, the administration's quiet efforts to persuade southern governors not to openly resist the Supreme Court's order in *Smith v. Allwright* and to open the Democratic primary to black voters were largely successful. But the visible participation of black voters in the election process soon produced a significant backlash in several southern states, where candidates pledged to bring back the state's white primary if elected. Theodore Bilbo, seeking reelection to the Senate from Mississippi, called on "red-blooded Anglo Saxon" men to "resort to any means to keep . . . Negroes from the polls." Eugene Talmadge, seeking to return as governor of Georgia, promised that if he was elected, blacks "won't be voting in our white primary in the next four years." Within days following the race-tinged Georgia Democratic Party primary, an army veteran, Maceo Snipes, was murdered in Taylor County, Georgia, and four black men and women were slaughtered in the infamous mass lynching at Moore's Ford. The Truman administration's plan to quietly finesse civil rights issues was clearly not practical, and Attorney General Clark announced a full federal investigation into the Moore's Ford incident.[12]

Announcing an investigation was the easy part; getting real results proved to be far more elusive. Federal grand juries impaneled to review the incidents in Columbia, Tennessee, and Monroe, Georgia, failed to issue indictments. The federal government's civil rights enforcement efforts appeared feckless to the civil rights community while stirring anger and resentment among southern whites.

When reports of the Isaac Woodard blinding began circulating in July 1946, civil rights leaders called for a vigorous investigation and prosecution of the persons responsible. On July 30, members of the National Association of Colored Women's Clubs picketed the White House, with one of the picketers carrying a sign that stated "Speak! Speak! Mr. President." To increase the pressure on the Truman administration to act, the NAACP pulled together forty civil rights, labor, and religious groups to establish an umbrella organization, the National Emergency Committee Against Mob Violence, and requested an audience with the president. A meeting was scheduled for September 19.

Senior White House staff met with Truman in advance of his planned meeting with civil rights leaders to explain the obstacles confronting any federal efforts to attack the recent incidents of racial violence across the South. In particular, successful criminal prosecutions were unlikely because of the hostile political and legal environments in which those cases had to be tried, and Congress appeared to have no appetite for new civil rights legislation. The clear message from Truman's staff was that despite his personal desire for the federal government to do more, there was little the president could do to obtain justice for the victims of racial violence.[13]

The civil rights leaders opened the September 19 meeting by imploring Truman to take vigorous action against lynch mobs and other racially motivated violence across the South. They urged the president to call Congress into special session to adopt federal anti-lynching legislation. After listening sympathetically, Truman told them, "Everyone seems to believe the president by himself can do anything he wishes to on such matters as this. But the president is helpless unless he is backed by public opinion."

Truman's closest ally in the room, Walter White, sensed that the president did not appreciate the gravity of the situation. Rather than continuing the discussion on proposals for presidential action, he began sharing with Truman, in graphic detail, the beating and blinding of Isaac Woodard. As the story unfolded, Truman sat riveted and became visibly agitated and angered. One observer later described his face as "distorted in horror." Casting his staff's advice aside, an obviously distressed president responded, "My God! I had no idea it was as terrible as that! We have got to do something."

David Niles, Truman's assistant responsible for civil rights, suggested the creation of a blue-ribbon committee to make recommendations for federal action. A serious and distinguished blue-ribbon committee to study the situation and to make proposals appealed to Truman because it was clear—from his discussions both with his staff and now with civil rights leaders—that there was a dire need for fresh ideas to deal with the country's seemingly intractable racial problems. Some in attendance were initially resistant to the idea, fearing this would be just another excuse to do nothing, but Truman promised that the committee could be formed immediately, with a mandate to deliver a report for action before the next Congress convened in January 1948. He also assured them that he would draw from the president's contingency fund for the civil rights committee's operations, thus avoiding a bruising fight in Congress to obtain an appropriation. Walter White warmed to the idea and pledged to work with the president's staff to put together a first-rate committee.[14]

———

Clearly shaken by the account of Woodard's beating and blinding, Truman wrote a personal letter to Attorney General Clark on September 20, 1946, the day following his meeting with civil rights leaders. He shared with Clark the story of the "Negro Sergeant" from South Carolina "who had been discharged from the Army just three hours, was taken off the bus and not only seriously beaten but his eyes deliberately put out." He stated that he was "very much alarmed at the increased racial feeling all over the country."

Truman proposed to his attorney general the creation of the first presidential committee on civil rights "to analyze the situation and have a remedy to present to the next Congress." He indicated that he was aware the Justice Department was "looking into the Tennessee and Georgia lynchings" as well as an incident in Louisiana, "but I think it is going to take something more than the handling of each individual case after it happens." The president indicated he believed "it is going to require the inauguration of some sort of policy to prevent such happenings." He sent another note the same day to David Niles, attaching a copy of his letter to the attorney general and stating, "I am very much in earnest on this thing and I'd like very much to have you push it with everything you have."[15]

Truman's letter to Clark landed like a bombshell in the Department of Justice. The simple truth was that in the face of murders, mass lynchings, and other racial incidents over the past eight months, not a single criminal prosecution had been brought by the Justice Department in these highly publicized cases. The Truman letter was clear: the time for action had arrived.[16]

The president's request that the Justice Department prepare appropriate documents for the creation of a presidential commission on civil rights was a relatively uncomplicated task. The attorney general assigned staff to prepare an executive order creating the committee, and within a few weeks a draft was submitted to the White House for review.[17] The more complicated issue was the initiation of federal civil rights prosecutions, and the small staff within the Civil Rights Section continued to offer endless reasons why this was not possible.

Circumstances had now changed. The president was focusing on the department's civil rights efforts (or, more precisely, on the lack of action), and key civil rights leaders were publicly complaining about the absence of prosecutions. Added to these obvious pressures was a new and looming political imperative, the 1946 congressional elections. The Democrats had held both houses of Congress since President Roosevelt's election in 1932, but the political winds appeared to be shifting away from them. A loss of either house of Congress would be politically embarrassing to the new president and a suggestion of major political vulnerability.

———

On Wednesday, September 25, 1946, just three business days after the president's letter was delivered to Attorney General Clark, the Civil Rights Section initiated criminal charges against Lynwood Shull in the blinding of Isaac Woodard. The section chief, Turner Smith, called Claud Sapp, the U.S. attorney for the District of South Carolina, to advise him that legal documents were being forwarded to him for arrival the next day for the filing of criminal charges against Shull.

Under normal circumstances, the U.S. attorney would be provided with investigative documents by the FBI or other federal law-enforcement agencies relating to a possible criminal prosecution. The U.S. attorney would review the material and then, in consultation with the investigating agents, make the discretionary call about whether to present the case to the federal grand jury for indictment. If the U.S. attorney decided to proceed with the case, he would present it at the next meeting of the federal grand jury and obtain a "true bill" or "no bill" regarding a proposed indictment. A true bill could be returned only if twelve federal grand jurors (out of a total that can be as small as sixteen or as large as twenty-three) voted in favor of issuing the indictment. This process of local U.S. Attorney Office review and presentment to a federal grand jury took time and could not be accomplished in a few days or even a few weeks. Further, it was not uncommon in civil rights cases in the South for local federal grand juries to refuse to return indictments against white persons alleged to have violated the civil rights of minority citizens.

Turner Smith advised Sapp that this normal process would not be followed in the Shull case. Instead, the criminal case against Shull would be brought as a misdemeanor with a maximum punishment of one year, which avoided the legal requirement to present the case to a South Carolina federal grand jury. The case would be brought on what was known as an Information, with the U.S. attorney initiating the criminal prosecution simply by filing the charging document with the clerk of the district court. At the time of the call from Smith, Sapp was unaware of the FBI's investigation of Shull and had not received any of the bureau's field reports or the Justice Department's legal analysis of the case.

Expecting that the final decision to initiate the prosecution would be his, Sapp informed Smith that after he reviewed the materials from the Justice Department, he would make a determination if a criminal case should be filed. Smith firmly responded that this call was not a request but an order. Sapp was to receive and file the Information charging Shull the very next day, as soon as the documents were received in his office. Further, he was directed to advise Smith promptly by telephone when the Information was filed.[18]

Recognizing that Sapp was being directed to file criminal charges without the benefit of the investigative record, Smith promised Sapp that he would have the investigating FBI agents promptly forward their field reports and other relevant documents. Smith assured Sapp that after he had an opportunity to review these investigative records, Sapp could make a decision about whether the case would continue or be dismissed. Reading between the lines, Sapp interpreted Smith's comments to indicate that the Justice Department wanted the benefit of immediate publicity relating to the Shull case but that later he would be free to dismiss the case if that was his wish.[19]

Claud Sapp was not an inexperienced federal prosecutor and was certainly not accustomed to receiving such orders from Justice Department officials. He was the former chairman of the South Carolina Democratic Party and an early and prominent supporter of the Roosevelt for President campaign. He had traveled across the South organizing "Roosevelt for President" clubs and served as Roosevelt's southern floor manager during the 1932 Democratic National Convention. After Roosevelt's election, Sapp was offered the plum position of U.S. attorney for the Eastern District of South Carolina, which he had now held for more than a decade. He was also a legendary trial lawyer with a great ability to give a stem-winding closing argument or capture a complex concept with a folksy turn of phrase.[20]

Although Sapp would later claim he objected to filing the Information in the manner directed by the Justice Department, the record shows he obediently followed orders and filed the criminal charges in the case of *United States v. Lynwood Lanier Shull* the following day, September 26, 1946. Sapp, as instructed, promptly advised Smith that the charges were filed. Later that same day, Attorney General Tom Clark issued a press release announcing that "criminal charges have been filed against Lynwood Lanier Shull, Batesburg, South Carolina Chief of Police," for violating the right of Isaac Woodard Jr. "not to be beaten and tortured by persons exercising the authority to arrest." The following day, reports of the Justice Department's action and Clark's statements were prominently covered in major newspapers across the country.[21]

The newspaper accounts of the Justice Department's prosecution of Shull caught many by surprise, perhaps none more so than the Savannah-based FBI agents who had conducted the field investigation. The special agent in charge of the Savannah office, D. K. Brown, attempted to call Sapp immediately after press reports broke to obtain some explanation for this unexpected turn of events. Brown was informed that Sapp and his assistant were out of the office, but a stenographer in the U.S. attorney's office confidentially shared with him details of Smith's call to Sapp, including the direct order to file the charges the day after the paperwork was received by the office. Agent Brown then promptly reported this conversation to Hoover in a "most urgent" telex.

A few days later, another Savannah-based FBI agent, Ralph House, met privately with Sapp. He shared with House the details of his telephone conversation with the Justice Department. Sapp told House that "he gathered . . . that the Department was not concerned whether he entered a nolle prosequi [a dismissal] . . . as long as they got their publicity." House presumably shared with Sapp the investigating agents' dim view of the charges brought against Shull. Sapp informed House that he would "call the Department of Justice and advise them it was his intention to dismiss the Information in this case and to take no further prosecutive action." A summary of this conversation between Sapp and House was soon distributed to the leadership of the FBI, including Director Hoover.[22]

The announcement of the Shull prosecution produced another surprise. The Associated Press reported an interview with Shull in which he claimed that he had earlier informed local FBI agents of the Woodard incident and was told "to keep quiet about it." Shull claimed he reported the incident because Woodard was in uniform at the time of the encounter and later stated he could not see. Senior staff at FBI headquarters in Washington demanded immediate written explanations from the agents involved.[23]

Two FBI special agents, Ralph House and Leroy Steiner, submitted lengthy statements acknowledging that in early May 1946 they had a discussion with Shull while handling another matter in Batesburg. The agents stated that they observed a spring dangling from Shull's blackjack, indicating the weapon was broken. One agent joked that it looked as if someone had gotten the better of Shull. Shull responded that a drunken black man had attacked him and there had been a struggle for control of the blackjack. Shull claimed that he regained control of his blackjack and gave the man "one lick" across the head. The agents denied being told the man struck was a soldier in uniform and claimed the entire conversation was informal and informational only. They also denied telling Shull to keep quiet about the allegations.[24]

The Shull prosecution produced a storm of protest in South Carolina. The U.S. senator Olin Johnston denounced the prosecution, stating that he was "worked up" about the Justice Department's actions and "sick and tired of the federal government butting in on everything." Lexington County's sheriff, Henry Caughman, whose jurisdiction included the town of Batesburg, announced that he had conducted his own investigation and concluded that Shull had acted "entirely in defense of himself and did his duty in handling the case." Caughman further stated that he "deplore[d] the fact that federal authorities have seen fit to come into

Lexington County" when the case could have been handled, "if handling was required," by "our competent South Carolina authorities."[25]

Dorchester County's sheriff, H. H. Jensen, announced that he had proposed a resolution to the South Carolina Law Enforcement Officers' Association that FBI agents be barred from the organization's annual summer meeting because of the Shull prosecution. Columbia's police chief, Lyle Campbell, opposed the Jensen resolution, observing that the decision to prosecute Shull came from elsewhere and the FBI was just following orders. The resolution to bar the FBI from South Carolina law-enforcement meetings was ultimately defeated, but the association publicly condemned the Shull prosecution and voted to provide $2,000 for legal defense costs for Shull and any other South Carolina law-enforcement officer charged in a federal civil rights prosecution. Director Hoover reported to Douglas McGregor, assistant to the attorney general, that there was strong sentiment among the South Carolina law-enforcement officers that the Department of Justice "had yielded to pressure from northern negroes and radical groups in this case and were prosecuting Chief Shull purely for political reasons."[26]

The vocal criticism by South Carolina law-enforcement officials was viewed with great alarm by locally assigned FBI agents, who worried that the Shull prosecution would damage the FBI's working relationship with local police agencies. Special Agent Brown asked his superiors if he was free to explain to local law-enforcement officials that the FBI's investigation had actually helped Shull. Brown proposed to tell the local officers that the FBI fieldwork had left Shull "in a better defensive position than he would have been had he been charged and tried solely on the basis of the facts presented by the NAACP since at that time witnesses having information favorable to the defense were not known." Brown was advised "specifically that he should not mention that point" because the bureau had recently been criticized by "various pressure groups" for not providing investigative information to assist black defendants charged by the state in the Columbia, Tennessee, incident. Brown was told, however, that he could tell South Carolina law-enforcement officers, if asked, that the FBI conducted civil rights investigations only on the "explicit instructions" of the Justice Department.[27]

———

Under normal circumstances, the Shull prosecution would have been tried by the Columbia-based U.S. district judge, George Bell Timmerman, because Batesburg fell within the Columbia Division of the Eastern District of South Carolina. But Timmerman had many reasons to avoid this case. He was a passionate segregationist and opposed federal civil rights prosecutions of police officers. Further, Timmerman resided in Batesburg and was personally acquainted with Shull, creating a potential conflict of interest. Judge Timmerman requested that his Charleston-based colleague, U.S. District Judge J. Waties Waring, accept the case assignment. Waring agreed to the case transfer and made plans to come to Columbia to try the case during a criminal trial term previously scheduled for the week of November 4, 1946.

As the trial attorneys within the Civil Rights Section of the Justice Department examined more closely the FBI's field reports while preparing for their November trial, they realized, apparently for the first time, that there were significant deficiencies in the bureau's field investigation. Justice Department lawyers observed that it was of "particular importance in this case to determine whether or not the victim did actually suffer a series of licks," as Woodard asserted, or whether he had been struck on only one occasion, as Shull claimed. Sapp was asked by Assistant Attorney General Caudle on October 23, less than two weeks before the beginning of the impending criminal trial term, to request a continuance beyond the court's November trial term to allow time to conduct further investigation into this and other matters. This request for a continuance likely suited Sapp because he was continuing his efforts to dismiss the case. Because district judges in the federal court system control their criminal dockets, Sapp traveled to Charleston to discuss with Judge Waring the Justice Department's request for a continuance.[28]

At this time, Waties Waring had served on the federal bench for

nearly five years, after a distinguished career as one of Charleston's premier civil litigators. Waring was known to have close ties to the state's
political establishment, having been nominated to the federal bench in
1942 with the support of South Carolina's two U.S. senators, Ellison
"Cotton Ed" Smith and Burnet Maybank. Sapp was confident he could
speak candidly to the judge about his opposition to the Shull prosecution
and his efforts to dismiss the case.[29]

Judge Waring had followed the press reports about the case. He was
aware of the active role of the NAACP and Orson Welles in promoting
the prosecution of Shull and the vocal opposition to the case by local political leaders and law-enforcement officials. Sapp disclosed to Waring
details of his call with the Justice Department prior to the filing of the
criminal charges. He acknowledged that he still had made no independent review of the case and had little knowledge of the facts. He shared
with Waring his desire to get the case dismissed and the Justice Department's request for a continuance to conduct further investigation.[30]

If Sapp expected a sympathetic response from Judge Waring, he was
surely disappointed. Waring let Sapp know that he was highly offended
by the conduct of the Justice Department in this matter and suspected
that the whole case was a publicity stunt by the Truman administration in
advance of the November congressional elections. To Sapp's apparent
amazement, Waring advised him that the request for a continuance was
denied. He further told Sapp that if the Justice Department was not ready
to proceed when the case was called in early November, he would dismiss
the prosecution and publicly disclose in a written order what he believed to be professional misconduct by the department. Waring's trial
schedule would force the Justice Department to try the case by Election
Day or face the political consequences of the judge's dismissing the case
with an embarrassing judicial order.

Anticipating that the government would not be ready to proceed,
Waring drafted an order dismissing the Shull prosecution. The draft order
questioned the need for filing the case one day after the documents were
sent from Washington, wondering about the "haste in starting a prose-

cution." Waring referenced public statements made on radio and in the newspapers about the case and observed that the case "had gone beyond the bounds of an ordinary criminal prosecution." He went on to state that "a criminal prosecution in the courts of this country should [not] be influenced one way or the other by the desire of any of the parties for publicity" or political benefit. He concluded that the blinded victim should not "be used as a football in a contest between the box office and the ballot box."[31]

When Sapp reported to the Justice Department Judge Waring's denial of the continuance and intention to dismiss the case with an order denouncing the department, he was advised that the department would be ready to try the case when it was called. Waring's draft order was, therefore, never issued. Instead, Sapp's office rushed to issue subpoenas to the witnesses whose names were only now supplied by the Justice Department. An apparently perplexed Special Agent Brown advised Hoover in a "personal and confidential" note of October 30, 1946, that the Justice Department "was definitely determined to carry through the prosecution of this case despite the apparent reluctance on the part of Mr. Sapp."[32]

Because Sapp was wholly unfamiliar with the facts of the Shull case and had never tried a civil rights prosecution, the Justice Department agreed to send an attorney from the Civil Rights Section to be lead counsel and to allow Sapp to serve as second chair. But this plan had its own challenges because the Justice Department staff attorney assigned to the case, Fred S. Rogers, was not scheduled to arrive in Columbia until Monday morning, November 4, 1946, after driving all night from Washington. Rogers and Sapp would then interview the key witnesses in the case, whom neither had ever met. The trial was anticipated to commence the following morning, Tuesday, November 5.[33]

Thus, the case of *United States v. Lynwood Shull*, the first major civil rights prosecution in the postwar era, was now scheduled to go to trial under less than ideal circumstances. The attorneys responsible for prosecuting the case were unprepared and would have essentially twenty-four hours to meet the witnesses and prepare a joint trial strategy. The case was to be tried in a Deep South city where prominent elected and law-enforcement officials had publicly denounced the prosecution as federal meddling tainted by improper political considerations. It was likely that the more informed members of the jury panel would be aware of these public criticisms. Further, the department's investigation was woefully incomplete, and the veteran U.S. attorney was actively scheming with FBI agents to get the case dismissed. It is hard to imagine a less promising scenario.

6.

THE ISAAC WOODARD
ROAD SHOW

FROM HIS DISCHARGE from the U.S. Army on that hopeful afternoon of February 12, 1946, until the announcement of federal criminal charges against Lynwood Shull some seven and a half months later, Isaac Woodard had been on an extraordinary roller-coaster ride. He had experienced the joyful moments of a returning decorated veteran about to visit his wife and family and the desperate low of waking up in a small-town southern jail blinded and wondering if this was a nightmare. The lows continued with a finding by his doctors that his blindness was irreversible and a decision by the Veterans Administration that he was eligible only for a partial and inadequate pension because he was, although still in uniform, technically not in military service when he was blinded.

Woodard struggled for two months in the VA Hospital in Columbia,

South Carolina, dealing with the physical and psychological scars of his injuries and blindness. Abandoned by his wife, Rosa, and having no adequate means of support, he retreated to his family's new home in the Bronx. He suffered from severe headaches and had little physical independence because he had received no training to assist him with adapting to his new disability.[1]

After the story of Woodard's blinding was spread across the nation through press reports and the Orson Welles radio broadcasts, everyone seemed to want a piece of Isaac Woodard. Activist groups, including the American Communist Party and black veterans organizations, embraced his cause, and good-hearted citizens began appearing uninvited at the Woodard home offering to lend a hand. The *Amsterdam News* promoted a celebrity-filled benefit concert, and Woodard received offers for compensated speaking engagements. In the midst of what was fast becoming a public circus, the NAACP leadership saw its control of the story and of Woodard potentially slipping away.

The NAACP had an understandable interest in preserving its relationship with Woodard because the organization's staff had played such an important role in initially publicizing the incident. The NAACP and Woodard entered into a written representation agreement, which made the organization his exclusive representative for all legal and fund-raising matters. The *Amsterdam News* concert was already off and running, and C. B. Powell was unwilling to relinquish to the NAACP his control of the program or of funds raised. This created palpable tension between two titans of the black community in America, Walter White and C. B. Powell. White informed the *Amsterdam News* staff that he was unwilling to participate in the all-star celebrity concert because no agreement had been reached with the NAACP about the disposition of the funds raised, which resulted in his notable and somewhat embarrassing absence at the blockbuster event in Harlem on August 18, 1946.[2]

Because Isaac Woodard had no means of support other than a $50-per-month pension payment, he was eager to respond to offers for compensated speaking engagements. This forced the NAACP to decide whether it would organize its own speaking tour for Woodard or turn him loose to make his own arrangements with other organizations. In late August 1946, Walter White advised his senior staff that the NAACP would sponsor its own national speaking tour for Woodard and directed them to immediately present him with a comprehensive plan. White stated that the "tour should be arranged exclusively under the auspices of the NAACP for further stirring of public opinion on the issue of mob violence and to raise funds both for the prosecution of the Woodard case and for the whole fight against mob violence."[3]

Planning a multi-city coast-to-coast speaking tour in 1946 was a daunting task. NAACP staffers contacted branch presidents asking whether their local chapters would be willing to sponsor a Woodard event. A common question soon arose as to whether the branches would receive a cut of any proceeds raised. Meanwhile, rumors were spreading that the NAACP was taking money raised for Woodard to support its expanding budget. Walter White, highly sensitive to such rumors, publicly announced that funds raised on Woodard's behalf would be placed in a separate trust fund. Local NAACP chapters were told they would not be sharing in the funds raised through the Woodard speaking tour. The NAACP executed a second written agreement with Woodard, promising he would receive one-half of the proceeds raised on the tour, with the other half going to defray expenses and to promote the association's campaign against mob violence.[4]

The suggestion that the NAACP was profiting from Woodard's misfortune was unfair. Were it not for the NAACP, Woodard's story would likely never have garnered the vast public attention it received. The association's legal staff expended countless hours promoting Woodard's pension claim, and tremendous organizational resources were applied to publicize the story. Any funds ultimately received by the NAACP from its efforts on Woodard's behalf covered only a fraction of the costs associated with the various Woodard-related activities. While the NAACP certainly benefited from its association with Isaac Woodard, the blinded veteran personally received great benefits from the relationship.

NAACP staffers confronted a number of practical problems in organizing a national speaking tour for Woodard, who continued to have significant physical and emotional problems resulting from his severe beating and blinding. As discussions evolved regarding the beginning date of the tour, Woodard candidly told association staff members that he was in no shape for a national tour. He pushed the start date back until mid-October 1946 as he continued to convalesce from his injuries.

Some association staff expressed concern that Woodard needed around-the-clock assistance because he had limited physical independence and would be undertaking an extensive cross-country trip that required frequent intercity train travel. One staff member, Madison Jones, recommended against the association's undertaking the Woodard speaking tour. She argued that Woodard was "not too well" and "totally blind" and could not "be left alone for very long." Another staff member, Ruby Hurley, expressed concern that "the young man has not been blind long enough to be completely adept at handling himself" and recommended that a relative be employed as a personal assistant for him on the tour. This recommendation was followed, and the association hired Woodard's cousin Willie Mabry, an army veteran, to accompany him.[5]

Beyond these challenges, there was a concern that Woodard was not an experienced or inspiring public speaker. In fact, his public orations to date had mostly been delivered in a flat monotone, with a tendency for his voice to dip so low that his audience had trouble hearing him. To address this potential problem, the national office advised the local branches to include in the program "dynamic orators" to excite the audience and to "make a stirring appeal for money."[6]

The call for the local branches to participate in the Woodard speaking tour was greeted with great enthusiasm. Support for the tour grew to a fever pitch when Attorney General Clark announced on September 26, 1946, that the Justice Department had filed criminal charges in Columbia, South Carolina, against Lynwood Shull. NAACP staffers had little trouble finding host cities for the tour, which began in Baltimore on October 20 and stretched over seven weeks across more than two dozen cities in the East and the Midwest and on the West Coast. The tremendous response from the local branches was a testament to both the resonance of Woodard's story and the skillful promotion by the NAACP.[7]

As the tour began in mid-October, Woodard had acquired celebrity status in black communities across the nation. Part of this came from the remarkable circumstances that led to his blindness. Also key was that, in Woodard's telling, his removal from the Greyhound bus and into the hands of Chief Shull had occurred because he insisted that the white bus driver speak to him with respect: "I am a man just like you." But a significant part of the Woodard mystique was the simple fact that he was a walking, talking survivor of southern racial violence. Most victims of racial violence did not survive, and those who did were usually too frightened to share their story. Woodard was very much alive and willing to speak out boldly against the violence that had taken his sight. For many black Americans, Isaac Woodard was a true American hero.

The NAACP staff did not depend exclusively on Woodard's celebrity status to produce large crowds for his appearances, and gave specific instructions to the local branches on ways to promote the tour and fill auditoriums and churches. Some branches were well organized and able to turn out big crowds with minimal effort, while others had been relatively inactive and needed something like the Woodard event to reinvigorate them.

Local leaders were instructed to print and distribute materials announcing the event and to issue press releases. Skillfully designed broadsides and other promotional materials urged attendance. One broadside stated, "See and Hear Isaac Woodard, [the] veteran whose eyes were gouged out by Batesburg, S. Carolina police." Another promotional piece stated, "Hear Woodard tell his story! Support the fight for justice." One branch used attractive women with sandwich boards stating, "Don't Forget Isaac Woodard," and including the time, date, and location of the event.[8]

According to the national office's instructions, the program needed to have a revival feel, with music and great oration, and a focus on the ongoing battle against mob violence. Churches were urged to sponsor

"Isaac Woodard Day" events on the Sunday before Woodard's appearance as a means of promoting attendance and obtaining "offering[s]" to
support the tour.

Recognizing that the national tour was costly, local branches were
tasked with raising "at least $1,000 in the collection over and above the
expenses." This was to be accomplished by "secur[ing] a good money-
raiser to take the offering" and by promising that any churches and other
organizations that raised funds would be recognized at the mass meeting.
Local leaders were informed that the fund-raising effort was both to benefit Woodard and to "continue the fight against discrimination, segregation and the denial of civil liberties in America."[9]

Although the tour was to have an informal, old-time church feeling, it
was organized with a high degree of skill. Strict accounting was made of
all funds raised, with daily reports airmailed to the national office. The
tour entourage included Woodard, Mabry, and a senior NAACP staff
member. Details were coordinated out of the national office with designated branch officials in each tour location. A precise train schedule was
set before the tour's commencement, with specific departure times set
for each city.

In addition to the core traveling group, the NAACP sent speakers from
the national office to participate. In some locations, Woodard's NAACP-
assigned attorney, Franklin Williams, would speak. At others, Thurgood
Marshall appeared. At the Washington, D.C., event, the speakers included
Orson Welles, the journalist Drew Pearson, and Walter White. Prominent
local ministers and civil rights leaders were given speaking roles. In some
locations, where religious and labor groups endorsed the event, a rabbi or
a labor leader would deliver an opening prayer or welcome. By all reports,
the various events were professionally organized and presented.[10]

The tour had its inaugural event in Baltimore on October 20, 1946,
and soon headed to such cities as Louisville, Indianapolis, St. Louis,
Pittsburgh, Milwaukee, and Wichita. The plan was for the tour to break
for a few days after the Wichita event on October 30 to allow Woodard
and his entourage to travel to the West Coast for events in Los Angeles,

San Francisco, Seattle, and other cities. These events had been heavily promoted by the West Coast NAACP branches, and large turnouts were anticipated.

Given the buzz associated with the Woodard story, it is not surprising that the speaking tour had overflowing, enthusiastic audiences. Typical was Woodard's appearance in Youngstown, Ohio, where seven hundred people packed into the large sanctuary at Oak Hill Avenue AME Church and still others heard the program piped into the church's lower-level Sunday school classrooms. Local NAACP leaders and Franklin Williams spoke to the gathering, but the highlight of the evening was Woodard's dramatic recitation of the events that had led to his blinding. Woodard, dressed in his army uniform and wearing sunglasses to cover his devastated eyes, was guided to the podium after being introduced by Williams. A rapt audience sat riveted to the sergeant's words. He stated, "I spent three and a half years in service of my country and thought I would be treated as a man when I returned to civilian life but I was mistaken. Five hours after I was discharged and while still in the uniform of my country, I was assaulted and my eyes were gouged out by a South Carolina police officer." He went on to state that he would "gladly give my sight if it will mean that my people will unite and fight such things."

Among those present at the Youngstown event was a recently returned army veteran, Nathaniel Jones, who covered the event for the local black-owned newspaper, *The Buckeye Review*, and interviewed Woodard after his talk. Remembering the event more than seventy years later, Jones recalled the Woodard appearance in detail, explaining that the sergeant's very survival and courage in the face of unspeakable evil were seared forever in his memory. Jones would later attend law school and devote much of his legal career to civil rights work, ultimately serving for a decade as general counsel of the NAACP. In 1979, President Carter nominated Jones for a position on the Sixth Circuit Court of Appeals, where he served until his retirement in 2002.[11]

As the tour moved across the country, a behind-the-scenes battle ensued between C. B. Powell and Walter White concerning the disposition of funds raised for Woodard's benefit. Initially, Powell proposed devoting the funds to the purchase of a restaurant, but Woodard's blindness and lack of business experience caused that idea to be rejected. Next he favored devoting the funds to purchase a multifamily home for Woodard, which would provide him with a cost-free place to live and allow him to generate rental income. But the NAACP staff strongly opposed Powell's proposal, arguing that Woodard would likely be victimized by unscrupulous characters and lose the property. The association favored the purchase of a lifetime annuity that would provide Woodard with a monthly income.

In the end, Powell and the NAACP decided to go their separate ways. Powell personally visited potential homes with Woodard's mother, and they located a suitable multifamily property at 1075 Forest Avenue in the Bronx. Applying proceeds from the benefit concert, Woodard was able to acquire the home in an all-cash transaction of $11,752.85. The NAACP elected to use the proceeds from Woodard's national speaking tour, which ultimately reached $10,500, for the purchase of a lifetime annuity, which initially generated $50 per month. Combined with his VA disability pension, Woodard now had a monthly income of $100, equivalent today to approximately $1,325 per month. In making the argument that Woodard would benefit from a monthly annuity, the NAACP staffer Madison Jones astutely observed the need for lifetime income because "right now he is riding the crest of a wave of popularity but ten years from now no one will remember Woodard."[12]

As the tour progressed, an unexpected development disrupted the schedule. Late in the week of October 28, 1946, the NAACP legal counsel's office was informed that U.S. District Judge J. Waties Waring, the presiding judge in the Shull prosecution, had denied the Justice Department's request for a continuance. U.S. Attorney Sapp sent word that he needed Woodard in Columbia, South Carolina, on Monday morning, November 4, to meet with prosecutors to prepare for trial. The demand that

Woodard immediately appear in South Carolina could not have come at a more inconvenient time. Staffers responsible for organizing the tour were confused about what Woodard should do because elaborate and costly plans had been made for the West Coast tour events. But Robert Carter let it be known that there was really no choice. If Woodard failed to appear, Sapp would surely dismiss the charges against Shull.[13]

Confronting reality, the NAACP reluctantly canceled the West Coast leg of the tour, which was to run from November 3 to 11, with the plan to pick the tour back up in Denver on November 15. Meanwhile, Thurgood Marshall made contact with local association officials in Columbia to find a suitable place for Woodard and Franklin Williams to stay, beginning on Sunday, November 3. Woodard and Williams made their way to Columbia, arriving mid-afternoon on Sunday and registering at a segregated downtown hotel in preparation for their meeting with the government prosecutors the next morning. They were about to have an experience that they, and many others present for the trial of *United States v. Shull*, would never forget.[14]

7.

THE GRADUALIST

TRYING **CIVIL RIGHTS CASES** in southern federal courthouses in the 1940s was, to say the least, a challenging experience. Federal district judges presiding in the South were frequently hostile and almost always unreceptive to civil rights claims, and even the most meritorious cases had to be won on appeal after suffering an initial defeat at the trial court level. This hostile environment reflected the political culture of the South during this era and the process by which federal judges were selected.

Federal district judgeships, which are lifetime appointments, have long been highly sought-after nominations, traditionally held by the closest and most loyal political allies of a state's U.S. senators. Federal judges are nominated by the president on the recommendation of their state's senators and must be confirmed by the full U.S. Senate. Under long-standing Senate custom, a district judge's nomination does not go forward for confirmation unless both of the state's senators have indicated their approval through the submission of a document known as a blue slip. In the 1940s, essentially every U.S. senator from the South was publicly committed to racial segregation, and it was unthinkable that any lawyer who questioned the racial status quo would ever have been considered for appointment to the federal bench from any of the former states of the Confederacy. Simply put, the racial views of the federal judges of that era were generally a reflection of their Senate sponsors.

The district judge assigned to the case of *United States v. Lynwood Shull*, George Bell Timmerman, fit the profile of the unsympathetic federal judge NAACP lawyers routinely encountered in the South. But Judge Timmerman decided to recuse himself and to have the case tried by his colleague Judge J. Waties Waring. This, for the NAACP, was an interesting development. Although Judge Waring seemed to be thoroughly steeped in the social and political culture of South Carolina, Thurgood Marshall had seen a glimmer of something from Waring in earlier cases that suggested there might be something different about this Charleston patrician.

———

Waring was an imposing figure. Over six feet tall, he had steely blue eyes and spoke with an upper-class Charleston cadence. He commanded his courtroom with a firm hand and was respected by the federal bar for his efficiency, decisiveness, and hard work. His path to appointment to the federal bench in 1942 had been thoroughly conventional, without the slightest suggestion that he questioned the racial status quo.

Judge Waring was an eighth-generation Charlestonian with family roots that reached back into the earliest days of the Carolina colony. Benjamin Waring, the first generation of Warings to arrive in the state, acquired 700 acres on the Ashley River in 1683. His mother's family, the Watieses, settled in the Charleston area from Wales in 1694 and acquired 250 acres. Multiple generations of Warings and Watieses were slaveholders. Waring's maternal great-grandfather, Thomas Waties, held the prestigious position of chancellor of the South Carolina Court of Equity. Waring's father, Edward Perry Waring, was a Confederate veteran "thoroughly saturated with the southern cause." An uncle, one of his father's brothers, died in battle during the Civil War.[1]

Waties Waring was born in Charleston in 1880 and was the youngest of four children. He was raised during an economically challenging time for the city. Charleston was once a thriving and wealthy port city, but the devastation wrought by the Civil War left the city a shadow of its former self. The once grand houses of the Battery, the waterfront promenade that in antebellum years had been one of the wealthiest streets in America, were now mostly threadbare and deteriorating under the stress of inadequate maintenance in the semitropical climate. Waring described the Charleston of his childhood as living "completely" in the "Confederate southern tradition," sustained by "rice and recollections." In this environment, free thought was neither welcomed nor tolerated.

Like that of many white Charlestonians of this era, the luster of the Waring family's past was a bit faded. Waring's father was a middle manager in a small railroad company, and family fortunes tended to rise and fall with the economy. The elder Waring periodically found himself out of work and struggled to maintain a middle-class lifestyle for the family. Waring's mother, Anna Waties Waring, who had been orphaned as a child, was an avid reader and instilled in her four children (three boys and one girl) a great love of learning. Waring's eldest brother, Thomas, excelled as a student and received a full scholarship to Hobart College, a small Episcopal school in upstate New York. Thomas was a mentor to Waties, who was nine years his junior and the baby of the family. When Waties Waring finished high school, his family had no funds to send him away to college. He entered the local city college, the College of Charleston, while continuing to live at home. Waring's college studies focused on the classics, and he proved to be a gifted student, ultimately finishing number two in his class.[2]

Waties Waring was raised with the assumption that he would one day become a lawyer. His father often referred to him as "Judge," and it was anticipated that he would restore the family's legacy in the law. When Waring finished his studies at the College of Charleston in 1900, his family's economic circumstances prevented him from attending the law school at the University of South Carolina in Columbia. Instead, Waring studied law in the "old style," which required the aspiring attorney to read traditional legal texts and other materials on his own while working as a sort of apprentice or in an observer capacity in a local law office. Waring took the process seriously, rigorously studying such challenging materials as the multivolume treatises Blackstone's *Commentaries* and Kent's *Commentaries*. He also assisted in a law office on Broad Street, which was Charleston's "legal street." After two years of "reading law," Waring took and passed the South Carolina Bar in 1902. His path to the bar was not unusual for the era: such notable South Carolina public officials as James F. Byrnes and Strom Thurmond obtained their law licenses in the same way.[3]

Initially sharing space in the office where he had read law, Waring slowly but steadily built his own practice. He received referrals involving minor legal disputes from older attorneys and represented various small businesses. He tried cases in magistrate's court, where the fees were not large enough for the more experienced attorneys. Waring's initial aspirations were modest. He hoped to make a "mark in the legal fraternity in Charleston and take my part and trade blows with other lawyers." Waring also was active in local Democratic Party politics, doing behind-the-scenes work for candidates rather than seeking public office himself.

In 1913, after an extended courtship, Waring married Annie Gammell, a distant cousin by marriage with deep Charleston roots. Both were in their thirties. Before the marriage, Annie had studied acting in New York and lived for a number of years in Paris, where she had what was essentially a daughter-mother relationship with the renowned actress Sarah Bernhardt. Years later, Bernhardt would become the godmother of the Warings' only child, Anne. The new couple soon became part of the active and very insular Charleston social scene and members of the city's highly selective social clubs.[4]

Waring's political work paid off in 1914, a year after his marriage, when he was appointed assistant U.S. attorney in Charleston. He was essentially a one-man show in the Charleston office, with his boss, U.S. Attorney Francis H. Weston, working out of the federal courthouse in Columbia, some two hours away. Weston gave Waring a free hand to run the Charleston office, which allowed him to try a wide variety of civil and criminal cases and to argue the office's appeals before the Fourth Circuit Court of Appeals in Richmond, Virginia. It is hard to imagine a better training ground for an able young attorney.

A special benefit of Waring's relationship with Weston was the U.S. attorney's close friendship with the state's senior U.S. senator, Ellison "Cotton Ed" Smith. Weston had previously served as Cotton Ed's campaign manager, and Waring's work with Weston brought him into the senator's inner circle. Cotton Ed had a well-earned reputation for racially inflammatory campaigns, and his "racist rhetoric," as one historian observed, "made Klan kleagles sound like Boy Scouts by comparison." Waring, while later acknowledging that Cotton Ed was a demagogue who fired up the "backwoods boys" with "race talk," admitted a "sneaking fondness" for him personally and for his innate political skills.[5]

Waring left the U.S. Attorney's Office in 1921 with the election of a new Republican president. By this point, he had developed a reputation as a skilled and experienced federal litigator and had opened a law practice with D. A. Brockington. He was also becoming known as someone with good political connections, certainly enhanced by his sister's husband, Wilson G. Harvey, who served as lieutenant governor and governor of South Carolina in the 1920s. Waring would eventually build a silk-stocking law practice representing some of the city's most prominent business interests, including the local newspaper company (where his brother Thomas served as an editor), major shipping interests, and insurance companies.

Waring continued his active involvement in local politics, throwing himself fully into the successful effort of an upstart businessman and city councilman, Burnet Maybank, in his 1930 campaign for mayor of

Charleston. When Maybank took office, he gave Waring the plum appointment of corporation counsel, or city attorney. Waring would hold this prestigious part-time position for a dozen years, until he resigned to become U.S. district judge.

Mayor Maybank inherited an insolvent city government with its economy deeply distressed by the Depression. With Waring's able legal assistance, Maybank designed innovative programs to rescue the city government and provide critical services to its citizens. When the city's coffers ran dry and the banks would not make loans to help it make payroll, he arranged for Charleston to issue script to pay its employees. Maybank was an early supporter of Franklin Roosevelt's and used his close connections to the White House to obtain major federal grants for large public works projects, which helped keep the struggling city afloat.[6]

Waring had long nursed an ambition to be the U.S. district judge assigned to the Charleston Federal Courthouse. His prior federal service, successful law practice, and close relationships with various political big shots made this a seemingly realistic ambition. All Waring needed was a new Democratic administration in Washington, and with some luck the position might be his. With the election of Franklin Roosevelt in 1932 and an opening in the Charleston federal judgeship in 1934, it appeared the stars might be lining up for Waties Waring.

Cotton Ed endorsed Waring's nomination to the district court bench, and many Charleston lawyers wrote to the Justice Department in support of Waring's appointment. To the astonishment of Waring and many others, the nomination went to Frank K. Myers, a county judicial officer, the master in equity, who had never practiced in federal court. But Myers had the benefit of being the former law partner of the junior U.S. senator, James F. Byrnes, who had a very close relationship with the Roosevelt White House. Myers also happened to be the father-in-law of Mayor Maybank, and Waring harbored the suspicion that his closest political friend had sold him out.[7]

Waring, likely continuing to pursue his judicial ambitions, agreed to serve as the Charleston County campaign manager for Cotton Ed's

1938 reelection campaign. This was politically an unlikely place for an urbane and socially connected Charlestonian like Waring with a flourishing upscale law practice and close ties to many New Dealers. By 1938, Cotton Ed was one of Roosevelt's most outspoken critics, and the president had taken the unusual step of endorsing his opponent in the Democratic primary, Governor Olin Johnston. Most of South Carolina's politically active Roosevelt Democrats backed Johnston, and Roosevelt personally visited the state to stump for Johnston. There appeared to be little doubt that Cotton Ed was about to suffer a humiliating defeat.

Cotton Ed doubled down on his racial rhetoric in the 1938 campaign, regaling his rural supporters with the story of how he walked out of the 1936 Democratic National Convention in Philadelphia when a black minister was allowed to deliver the opening prayer. When Cotton Ed once attempted to talk about agriculture policy during a stump speech, one of his supporters yelled out, "Aw, cut all of that out, Ed, and tells us about Philadelphy." Cotton Ed won the Democratic primary after receiving a surprisingly strong vote in Charleston County. Waring was credited with playing an important role in Smith's unexpected reelection victory.[8]

In that same year, Burnet Maybank parlayed his highly successful career as mayor of Charleston into election as governor of South Carolina. He filed to run for the U.S. Senate in 1941 in a special election caused by Senator Byrnes's appointment to the U.S. Supreme Court. Soon after entering the race, Maybank dropped by Waring's Broad Street office to ask him to serve as his Charleston County campaign manager for the Senate race. Waring had heard rumors that Maybank had already promised any future federal judgeship openings to others and, remembering the prior episode with Maybank's father-in-law, asked for a personal commitment from the governor for a future federal judicial appointment. When Maybank declined to make that commitment, Waring curtly declined to serve as Maybank's Charleston County campaign manager. Maybank left Waring's office in a huff, and Waring's judicial possibilities seemed to have walked out the door with him.[9]

But politics can produce unpredictable results. Shortly after Maybank's successful election to the U.S. Senate, federal district court judgeships opened in both Columbia and Charleston. Cotton Ed was persona non grata in the Roosevelt White House, but his blue slip was necessary to obtain confirmation for any South Carolina district court appointment. Maybank, with his close Roosevelt ties, acted as a middleman in an effort to nominate candidates for both openings acceptable to the White House, Cotton Ed, and himself. For political reasons, Maybank wanted to nominate George Bell Timmerman for the Columbia seat and seemed to have a lesser interest in the Charleston slot. Both Maybank and Smith submitted numerous names to the Justice Department as potential nominees for the Charleston judgeship. The one name in common on the senators' lists was J. Waties Waring. Thus, apparently out of the blue, Senator Maybank called Waring late one evening to advise him that President Roosevelt would soon nominate him as U.S. district judge, with the formal announcement made by the White House on December 18, 1941. A little over a month later, at high noon on January 26, 1942, Waties Waring took the oath of office as a U.S. district judge for the Eastern District of South Carolina. He was then sixty-one years old, a little on the old side for a newly appointed federal judge. The state's two U.S. senators, Maybank and Cotton Ed, proudly claimed credit for Waring's nomination, and the federal bar generally viewed Waring as a solid choice for the Charleston judgeship.[10]

Waring assumed his judicial duties with vigor, quickly attacking the badly congested Charleston federal court trial roster, where some cases had languished for more than a decade. He summoned lawyers to frequent roster calls and set the oldest cases for trial. Most of the cases settled, and Waring tried the few that were not resolved. In short order, he had in place a very current trial docket, which he maintained until his retirement a decade later.[11]

In subsequent years, some Waring critics would claim that he had always secretly harbored unorthodox racial views and committed a sort of fraud to obtain his judgeship. This was surely not the case. But the critique suggested that there was a single fixed view on race held by white southerners at the time when, in fact, there was some nuance and subtlety among whites on the racial issue. Without a doubt, no rational white southerner in public life would openly question racial segregation or black disenfranchisement. When a random minister, college professor, or newspaperman would seem to challenge these racial orthodoxies, the vehement response and inevitable retaliation from segregationists would persuade other like-minded southerners to keep their opinions to themselves. But among those in the political and social mainstream of the South at the time, there were differences in both style and substance on the race question. Some more progressive whites, while not challenging the separate but equal doctrine of *Plessy*, believed that greater funding should be provided to public services for blacks, particularly in the area of the public schools, and that black public servants, such as schoolteachers, should receive equal pay for equal work. These self-described southern liberals supported Jim Crow without all the vitriol, which meant in effect that they supported the *Plessy* separate but equal doctrine.

The far more predominant view, however, was that white hegemony should be vigorously maintained through strict adherence to Jim Crow laws and that no more than minimal financial support should be given to the segregated black public schools, on the theory that whites paid most of the taxes and should get most of the benefits. Suffused in this view was an inherent hostility toward African Americans and an unquestioned premise that they posed a persistent threat to white security and control. Most of the white elected officials in the South toed this line, vocally opposing federal anti-lynching legislation and any other efforts that might be perceived as encroaching on white control. This approach essentially provided for separate and *un*equal.

As Waties Waring donned the black robe of his new judicial office in January 1942, he had never given much thought to these racial issues. By background and temperament, he was attuned to the more progressive southern view on race, but this did not prevent him from playing a key role in Cotton Ed's 1938 reelection campaign. Waring later explained his views on race prior to assuming his judgeship: "We didn't give them any rights, but they never asked for any rights, and I didn't question it."[12]

———

In the 1940s, civil rights litigation brought by the NAACP was coming into its own, with a major U.S. Supreme Court victory overturning the Texas all-white Democratic primary in *Smith v. Allwright* (1944) and the Fourth Circuit Court of Appeals in Richmond, Virginia, declaring a discriminatory teacher pay system unconstitutional in *Alston v. School Board of City of Norfolk* (1940). As the NAACP sought to build on these legal successes, South Carolina was on the front lines in many of its cases.

At the time, South Carolina had three federal judges covering two judicial districts in the state. One judge presided in the Eastern District, one in the Western District, and the third, a "roving" judge, handled cases in both districts. Judge Waring was assigned to the Eastern District and was responsible for cases in the federal courthouse in Charleston and in smaller courthouses in Orangeburg and Florence. Judge Charles Cecil Wyche was assigned to the Western District seat in Greenville and handled cases in upstate. Judge Timmerman, the roving judge, presided in the courthouse in Columbia. It was an open secret that Timmerman disliked handling civil rights cases and opposed the recent Supreme Court civil rights decisions. He routinely recused himself from civil rights cases on the basis of some perceived conflict of interest, or he found other means to transfer these cases off his docket. Because most of the South Carolina civil rights cases arose in the Eastern District, which had the highest percentage of African American population, Timmerman's cases were reassigned to the other Eastern District judge, Waties Waring.[13]

Waring's first significant civil rights case, *Duvall v. Seignous*, was filed in November 1943 and involved a challenge by a black Charleston chemistry teacher, Viola Duvall, who complained that she was paid 30 percent less than similarly situated white teachers. Duvall brought her suit on behalf of herself and a class of similarly situated black teachers in the Charleston city school district. Except for the racial issues raised in the litigation, this should have been an easy case. In 1940, the Fourth Circuit Court of Appeals, which handled cases from the federal courts from Maryland to South Carolina, struck a similar race-based pay scheme in Norfolk, Virginia, in its landmark *Alston* decision, finding that such a pay disparity based upon race violated the separate but equal doctrine of *Plessy v. Ferguson*.[14]

The *Alston* decision was authored by the Fourth Circuit's chief judge, John J. Parker, the most eminent and respected federal judge in the South. Nearly twenty years earlier, Parker's nomination to the U.S. Supreme Court was defeated in the Senate by a vote of 41 to 39, with the attack on Parker based primarily on comments supporting black disenfranchisement he had made as a candidate for governor of North Carolina in 1920. The rejection of his Supreme Court nomination remained a source of great personal embarrassment to the judge, and Parker spent much of his remaining judicial career trying to demonstrate that the characterizations of him during the confirmation battle were unfair and undeserved. Notwithstanding Parker's relatively progressive views on race reflected by his order in *Alston*, he remained to many white southerners a hero and martyr to the southern cause, unjustly victimized by northern liberals and civil rights activists.

Duvall's attorney, Thurgood Marshall, was under no illusion about winning his case in the Charleston Federal Courthouse. Despite the strong Fourth Circuit precedent, Marshall understood the unwritten rule that federal district judges sitting in the South did not side with plaintiffs in civil rights cases. If civil rights plaintiffs were to get relief, they had to absorb defeat at the district court level and then persuade a federal court of appeals or the U.S. Supreme Court to reverse that decision.

Marshall arrived in Charleston to try the *Duvall* case in early February 1944 expecting, he would later admit, "the usual legal head whipping before I went along to the court of appeals." Prior to the trial, Marshall met with John McCray, a civil rights activist and editor of the local black-owned newspaper, *The Lighthouse and Informer*, and discussed the difficult challenge presented at the district court level. Marshall told McCray that he had come to Charleston "loaded for bear," but all understood that the chance for victory at the trial court level was slight. Indeed, McCray thought a win so improbable that he told Marshall, who famously loved scotch but never drank before a trial, that he would buy him a bottle of the best scotch in Charleston if he won the *Duvall* case. Neither seriously thought McCray would have to deliver on his offer.

When the trial opened on February 10, 1944, Marshall had his first encounter with Judge Waring, who he assumed "was just another southern jurist" who would fit the mold of the deeply unsympathetic federal district judges that he regularly appeared before in the South. The opening moments of the proceedings did nothing to cause Marshall to question that assumption. Waring directed a question to the school district attorney, asking him for the date of the *Alston* decision. As the school board lawyer dug into his files looking for the answer, a helpful Marshall stood to provide the court with the information because he had handled the *Alston* case. Waring directed Marshall to sit down, indicating that he had asked the school board attorney the question. The school board attorney then advised the Court that the *Alston* case had been decided in 1940. Waring asked the school board lawyer what year an earlier and similar federal court decision in Maryland had been decided. As the school board lawyer dug into his files to answer this inquiry, Marshall again stood to provide Waring with the requested date because he had also handled the Maryland equal pay case. This time, even more sternly, Waring informed Marshall he had directed his question to the school board lawyer. A friend of the plaintiff's sitting behind Duvall loudly lamented, "They won't even let her lawyer speak." When the school board's lawyer announced that the Maryland case was decided in 1939, Waring turned to Marshall and stated, "I don't want you to think I was being rude in not permitting you to answer those questions. I knew you knew the answers. I was trying to determine how long it had been that the school board in Charleston has known that it must pay equal salaries." Waring's comments stunned the school board attorney, who had assumed his local judge would rule with him.[15]

The trial of the *Duvall* case was conducted before Judge Waring without a jury. Marshall called Duvall as his first witness. She detailed her educational background and duties as a classroom teacher, demonstrating that she was performing work equal to that of similarly situated and trained white teachers. She further testified that despite her equal training and duties, she was paid a markedly unequal wage. The school district's accountant testified next, and admitted under questioning by Judge Waring that the disparity in the salaries of black and white teachers was based entirely upon race. After the accountant stepped off the witness stand, the school board attorney, sensing things were not going well for his client, asked the court for a recess to discuss a potential settlement with Marshall. Shortly thereafter, the parties advised Waring that a settlement had been reached. The settlement was formalized in a court order signed by Waring, which found that the district's "official policy and official acts" of paying "Negro teachers and principals . . . smaller salaries" than those paid to their white colleagues constituted a "violation of the equal protection clause of the Fourteenth Amendment." The school district agreed to eliminate any race-based disparities in the teacher salary schedule but was given two years to do so.[16]

The consent decree in the *Duvall* case, implementing the parties' settlement agreement, marked an important milestone for the civil rights movement, with a victory by an African American plaintiff at the district court level in the South. Waring's tough questioning of the school board counsel and respectful treatment of Marshall were also notable. Marshall later remembered that *Duvall* was "the only case I ever tried with my mouth hanging open half the time" because "Judge Waring was so fair." On the night of February 10, 1944, having achieved an unexpected victory for Duvall and the other black schoolteachers of Charleston, Marshall received, as promised, a bottle of the city's best scotch from John McCray, and he and the city's NAACP leadership toasted their surprising success.[17]

The *Duvall* consent order did not go unnoticed by state legislative leaders. South Carolina's NAACP president, James Hinton, reported to

Marshall on March 17, 1944, that "the Charleston decision really turned [the] General Assembly upside down." Legislators demanded a new certification system that would justify continued pay disparities between black and white teachers without running afoul of Judge Waring's order. The new scheme devised was the use of the results of the National Teachers Exam (NTE) to establish a schedule of graded certificates, with the higher grades receiving the highest pay. The assumption was that white teachers would perform better on the standardized tests and this would provide a racially neutral standard to justify paying them at a higher rate. In reality, the new certification plan produced a chaotic result in which similarly trained and experienced teachers, both black and white, were paid vastly different amounts simply because of a result on a single standardized test. But at that time, the use of a racially neutral standard to set salaries was sufficient to survive legal challenge. The General Assembly also adopted a new law requiring any challenge to a teacher's pay be presented first to the school board and then on appeal to state court. This was an effort to prevent future federal court reviews of a school district's discriminatory teacher salary schedule.[18]

Soon after the *Duvall* case was concluded, Albert Thompson, an African American teacher in Richland County School District One, brought an equal pay suit on behalf of himself and a class of all black teachers in his school district, which included South Carolina's capital city of Columbia. The case, *Thompson v. Gibbes*, was initially assigned to Judge Timmerman, but he requested that Waring take the case because of his recent experience in handling the *Duvall* litigation.

The lawyers representing Richland One decided to take a more aggressive approach than had been taken by the Charleston School District in *Duvall* and vigorously contested the plaintiff's claims on both procedural and substantive grounds. The plaintiff in the Richland One case, Thompson, challenged the newly adopted state salary schedule, which relied on NTE scores, and a local salary supplement that continued to use race as a factor in setting teacher pay. The defendant's effort to mount a serious defense to its race-based local salary schedule was undermined, however, by the forthright responses of the school board's chairman, Dr. J. Heyward Gibbes, and the district superintendent, Dr. A. C. Flora, to Judge Waring's questioning regarding the district's pay practices. Later explaining that he was not prepared to "sit there like a mummy . . . and take what's handed to you," Waring conducted what was effectively a cross-examination of the witnesses, asking for an explanation of why a black teacher at a particular school was paid less than a similarly situated white teacher at another school. Flora responded, "One's a white school and the other's a Negro school." Flora testified that both teachers performed satisfactorily and were paid different salaries because "the school board orders me what to pay them. I pay what the school board says." Both the board chairman and the superintendent admitted that black teachers should be paid a wage equal to that of white teachers and that the school district's compensation scheme was not what it should be.[19]

The candor of the trial testimony of Flora and Gibbes impressed Waring, who was irritated by the tedious and officious arguments of the school board's lawyers. The straightforward federal court testimony provided by Flora and Gibbes was not the first time these men had taken public stands advocating a more progressive approach on racial issues. Both had been among twenty white South Carolinians who signed a controversial public call in March 1944 for a more humane and just state policy on race relations. Titling their appeal "A Statement on the Race Problem in South Carolina," the signers advocated greater resources be devoted to African American schools and communities and the appointment of blacks as police officers and to public boards affecting the black community. The statement did not challenge black disenfranchisement, observing that "Negro suffrage in South Carolina has no immediate solution," but commented that denial of African Americans' access to the ballot could not "endure indefinitely." The signers also made clear that their proposals did not include "social equality," racial code words for integration, and sought only to achieve a form of "white supremacy which is worthy of the name," one that "exists because of virtue, not power."[20]

Unlike his brief consent decree in *Duvall*, Waring issued a detailed order in *Thompson* on May 26, 1945, which addressed the numerous legal and factual defenses asserted by the school district. He quickly dismissed the argument that the newly established state law, which required that a teacher submit any salary dispute first to his local school board and then to state court, could deny the federal court's jurisdiction. Waring ruled that a state "cannot deprive the federal courts of jurisdiction granted them under the Constitution and laws of the United States." He indicated that he had no problem with the newly adopted state pay and certification system based on NTE results, even if it could be shown that black teachers were hurt by the use of the new system. Waring observed that "the concern of this court is whether it is free from the tinge of race prejudice, and I find it so to be."[21]

But Waring found that the present pay system was still infected with racially discriminatory elements. Approximately one-half a teacher's salary in Richland District One was based on a local salary supplement, and the local salary schedule still differentiated pay levels on the basis of race. Further, Waring was concerned that the state's new pay schedule had been adopted for only one year. The judge stated clearly that if the school district adopted and permanently implemented the state's newly created pay system, which relied on NTE scores to set salary levels, and abandoned any pay scheme that differentiated teachers on the basis of race, this would meet *Plessy*'s separate but equal standard.[22]

Waring made repeated positive references in the *Thompson* order to the testimony of Gibbes and Flora, noting that he "was greatly impressed" by their "desire to be just and fair to all parties." He observed that they had inherited a racially discriminatory pay system and had been "trying to eliminate gradually the disparity." Although not doubting the sincerity of the board chairman and the superintendent, he observed that a court order was necessary in the event that their "desires . . . are not backed up and followed by the Board."[23]

Waring's praise for the Richland One board chairman and superintendent reflected his personal identification with their desire to promote moderate and gradual progress on the racial front. Following his decision, Waring wrote Gibbes a private letter, dated June 12, 1945, indicating that he had seen in him and Flora "sympathetic and understanding persons" who understood that racial progress needed to be made in South Carolina. Waring lamented, "I am afraid that we are in the minority and the people of our state are going to be hard to educate along these lines." He went on to state, "We liberal minded southerners may be able to eventually cure this situation, not by the radical methods of the Eleanor Roosevelt–Wendell Willkie school, nor by the reactionary methods of the old slave owners, but by moderate, gradual and understanding action." In Waring's view at that time, racial progress in the South had to be directed by the better class of white southerners deliberately and gradually, without undue pressure from the federal government, the courts, or national civil rights groups.[24]

Waring's order in *Thompson* stirred little public criticism of the judge. In fact, his decision produced a favorable editorial in *The Columbia Record*, titled "Eliminating Discrimination," and he received a complimentary letter from Senator Edgar Brown, the president pro tempore of the South Carolina Senate and one of the state's most powerful legislative leaders. Brown's letter to Waring, addressed "Dear Waites," reflected the fact that the *Thompson* decision had not taken Waring outside the state's political mainstream on race. Waring responded to Brown's letter by telling him that he "was much impressed with the recertification plan" that had been adopted by the South Carolina General Assembly and that he believed the legislators had "hit on something that may prove very useful." Waring observed, "It is likely that at first the negro teachers are going to suffer . . . because of the inadequacy of preparation, and frankly, because most of them haven't an equal ability." Waring observed that "we should do all that we can to try and relieve" the state's overtly race-conscious pay scheme, and "if we can approach this from a moderate standpoint we shall do much."[25]

But Waring would later observe that the *Thompson* and *Duvall* trials affected him "internally," because "every time you looked into one of these things, the less reason you can see for resistance to what we commonly call the American creed of equality of all citizens of this country." Waring referred to the school district defenses in these cases as "old sophistry" that resulted in blacks not being "treated as ordinary American citizens, but were put in a separate classification." He later remembered that "the whole thing worried me a great deal, and I knew the thing was coming to a showdown someday" with issues far more difficult to resolve quietly and without controversy. He privately wondered whether, when a really difficult and controversial racial justice question was presented in the future, "I should dodge it or meet it."[26]

Waring's decisions in *Duvall* and *Thompson* carried great practical and symbolic significance to South Carolina's African American schoolteachers. As the former teacher and community activist Ruby Cornwell later observed, the salary increases resulting from Waring's two orders provided raises that allowed many black teachers to afford homes, cars, and other aspects of a middle-class lifestyle for the first time. The decisions also ended the indignity of college-educated professionals being paid a discriminatory wage for equal work performed. Further, the NAACP's success in the equal pay cases created a sense of hope and optimism in the South Carolina civil rights community that the state's federal district courts might become an effective forum to vindicate minority rights guaranteed by the U.S. Constitution.[27]

———

In the midst of handling the *Thompson* case, Waring confronted a profound crisis in his personal life. After thirty-two years of marriage, he came home from his office one February evening in 1945 to inform his wife, Annie Gammell Waring, that he had fallen in love with another woman and wanted a divorce. Waring's announcement stunned his wife and the couple's friends and family.

The other woman was Elizabeth Avery Mills Hoffman, the granddaughter of a Michigan lumber baron and the present wife of an elderly Connecticut textile manufacturer, Henry Hoffman. The Hoffmans wintered in Charleston and owned a home on historic Tradd Street. They were very much part of the Charleston social scene. As Elizabeth would later explain, prior to her divorce and marriage to Waring, she was the "toast of the town" because Charlestonians loved "rich northerners." Among the Hoffmans' many social acquaintances were the Warings, who were regular bridge partners. Little is known regarding exactly when Waties Waring and Elizabeth Hoffman went from being bridge partners to lovers, but in early 1945 both wanted divorces from their spouses so they could marry.[28]

Judge Waring's effort to divorce Annie was not without its difficulties under South Carolina law. At the time, South Carolina was the only state that did not allow divorce, and those South Carolinians seeking to end their marriages had to have one of the marriage partners acquire residence in another state to obtain a divorce. Judge Waring persuaded his shocked and devastated wife to move to Florida for ninety days to acquire state residency and then to file for divorce. Annie meekly acceded to her husband's request, moving to Florida on March 1, 1945, and petitioning for a divorce in early June. A Florida judge granted the divorce on June 7, 1945. Meanwhile, Elizabeth obtained a divorce from Henry Hoffman. On June 12, just five days after the Warings' Florida divorce was finalized, Elizabeth and Waties Waring were married by a municipal judge in Greenwich, Connecticut. As the word spread in Charleston's social circles of the Warings' divorce and the judge's immediate remarriage, shock was soon replaced with sympathy for Annie and resentment toward Elizabeth.[29]

Prior to the divorce, Judge Waring and Annie were members of various exclusive clubs and societies that drew their membership primarily from wellborn Charlestonians who could trace their ancestors back to the earliest days of the Carolina colony. Many resided in stately South of Broad homes and were dubbed the "S.O.B.'s." This group, which numbered perhaps in the hundreds, was insular and deeply conservative and made up most if not all of the judge's and Annie's social circle. Hardly a picture of tolerance, these exclusive Charleston societies banned divorced persons from membership. One reporter observed that divorce in Charleston during this era was about as welcome as the measles.

Elizabeth Waring did not fit the profile of a typical member of Charleston's society of that era. Educated at boarding schools in the Northeast and in Paris, she married a considerably older, prominent Detroit banker, Wilson Mills, when she was twenty, and they had three children together. After eighteen years of marriage, she informed her very surprised husband in 1933 that she wanted a divorce to marry Hoffman. Now, twelve years later, she informed Hoffman that she wanted a divorce to marry Judge Waring.

At age fifty, Elizabeth was attractive and stylish, often sporting the most current New York designer dresses. One reporter described her as "tall, blue-eyed, fiftyish, and simply dressed in black." Elizabeth was brash and self-confident and could be at times a mercurial personality. She was not, as some of her Charleston critics would later claim, a closet integrationist with a personal agenda to overturn the southern racial order. In fact, at the time of her marriage, Elizabeth had no particular interest in racial issues or in any other public policy questions. Her great passion was the arts, particularly opera, and she was an avid reader.[30]

Charleston high society froze out Judge Waring and his new wife. Party invitations were no longer received, and Waring was informed that as divorced persons he and Elizabeth were not eligible for membership in the exclusive societies of Charleston. When the judge and Elizabeth hosted a party at their home to celebrate their marriage, few of the invitees appeared. Long active participants in the Charleston social scene, Waties and Elizabeth Waring found their exile from Charleston society jarring and unexpected. This exclusion did not extend to Columbia or Florence, where the couple was invited to attend events when the judge was in town holding court. Further, this social isolation did not affect Waring's high standing in the general community in Charleston, where his position as the local federal judge continued to provide him with a level of respect and prominence.[31]

———

When Waring assumed responsibility for the *Shull* case in the fall of 1946, a little more than a year after his divorce and remarriage, he still did not question either racial segregation or black disenfranchisement and favored a slow and gradual change in southern race relations. He was also highly skeptical of an aggressive federal role in promoting civil rights, believing this would produce a strong local backlash. Like many prominent South Carolinians, Waring initially viewed the *Shull* prosecution with considerable suspicion. When U.S. Attorney Sapp came to him to request a continuance of the *Shull* case and privately revealed his desire to have the case dismissed after the November elections, Waring was greatly offended by what appeared to be political considerations in the prosecution. He therefore insisted the case be tried before or on Election Day or face summary dismissal.[32]

But whatever impression Waties Waring might have had about the merits of the *Shull* case before the trial commenced, the moving testimony of Isaac Woodard as the opening witness made him realize there was much more to this case than he had appreciated. With Elizabeth observing in the courtroom, both Warings saw for the first time the ugly underbelly of southern racial practices. Unable to avert their eyes, they were forced to stare into the southern racial abyss, a view that would forever transform them both.

8.

A "BAPTISM IN RACIAL PREJUDICE"

A s the attorneys and witnesses gathered in South Carolina in preparation for the trial of Lynwood Shull, the top staff of the NAACP remained highly skeptical about the resolve and commitment of the Department of Justice. In a forum in New York sponsored by the *New York Herald Tribune* on October 28, 1946, the NAACP's director of public relations, Ollie Harrington, publicly challenged Attorney General Tom Clark about the department's lack of progress in federal prosecutions of racial hate crimes. Harrington declared that "for the crime of racial hate and lynching, there has hardly ever been a conviction in the history of the United States." Clark defended the Justice Department's ongoing civil rights enforcement efforts and placed special emphasis on the upcoming *Shull* trial, in which he promised a "vigorous prosecution."[1]

Thurgood Marshall was unconvinced. On November 4, he sent Harrington a memorandum telling him that the *Shull* case had been officially called in federal court in Columbia, South Carolina, that morning and would likely be tried during the week. He urged Harrington to persuade the New York press to cover the trial, "because, as you know, the Department of Justice might 'take it easy.' I doubt they will do so if the case is fully covered." Marshall also dispatched his assistant counsel, Franklin Williams, to attend the trial to keep an eye on the prosecution team.[2]

When Williams and Isaac Woodard arrived at the federal courthouse in Columbia on Monday, November 4, for a scheduled 10:00 a.m. meeting, they were ushered into the well-appointed offices of the U.S. attorney to join a group already gathered. In attendance at this first meeting with Williams and Woodard were the Justice Department's special counsel Fred S. Rogers, the U.S. attorney Claud Sapp, and the FBI special agent Ralph House. House and the other Savannah-based agents involved in the Shull investigation were continuing their efforts to undermine the prosecution, even using a confidential source in the Columbia U.S. Attorney's Office, a stenographer, to keep them informed of the prosecutors' internal deliberations. This information was then being sent directly to FBI Director Hoover. Meanwhile, Sapp, having made unsuccessful efforts to dismiss this locally unpopular case, was, at best, a reluctant participant. Special Counsel Rogers, a long-serving government lawyer, was quickly coming to appreciate that he had stepped into something of a snake pit, with investigating agents and the U.S. attorney scheming against the prosecution. Shortly after meeting Franklin Williams, Rogers privately stated to him, almost apologetically, "You realize my position." Williams later confessed to Marshall that at the time it was a comment "I could not fully understand."[3]

The meeting with the prosecutors, Woodard, and the FBI special agent began with a discussion of the witnesses the government should call at trial. Williams recommended that the government offer the testimony of two eyewitnesses on the Greyhound bus, McQuilla Hudson and Lincoln Miller. Miller was, in Williams's view, a particularly critical witness because he observed Shull striking Woodard with his blackjack shortly after the sergeant stepped off the bus and without any apparent provocation. Rogers responded that Miller's testimony was problematic because he had given the FBI a statement that he had seen Woodard drinking on the bus, which Woodard had denied. Rogers then turned to Woodard and asked him directly whether he had been drinking on the bus that evening. Before Woodard could answer, Williams interjected, "No, he had not taken a drink." Rogers, unsatisfied with the attorney's response, insisted that Woodard personally answer the question. Woodard then stated he had not been drinking on the bus that night, a comment no one else in the room, except Williams, appeared to believe. As Sapp later observed, if he had just been discharged from the army, he certainly would have been drinking.[4]

Rogers stated that in light of Woodard's insistence that he had not been drinking on the bus, Miller would not be called as a witness for the government. Williams vigorously protested, wondering why the drinking issue was such an important matter when what was critical in the case was what Shull did after Woodard got off the bus and not what Woodard consumed while on the bus. Sapp, apparently attempting to avoid this brewing conflict between Williams and Rogers, suggested that all of the participants adjourn to review the FBI file in more detail and reconvene at 1:00 p.m.[5]

After Williams left the U.S. attorney's office, Rogers approached Special Agent House concerning his disagreement with Williams over the drinking issue. Rogers stated that he was "very much concerned over this question" and inquired whether House "was not worried about this particular point." Agent House curtly responded that the FBI investigation had unquestionably established that Woodard was drinking on the bus and he "was not personally concerned over any of the issues." The agent's obvious hostility toward the government's case prompted Rogers and Sapp to exclude him from further trial preparation sessions. This suited Agent House just fine, and he elected not to sit with the prosecution or to assist the government attorneys during the trial, as the investigating FBI agents routinely did.[6]

After the morning discussion with prosecutors, it was apparent to

Williams that Rogers and Sapp were not very familiar with the facts of the case. They also seemed to be unconcerned about whether the witnesses the government had subpoenaed to appear at the courthouse that morning were actually present. Williams walked around the Columbia federal courthouse in search of the subpoenaed witnesses. He found one of them, McQuilla Hudson, sitting alone in the empty courtroom. Hudson informed Williams that he had not yet been interviewed by the prosecutors. Williams sat with Hudson and had the army veteran summarize his testimony. Williams was also on the lookout for Lincoln Miller, but he was nowhere to be found. He then learned that in the government's haste to issue subpoenas the prior week, the U.S. Attorney's Office sent Miller's subpoena to the wrong address. Apparently because of the controversy over the drinking issue, the prosecutors elected not to issue a new subpoena or make any effort to locate Miller.[7]

Williams and Woodard returned to the U.S. attorney's office at 1:00 p.m., as instructed, and were told that Sapp was tied up in court. The prosecutors and Woodard finally met at 3:00 p.m., when Sapp and Rogers heard Woodard's account of his beating and blinding directly from him for the first time. They also interviewed McQuilla Hudson and another witness, a white soldier, Jennings Stroud. Stroud informed the prosecutors that, as he had told the FBI, he had observed Woodard step off the Greyhound bus in Batesburg and almost immediately be struck by Shull in the head with a blackjack. Stroud's account clearly contradicted Shull's sworn statement to the FBI that he did not strike Woodard with his blackjack until after he and Woodard left the bus station, walked several blocks, and were approaching the town jail. The fact that Stroud was a white veteran with no past relationship with Woodard made him, in these racially charged times, a potentially critical witness.[8]

In the U.S. Attorney's Office's rush to prepare for trial, subpoenas had been issued for three physicians interviewed in the Woodard investigation by the FBI, apparently without regard for trial strategy or the opinions of the physicians. One of those physicians, Dr. W. W. King, the Batesburg town doctor, made no secret of his efforts to assist the Shull defense. In his FBI interview, King offered the dubious theory that Shull might have blinded Woodard by simultaneously hitting one eye with the blackjack and the other with his knuckle. Why the government would subpoena such a witness and then call him in the government's case is a mystery.[9]

As the prosecutors completed their witness interviews late on the afternoon of November 4, Sapp directed Woodard and the others present to arrive at the courthouse first thing the next morning prepared to testify. This contradicted various public reports that the trial would begin on Wednesday, November 6. The announcement of the later trial date was apparently an act of misdirection by the U.S. Attorney's Office in response to rumors that a group of Georgia ruffians, supporters of Governor Eugene Talmadge, were planning to attend the trial to "heckle witnesses for the prosecution." Judge Waring directed the U.S. Marshals Service to be on alert for any trouble and to bring any person attempting to disrupt the trial to him for immediate contempt proceedings. The judge also warned the marshals "to be particularly careful and allow no harm to come to Woodard at any time under any conditions." Whether these rumors reflected a genuine scheme or just loose talk will never be known, but no Georgians were reported to be in attendance when the trial commenced the next morning.[10]

Jury selection in *United States v. Shull* began the next morning, Tuesday, November 5, at 10:30. The pool of prospective jurors, known as the jury venire, was all white, even though South Carolina's minority population was approximately 40 percent, the highest percentage of any state except Mississippi. This was the product of the state's systematic policies and practices of black disenfranchisement, because the jury pool was drawn from registered voter lists.[11]

The defense attorneys for Shull, Jefferson Davis Griffith and Jack D. Hall, wasted no time injecting race into the proceedings. Griffith was the elected solicitor, or chief prosecutor, for the state judicial district where Batesburg was situated and was one of the premier trial attorneys in the area. Hall was an attorney practicing in Batesburg. As jury selection began, defense counsel asked Judge Waring to inquire to the jury venire if any was "a member of the Association for the Protection of the Colored Race or any other association or organization interested in race relations." Because the jury pool was all white, the possibility that any prospective juror might be a member of the NAACP or any other civil rights organization was somewhere near zero. To Franklin Williams's surprise, the government did not object to this question or request that the jury panel be asked about membership in the Ku Klux Klan or other similar organizations, a far more likely problem for the prosecution when drawing a jury at the time in South Carolina.[12]

After Judge Waring went through his standard questions for jury qualification and asked the defense's requested inquiry regarding NAACP membership, the court proceeded to jury selection. Both the prosecution and the defense had the right to make peremptory challenges, which allowed the dismissal of a limited number of prospective jurors without a stated cause. Court rules also allowed either party to move for the removal of a prospective juror for cause, which could include such reasons as racial prejudice or bias in favor of the white law-enforcement defendant. The defense made two peremptory challenges; the government made none. No requests for strikes for cause were made by either party. Williams, amazed and astounded by the government's passivity in jury selection, wrote in his trial notes, "No [government] challenges at all!" He subsequently observed to Thurgood Marshall that the prosecutors seemed wholly unconcerned about who their jurors would be. Rogers later claimed that he had deferred to Sapp and his staff, who had reviewed the juror list and "concluded the jury panel would be fair to the government and the defendant alike."[13]

After the jury was selected, the attorneys made brief opening statements. The courtroom was packed, with white farmers and businessmen from Lexington County appearing in support of Lynwood Shull and black college students from nearby Allen University and Paine College attending in support of Isaac Woodard. To Williams's irritation, Sapp mispronounced Woodard's name in the opening statement, repeatedly referring to him as "Woodward."[14]

Isaac Woodard was called as the government's first witness. He wore a brown suit and green sunglasses and had to be led to the witness chair by court staff. Woodard described his disagreement that fateful evening with the Greyhound bus driver over his request to step off the bus during a stop to relieve himself. Woodard stated that the bus driver cursed him, and he cursed back, insisting that he "talk to me like I'm talking to you. I'm a man just like you." Woodard testified that he was summoned off the bus at the next stop and came face-to-face with the police chief Lynwood Shull. He stated that when he attempted to explain what had happened, Shull struck him on the head with a blackjack, arrested him, and led him down the street to the town jail several blocks away with his arm twisted behind his back.

Woodard testified that after they had turned the corner and were no longer in sight of the bus stop, Shull asked him if he had been discharged from the army. Woodard stated that when he responded "yes," Shull struck him a second time on the head with his blackjack, telling Woodard the correct answer was "yes, sir." Woodard acknowledged that he then attempted to take the blackjack away from Shull to prevent any additional unprovoked strikes. He testified he was able to obtain control of the officer's blackjack. At that point, he testified, another officer appeared with his gun drawn and demanded that Woodard drop the blackjack or he would drop Woodard. He testified that Shull regained control of his blackjack and furiously began beating him about the head until he was unconscious. Woodard stated that when he regained consciousness, Shull directed him to stand up. As he attempted to comply, Woodard testified, Shull drove the handle end of the blackjack into each eye repeatedly. Woodard stated he was then taken to the town jail, was placed in a cell in a semiconscious state, and drifted to sleep.[15]

Woodard stated that when he awoke the next morning, he realized he could not see. He stated that Shull informed him that he had a trial set that morning in town court on the charge of drunk and disorderly conduct. Because he was unable to see, Woodard stated, Shull had to escort him to the nearby town courtroom. Woodard testified that he tried to explain to the town's judge what had happened. Shull interjected that Woodard had attacked him. The judge responded that they did not allow such conduct around his town and promptly found Woodard guilty. He imposed a fine of $50 or thirty days on the chain gang. When Woodard was able to produce only $44 in cash, the balance of the fine was suspended and he was then free to leave. Woodard stated that he told Shull he felt ill and was escorted back to the jail, where he lay down. Later that day, when his condition did not improve, Shull transported him to the VA Hospital in Columbia, where he was left.[16]

Woodard held his own on cross-examination from defense counsel, who mostly focused on the sergeant's conduct while on the bus rather than his encounter with Shull. As defense counsel questioned Woodard, he referred to him as "Isaac," a common custom at that time in which whites denied blacks the courtesy of addressing them as "Mr." or "Mrs." Woodard was pressed on cross-examination about whether he had been drinking on the bus and whether he had been so profane that a white passenger had asked the bus driver to remove him. The questioning suggested that if Woodard had been drinking on the bus, he later received a beating he deserved. Woodard denied drinking on the bus or using profanity beyond his exchange with the bus driver.[17]

The government next called to the stand Dr. King, who described the physical injuries he observed when he examined Woodard in the jail on the afternoon of February 13, one day after he was struck by Shull. Clearly cooperating with the defense, King was asked on cross-examination by defense counsel whether Woodard's injuries were possible with a single strike of a blackjack. After being handed a blackjack to examine, King offered the opinion that Woodard "could have" been blinded in both eyes with a single blow. Now in a position of having to challenge his own witness, Rogers asked King whether such an injury with a single strike was improbable. King admitted that Woodard's blinding could have occurred with a single strike from the blackjack only with a "perfectly timed" blow.[18]

The government then called the two VA doctors who examined

Woodard, Dr. Arthur Clancy and Dr. Mortimer Burger. Both physicians provided clinical descriptions of Woodard's eye injuries. The prosecutor did not, however, elicit from Clancy the opinion he had offered the FBI in a field interview that "the victim appeared to have been struck with more than one blow inasmuch as the bone structure surrounding the eye would make it rather difficult to strike both eyeballs at one time with one blow." He also did not elicit from Burger the information he had given the FBI regarding the multiple facial injuries detailed in his physical examination report prepared on the morning of February 14. Such evidence would have supported Woodard's testimony that he was struck multiple times by Shull and undermined Shull's defense that he had blinded Woodard in both eyes with a single strike of a blackjack.[19]

With the completion of Burger's testimony, the government rested its case at 12:25 p.m., just one hour and twenty-five minutes after it had opened its case. Franklin Williams was almost apoplectic. The government had not called Jennings Stroud, the white veteran who had observed Shull strike Woodard unprovoked shortly after exiting the bus, or McQuilla Hudson, who was prepared to testify that Woodard was not disruptive or boisterous on the bus. Williams also realized that the government had never subpoenaed Woodard's medical records from the VA, which he was confident would document more injuries than described by the doctors from the witness stand. In his handwritten notes made while observing the trial, Williams wrote, "Where are hospital records!! Why not subpoenaed? Gov't rests!!"

Williams angrily confronted Rogers during a court recess, challenging his decision not to call Stroud and Hudson in the government's case in chief. Rogers responded that it would be better to call these witnesses in rebuttal. In a criminal prosecution, the government is required to put up its entire case initially, in what is called the case in chief. The defendant is then allowed to offer evidence in his defense. The government thereafter is entitled to offer rebuttal or reply testimony, which must be evidence responding to the offered defense. Because the defendant is not allowed another opportunity to offer evidence after the government's rebuttal stage, trial judges commonly place strict limits on the type of evidence the government can offer for the first time in the rebuttal phase. Thus, the prosecutors' decision to hold back the testimony of Stroud and Hudson until the rebuttal phase of the trial was a very risky strategy with little seeming upside.

Williams also expressed astonishment to Rogers that the government had not obtained a copy of Woodard's medical records. Williams asked Rogers for some explanation for this glaring failure to collect the most basic evidence in the case. According to Williams, Rogers's response was "evasive and unsatisfactory."[20]

Shull's defense team began their case by calling the bus driver, Alton Blackwell, as their first witness. Blackwell described Woodard as boisterous, drunk, and profane on the bus and stated he resolved to have the soldier removed after a white couple complained about his language. He also testified that Woodard put him behind schedule by repeatedly exiting the bus at each stop to relieve himself. On cross-examination, Sapp brought out inconsistencies between Blackwell's testimony and his earlier sworn statement given to the FBI.

Agent House, observing the trial from the audience, became enraged by Sapp's cross-examination of the bus driver. During a subsequent court recess, House bitterly complained to Sapp that his questioning of Blackwell was misleading because any discrepancies between the bus driver's statement to the FBI and his trial testimony were inconsequential. House contended that Shull's lawyers had insinuated that the FBI had taken some liberties in preparing Blackwell's affidavit. House asserted that the FBI had "received undue criticism and publicity about this case" from local law enforcement, and he wanted Sapp to protect the FBI's reputation by having Blackwell's full statement read into the record. To their credit, the prosecutors refused.[21]

The defense next called Officer Elliot Long, the other half of Batesburg's two-man police department. Long testified that he had personally retrieved Woodard from the bus and observed that Woodard was loud and intoxicated. He further testified that he appeared at the jail as Woodard arrived and there was no evidence that he had been beaten or injured in any way. Long also denied having pulled his gun on Woodard or being present when Shull beat him with a blackjack.

Long stumbled during cross-examination when he was confronted with his prior statement to the FBI that Shull, not he, had taken Woodard off the bus. Long attempted to explain this discrepancy by stating, "I studied the case and later learned that I did." When pressed by Sapp for a better explanation, Long stated, "I didn't have a chance to think it up."[22] With that curious response, the officer left the stand around 1:20 p.m., and Judge Waring recessed the trial for lunch until 3:00 p.m.[23]

As soon as the trial resumed, Shull took the stand in his own defense. He described Woodard as intoxicated and loud when he came off the bus. Shull claimed he arrested Woodard not for his conduct on the bus but for his behavior at the bus stop. He denied striking Woodard at that point but stated that he took him by the arm and headed to the town jail a few blocks away. Shull testified that after he and Woodard turned the corner and were out of sight of the bus stop, Woodard suddenly attacked him without provocation. According to Shull, Woodard grabbed his blackjack, which was connected to Shull through a leather wrist strap, and the two struggled over control of the weapon. It was then, Shull testified, that he had struck Woodard a single blow with the blackjack. Shull explained that in the frenzy of the moment he had no opportunity to aim the blackjack and did strike the veteran in the head. Shull stated, "I had no intention of blinding him in the eyes. I merely struck him in my own defense. I could even have stuck my fingers in his eyes, but I couldn't be sure, and in a similar scuffle, I don't suppose anyone could be." Shull concluded, "If my blow blinded him, I'm sorry. I hit him in self-defense, and to keep him off of me."

Shull testified he then took Woodard to the town jail and the soldier gave no indication of having suffered any serious injury. The next morning, Shull stated, he took Woodard to the town court to be tried on a charge of drunk and disorderly conduct. Although one of Woodard's eyes was swollen, Shull claimed, Woodard was able to see and function independently. According to Shull, Woodard stated that he "reckoned he drunk too much" and pleaded guilty to the charge. The judge fined Woodard $50, later lowered to $44 because that was all the cash Woodard had on him.

Shull testified that Woodard did not complain of an inability to see until after the town court proceeding. Shull stated that Woodard informed him he felt "sick at the stomach" and was allowed to return to the jail to lie down. As Woodard's left eye became more swollen, Shull stated, he sought the assistance of the town physician, Dr. King, but King was then unavailable. Later, after King appeared and examined Woodard, Shull testified, he followed the doctor's instructions and took Woodard to the VA Hospital in Columbia, some thirty-five miles away.[24]

Sapp began his cross-examination of Shull by dangling Shull's sworn statement to the FBI in the air and having him confirm he had given and signed the statement. Sapp then asked Shull if FBI agents would have any reason not to have recorded his statement accurately and completely. Shull responded that he did not think "those FBI boys would try to trick" him. Shull's attorney, almost in a panic, came across the courtroom to where Sapp was standing and demanded that he be shown Shull's prior statement. Judge Waring denied the defense counsel's objection and ruled Sapp had no obligation to provide Shull with a copy of his prior statement.[25]

There was a difference in Shull's trial testimony and the sworn statement on the single-strike issue. In the FBI statement, Shull had stated that after he and Woodard turned the corner, Woodard refused to proceed any farther and Shull then shook his blackjack at him and "bumped him lightly with the blackjack on the side of the head." Woodard responded to this, according to the Shull statement, by attacking him and trying to wrestle away the blackjack. Shull's trial testimony was that there was only a single strike of the blackjack that had followed a surprising and unprovoked assault by Woodard.

When Shull was confronted with this inconsistency, he responded unexpectedly, by admitting that he struck Woodard with his blackjack at the bus stop. This is something he had consistently denied until that moment. Shull's new admission did not go directly to the issue of whether he had brutally beaten Woodard into unconsciousness and then jammed the blackjack handle into his eyes, but his changing testimony about where and how many times he struck Woodard had the potential of undermining his credibility.

After having made a dramatic use before the jury of Shull's prior FBI statement and obtaining a new admission from Shull about striking Woodard at the bus stop, Sapp gave it all away by announcing in a joking manner that the defense had nothing to worry about because Shull's FBI statement and his trial testimony were "substantially the same." Sapp's statement produced widespread laughter from Shull's supporters in the courtroom, but Franklin Williams was incensed. He believed that Sapp had intentionally undermined a legitimate point of inconsistency in Shull's testimony in an effort to go soft on him.[26]

Following Shull's testimony, the defense called Batesburg's mayor, H. E. Quarles, who doubled as the town's judge. He testified that Woodard pleaded guilty at his trial and admitted he had drunk too much the night before. Quarles stated that Woodard was able to see and function independently and did not ask for medical attention. Another witness, G. C. Shealy, a local furniture salesman, testified he happened to be present at the town court proceedings on the morning of February 13 and heard Woodard plead guilty. This testimony was followed by four character witnesses, including the Lexington County sheriff, Henry Caughman, and a black contractor from Batesburg, Archie Beechem. After Beechem testified that he had known Shull for twenty years and stated that he treated black citizens "extra fine," Franklin Williams wrote in his notes, "Judas." At 4:30 p.m., the defense rested.[27]

The government prosecutors then attempted to call Jennings Stroud as a rebuttal witness. Shull's attorneys strenuously objected, arguing that such testimony should have been offered in the prosecutor's case in chief and was beyond the scope of rebuttal evidence. Judge Waring sustained the defense objection, a not surprising ruling under the circumstances.

Because the government elected not to issue a new subpoena to Lincoln Miller when the first subpoena was sent to the wrong address and failed to offer Stroud's testimony in its case in chief, the jury never heard from two eyewitnesses who observed Shull's unprovoked and violent striking of Woodard just as he stepped off the Greyhound bus.[28]

The defense moved for a directed verdict of acquittal. Judge Waring denied the motion and directed counsel to present closing arguments. Special Counsel Rogers, leading off for the government, told the jury that he was a southerner, from Texas, and understood what they might feel about a civil rights case. He felt obligated to tell the jury that he was not a member of the NAACP. Rogers stated he was not ashamed of this assignment because he was an upholder of justice regardless of race and was convinced that Shull had acted "in pure malice." After reviewing the evidence offered at trial, he asked the jury to return a verdict of guilty.[29]

The defense counsel, Hall and Griffith, split their thirty-minute argument, unleashing a rash of racially charged arguments that Judge Waring would later describe as "pretty dreadful." Announcing that the people of South Carolina resented this federal civil rights prosecution, Hall argued that "if a decision against the government means seceding, then let South Carolina secede again." He argued that a guilty verdict would render nil the ability of law-enforcement officers to protect the public, which triggered an objection from the prosecutors and an instruction from Judge Waring that the argument was improper because law enforcement was not on trial. The defense further argued that Woodard belonged to "an inferior race that the South has always protected" and that Woodard's admission that he spoke back to the white bus driver demonstrated he was intoxicated because "that's not the talk of a sober niggra in South Carolina." The defense argument concluded with a request that the jury return a verdict of not guilty.[30]

Claud Sapp then stepped forward to make a brief final closing argument for the United States. He told the jury members he had fulfilled his duty as U.S. attorney by presenting this case and "whatever verdict you gentlemen bring in, the government will be satisfied with." Departing from well-established custom, Sapp did not ask the jury to return a verdict of guilty.[31]

Judge Waring charged the jury for twenty-four minutes, laying out the requirement that the defendant must be found guilty beyond a reasonable doubt and explaining to the jurors the legal requirements for a conviction under the civil rights statute. Acknowledging the controversy and publicity about the case, Judge Waring instructed the jury to disregard the opinions of various groups and individuals and what they might say about the verdict. Instead, he instructed the jury members to base their verdict on the evidence and not to consider race or the fact that the defendant was a law-enforcement officer. Referring to the closing argument by defense counsel to which he had sustained an objection, Waring told the jury that one man, not all of law enforcement, was on trial.[32]

Judge Waring sent the jury out at 6:28 p.m. to begin its deliberations. In order to avoid the indignity of a five-minute verdict in the case, he advised the deputy marshal that he was going for a walk and would return to the courthouse in twenty minutes. The marshal replied, "But, Judge, that jury ain't going to stay out for twenty minutes." Waring responded, "They're going to stay out twenty minutes because they can't come out until I come back, and I'm not going to be back for twenty minutes."

Waring took a leisurely early evening walk in downtown Columbia, returning to the federal courthouse twenty-five minutes later. He was advised that the jurors had been banging incessantly on the jury room door, insisting they had reached a verdict. At 6:56 p.m., twenty-eight minutes after they had filed out of the courtroom to begin deliberations, the jury returned to the courtroom, and the clerk published the jurors' unanimous verdict of not guilty. As Shull's supporters celebrated, few noticed Elizabeth Waring quietly leaving the courtroom in tears. A disappointed Isaac Woodard told Franklin Williams that "the right man hasn't tried [Shull] yet."[33]

In the weeks following the acquittal, civil rights activists criticized the performance of the government prosecutors in *United States v. Shull*.

In a letter to Attorney General Tom Clark on November 14, 1946, Thurgood Marshall asserted that there was a "failure vigorously to prosecute" Shull by U.S. Attorney Sapp and Special Counsel Rogers. He pointed to the prosecutors' failure to request that the judge inquire into prospective jurors' affiliations with the Klan or other segregationist organizations and to Sapp's failure to ask the jury to return a verdict of guilty. Instead, Marshall observed, Sapp told the jury that the government would be "satisfied with whatever verdict the jury should return," which Marshall said was "an invitation to the jury to bring in a verdict of acquittal." The legendary civil rights leader A. Philip Randolph wrote to Clark, criticizing Sapp's failure to request a verdict of guilty and the prosecutors' failure "to place on the stand two eyewitnesses who saw Woodard beaten." An article in *The Pittsburgh Courier* of November 16 voiced some of the same criticisms and also referenced the prosecutors' failure to exercise any of their peremptory challenges.[34]

There was considerable merit to the criticisms voiced by the civil rights community. A good example was the government's failure to request that Judge Waring ask the jury panel questions about potential bias or to exercise any of its preemptory challenges. The Justice Department's decision to charge Shull only with a misdemeanor (and thus avoid presentation of the case to an all-white South Carolina federal grand jury for a felony indictment) was based on the assumption that there was so much local bias that the grand jury would likely refuse to return an indictment. In light of that reasonable assumption, the failure to request that the judge carefully question the jury panel about bias is inexplicable. Similarly, Sapp's failure in his closing argument to ask the jury to return a verdict of guilty and his suggestion that the jurors do what they thought was right clearly communicated that he had no expectation of a guilty verdict.

The prosecutors also blundered in failing to present in their case in chief the eyewitness testimony of Jennings Stroud and Lincoln Miller that they observed Shull inflict a serious and unprovoked blow to Woodard's head moments after the soldier stepped off the bus. This testimony was certainly in conflict with Shull's claim that he had struck Woodard once and only in self-defense, and suggested a level of animus and gratuitous violence by Shull inconsistent with his FBI statement and trial testimony. The eyewitness testimony of the soldiers on the bus was never heard by the jury because of the ill-advised decision to hold Stroud's testimony until the government's reply, clearly a risky move, and the failure to locate Miller after his first subpoena was sent to the wrong address.

There is little question that Woodard's insistence that he was not drinking on the bus presented practical problems for the prosecutors. But this was not a case charging Woodard with consumption of alcohol on a bus, and all of the soldier witnesses on the bus, both black and white, told the FBI that Woodard was not disruptive or obviously intoxicated. The investigating FBI agents and Special Counsel Rogers obsessed over the dispute about Woodard's drinking on the bus, suggesting that if Woodard's pre-assault conduct was not perfect, Shull could not be culpable for the use of excessive force. The critical issue was not whether Woodard had been drinking before his arrest but whether Shull had used excessive force after taking Woodard into custody. This very point was made by James Hinton, the South Carolina president of the NAACP, shortly after the trial when he stated in a letter to the editor of *The State*, "We have no hate for Mr. Shull, nor do we condone any wrong Isaac Woodard might have done, but we do know that more physical force was used against the veteran than was necessary."[35]

In the end, the fundamental flaw in the government's prosecution of Lynwood Shull was the FBI's failure to determine through independent medical experts the nature and amount of force actually used by Shull to blind Woodard. Common sense suggested that Shull's claim of a single defensive strike to the head producing bilateral blindness was improbable. Initial interviews with Woodard's VA doctors certainly raised doubts about Shull's single-strike claim. But despite these important leads, the FBI failed to obtain an independent specialist evaluation of Woodard, which would have revealed that the globes of both of his eyes had been crushed, something that a single strike to the head under these circumstances could not have produced. The prosecutors also failed to have the medical evidence in the case assessed by forensic medical experts, who could have reconstructed the nature and number of strikes necessary to produce Woodard's injuries. The most advanced forensic department then existing in the world, the Armed Forces Institute of Pathology, was located just blocks from the Department of Justice in Washington and could have been called upon by prosecutors or FBI agents to assist. The agents' failure to obtain a copy of Woodard's VA Hospital records, an essential starting point to investigate the cause of his blindness, speaks volumes about the FBI's myopic and incomplete investigation.[36]

The harshest critic of the government's prosecution, Judge Waring, held his tongue at the time but after his retirement shared with a historian a devastating critique. Waring described the government prosecutors as ill-prepared and the investigation far from thorough. He stated, "I was shocked at the hypocrisy of my government . . . in submitting that disgraceful case before a jury [and was] hurt I was made a party to it." Waring was convinced there was a stronger case that could have been presented. He acknowledged, however, that he was not sure there would have been a conviction before an all-white federal jury in South Carolina in 1946 even if the government had presented twenty eyewitnesses.[37]

Waties Waring returned to his hotel room the night of the Shull verdict deeply troubled about the trial. He found his wife tearful and emotionally traumatized by the events of that day. Having lived a life of privilege, shielded from the underbelly of southern racial practices, Elizabeth Waring struggled to process what she had just witnessed. For his part, Waring was "tortured" by the fact that a police officer, who had appeared to be a "fine young man," inflicted a vicious beating on a returning American soldier and that the criminal justice system had failed to hold the police officer accountable. Elizabeth Waring bluntly told her husband she had never heard or seen such a "terrible thing" and privately shared her distress with a South Carolina–born friend a few days later. The friend responded, "That sort of thing happens all the time. It's dreadful, but what are we going to do about it?"[38]

Judge Waring would later describe the *Shull* trial as his wife's "baptism in racial prejudice" and his own "baptism of fire." It was a transformative event in the life of the Warings, causing them to see and sense the world around them in a fundamentally different way. The world of Jim Crow now suddenly came into focus. For the first time in his sixty-six years, Waties Waring began to doubt his basic assumptions about the southern way of life. Responding to the question of Elizabeth's friend, "What are we going to do about it?," the Warings began a period of serious study and reflection on the issue of race in America and a federal judge's personal responsibility to uphold the rule of law. This period of study and introspection would take Waties Waring on a journey in which he ultimately resolved that it was his sworn duty to boldly and forthrightly confront racial injustice, whatever the personal consequences. Soon he would begin issuing landmark civil rights decisions that would shake the political foundations of his native state and alter the course of American history.[39]

THE CALL TO ACTION

9.

"I SHALL FIGHT TO END
EVIL LIKE THIS"

NOVEMBER 5, 1946, was an inauspicious day for the Truman administration. Republicans trounced the Democrats in the congressional elections, winning fifty-five additional seats in the House and eleven in the Senate and gaining control of both houses of Congress for the first time since the Hoover administration. This electoral sweep was accomplished with large gains by Republicans in the Northeast, the Midwest, and the West. Only the South was unmoved by this political earthquake, with white southerners remaining steadfastly loyal to the Democratic Party. Adding salt to these deep political wounds, an all-white federal jury in Columbia, South Carolina, acquitted Lynwood Shull on that same day in the blinding of Isaac Woodard.

A less resolute and self-confident man than Harry Truman might have found these developments crushing and demoralizing, but the president took it all in stride. After fourteen years of Democratic control of the national government, Truman understood that the postwar and post-Depression electorate was restless and looking for change. A year earlier, the British had voted out Winston Churchill after he heroically led the nation from the brink of defeat to a triumphant victory over fascist Germany. In Washington, the Democratic Congress, dominated by mostly elderly committee chairs seemingly resistant to any progressive action, offered little inspiration or vision to the electorate.[1]

In the midst of these political setbacks, a convergence of events and political realities brought the issue of civil rights to the top of the Truman administration's agenda. No recent administration had been willing to confront the deeply divisive issues of racial segregation and black disenfranchisement. While Franklin Roosevelt, the most skillful politician of his generation, gave private encouragement to civil rights leaders and quietly included African Americans in New Deal social programs, he was reluctant to make too much of a public show on civil rights issues, recognizing the risk it would pose for his New Deal coalition. As Truman's adviser Clark Clifford observed, Roosevelt's supporters were an "unhappy alliance" of southern segregationists, western progressives, big-city labor, and urban African American voters. The fact remained that any suggestion of federal government engagement on civil rights, no matter how modest, produced immediate and vigorous opposition from southern elected officials.

But realities on the ground made neglect of civil rights no longer an acceptable option. The widely reported incidents of racial violence inflicted on returning African American veterans in the Deep South galvanized civil rights activists and brought demands for effective federal engagement. With the growing African American presence in major urban centers in swing states, black voters were now a prized target for both Democrats and Republicans. Governor Thomas Dewey of New York, the likely Republican presidential candidate in 1948, had an exemplary record on civil rights and seemed to many in the civil rights community to be a reasonable alternative to the southern-dominated congressional Democrats who obstructed even the most modest proposals to combat racial mob violence.[2]

Beyond the political considerations, Truman was profoundly troubled by the reports of violence inflicted on returning African American veterans. He remembered the rise of similar incidents after World War I and had no intention to sit idly back and allow a repeat of such actions on his watch. As one of Truman's African American staffers, Truman Gibson, later remembered, the president "had these deep feelings, and he didn't really care what other people thought" or what the polls reflected. After hearing the details of the blinding of Isaac Woodard, the president told Gibson, "Enough is enough. Dammit, I'm going to do something immediately."[3]

―――――

But what could a president do that would make a real difference regarding civil rights?

Congress was unwilling to act, and as the Shull trial demonstrated, federal civil rights prosecutions in the South were a long road to nowhere. Truman needed to develop a new strategy that would allow him to use his executive powers and did not depend on congressional action or all-white southern juries to be successful. The idea of a presidential committee on civil rights, first floated in a meeting with civil rights leaders in September 1946, was pursued because it was a definitive step Truman could take immediately, and there was some hope that proposals recommended by a blue-ribbon panel of business and civic leaders might help change the public discourse on civil rights.[4]

Truman staffers and civil rights advocates appreciated that a presidential committee on civil rights would be only as good as its members, and serious discussions ensued over potential candidates. Walter White was invited to propose names and ultimately recommended five of the fifteen committee members, including its chairman, Charles E. Wilson. White was unsuccessful in obtaining the appointment of a more controversial figure, Orson Welles. In a letter to the Truman staffer David Niles, White urged Welles's appointment as being "particularly important because of the attacks on him for his broadcasts about the Isaac Woodard case." He explained that as a result of these broadcasts "they are boycotting his pictures in South Carolina and he is being removed from the air because of Ku Kluxers' protests." White House officials opted to sidestep Welles and the additional controversy his appointment would undoubtedly bring.[5]

By any measure, Truman's appointees to his civil rights committee were impressive. They included the heads of two major corporations (General Electric's president, Charles Wilson, and Lever Brothers' president, Charles Luckman), two labor leaders (the CIO secretary treasurer, James Carey, and the AFL economist Boris Shishkin), two college presidents (Dartmouth College's John Dickey and the University of North Carolina's Frank Porter Graham), two African Americans (the Philadelphia city solicitor Sadie Alexander and the former NAACP board member Channing Tobias), two women (Sadie Alexander and the Southern Regional Council's field secretary Dorothy Tilly), and two white southerners (Dorothy Tilly and Frank Porter Graham). Some referred to the commission as "Noah's ark" because there seemed to be two appointees from distinct categories. There were also religious leaders from Protestant, Catholic, and Jewish faiths and a very recognizable name, Franklin D. Roosevelt Jr. Additionally, Dr. Robert K. Carr, a highly respected scholar and chair of the Department of Government at Dartmouth, was appointed as the commission's staff member and was tasked with drafting the final report.[6]

It was notable that all of Truman's appointees had long histories of advocacy of civil rights, and there was no effort to balance the committee with defenders of the racial status quo. In fact, the two arguably most conservative members of the committee, Graham and Tilly, were prominent voices in the southern civil rights community. By taking this approach, Truman avoided the endless and divisive debates over race and Jim Crow practices that paralyzed congressional progress on civil rights.[7]

Although much of the staff work necessary to create the committee was completed in October 1946, Truman did not formally announce its creation until December 5, exactly one month after the disastrous congressional elections. This delay was hardly an oversight, because civil rights remained a profoundly unpopular issue among white Americans. Truman issued an executive order establishing the President's Committee on Civil Rights, explaining that "the preservation of civil rights . . . is essential to domestic tranquility, national security, the general welfare, and the continued existence of our free institutions." The executive order emphasized the recent incidents of racially inspired mob violence, noting that such actions were "subversive to our democratic system of law enforcement and public criminal justice, and gravely [threaten] our form of government." The committee was charged with making recommendations for "more adequate and effective means and procedures for the protection of the civil rights of the people of the United States."[8]

The committee first met on January 15, 1947, in the Cabinet Room, to highlight the importance that Truman placed on its work. Truman appeared at the committee's opening session to charge the members as they undertook what he described as their "vitally important job." He recalled his experience as a first-time candidate for public office in 1922 in Jackson County, Missouri, where there was an organization "that met in the hills and burned crosses and worked behind sheets. There is a tendency in this country for that situation to develop again, unless we do something tangible to prevent it." Truman went on to state, "I don't want to see any racial discrimination. I don't want to see any religious bigotry break out in this country as it did then." He candidly told the members that they "may get more brickbats than bouquets" for their work. The president stated that the committee's work was not limited to studying instances of racial violence but included determining "just how far the federal government under the Constitution has the right to go in these civil rights matters." Truman explained that while he was a believer in local sovereignty, "there are certain rights under the Constitution of the United States which I think the federal government has a right to protect." He set an ambitious goal for the committee to complete its work and issue a report before the beginning of the 1948 congressional session, just twelve months away.[9]

The committee set about its work with a flurry of activity, conducting public hearings and gathering detailed information on recent episodes of mob violence, barriers to African American voting, the persistence of racial segregation, and the denial of equal protection of the law to black citizens. Prominent officials, including the FBI director, J. Edgar Hoover, testified before the committee. Following Truman's lead, the committee read its mandate broadly, as including a wide range of issues related to civil rights rather than a simple focus on instances of mob violence. This was done, as the committee later explained, "because these individual instances are only reflections of deeper maladies. We believe we must cure the disease as well as treat its symptoms."[10]

Shortly after the committee's first meeting, a lynching occurred in South Carolina on February 17, 1947, when a white mob seized a black criminal defendant, Willie Earle, from a jail in Pickens, South Carolina, where he was being held on murder charges. The mob viciously beat Earle and then shot him to death. The State of South Carolina prosecuted thirty-one members of the mob, who were all acquitted on May 21 after a jury trial. The occurrence of such an incident while the President's Committee on Civil Rights was investigating prior episodes of racially inspired mob violence, and the failure of the criminal justice system to hold the wrongdoers accountable, reinforced the need for definitive federal action to protect the rights of minority citizens.[11]

———

On June 29, 1947, while the President's Committee on Civil Rights was actively conducting its work, Truman delivered the keynote address at the annual meeting of the NAACP. At that time, no president had ever spoken at a meeting of the nation's preeminent civil rights group, and mere membership in the NAACP was then cause for termination of black teachers in many Deep South communities. The address was to be delivered from the base of the Lincoln Memorial. Platform guests included the former First Lady Eleanor Roosevelt, Attorney General Tom Clark, Chief Justice Fred Vinson, and the NAACP's executive secretary, Walter White. The speech was carried live on four national radio networks and was then the most widely heard civil rights address in American history.

Truman staffers appreciated the significance of this historic moment and arranged for Robert Carr, the staff director of the President's Committee on Civil Rights, to actively participate in the preparation of the address. Truman personally solicited input from Walter White, who jokingly told the president that "if he included one half of the things" he thought ought to be included, "the southern Democrats would probably want to run [you] out of the country." The speech went through four drafts, with Truman personally adding language to emphasize his commitment to the cause. On the day prior to the speech, Truman wrote to his sister, Mary Jane, advising her of the address and observing, "Mama won't like what I have to say . . . but I believe what I say."[12]

With an audience of thousands present in Washington and millions listening on the radio, Harry Truman stepped to the microphone at 4:30 p.m. and, in a twelve-minute address, redefined the role of the modern national government as the protector of the constitutional rights of its minority citizens. After brief preliminary remarks thanking the NAACP for its invitation, Truman stated, "It is my deep conviction that we have reached a turning point in the long history of our country's efforts to guarantee freedom and equality to all of our citizens." He noted that "recent events in the United States and abroad have made us realize that it is more important today than ever before to insure that all Americans enjoy these rights." He then added his penciled-in addition: "When I say all Americans, I mean all Americans."

Referencing America's early resistance to imperial authority, Truman stated it was no longer sufficient to view the role of the federal government as limited to protecting against "the possibility of tyranny by the government. We cannot stop there." "We must," Truman continued, move forward with "new concepts of civil rights to safeguard our heritage. The extension of civil rights today means, not protection of the people against the government, but the protection of the people by the government."

Truman then moved from the general to the specific, declaring that "our immediate task is to remove the last remnants of the barriers that stand between millions of our citizens and their birthright" as Americans. He maintained there was "no justifiable reason for discrimination because of ancestry, or religion, or race, or color." He asserted that the rights of American citizenship included the right to a decent home, a quality education, adequate medical care, a worthwhile job, equal access to the ballot, and a fair trial in a fair court.

The president turned to the recent episodes of mob violence and acknowledged that the legal machinery had not yet "secured to each citizen full freedom from fear." Noting the urgency of the moment, he stated that America "cannot wait another decade or another generation to remedy these evils . . . We can no longer afford the luxury of a leisurely attack upon prejudice and discrimination" and "await the growth of a will to action in the slowest state or the most backward community." Instead, he declared, "we must strive to advance civil rights wherever it lies within our power."

Truman concluded by expressing confidence that while the "way ahead is not easy," "we can reach the goal . . . [with] skillful and vigorous action." Referencing the principles of the Declaration of Independence, the U.S. Constitution, the Emancipation Proclamation, and the proposed United Nations International Bill of Rights, he concluded that with these "noble charters to guide us . . . we shall make our land a happier home for our people, a symbol of hope for all men, and a rock of security in a troubled world."[13]

As Truman sat down, an amazed Walter White privately congratulated him on his extraordinary address. Truman responded, "I said what I did because I mean every word of it—and I am going to prove that I do mean it." The audience was stunned that this former haberdasher and machine politician, raised in a portion of Missouri known for its Confederate sympathies, had delivered such a visionary message. As one historian later observed, "No one expected it would be this man who would be the first president to publicly advance a bold civil rights agenda for America."

The NAACP's magazine, *The Crisis*, called the address "the most comprehensive and forthright statement on the rights of minorities in a democracy and the duty of the government to secure safeguards that has ever been made by a president of the United States." Walter White would later observe in his autobiography that if Truman "had any premonition of the savage assaults which were destined to be made upon him" by southern elected officials or "fear of the consequences" of his proposals, "he showed no signs of it" that day. White compared Truman's call for federal action to Lincoln's Gettysburg Address, "but in some respects it had been a more courageous one in its specific condemnation of evils based on race prejudice . . . and its call for immediate action against them." Members of the President's Committee on Civil Rights, preparing to meet, huddled around their radios to hear the address and buzzed with excitement over Truman's inspiring message. African American troops, hearing the broadcast over shortwave radio from a remote island in the Pacific, were so moved that they passed the hat to make a contribution to the NAACP.[14]

Two seminal events in the fall of 1947 secured the place of civil rights at the top of the Truman administration's domestic agenda. Clark Clifford, among the most influential of Truman's senior advisers, submitted to the president a fifty-five-page memorandum on November 19 that set the "course of political conduct for the Administration extending from November, 1947 to November, 1948." Clifford, who had practiced law in St. Louis for over a decade before entering the navy with the outbreak of World War II, was initially assigned to Truman as the president's naval adviser. As their relationship grew closer, Truman named Clifford as White House counsel, and he assumed responsibility for developing the president's reelection strategy.

The Clifford memorandum, which is now the stuff of political legend, laid out a detailed plan in which the political underdog, President Truman, would defeat the heavily favored Thomas Dewey in the 1948 election. Clark described the critical need for Truman to shore up his support among several essential Democratic Party constituencies, including western farmers, labor unionists, and urban black voters. The solid South was taken as a given for the Democrats in light of its fierce loyalty in the disastrous 1946 congressional elections.

Clifford noted the history of Franklin Roosevelt's wooing away black voters from the Republican Party, referencing the "classic remark" that blacks should "turn your picture of Abraham Lincoln to the wall—we have paid that debt." He observed that in recent years Dewey and the Republicans had undertaken "the assiduous and continuous cultivation of the New York Negro vote" and civil rights leaders were fully aware that southern Democratic congressional leaders were preventing any progress on the legislative front. Clifford made specific reference to Walter White, describing him as "intelligent, educated and sophisticated" and a "cynical and hardboiled trader" for the advancement of the civil rights agenda.

Clifford warned that "unless the administration makes a determined campaign to help the Negro" with "new and real efforts," the African American vote would be lost by the Democrats and Thomas Dewey would be elected president. He cautioned that "mere political gestures" by the Truman administration would not be enough and were "thoroughly understood and strongly resented by sophisticated Negro leaders." He concluded that it "would appear to be sound strategy to have the President go as far as he feels he possibly could in recommending measures to protect the rights of minority groups." Clifford acknowledged this approach might "cause difficulty with our southern friends, but that is the lesser of two evils."[15]

Clifford is widely credited as the architect of Truman's improbable 1948 election victory and a visionary regarding the critical role urban minority voters had begun to play in important swing states. Clearly, his advice regarding the administration's need to put forth new and effective federal measures to promote civil rights was heeded and became an important factor in Truman's advancement of the civil rights cause. But Clifford badly miscalculated the tolerance of southern white voters for the administration's civil rights agenda and did not envision the third-party efforts of the southern states' rights Democrats. As Clifford later acknowledged, "I thought we had not pushed the South beyond the limit that they would accept [and] I was wrong."[16]

The second seminal event on the civil rights front was the issuance on October 29, 1947, of the final report of the President's Committee on Civil Rights, titled *To Secure These Rights*. The report represented a carefully crafted effort to provide a thoughtful and candid assessment of America's ongoing struggle with racial injustice and to recommend solutions. This was not an easy report to issue to a nation in which a majority of states had some form of Jim Crow laws, the great majority of African Americans in the South were disenfranchised, and residential segregation existed in virtually every region of the country. Moreover, despite the military service of African Americans in the two world wars, the armed forces of the United States remained segregated. This entire scheme of disenfranchisement and government-mandated racial segregation was grounded upon legal doctrines explicitly sanctioned by the U.S. Supreme Court, despite the provisions of the Thirteenth, Fourteenth, and Fifteenth Amendments requiring the elimination of the last vestiges of slavery, the equal protection of the laws, and the right to vote for all citizens.

To Secure These Rights began by recognizing four "essential rights" of American citizenship: "the right to safety and security of the person," "the right to citizenship and its privileges," "the right to freedom of conscience and expression," and "the right to equality of opportunity." From these broadly stated goals in which few would find offense, the committee diagnosed the ills of America in a remarkably forthright way. The committee reported that citizens were not secure in their homes and communities because of the fear of mob violence. The report gave as specific examples the recent lynching episodes in Georgia, Louisiana, and South Carolina. It characterized lynching as "a terrorist device" and observed that the "devastating consequences of lynchings go far beyond what is shown by counting the victims." The report lamented the "almost complete immunity from punishment enjoyed by the lynchers" and concluded that "lynching is the ultimate threat by which [the black man's] inferior status is driven home" and "reinforces all of the other disabilities placed upon him."[17]

The report was equally frank about the "widespread" problem of police brutality. Numerous episodes of racially inspired police violence against defenseless citizens were detailed, including jail beatings and assaults by officers with blackjacks. FBI Director Hoover testified before the committee about racially inspired beatings at a particular jail, stating that "it was seldom that a Negro man or woman was incarcerated who was not given a severe beating, which started off with a pistol whipping and ended with a rubber hose." The report observed that it was difficult to accept "at face value" the common claim of police officers that they used force only in self-defense and to prevent escape. "The total picture," the committee concluded, was a "serious reflection on American justice," and the "incidence of police brutality against Negroes is disturbingly high."[18]

The committee bluntly addressed black disenfranchisement, noting that it was difficult to list all of the devices used to prevent blacks from voting because "at different times, different methods have been employed." These included the all-white primary, "understanding clauses," the poll tax, and "terror and intimidation." A chart titled "Suffrage in the Poll Tax States" showed that in the forty states without poll taxes 68 percent of the voters cast a ballot in the 1944 presidential election compared with 18 percent who voted in the eight (southern) states with a poll tax.[19]

The report was unsparing in its criticism of discrimination in the U.S. armed forces. This included widespread segregation in the traditional armed forces and the National Guard, an absolute cap on the number of black soldiers allowed in certain branches of the service, concentration of black soldiers in the lowest ranks and in the most menial jobs, and limited opportunity for promotion by black soldiers into the officer corps. The navy was noted to have a ratio of one white officer to seven white enlisted men and one black officer to *every ten thousand* black enlisted men. The committee observed that the armed forces had the ability to be a laboratory for the advancement of equal opportunity and to educate the public on the "practicability of American ideals as a way of life."[20]

A broad range of other discriminatory practices was analyzed and critiqued, including discrimination in funding of segregated schools, government enforcement of restrictive racial covenants, discrimination in the delivery of federal services, and systemic racial discrimination in the District of Columbia. But the committee reserved its harshest criticism for government-directed and government-enforced racial segregation, which it characterized as providing the "cornerstone of the elaborate structure of discrimination against some American citizens." In a section of the report titled "Segregation Reconsidered: The 'Separate but Equal' Failure," the committee made no secret of its disdain for the U.S. Supreme Court's decision in *Plessy v. Ferguson* and belief that its holding was incompatible with the Fourteenth Amendment's guarantee of equal protection under the law. Citing recent social science research, the report stated that the "separate but equal doctrine stands convicted on three grounds," because it "contravenes the equalitarian spirit of the American heritage," produces "inequality of services," and keeps "groups apart despite indisputable evidence that normal contacts among these groups promote social harmony." The committee concluded that "no argument or rationalization can alter [the] basic fact" that government-mandated segregation "creates inequality by imposing a caste status" on black Americans.[21]

The committee did note some modest but promising signs of recent progress, referencing new civil rights laws in New York, court victories on access to the ballot, the ending of segregated schools in Trenton and St. Louis, and the welcoming of black workers into the labor movement. The report also addressed the breaking of the color line in Major League

Baseball, with Jackie Robinson joining the Brooklyn Dodgers in April 1947, and praised the "firm" resolve of the president of the National League to suspend any player who refused to play with Robinson.[22]

Committee members, mindful of President Truman's charge to determine "just how far the federal government . . . has the right to go in these civil rights matters," recommended dozens of bold actions to attack America's ongoing struggle with racial equality at its roots. Some of the proposals directly challenged Jim Crow, including desegregating the armed forces and federal government employment, prohibiting the poll tax and other barriers to the ballot, and banning restrictive covenants in housing and segregation in interstate travel. Significant new government initiatives were proposed, including a permanent agency to enforce prohibitions against discrimination in private employment, expanded resources and authority for the Justice Department's Civil Rights Section, and home rule for the District of Columbia. New federal laws were proposed to prohibit discrimination in public accommodations and to impose criminal sanctions for lynching.[23]

Recognizing that civil rights enforcement procedures that required trial by jury in the South were destined to be ineffective, the committee recommended various alternatives. These included granting federal agencies authority to withhold federal aid to state and local governments that practiced racial discrimination and federal judges' broad equitable powers in civil rights cases, through the use of declaratory judgments, cease and desist orders, and injunctive relief. The recommendation to use the federal government's grant authority to force compliance with civil rights requirements provoked some of the most heated region-based divisions among committee members, with the two southern members, Tilly and Graham, arguing that this would be too punitive and would punish those who needed federal assistance the most. The committee's southerners ultimately dissented from this proposal while joining the balance of the report.[24]

The committee, clearly concerned with the Justice Department's lack of vigor and initiative in civil rights enforcement, closely questioned department officials about their failure to file amicus (friend of the court) briefs in important civil rights cases supporting the positions of private litigants. The civil rights committee viewed this as an effective way to lend the prestige of the United States to the NAACP's highly skilled litigation efforts. It was an idea that apparently had not occurred to the department's attorneys and was promptly adopted by the Justice Department with truly remarkable results.[25]

Despite the groundbreaking findings and recommendations of the President's Committee on Civil Rights, *To Secure These Rights* did not initially receive widespread public attention. The NAACP leadership, however, immediately grasped the report's significance. Walter White called the report "the most courageous and specific document of its kind in American history," and Thurgood Marshall predicted that it would "go down in history as one of the most important documents yet produced in this field." Truman's attorney general Tom Clark later described the issuance of the committee's report as "one of the brightest days in Mr. Truman's administration" because it provided a "blueprint of most everything that's been done on civil rights since that time." John Egerton, in his classic history, *Speak Now Against the Day*, observed that although "the nation hardly took notice at all" of the committee's report, its issuance marked "a day to remember in the nation's long pursuit of its venerable and elusive ideals" because "never before had an official agency of the United States government uttered an explicit rejection of racial segregation and its philosophical and legal foundations."[26]

Truman made his first substantive statement regarding the committee's report during his State of the Union speech before a joint session of Congress. He declared that our "first goal" must be "to secure fully the essential human rights of our citizens" and acknowledged that "some of our citizens are still denied equal opportunity for education, for jobs and economic advancement, and for the expression of their views at the polls." He declared that racial discrimination was "utterly contrary to American ideals of democracy" and pointed to the proposals in the report as showing "the way to corrective action." He promised to address Congress on the subject in greater depth in the coming weeks.[27]

On February 2, 1948, Truman delivered his first special message to Congress on civil rights. He unequivocally endorsed the findings and recommendations of the President's Committee on Civil Rights, observing that there was a "serious gap between our ideals and some of our practices. This gap must be closed." Leaving no ambiguity on his position, he embraced the committee's recommendations to abolish the poll tax and other barriers to full voting rights for minorities, end segregation in interstate transportation, declare lynching a federal crime, and establish a federal commission to protect minorities from discrimination in private sector employment. He recommended strengthening federal civil rights statutes and providing more resources for their enforcement. Truman also alerted Congress that he intended to use his executive authority to end discrimination in the armed forces and federal service. The president concluded his message with a reference to the national security implications of his civil rights program, stating that "if we wish to inspire the peoples of the world whose freedom is in jeopardy . . . , we must correct the remaining imperfections in our practice of democracy."[28]

The response of southern elected officials to Truman's civil rights proposals ranged from shock to hysteria. Mississippi's governor, Fielding Wright, accused Truman of attempting "to wreck the South and its institutions," and Senator Harry Byrd of Virginia described the proposals as "a mass invasion of states' rights" unprecedented in American history. Senator W. Lee "Pappy" O'Daniel of Texas accused six members of the President's Committee on Civil Rights of being associated with communist-front organizations, and South Carolina's congressman Mendel Rivers called the committee's report "a brazen and monumental insult to the Democratic South and the southern way of life for both white and colored."[29]

Rumors of a third-party effort to challenge Truman's reelection soon emerged, and southern congressional Democrats were in open revolt.

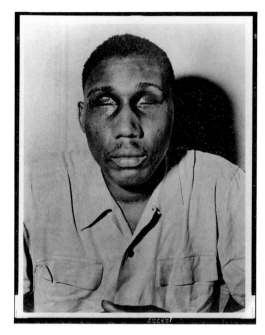

Just hours after being discharged from the U.S. Army on February 12, 1946, Sergeant Isaac Woodard was removed from a Greyhound bus after he insisted that the driver speak to him with respect. He was arrested by Batesburg, South Carolina, police chief Lynwood Shull. While in Shull's custody, Woodard was beaten so badly that he was blinded in both eyes.

(Photograph by J. DeBisse. Library of Congress, Prints & Photographs Division, Visual Materials from the NAACP Records [LC-USZ62-128327])

Shull (second from right) claimed that he struck Woodard only once with his blackjack and that Woodard's blinding was an unfortunate accident.

(*The Twin-City News*)

Racial mob violence and police brutality were reported with regularity both before and after World War II, especially in the rural South. The NAACP flew its "Lynch Flag" from its New York City headquarters whenever an incident was reported.

(Library of Congress, Prints & Photographs Division, Visual Materials from the NAACP Records [LC-DIG-ppmsca-09705])

Orson Welles, one of the most influential personalities of the era, reported details of the Woodard incident on his national radio program and demanded justice for the blinded sergeant.
(AP Photo)

Judge J. Waties Waring, an eighth-generation Charlestonian, had no record of questioning the racial status quo. But after presiding over the trial of Lynwood Shull, in which an all-white jury acquitted the police chief, Waring engaged in a period of intense study and reflection regarding the issues of race and justice.
(Courtesy of the South Caroliniana Library, University of South Carolina, Columbia, S.C.)

As nearly 900,000 African American veterans returned home and again confronted black disenfranchisement, membership in the NAACP grew exponentially. Walter White (center) was the organization's executive secretary; Thurgood Marshall (right), its general counsel; and Roy Wilkins (left), White's top assistant.
(Library of Congress, Prints & Photographs Division, Visual Materials from the NAACP Records [LC-DIG-ds-11196])

The September 19, 1946, meeting at which President Harry S. Truman (center) learned from Walter White (third from left) the details of the blinding of Isaac Woodard. Truman became visibly agitated. "My God!" he said. "I had no idea it was as terrible as that! We have got to do something."
(Courtesy of the South Caroliniana Library, University of South Carolina, Columbia, S.C.)

Woodard and his mother, Sarah Woodard, in a photograph dated July 12, 1946. After several months in a VA hospital, the sergeant was discharged to his parents, who were then living in the Bronx, New York. His wife had left him, and VA rules disqualified him from receiving full pension benefits.
(Special Collections and Archives, Georgia State University Library)

LEWISOHN STADIUM

137th Street & Convent Avenue, NYC

ISAAC WOODARD BENEFIT SHOW

Sponsored by Citizens Committee

FRIDAY, AUGUST 16, 1946

8 P. M.

for

Amsterdam News Welfare Fund
To Aid Isaac Woodard

MAYOR WILLIAM O. DWYER   JOE LOUIS - CAROL BRICE
Honorary Chairman   .   Co-Chairmen

Artists

JOE LOUIS	CAB CALLOWAY
CAROL BRICE	CANADA LEE
LOUIS JORDAN	COUNT BASIE
KING COLE TRIO	MAXINE SULLIVAN
PEARL BAILEY	BILLY HOLIDAY

Price . . . . . $1.20 (inc. tax)

Tickets sold at:—
Harlem YMCA — 135th Street off 7th Ave.
Harlem YWCA — 137th Street off 7th Ave.
Franks Restaurant — Bet. 8th Ave. & St. Nicholas
Palm Cafe — 125th Street and 7th Ave.
March on Washington Movement—Bookstore
Amsterdam News, 2340 — 8th Ave.

New York's *Amsterdam News* sponsored a benefit concert that included performances by Nat King Cole, Billie Holiday, and Count Basie. World heavyweight champion Joe Louis co-chaired with New York mayor William O'Dwyer. The concert was a sellout (at $1.20 a ticket), with more than twenty thousand attending.
(Courtesy of the New York *Amsterdam News*)

Louis (left) arrives with Woodard (center) at an August 9, 1946, press conference promoting the benefit. Said Louis, "This is the kind of thing I like to be involved in because I am always in my people's corner."
(Ossie LeViness / New York Daily News Archive / Getty Images)

President Truman addresses the annual meeting of the NAACP, June 29, 1947. Truman told the thousands assembled and the millions listening on the radio, "We can no longer afford the luxury of a leisurely attack upon prejudice and discrimination ... We must strive to advance civil rights wherever it lies within our power."
(Photograph by Abbie Rowe, National Park Service, Courtesy of the Harry S. Truman Library & Museum)

Judge J. Waties and Elizabeth Waring. After the jury verdict in the Shull trial, Elizabeth Waring left the courtroom in tears. Judge Waring called the trial his "baptism of fire" and his wife's "baptism in racial prejudice." (AP Photo)

Facing ostracism themselves, the NAACP's executive secretary, Walter White, and his wife, Poppy Cannon White, found deep kinship and friendship with the Warings.

OPPOSITE: Vilified and ostracized by their white neighbors, the Warings entertained African Americans in their home, an act that the News and Courier characterized as "an extraordinary and all but unique development in Charleston." The Warings hosted, among others, Septima Clark (to Judge Waring's left, laughing), a fiery civil rights activist dubbed by Dr. Martin Luther King Jr. the "queen mother of the civil rights movement." Ruby Cornwell (third from the right of Judge Waring) was the matriarch of the Charleston civil rights movement.

EXTRA — By Executive Order

PRESIDENT TRUMAN WIPES OUT SEGREGATION IN ARMED FORCES

2nd Order Sets Up FEPC In All Government Jobs

NATIONAL Edition

Chicago Defender
WORLD'S GREATEST WEEKLY

10¢ PAY NO MORE

In a dramatic and historic move, unprecedented since the time of Lincoln, President Harry Truman issued Monday afternoon two executive orders which doom forever Jim Crowism in the Armed forces of the United States and guarantee equal job opportunities in the Federal government and all of its branches.

VOL. XLIV, No. 16 — CHICAGO, ILL., SATURDAY, JULY 31, 1948

Executive Order No. 1

Establishing President's Committee on Equality of Treatment and Opportunity in the Armed Services.

Under 'States' Rights'

Posse, Bent On Lynching, Searches Woods For Prey

Rumor Negroes Would Resist

Intended Victims Escape; 2 Whites Shot As Prowlers

HAZELHURST, Miss.—

Come Back And Do A Job Is Truman Edict

GOP Must Decide What Comes First, Party Or Nation

WASHINGTON.—The Republican commanded 80th Congress is on the spot.

Aubrey Williams Bids Dixie Demos Farewell: 'Get Out And Stay Out'
By JOHN LEFLORE

MONTGOMERY, Ala.—Continuing his attack on Dixiecrats who reveled out of the Democratic convention over President Truman's civil rights program, Aubrey Williams, militant southern liberal, last week let loose another blast in the form of an editorial in the Southern Farmer.

Baltimore Sidesteps Court Order Ending Golf Link Jim Crow

BALTIMORE—A recent court order here enforcing segregation on all municipal golf courses was side stepped by means of employing separate playing time for whites and negroes.

Wallace Says He'll Stay In Race, But Won't Predict Victory In '48
By VENICE T. SPRAGGS

PHILADELPHIA—Henry A. Wallace has no intention of abandoning his "people movement" whose followers approved his presidential candidacy at the founding convention of the new Progressive Party which attracted a wide and eye-opening attendance.

Asks Integration Department In U. S. Department

Leaders To Help Raise Funds For Demo Campaign

Demand Return To Dixie Of Coast Businessman Freed 21 Years Ago

OAKLAND, Calif.—Following unusual procedure, Gov. Earl Warren last week slated for July 27 a public hearing of the case of Wiley King, 48, well known local business and churchman, whom the state of Mississippi demands be extradited for what King supporters claim was a self-defense slaying pardoned many years ago.

Hint L. Lomax Jr. To Marry Writer Almena Davis Soon

Snub Truman's Wife; Friends Are Too Dark

Judge Moore's Reappointment Wins Bar Nod

6 Killed, 19 Hurt As Trucks Collide On Memphis Highway

FRENCHMAN'S BAYOU, Ark.—Six workers, including two women, were killed, and nineteen others were injured.

WRITE YOUR CONGRESSMAN—TODAY
— Urge Him To VOTE FOR —
PRESIDENT TRUMAN'S CIVIL RIGHTS LEGISLATION
Civil Rights Mean A Guarantee of Human Rights to You!
WRITE YOUR Congressman in Washington TODAY!

Klan Increases Members To Scare Negroes From Voting

STONE MOUNTAIN, Ga.—Garbed in bedsheets.

On July 26, 1948, President Truman issued Executive Order 9981, mandating the end of segregation in America's armed forces. This marked the beginning of the end of Jim Crow in America. *The Chicago Defender* was one of the leading African American newspapers at the time, with a circulation exceeding 200,000.

(*Chicago Defender*)

Thurgood Marshall arrives in Charleston to try one of his groundbreaking civil rights cases before Judge Waring. From 1944 to 1951, Marshall tried cases involving equal pay, fair access to legal education, voting rights, and the end of public school segregation. The plaintiffs ultimately prevailed in each of these cases. One of the most notable was *Briggs v. Elliott*, one of the four cases consolidated before the U.S. Supreme Court under the title *Brown v. Board of Education*.

(Photograph by Cecil J. Williams)

Elizabeth Waring (far right) on *Meet the Press*, February 11, 1950. She defended her statement that white southerners were "morally weak and low" as being necessary "shock treatment" to attack white supremacy.

(Courtesy of the Moorland-Spingarn Research Center, Howard University Archives, Howard University, Washington, D.C.)

George Elmore, a Columbia businessman, successfully challenged the exclusion of black voters from the South Carolina Democratic primary in *Elmore v. Rice*. His suppliers and creditors blacklisted him, and he eventually lost his once-thriving businesses and died penniless.

(Photograph courtesy of the Elmore family. May not be reproduced or distributed in any form, or used by anyone for any other purpose, without the express written authorization of the Elmore family.)

WU C135 PD=

=COLUMBIA SOCAR

APR 19 236P

ATTORNEY THURGOOD MARSHALL NAACP=

317P.

Rcd. APR 19 1948

Rfd. to ...

=CONGRATULATIONS FOR YOUR OUTSTANDING
VICTORY IN OPENING THE DEMOCRATIC PRIMARIES TO NEGROES IN SOUTH
CAROLINA IT IS THE NEW EMANCIPATION TO THOUSANDS OF NEGROES IN
SOUTH CAROLINA RAISING THEM TO FIRST CLASS CITIZENSHIP=

=J M HINTON.

Judge Waring ruled on July 12, 1947, in *Elmore v. Rice* that the exclusion of African Americans from voting in the South Carolina Democratic primary was unconstitutional. James Hinton, the state NAACP president, sent Thurgood Marshall a congratulatory telegram on April 19, 1948, when the U.S. Supreme Court denied review, making Judge Waring's decision final.
(Library of Congress, NAACP Collection, *Elmore v. Rice* File)

South Carolina Democratic Party officials attempted to obstruct Waring's order in *Elmore*, but Waring made it clear that defiance would result in immediate incarceration. African Americans across the state began registering to vote.
(Alex M. Rivera Collection, J. E. Shepard Memorial Library, NCCU Archives, Records and History Center)

The Reverend Joseph A. DeLaine led the effort to equalize educational facilities in the profoundly unequal Summerton, South Carolina, school district. As a consequence, the school district fired DeLaine, his wife, his two sisters, and his niece. (Courtesy of the DeLaine family)

Rev. DeLaine and his family inspect the remains of their home, which burned while volunteer firemen watched. (Courtesy of the DeLaine family)

George McLaurin (left), a graduate student at the University of Oklahoma. The Supreme Court ruled on June 5, 1950, in *McLaurin v. Oklahoma State Regents* that the plaintiff's education was separate but it was certainly not equal.
(Bettmann / Getty Images)

Members of the NAACP trial team prepare for *Briggs v. Elliott* at the home of the Charleston civil rights activists Reginald and Eva Boone. (From left) Local NAACP counsel Harold Boulware, Thurgood Marshall, South Carolina NAACP president James Hinton, and Virginia attorneys Spottswood Robinson and Oliver Hill.
(Alex M. Rivera Collection, J. E. Shepard Memorial Library, NCCU Archives, Records and History Center)

The plaintiffs in *Briggs v. Elliott* on the opening day of the trial, May 28, 1951.
(Alex M. Rivera Collection, J. E. Shepard Memorial Library, NCCU Archives, Records and History Center)

As the sun rose on the morning of May 28, 1951, African Americans lined up in front of the Charleston federal courthouse as far as the eye could see in the hope of getting a seat for the opening day of *Briggs v. Elliott*. Judge Waring described the "interesting and dramatic situation" as a "little breath of freedom."
(Alex M. Rivera Collection, J. E. Shepard Memorial Library, NCCU Archives, Records and History Center)

Thurgood Marshall (center, in short sleeves) and his trial team prepare their witnesses on the opening day of *Briggs v. Elliott*. To Marshall's left are Arthur Shores, a Birmingham, Alabama, attorney; Robert Carter, associate general counsel of the NAACP; Spottswood Robinson, a Richmond, Virginia, attorney; and Dr. Kenneth Clark, who hours later would offer historic testimony using his doll studies to demonstrate the effects of segregation on African American children.
(Alex M. Rivera Collection, J. E. Shepard Memorial Library, NCCU Archives, Records and History Center)

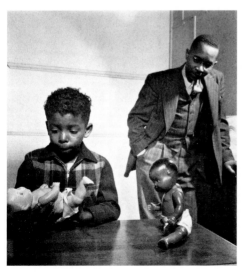

The New York social psychologist Dr. Kenneth Clark had conducted pioneering research on the effects of segregation on black children using black and white dolls. The Supreme Court later cited Dr. Clark's studies in *Brown v. Board of Education* as new evidence not available to the Court at the time of *Plessy v. Ferguson*.
(Photograph by Gordon Parks, courtesy of and copyright the Gordon Parks Foundation)

ISAAC WOODARD: *America's* *Forgotten Man*

Holding GI photo of self, Isaac Woodard remembers when he served country.

In the shadow of a New York skyscraper, a tall, husky man rises early each morning, feels his unseen way down the three flights of stairs from his tiny apartment, and weaves cautiously through traffic-choked streets for a stroll.

Neighborhood children wave to him, and passing housewives exchange pleasantries. Sometimes he pauses on his morning rounds to chat with a friend at a corner newsstand, or to purchase his daily cigaret ration from a nearby confectionery.

Everybody knows he is sightless. But few know him for who he is: America's forgotten man, Isaac Woodard, whose name 10 years ago this month was on 10 million tongues as the soldier whose eyes were gouged out by a Dixie cop in an unprovoked attack.

It was the wintry night of February 12, 1946, when Woodard, with an Army discharge, $46 in cash and a check for $790 in mustering-out pay stuffed in his pocket, was en route home to The Bronx, N. Y., from an Army separation center in Georgia. North Carolina-born Woodard boarded a bus at Camp Boyd, Ga., sat in the prescribed rear until near Aiken, S. C., when he asked the driver for a rest stop. At first, the driver refused to speak, later turned down the request. The two argued.

At Batesburgh, the driver called in police and Woodard was ordered off the bus and accused of creating a disturbance. "It was the worst few hours of my life," recalls the 36-year-old ex-infantry soldier. "For no reason at all that policeman—I remember his name was L. C. Shaw—knocked me down with a pis-

Getting glass of milk, Woodard is aided by his mother.

tol butt three times. I stayed down the third time and that is when he ground his night stick into my eyes. I had done nothing but ask the driver for a rest stop."

Blinded and bloody, Woodard spent the night in jail without medical attention. "I was unconscious for a while," he remembers, "but every few minutes I would wake up, then black out again. I was bloody from head to foot. Some time during the night,—I'll never know

Sightless, Woodard misses fun of reading to his son, Isaac III.

12

13

Isaac Woodard soon faded into obscurity. He was featured in a March 1956 article in *Jet* magazine as "America's forgotten man." According to family members, Woodard was never aware of the impact his beating and blinding had on President Truman or Judge Waring. Woodard died in the Bronx on September 23, 1992, at age seventy-three.

Senator Tom Connally of Texas, long identified as a close Truman friend, described the president's civil rights package as "a lynching of the Constitution," and Senator Olin Johnston of South Carolina boycotted a Jefferson-Jackson Day dinner honoring Truman, explaining that he and his wife might be seated beside a "niggra." A Gallup poll showed that 82 percent of Americans opposed Truman's civil rights program.[30]

Despite this avalanche of criticism, Truman refused to back down. He responded to the low poll numbers by observing, "I wonder how far Moses would have gone if he had taken a poll in Egypt." Long known for the famous statement on his desk, "The buck stops here," Truman also kept another quotation nearby: "Always do right. This will gratify some people and astonish the rest." When a group of southern congressional leaders approached the president with an offer to quell the third-party rebellion if he would soften his position on civil rights, Truman responded that "my forebears were Confederates" and "every factor and influence in my background . . . would foster the personal belief that you are right." But "whatever my inclination as a native of Missouri might have been, as president I know this is bad. I shall fight to end evil like this." Responding to the demands of a Democratic National Committee woman from Alabama at a White House banquet that the president assure the South that he was not "ramming miscegenation down our throats," Truman pulled a copy of the Constitution from his pocket and began reading her the Bill of Rights. He then stated to those assembled, "I take nothing back of what I proposed and make no excuses for it."[31]

As Truman's support in the South continued to erode, the architect of his grand political strategy, Clark Clifford, came to the president to suggest that perhaps it was time to modify his stand on civil rights. Recalling his discussions with Truman years later, Clifford admitted with some embarrassment that he advised the president that "we ought to be very careful not to drive the South away." Truman responded by telling Clifford "he was not going to retreat one inch from his civil rights program. And by God that's the way it was, and that's the way he was going to stay with it. And he did stay with it. He did not budge an inch."[32]

As the spring of 1948 turned to summer, Truman's political position appeared increasingly precarious. His legislative agenda was going nowhere. Word of a likely third-party effort by states' rights Democrats spread widely, and a fourth-party effort by Henry Wallace, the former Roosevelt vice president, also emerged. Each of these campaigns threatened to drain critical votes from the old New Deal coalition, which could seal Dewey's victory and Truman's defeat. Political polling, widely used for the first time in this presidential campaign, confirmed a commanding lead for Dewey and disillusionment with Truman's leadership.

Dewey's political advisers recognized that key elements of Truman's legislative program enjoyed widespread public support and included many of Truman's issues in the Republican Party platform, among them proposals for federal initiatives in public education, housing, and wages. In an effort to attract African American voters, the Republican platform had a progressive civil rights plank, which included a federal prohibition of lynching and poll taxes. Truman immediately appreciated that the Republican platform was at war with the Republican congressional leadership, who often joined southern Democrats in defeating civil rights legislation. In this conflict between the Republican platform and the party's congressional leadership, Truman sensed real political opportunity.[33]

As Democrats gathered in Philadelphia for their national convention, there was widespread despair and low morale. The threat of a southern walkout hung over the convention, and efforts were made to bring the warring factions back together in the Platform Committee. One idea acceptable to Truman was to downplay the civil rights issue by simply readopting the party's reasonably progressive but nonspecific 1944 civil rights plank. This provision guaranteed the right of all citizens "to live, develop, and vote equally . . . and share the rights guaranteed by our Constitution. Congress should exert its full constitutional powers to protect those rights." A number of delegates, rallying around the mayor of

Minneapolis, Hubert Humphrey, proposed that the party platform include the specific recommendations the president had endorsed in his special civil rights message to Congress. When the Platform Committee readopted the 1944 civil rights platform, Humphrey issued a minority report and promised a vigorous fight on the convention floor.

With little other drama at the convention, the battle over the civil rights platform became the focus of the delegates. Southerners promised to bolt if the Humphrey proposal was adopted. Civil rights proponents, labor union members, and liberal activists coalesced in support of the minority report. Truman endorsed the Platform Committee's proposal in an effort to avoid a complete break with the southern delegates, but this placed him in the awkward position of opposing a platform that simply detailed his own civil rights program. As Clark Clifford later explained, Truman's convention strategy made political sense because the precise wording of the party platform was not particularly important. In a dramatic and close vote, the minority report was adopted by the convention. Numerous southern delegates, including the entire Mississippi delegation, walked out.[34]

The battle over the civil rights platform delayed Truman's speech accepting the nomination until 2:00 a.m., long after most Americans had gone to bed. The delegates and the national radio audience tuning in were treated to a fiery and feisty Truman, who railed against the "do-nothing" Congress that had failed to address the country's problems with inflation, wages, housing, and education. He contrasted the Republican-controlled Congress's inaction on his proposals in these areas with the Republican Party platform, which he derided as "such poppycock." He noted that while the Republican platform embraced a progressive civil rights program, the Republican-controlled Congress had failed to pass a single proposal from his special civil rights message. As Truman railed against the do-nothing Republican Congress, the formerly morose delegates roared with approval and excitement.

Truman then announced that in light of this "long list of . . . promises in the Republican platform" and the absence of any progress on these issues by Congress, he was calling Congress back into special session on July 26, eleven days hence, to pass the programs and policies endorsed in the Republican platform. Truman noted that the day he was calling Congress back into session was known as Turnip Day in Missouri. He would thereafter dub the Republican majority the "Turnip Day Congress." The convention delegates were ecstatic, with *The New York Times* reporting that Truman had "set the convention on fire."[35]

Republicans denounced Truman's calling of a special session of Congress as pure politics and "the last hysterical gasp from an expiring administration." But Truman understood that the Republican leadership in Congress was not remotely interested in passing the progressive Republican Party platform, and Congress's inaction in the special session would drive a wedge between the party's presidential nominee and its congressional leadership. This would also reinforce Truman's message against the do-nothing Congress, turning the focus away from him to the even more reviled Congress. The Republican Speaker, Joe Martin, would later concede that Truman's strategy was "devilishly astute."[36]

Two days after the Democratic Party convention adjourned, a group of southern Democrats convened in Birmingham, Alabama, and established the States' Rights Democratic Party, dubbing themselves the Dixiecrats. Party leaders attacked Truman's civil rights proposals as seeking "to reduce us to the status of a mongrel, inferior race." One of the organizers of the new party was blunt about his opposition to Truman: "He thinks too damn much of the nigger." Governor Strom Thurmond of South Carolina was nominated for president and Governor Fielding Wright of Mississippi for vice president. Recognizing that the party could never win a national election for president, its strategists hoped to win enough electoral votes to throw the election to the House of Representatives, where southerners hoped to extract concessions on civil rights from Dewey. When a reporter questioned Governor Thurmond regarding his opposition to Truman when the president had supported the same civil rights platform as Roosevelt, Thurmond responded, "I agree, but Truman actually means it."[37]

Several days after Thurmond's nomination, a second splinter group, calling itself the Progressive Party, convened in Philadelphia and nominated Henry Wallace for president. Wallace had served as Roosevelt's vice president and was briefly a member of Truman's cabinet as secretary of commerce until Truman fired him for opposing his efforts to contain the Soviet Union. Wallace's candidacy was strongest among liberals in the major urban centers, and Democratic Party regulars dismissed his campaign as a front for the Communist Party. Although his platform appealed to the hearts of many liberal Democrats, Wallace had no realistic possibility of winning a national election. His greatest potential electoral impact was taking critical votes from Truman in swing states, thereby tipping those states and potentially the election to Dewey. As the campaign progressed, many early Wallace supporters migrated to the Truman campaign to avoid inadvertently putting Dewey in the White House.[38]

On July 26, 1948, an ill-tempered Republican-controlled Congress returned from interrupted summer vacations to a hot and muggy Washington, D.C., to open the special "Turnip Day" session. As the congressmen arrived, they were in for an even greater surprise—Truman's issuance of two blockbuster executive orders on the day the special session opened. Executive Order 9981 mandated equality in the policies of the U.S. armed forces, which Truman made clear meant the end of segregation in America's military. Executive Order 9980 prohibited discrimination in federal employment, effectively ending segregation in federal offices and facilities. In relying on his executive powers over the armed forces and the federal government, Truman acted with amazing decisiveness and effectiveness in implementing arguably the most important recommendations of his civil rights committee, and he did this without consulting or obtaining the approval of Congress.[39]

The congressional resentment was palpable when Truman appeared to speak to Congress at the opening of the special session, with a number of members staying in their seats rather than standing when he was announced. Truman wrote to his wife, Bess, "They sure are in a stew and mad as wet hens. If I can make them madder, maybe they'll do the[ir] jobs." Following the Truman script, the special session accomplished nothing during its two-week run except reinforcing the Democratic Party's message that the last thing Americans wanted to do was to give the Republicans control of the national government.[40]

After Congress adjourned the special session, Truman and his top campaign advisers completed plans for a demanding barnstorming campaign across the country that would allow the president to speak directly to farmers and other midwestern and western voters who held the key to a Truman victory. Truman was confident that if given the opportunity to speak directly to the voters, just as he had done in his two successful U.S. Senate races, he would win the election. The plan was for him to travel primarily by train, which would allow him to speak in numerous communities on a single day. Truman called his campaign the Whistle Stop Tour.

As he prepared for the arduous campaign trip, he received a private letter from an old friend, Ernest W. Roberts, a Missourian and a member of Truman's battery during World War I. Roberts offered Truman some unsolicited advice: drop your support for the "Equal Rights Bill" and "let the South take care of the Niggers." He observed that Truman could win the South without the civil rights issue but could not win it if he continued to advocate his civil rights platform. Roberts suggested that "if the Niggers do not like the southern treatment, let them come to Mrs. Roosevelt."

Truman responded in a private letter, which he later instructed not to be publicly released until after his death. Beginning his letter "Dear Ernie," he thanked Roberts for writing to him so he would have "a chance to tell you what the facts are." Truman explained that he was not "asking for social equality . . . but I am asking for equality of opportunity for all human beings and, as long as I stay here, I am going to continue that fight." He then referenced the blinding of Isaac Woodard, explaining that the failure of South Carolina officials to prosecute the police officer who inflicted the vicious beating on the "negro Sergeant" was "radically wrong." Truman referred to the lynching at Moore's Ford and other incidents of mob violence. He stated, "I can't approve of such goings on and I shall never approve it . . . I am going to try to remedy it and if that ends up in my failure to be reelected, that failure will be in a good cause."[41]

As Truman prepared to leave Washington on September 17, 1948, for his Whistle Stop Tour, he left behind a political class convinced that the election was a formality and that he was heading for a humiliating defeat. A Gallup poll reported that Dewey led Truman 48 percent to 38 percent, and anecdotal reports from across the country confirmed that this was going to be a Republican year. But even before the Whistle Stop Tour had departed, there was evidence that this assumption of a Republican landslide might not be correct. On Labor Day, Truman appeared at a rally in Detroit, where a reported crowd of 100,000 wildly cheered him. On his first full day on the Whistle Stop Tour, he drew large crowds across Iowa, in the Republican strongholds of Des Moines, Davenport, Iowa City, and Grinnell. *The Des Moines Register* reported that at each of these stops "the listeners massed for his rear platform talk were larger than the town's population."

Over thirty-three days, the president's train rumbled across the Midwest and the West, often making more than a dozen stops in a single day. Many if not most of these stops were in communities in which a president of the United States had never appeared. Truman would spend about ten minutes at each stop, mostly focused on the do-nothing Congress and its failure to address the nation's most urgent problems because of the influence of powerful special interests. He also introduced his wife, Bess, and his daughter, Margaret, and they always received enthusiastic welcomes.

Many stops had crowds in the thousands waiting hours to see their president, and few seemed to leave disappointed with his fiery attacks on the Republican Congress. The cry "Give 'em hell, Harry" could be heard from the audience. When Truman campaigned in Texas, a critical state he needed to win, with its twenty-three electoral votes, large crowds met his train despite the controversy over his civil rights platform. Truman sensed that, notwithstanding the polling and prognostications, he was going to win this race.[42]

———

Dewey also campaigned by train but had fewer stops and smaller crowds. His aloof and distant manner seemed to excite few voters, but there was an unmistakable sense among political pundits that his victory was inevitable. A popular parlor game in Washington was to guess the members of Dewey's first cabinet. A survey of the fifty most prominent political reporters conducted by *Newsweek* indicated that every person surveyed predicted a Dewey victory. Even when late polling results suggested that Dewey's lead was narrowing, his advisers counseled a low-key approach to avoid rocking the boat on this sure win.[43]

Truman made little effort to raise the civil rights issue during the presidential campaign, recognizing that it had little popular appeal among white voters. After he returned to Washington in late October, he insisted that the campaign schedule a rally in Harlem, in an effort to beat Dewey in his own backyard. On October 29, just days before the election, Truman appeared before a massive cheering crowd in Harlem, making him the first president ever to campaign there.[44]

As the early votes came in on election night, November 2, 1948, Truman took a lead in the national vote. Because the results in key states remained unsettled, reporters continued to predict a decisive Dewey victory. At midnight, NBC Radio reported that Truman had a lead in the national vote by 1.2 million voters but was still "undoubtedly beaten." As dawn broke, Truman had slim leads in the critical states of Illinois, Ohio, and California. His lead in the national vote now exceeded 2 million. At 8:30 a.m., Ohio was declared for Truman, putting him over the 270 electoral votes required for victory. In the end, Truman would win 303 electoral votes and the popular vote by 2.1 million. He also had long political coattails, with Democrats recapturing the House and the Senate.

Only Henry Wallace's votes, draining off traditionally Democratic supporters, prevented Truman from beating Dewey in New York.[45]

Truman's vote totals were particularly impressive in the South, where
he decisively outpolled Dewey and Thurmond, winning eight of the
twelve southern states. In Texas, which was thought to be hotly contested, Truman carried every county in the state. Sam Rayburn, the legendary Texas congressman, observed that "those Dixiecrats are as welcome
around here as a bastard at a family reunion."[46]

A postelection review of the returns revealed that Truman's narrow
victories in the key states of Illinois, Ohio, and California were the result
of massive African American turnout in major cities. Clark Clifford's strategy of appealing to African American voters by promoting an aggressive
program on civil rights had worked, resulting in the improbable reelection
of Harry Truman. American politics would never be the same.[47]

10.

"WE KNOW THE WAY.
WE NEED ONLY THE WILL."

DESPITE THE PRESIDENT'S convincing 1948 election victory and the Democrats' recapturing both houses of Congress, Truman was still unable to persuade congressional leaders to adopt his civil rights program. The alliance of southern Democrats and conservative Republicans continued to tie up the Senate with filibusters on any legislation advancing the cause of civil rights. Early in his second term, Truman and Vice President Alben Barkley endorsed changes in the Senate filibuster procedures, known as Rule XXII, that would have made the overriding of filibusters easier. This critical reform effort was defeated in the Senate 46 to 41 on March 11, 1949. Thereafter, while Truman continued to mention civil rights in every State of the Union address for the remainder of his presidency and annually sent special civil rights messages to Congress, he turned his primary focus on civil rights to executive actions, which he could implement without congressional authorization.[1]

Truman's second term lacked the high-profile civil rights advocacy of his first term, but a reasonable argument can be made that his most important and enduring achievements in civil rights occurred during the second term. Much of the work was done outside the public eye and involved intense bureaucratic battles between a little-known presidential committee and the army brass over the full implementation of Truman's desegregation order. Meanwhile, a small group of brilliant lawyers in the Office of the Solicitor General prepared highly influential amicus briefs that were filed by the United States in some of the most important civil rights cases of the era, creating a powerful and timely alliance between the nation's premier civil rights organization and the U.S. Department of Justice.

———

Harry Truman's determination to fully implement his executive order ending segregation in the armed forces was evident within days of its issuance on July 26, 1948. The language of the executive order declared that the policy of the armed forces was to provide "equality of treatment and opportunity" to all citizens and made no explicit statement regarding the ending of racial segregation. A few days after the issuance of the order, press reports indicated that army staff did not believe that the president was mandating the end of racial segregation in the armed forces. The army's resistance became even more public when its chief of staff, General Omar Bradley, expressed the opinion that the military was no place to conduct social experiments and declared that the military would desegregate when the rest of society did so. The next day, Truman made it clear that his executive order required the end of segregation in the armed forces, and he summoned General Bradley to the White House for a dressing-down. The general promptly issued a public apology to the president and pledged his commitment to following the directives of his commander in chief.[2]

Recognizing that he would face significant institutional resistance

within the armed forces to his efforts to end segregation, Truman appointed a special presidential committee charged with reviewing and ap-
proving desegregation plans for each branch. The committee was officially
titled the Committee on Equality of Treatment and Opportunity in the
Armed Services. It was more commonly known as the Fahy Committee,
after its chairman, the former U.S. solicitor general Charles Fahy. Secretary of the Army Kenneth Royall lobbied against the appointment of any
member who had "publicly expressed the opinion in favor of abolishing
segregation in the Armed Services." Truman would have none of this.
Chairman Fahy was a highly skilled attorney with a well-earned reputation as a racial progressive. Two African American appointees, Lester
Granger, executive secretary of the National Urban League, and Robert
Sengstacke, publisher of *The Chicago Defender*, were nationally prominent civil rights advocates. In fact, all five members of the Fahy Committee were committed to the full enforcement of Truman's executive
order and the establishment of a multiracial military organization.[3]

Truman greeted the members of the Fahy Committee at their organizational meeting at the White House on January 12, 1949, and made it
clear that he expected the armed forces to provide "equal treatment," not
merely "fair treatment," for all of their members. These were code words
for the ending of segregation, and Truman let the committee members
know that he was prepared to exercise his power as commander in chief
to "knock somebody's ears down" if that became necessary. He expected
the Fahy Committee to "carry out the spirit, as well as the letter, of the
order" and hopefully to provide a model that could then be followed by
other federal agencies. Truman emphasized that this work "is not a publicity stunt. I want concrete results." With all of the branch secretaries
present, Secretary of the Air Force Stuart Symington spoke up, asserting
to the president that the air force's plan would "completely eliminate segregation." Notably, Secretary Royall remained silent.[4]

The Fahy Committee directed each branch of the military service to
submit a plan for ending segregation and providing equal opportunity
without regard to race. The air force, the newest and smallest military ser-

vice, promptly submitted its plan, and the Fahy Committee approved it. The navy, with some minor adjustments in its plan, soon won approval from the committee as well. But the army was resistant, arguing that the military should not be "an instrument of social evolution." Secretary Royall explained that the army's experience had been that black soldiers were not particularly well suited for combat units and were "peculiarly qualified" for manual labor. Integration, in Royall's view, would disrupt the army and interfere with its mission.

The army's plan was to maintain segregated units but to open access to a selective group of black soldiers for any duty assignment. The army also insisted on maintaining a cap on black soldiers at 10 percent of the total force. The army's plan was a nonstarter for the Fahy Committee, and a pitched political battle ensued within the Truman administration. The army brass elicited the support of such luminaries as the retired generals Dwight Eisenhower, George Marshall, and Mark Clark as well as various southern congressmen, to oppose the president's order. In the face of this public campaign, Truman made it clear that the army had no choice but to adopt a plan acceptable to the Fahy Committee. The president was dismissive of the retired generals' warnings that racial segregation was essential for military order and efficiency, calling it "just plain nonsense." Reports that the air force and navy desegregation plans had been successfully implemented undermined the army's increasingly tenuous position. After a year of submitted and rejected compliance plans, an exhausted army brass finally relented, agreeing to the full integration of all units and the removal of the racial cap for African Americans in military service.[5]

Progress was thereafter remarkably fast, and segregation ended in every branch of the military service with little disruption or loss of efficiency. Virtually every aspect of military life, including base housing, basic training, and public schools on military bases, was racially integrated. By 1953, 95 percent of the African American soldiers served in integrated units. With the removal of the racial cap on military service, black enlistment in the army climbed from 10 percent in 1949 to 16.1 percent by early 1953, an increase of more than 60 percent. As one historian observed, with the ending of segregation in the armed forces, "military life . . . developed a unique interracial character unlike that found in the other major institutions of American society." The successful ending of segregation in the armed forces, accomplished in the years immediately preceding *Brown v. Board of Education*, provided the U.S. Supreme Court with a powerful example of a post–Jim Crow world that undermined the segregationists' argument that racial integration was a practical impossibility. Members of the Supreme Court received the findings and reports of the Fahy Committee and reviewed in manuscript the first definitive work on the integration of the armed forces, *Breakthrough on the Color Front*, prior to the Court's landmark decision in *Brown*.[6]

Recognizing the potential impact that successfully integrated schools on military bases might have on the emerging judicial fight over public school segregation, southern congressional leaders inserted a late amendment into a school construction bill that required segregation of schools on military bases located in states where school segregation was mandated by law. Truman's executive order had already resulted in the desegregation of many schools on military bases. In what was a remarkably courageous act at that time, Truman vetoed the school construction bill on November 2, 1951, expressly citing the school segregation amendment as the reason. Noting the "rapid progress" that was being made in ending segregation in the armed forces and in the federal service, he explained that the amendment, "if enacted into law, would constitute a backward step in the efforts of the federal government to extend equal rights and opportunities to all people." He observed that the United States had "assumed a role of world leadership," and "we shall not impair our moral position by enacting a law that requires discrimination on the basis of race." The president requested that Congress readopt the school construction bill without the offending amendment, which it later did.[7]

━━━

While the Fahy Committee was engaged in its intense battle with the army's brass, a small cadre of lawyers in the Office of the Solicitor General quietly began implementing the recommendation of the President's Committee on Civil Rights that the United States file amicus briefs in important civil rights cases in which the government was not a party. The amicus brief program had much to recommend it. Through the submission of a brief, the Justice Department had the opportunity to weigh in on the major cases pending before the U.S. Supreme Court without the necessity of spending years identifying and litigating cases. Further, many of the key pending cases had been skillfully screened and litigated by Thurgood Marshall and his talented team of lawyers in the NAACP's General Counsel's Office, providing strong records upon which to advance key legal issues before the Court.

The amicus program was directed by Philip Elman, a former law clerk and confidant of the Supreme Court associate justice Felix Frankfurter. The solicitor general, the government's lawyer before the Supreme Court, filed his first civil rights amicus brief in December 1946 in *Shelley v. Kraemer*, just weeks after the issuance of the President's Committee on Civil Rights report recommending the adoption of the practice. *Shelley* challenged the long-standing practice of racially restrictive covenants, which commonly included prohibitions against the sale of a home or other property to a racial or religious minority. These restrictive covenants were enforced by state and local governments, thus creating the state action necessary to raise an equal protection question under the Fourteenth Amendment. Racially restrictive covenants were widely used across the nation.

The solicitor general argued that such covenants were "incompatible with the spirit and letter of the Constitution and laws of the United States" and violated the "fundamental principle" that "no agency of government should participate in any action which will result in depriving any person of essential rights because of race or color or creed." Residential discrimination was described as "rooted in ignorance, bigotry, and prejudice" and existed because "private racial restrictions are enforced by the courts." The government's brief quoted from President Truman's July 1947 speech to the NAACP, in which he stated that "our national government must show the way." Chief Justice Fred Vinson had been there on the rostrum when his close friend Harry Truman delivered his groundbreaking NAACP address. Months later, Vinson authored the unanimous opinion in *Shelley* declaring racially restrictive covenants unconstitutional.[8]

Two years later, the solicitor general filed an amicus brief in *Henderson v. United States* in support of a challenge to an order of the Interstate Commerce Commission permitting segregated seating in railroad dining cars traveling between states. The case had a certain historical resonance because *Plessy* had involved segregation on intrastate train travel. The solicitor general formally asserted for the first time in the *Henderson* amicus brief that the separate but equal doctrine of *Plessy v. Ferguson* should be "reexamined and discarded" because it was a "constitutional anachronism which no longer deserves a place in our law." Subsequently, the solicitor general filed a joint amicus brief in two higher education civil rights cases, *Sweatt v. Painter* and *McLaurin v. Oklahoma State Regents*, arguing that *Plessy* was "wrong as a matter of law, history and policy." The solicitor general urged the justices to "repudiate the 'separate but equal' doctrine as an unwarranted deviation from the principle of equality under law which the Fourteenth Amendment explicitly incorporated in the fundamental charter of this country." These amicus briefs were the first instances in which the executive branch had officially taken the position that *Plessy* should be overturned. The U.S. Supreme Court issued unanimous opinions in *Henderson*, *Sweatt*, and *McLaurin* on June 5, 1950, striking down the challenged practices in each of the three cases without mentioning *Plessy*.[9]

As the Truman administration was drawing to a close, the Justice Department on December 2, 1952, filed one last amicus brief, in the case of *Brown v. Board of Education*. The solicitor general called the question before the Court one of "first importance in our society" and urged the justices to accept their "special responsibility for assuring vindication of fundamental civil rights guaranteed by the Constitution." The issue was presented as a matter of national security: there existed a world struggle "between freedom and tyranny," and America's treatment of its black citizens had "an adverse effect upon our relations with other countries." The brief attacked the fundamental underpinnings of *Plessy* by declaring that the decision was "based upon dubious assumptions of fact combined with a disregard of the basic purposes of the Fourteenth Amendment." Recognizing that four of nine sitting justices had been appointed by Truman, the solicitor general quoted the president in the brief's concluding paragraph: "If we wish to inspire the people of the world whose freedom is in jeopardy, if we wish to restore hope to those who have already lost their civil liberties, if we wish to fulfill the promise that is ours, we must correct the remaining imperfections in our practice of democracy." The brief then ended with a poignant statement: "We know the way. We need only the will." A year and a half later, a unanimous Supreme Court overturned *Plessy* in *Brown v. Board of Education.*[10]

The Justice Department's amicus program was one of the "unheralded achievements" of the Truman administration's civil rights program. In the five civil rights cases before the U.S. Supreme Court in the late 1940s and early 1950s in which the Truman administration filed amicus briefs, civil rights plaintiffs won all of them by unanimous votes. The greatest share of credit for this remarkable run of Supreme Court victories must be given to the NAACP's skillful handling of these cases. But this was not the NAACP's victory alone, and there were important supporting roles played by others. The Truman administration's persistent and skillfully presented attacks on the *Plessy* doctrine certainly undermined the precedent and placed the executive branch unequivocally on the record as asserting that the separate but equal doctrine had no place in American constitutional jurisprudence.[11]

Truman issued a series of executive orders throughout 1951 prohibiting discrimination by federal contractors in a broad array of federal agencies, including the Department of Defense, the Department of Commerce, the General Services Administration, the Tennessee Valley Authority, and the Department of the Interior. On December 3, 1951, he issued an executive order establishing the Committee on Government

Contract Compliance to provide an effective mechanism to enforce the nondiscrimination provisions in federal contracts.[12]

Two years earlier, on October 21, 1949, Truman made a recess appointment of William Hastie to be a member of the U.S. Court of Appeals for the Third Circuit, making him the first African American to serve on a federal appellate court. This guaranteed Hastie his judgeship only until the end of the current congressional session. At the time of his recess appointment, Hastie was serving as the Truman-appointed governor of the Virgin Islands. A former editor of the *Harvard Law Review* and dean of the Howard University School of Law, he had impeccable credentials and had played an important role in the 1948 presidential campaign in persuading black voters across the East and the Midwest to support Truman's reelection.

The confirmation of Hastie by the U.S. Senate was by no means a foregone conclusion. Truman, with his deep understanding of Senate rules and customs, knew how to get it accomplished. When a group of senators approached the president to approve a package of new federal judgeships, which the senators sought in order to reward some of their most loyal friends and supporters, Truman stated that he could enthusiastically support the bill once Judge Hastie's nomination for a permanent position on the Third Circuit was confirmed. On July 19, 1950, with little fanfare, Judge Hastie's nomination was confirmed. Judge Hastie went on to have a distinguished judicial career, including service as chief judge of the Third Circuit.[13]

The Truman administration's stellar efforts with the President's Committee on Civil Rights, the Fahy Committee, and the amicus program of the Solicitor General's Office were not matched in other parts of the federal government. The Civil Rights Section of the Justice Department never performed effectively, because of weak leadership and limited resources. The FBI, under Director Hoover, frequently conducted ineffective investigations in civil rights cases, caught in a conflict between its mission to partner with local law-enforcement agencies and the need to investigate local law-enforcement officers who were often culpable.

The National Guard, the state-administered reserve force funded by the federal government, remained segregated despite the integration of all military units in the regular armed forces. The Federal Housing Administration, which had tremendous influence through its approval of FHA mortgages, redlined essentially all communities with significant minority populations, cutting off a large majority of prospective black homeowners from the program. Similarly, the Veterans Administration made few loans to black veterans, utilizing the same redlining policies as the FHA. In short, with the exception of the desegregation of the armed forces, the Truman administration realized limited success in rooting out the endemic racism that persisted in the federal government. It would take Lyndon Johnson's Great Society programs, a little more than a decade later, to make real progress in changing the racial practices of other federal agencies.[14]

Still, despite the Truman administration's mixed success in reforming the federal bureaucracy, there is little question that Truman was a transformative figure in America's civil rights history. As Richard Kluger observed of Truman in his classic work *Simple Justice*, "no president before or since Lincoln had put his political neck on the chopping block" for the advancement of civil rights like Truman. C. Vann Woodward, the dean of southern historians, credited Truman with breaking the bipartisan national policy on race, which had essentially allowed the South to ignore the mandates of the Civil War Amendments. Thurgood Marshall observed that "Truman proved that one man can be bigger than the statutes of his time—more forceful than the lawmakers." Despite the overwhelming hostility of American voters to his civil rights program, Truman persisted. As the legendary civil rights leader and congressman John Lewis observed, Truman never "put his finger in the air to see which way the wind was blowing. He did what he thought was right. He spoke from his gut, from his heart."[15]

When explaining his determination to act on civil rights or discussing the matter privately with staff and close associates, Truman would repeatedly mention his outrage over the treatment of returning black veterans and the failure of state officials to act to protect the safety and rights of these American heroes. As Clark Clifford remembered, Truman felt "it was outrageous that men could be asked to die for their country" but then be subject to racial discrimination by their own government. Invariably, Truman would tell the story of the "Negro Sergeant" from South Carolina and the injustice of local law-enforcement officials failing to punish the man responsible for his brutal attack and blinding. As Truman's biographer David McCullough observed, the Isaac Woodard story "made an everlasting impression on Truman, moving him in a way no statistics ever would." But unbeknownst to Truman, another federal official, the U.S. district judge sitting in Charleston, South Carolina, J. Waties Waring, was about to launch his own civil rights crusade inspired by the blinding of Isaac Woodard.[16]

11.

CONFRONTING THE AMERICAN DILEMMA

THE WARINGS RETURNED to Charleston following the *Shull* trial profoundly disturbed by the "viciousness" of the assault on Isaac Woodard and the judicial system's failure to hold the officer accountable. Elizabeth called it one of the "great shocks" of her life to "have sat in a courtroom in Columbia and see[n] a jury set free a man who beat out the eyes of Isaac Woodard." Judge Waring viewed the trial as his personal "baptism of fire." Both Warings struggled to find some effective response to this experience.[1]

The Warings had certainly long been aware that they lived in a Jim Crow world. Blacks were physically segregated in all public spaces and were deprived of their right to vote and struggled at the very bottom of the economic ladder. The Warings accepted these practices as built into the fabric of southern life and did not question them. What they had not recognized, or at least acknowledged to themselves, was that this entire discriminatory system was enforced by coercion, intimidation, and, where necessary, violence. The trial of Lynwood Shull forced them to acknowledge this basic truth.

Another basic truth of Jim Crow was that no dissent or questioning of the discriminatory practices was tolerated. The random iconoclast who questioned the morality or fairness of the racial status quo immediately felt the wrath of the segregationists, who essentially treated every voice of white dissent as an existential threat to white supremacy. Judge Waring would later describe southern life of that era as akin to living behind the Iron Curtain.[2]

Because race and justice were not topics white South Carolinians of this era openly discussed, the Warings resolved to undertake their own private study of race in America. Each evening after dinner, Elizabeth Waring would read out loud from a selected text, which allowed her husband to rest his eyes after a hard day at the office performing his judicial duties. After reading for a while, the Warings would take a drive around Charleston, one of their favorite evening activities, and discuss the text they had just read. Night after night, over many months, they undertook this ritual of reading, discussion, and reflection.[3]

The Warings began their studies with W. J. Cash's *Mind of the South*, a widely read and important book of the period. Published in 1941, the book conducted a sort of mass psychoanalysis of the white South, with a special focus on what Cash referred to as the "common white." Cash, who died at age forty-one shortly before the book was published, had worked as a newspaper reporter for *The Charlotte News*. He observed that some of the "best" traits of the "common white" southerner were pride, bravery, personal generosity, and courteousness. But, he noted, there was a "darker side" of the "common white" that included "the tendency toward violence" and "mob action," evidenced by "Negro lynching" and a murder rate in the South that greatly exceeded that of the rest of the country. In Cash's view, the "common white" was also characterized by intolerance ("greatly absorbed . . . by fears and hates"), an incapacity of analysis, an exaggerated individualism, an attachment to fictions and false values, and a "tendency toward unreality." These traits, Cash argued, made the "common white" unusually receptive to racial demagogues "of the more brutal sort."[4]

Cash characterized slavery as an "inescapably brutal and ugly" practice that placed African Americans in a "position of a mere domestic animal." This clearly deviated from the existing popular lore that slavery was a benign and civilizing institution for African slaves. Cash argued that the absolute power of whites bred "a savage and ignoble hate for the Negro." This hatred, he argued, produced exaggerated claims of sexual dangerousness of black men and made them "the obviously appointed scapegoat."[5]

Cash's candid discussion of racism and the portrayal of whites as victimizers of African Americans generated great criticism across the white South. Judge Waring, however, found *The Mind of the South* a liberating revelation. Cash, he observed, disclosed "the perverted and wrong method of thought of those who have carried out the persecution of the Negro." Waring initially found the book difficult to read because it challenged so many of his unquestioned premises about southern life, but he ultimately concluded it was "medicine to do it."[6]

Having studied Cash's harsh critique of southern racial customs, the Warings next tackled Gunnar Myrdal's fourteen-hundred-page study of race in America, *An American Dilemma: The Negro Problem and Modern Democracy*, published in 1944. This work, funded by the Carnegie Foundation, was a "comprehensive study of the Negro in the United States, to be undertaken in a wholly objective and dispassionate way as a social phenomenon." Myrdal, a Swedish economist and social scientist, was selected to conduct the study because of his renowned scholarship and his emotional distance from the American racial question. Eventually, forty researchers, including Ralph Bunche and Dr. Kenneth Clark, assisted in the preparation of *An American Dilemma*.[7]

The study clinically analyzed some of America's most delicate and often undiscussed racial practices and customs, including black disenfranchisement, racial mob violence, failures of the justice system, racial segregation, and the fear of interracial sexual relations and marriage. Myrdal asserted that the purpose of these racial practices was "to isolate the Negro and to assign them to a lower social status." In one of the most insightful sections of the study, Myrdal compared the "ranked order of discriminations" held by whites and blacks, which listed the most important aspects of Jim Crow practices to whites and the most critical issues of concern to blacks. For whites, the most important or "first rank" areas of concern regarding race relations were interracial sex and marriage. This was followed by concerns regarding direct social contact with blacks, such as eating and drinking together or using the same restrooms. Less important to whites were political disenfranchisement and discrimination in employment, credit, and public relief. For blacks, as victims of racial discrimination, the "ranked order of discriminations" was the same, but *in reverse*. Fair access to employment, credit, and public relief was at the top of concerns for blacks, followed by the right to vote. The areas of least concern for blacks were interracial sex and marriage.[8]

Myrdal, a future Nobel laureate with a deep faith in American democracy, observed that Americans were defined by a set of values he called the "American Creed." These included the essential dignity of each individual, the equality of all men, and the right to freedom, justice, and fair opportunity. Myrdal contrasted this American Creed with the treatment of southern blacks, which he described as a "moral lag in the development of the nation." He viewed America's racial difficulties as essentially the white man's problem that existed "in the heart of America," and the gap between the American Creed and the nation's treatment of its black citizens was the "American Dilemma." He called on America to courageously confront its racial practices because, after two world wars, "mankind needed . . . the youthful moralistic optimism of America." America's civil rights struggle, Myrdal maintained, was a great opportunity to perfect the nation and to give it "a spiritual power many times stronger than all of her financial and military resources."[9]

Myrdal had a dim view of southern liberals, whom he characterized as "inclined to stress the need for patience and to exalt the cautious approach, the slow change, the organic nature of social growth." Southern liberals, in Myrdal's view, excessively emphasized their "local and regional patriotism" and seemed desperate to "keep respectability" by treading "most cautiously around the negro problem." According to Myrdal, the southern liberal greatly feared "the deadly blow of being called a 'nigger lover,'" which produced a form of paralyzing timidity that left southern racial customs effectively unchallenged.[10]

Waring studied *An American Dilemma* with the same rigor and intensity with which he had first read law as an aspiring attorney more than forty years earlier. The book, which he described as "a great and monumental study," provided him with a historical and sociological lens through which to view his native South. He was particularly moved by Myrdal's concept of the American Creed, which soon found its way into his opinions and public statements. Waring shared Myrdal's view that the South's racial problems were a stain on America's international reputation in its battle against world communism. He also adopted Myrdal's skeptical view of southern liberals. Waring, who just years earlier proudly advocated southern gradualism, now disparaged "gradualists" as a major obstacle to meaningful social change.[11]

The Warings followed their study of Cash and Myrdal with additional evening readings in American history, anthropology, and sociology. A reporter for *The Christian Science Monitor* observed that the books in the Warings' library showed evidence of much use. Another reporter described Judge Waring's intense study of race as producing "a long night of soul searching" that resulted in "a new sense of meaning of the judge's function in a democratic order."[12]

The Warings' racial awakening coincided with a dynamic period in the racial history of the United States. African Americans, bolstered by returning World War II veterans, began to challenge Jim Crow practices and demand the right to vote. On April 15, 1947, America was mesmerized by the entry of Jackie Robinson into the lineup of the Brooklyn Dodgers, and his exciting exploits on the field made him a hero to young baseball fans, black and white. The emerging tensions between the United States and the Soviet Union heightened the concerns of many American leaders, including President Truman, that southern racial practices made America's claims for the superiority of democracy appear hypocritical.

There was also a discernible change in the attitude of the U.S. Supreme Court toward civil rights claims. In the Reconstruction and post-Reconstruction eras, the Supreme Court had been openly hostile toward the Civil War Amendments and their enabling statutes. Decisions in the 1870s, beginning with the *Slaughter-House Cases* in 1873, neutered the "privileges and immunities" clause of the Fourteenth Amendment, then thought by equal rights advocates to be the amendment's most significant provision. The Court ruled in an 1883 decision, the *Civil Rights Cases*, that Congress had no power to prohibit private acts of discrimination, tremendously limiting the ability of the federal government to combat racial discrimination undertaken by private citizens. The Supreme Court ruled in an 1877 decision, *Hall v. DeCuir*, that the states lacked the power to prohibit discrimination, but then ruled in the 1890 decision *Louisville, New Orleans & Texas Ry. Co. v. Mississippi* that states had the power to require segregation. The Court sanctioned racial segregation in interstate commerce in 1896 in *Plessy v. Ferguson*, under a doctrine later described as "separate but equal," and turned a blind eye to black disenfranchisement in the 1898 decision of *Williams v. Mississippi*, which sanctioned the use of literacy tests and poll taxes. For the next four decades, this body of case law delivered the unmistakable message that the federal courts were the place where civil rights claims went to die.[13]

In the late 1930s, however, the Supreme Court's antagonism toward civil rights cases began to abate. In *Gaines v. Canada*, a 1938 decision, a black applicant to the all-white University of Missouri Law School argued that under the *Plessy* doctrine he was entitled to admission to the historically white school because the state did not provide African Americans with a separate and equal program for legal training. The Supreme Court agreed, ruling that Missouri was required to either admit the plaintiff to the University of Missouri Law School or make "proper provision for his legal training within the state." Missouri elected to create a new, segregated law school for its black citizens.[14]

The Supreme Court took even bolder action six years later in the 1944 decision of *Smith v. Allwright*, which involved a challenge to the exclusion of black voters from the Texas Democratic Party primary. Prior Court decisions had held that a political party was a voluntary association that could exclude any persons it desired from its membership. The practical impact of these precedents was to exclude black voters from the only election that mattered in the one-party South. In a decisive 8–1 vote, the Supreme Court ruled that the Democratic primary was an integral part of the electoral machinery of Texas, as reflected by a detailed statutory scheme regulating the primaries, and "it may now be taken as a postulate that the right to vote [in a party primary] . . . without discrimination by the state, like the right to vote in a general election, is a right secured by the Constitution."[15]

Following the *Smith* decision, all southern states, save South Carolina and Georgia, agreed to allow black voters to participate in the Democratic primary. On October 12, 1945, U.S. District Judge T. Hoyt Davis, sitting in Macon, declared the all-white Georgia Democratic primary unconstitutional. The *Smith* decision was an important breakthrough victory for civil rights advocates because it began the slow but critical process of opening up the ballot to black southerners. Years later, reflecting on his remarkable legal career, Thurgood Marshall expressed the opinion that the Supreme Court's decision in *Smith v. Allwright* exceeded in importance even *Brown v. Board of Education* because, in his view, once African Americans obtained the franchise, they were able to resolve most other civil rights issues at the ballot box.[16]

The federal appellate courts in the South, the Fourth Circuit (extending from Maryland to South Carolina) and the Fifth Circuit (extending from Florida to Texas), also began to show a more sympathetic attitude toward civil rights cases. The Fourth Circuit's 1940 decision in *Alston v. School Board of City of Norfolk* declared racially discriminatory teacher salary schedules unconstitutional and ordered teacher pay equalized.

Civil rights advocates also viewed the Fifth Circuit's affirmance of Judge Davis's order in the Georgia white primary case as a promising sign.[17]

———

Judge Waring followed these emerging trends in the federal courts with great interest and began to look for opportunities to address civil rights issues on his own docket. He asked his clerk of court to monitor case filings in the Eastern District of South Carolina and to alert him whenever a civil rights case was filed. The clerk informed him in early 1947 that two significant civil rights cases had been filed in the Columbia Division. The first of these, *Wrighten v. Board of Trustees of the University of South Carolina*, involved a suit by a black applicant to the University of South Carolina Law School who asserted that he had been unlawfully denied admission because of his race. The second case, *Elmore v. Rice*, involved a challenge to South Carolina's all-white Democratic primary. Both of these cases were assigned to Waring's colleague Judge George Bell Timmerman because they were filed in the Columbia courthouse.

Timmerman contacted Waring to request that he accept responsibility for the law school case because he believed that his prior service on the university's board of trustees created a conflict of interest. Aware of Timmerman's general disdain for civil rights cases, Waring suggested that he also assume responsibility for the recently filed white primary case, on the dubious proposition that they were somehow related. Timmerman was "delighted" with Waring's suggestion and readily agreed to transfer that case to Waring as well.[18]

The law school admissions case proved to be straightforward. The facts presented bore a close resemblance to *Gaines v. Canada*, and there was no question that the State of South Carolina had a duty to provide its black citizens with equal access to professional training programs. The parties stipulated that the applicant, John H. Wrighten, was qualified for admission but for one fact, his race, and that the state's only law school, at the University of South Carolina, admitted only white students. Wrighten's attorneys informed Waring that they were not challenging *Plessy's*

separate but equal doctrine. Consequently, Waring ruled that his decision would not reach the "justice or injustice, propriety or impropriety, of
racial segregation in higher education." Waring observed that segregation
was a political question of whether a particular state wished as a matter of
policy to "sustain the financial burdens of segregation."[19]

Waring ruled on July 12, 1947, that Wrighten's right to equal protection of the laws was violated by the University of South Carolina's denial
of his admission to the state's only law school. He gave the state three options: admit Wrighten to the University of South Carolina Law School,
close the university's law school to all citizens, or establish a separate but
equal law school to provide legal training for Wrighten and two other qualified black applicants. The state selected the last option, undertaking the
burdensome duty of constructing a new law school on the campus of the
historically black South Carolina State College. The cost to South Carolina
taxpayers was $700,000 for the first year of the new law school's operations,
equivalent in today's dollars to $9 million. Waring later observed that it
"seemed like an absurdity to start a new law school" when the state could
have simply purchased a few more chairs for the qualified black applicants.

The opening of the South Carolina State Law School produced a
wholly unanticipated result. The law school graduated fifty-one students
from its opening in 1947 until it closed its doors in 1966, when the University of South Carolina admitted its first black applicants since Reconstruction. These State College law graduates formed a cadre of civil rights
attorneys who applied their legal training to dismantling Jim Crow in
South Carolina. Among the graduates were Matthew J. Perry, the chief
counsel of the South Carolina NAACP who was nominated by President
Jimmy Carter as the state's first African American federal judge in 1979,
and Ernest Finney, a skilled litigator and civil rights advocate who went
on to a distinguished state judicial career, including service as South Carolina's first black chief justice.[20]

Waring's decision in *Wrighten* produced little public outcry because
his order did not challenge one of the foundations of Jim Crow, the segregation of all public facilities. The same cannot be said of Waring's white

primary decision, which addressed another fundamental premise of Jim Crow, the disenfranchisement of black voters. The suit was brought by George Elmore, a prosperous owner of a small grocery store, the Waverly Five and Dime, and an adjacent liquor store. Elmore, who was light-skinned, had managed to register to vote on the mistaken belief that he was a white man but was then denied the right to vote in the Democratic primary. Party officials mocked Elmore, telling him that if he wanted to vote in a primary, he should start his own political party. But once Thurgood Marshall appeared as counsel for Elmore, state leaders viewed the litigation with considerable trepidation. Obviously, the case law was trending decidedly against the South Carolina Democratic Party. Further, unlike the separate but equal doctrine, the right to vote had no middle ground. Either a black citizen was entitled to vote or he was not. With South Carolina's black population approaching 40 percent, second only to Mississippi's, and concentrated in the former predominantly slaveholding regions of the Pee Dee and the Low Country, a free and open ballot would likely result in black majorities in numerous city, county, and legislative races. The white primary case, Waring observed, went to "the heart of political South Carolina."[21]

As most other southern states acquiesced in the Supreme Court decision in *Smith v. Allwright*, South Carolina's governor, Olin Johnston, vowed to preserve the state's white primary. He called the General Assembly into special session in April 1944 for the publicly declared purpose of evading the Supreme Court's white primary decision. The governor argued that because the Supreme Court in *Smith* had relied on the Texas statutory scheme governing the conduct of primary elections for its determination that the Democratic primary was part of the state's election machinery, South Carolina could evade federal court jurisdiction by repealing all state laws regulating the primary. Johnston summoned the state's sixteen elected solicitors (prosecutors) to Columbia to assist the state attorney general in searching the state election laws and removing all references to primary elections. Governor Johnston plainly stated in his proclamation, "White supremacy will be maintained in our primaries. Let the chips fall where they may." The South Carolina General Assembly convened and dutifully repealed 150 statutes governing the primary.[22]

South Carolina's effort to preserve the white primary through repeal of all state laws governing party primaries represented a serious threat to the NAACP's victory in *Smith v. Allwright*. Thurgood Marshall understood what was at stake and set about to prove that the state's repeal of the election law statutes did not (and could not) remove the state's obligation to establish and operate an election system to choose its public officials. Further, Marshall argued, the state had unlawfully delegated its duty to provide the machinery for electing federal and state officials to a private entity, the South Carolina Democratic Party. Marshall sent a draft of his pleadings in *Elmore* to William Hastie, who was then serving as the governor of the Virgin Islands. Hastie advised Marshall to emphasize the active role of the governor and the General Assembly in devising this latest election scheme for preserving the white primary, "since the state has an obligation to all of its citizens to uphold the guarantees of the federal Constitution which, on evasion, must be fulfilled by the federal court."[23]

Judge Waring observed the extraordinary lengths to which South Carolina's elected officials had gone to preserve the white primary and understood that any decision on his part that allowed African Americans to participate in the Democratic Party primary would likely produce a hostile, perhaps even violent, public response. He candidly discussed with Elizabeth the heavy price both might have to pay if he ruled for Elmore. Elizabeth Waring was unfazed, telling her husband she was there with him from "start to finish." Waring resolved that his choice was either "to be entirely governed by the doctrine of white supremacy" or to be "a federal judge and decide the law."[24]

The white primary case was tried before Judge Waring on June 3, 1947. The parties submitted proposed factual stipulations, which Waring accepted but found to be incomplete. On his own initiative, Waring admitted into evidence the governor's proclamation setting forth the purpose of the special session of the General Assembly and the present and former rules of the South Carolina Democratic Party. He also called as a court witness the Democratic Party chairman, William P. Baskin. Waring closely questioned Baskin about differences between the 1944 Democratic primary operated under the state statutory scheme and the 1946 primary operated exclusively under party rules. From this examination, Waring established that the Democratic Party's claim that the governance of the primary had materially changed as a result of the repeal of the election law statutes was "pure sophistry."[25]

Democratic Party officials argued that the party was a private association of consenting individuals who had the absolute right to determine their own rules for membership. They argued that South Carolina Democrats did not wish to associate with African Americans and possessed the right as free people to make that choice. Because South Carolina had repealed all laws relating to the primary, they contended that their primary was now a private activity and not an integral part of the state's election machinery. They compared the Democratic Party to a country club or patriotic society.

Judge Waring was not impressed. In an order dated July 12, 1947, he observed that the question before him was whether the Democratic Party was the equivalent of a "private business or social club with which the state and national governments have no concern" or was "the determining body in the choice of national and state officers in South Carolina." Said another way, Waring questioned whether the new primary system was simply "the same horse of a somewhat different color." He agreed that private organizations had the right to select their officers and members, but "private clubs and business organizations do not vote and elect a president of the United States, and the senators and members of the House of Representatives of our national congress." He went on to find that all citizens had a right to be involved in the selection of candidates for national office, and in South Carolina that meant the right to participate in the Democratic primary. Noting that every other southern state now allowed blacks to participate in the primary, Waring observed, "I cannot see where the skies will fall if South Carolina is put in the same class with these . . . other states."[26]

Echoing Gunnar Myrdal's American Creed thesis, Waring asserted that the United States' role as a world leader required a showing that the "American government and the American way of life is the fairest and the best that has yet been suggested." This required America to "take stock of our internal affairs" and "put our own house in order." He then quoted approvingly from President Truman's speech to the NAACP delivered just two weeks earlier, in which the president declared, "We cannot any longer await the growth of a will to action in the slowest state or the most backward community. Our national government must show the way."

Waring concluded the *Elmore* order by declaring that "it is time for South Carolina to rejoin the Union" and to "adopt the American way of conducting elections." This meant that "racial distinctions cannot exist in the machinery that selects the officers and lawmakers of the United States, and all citizens of this state and country are entitled to cast a free and untrammeled ballot in our elections." Waring ruled that the plaintiff was entitled to the relief requested and permanently enjoined the Democratic Party from excluding qualified voters from its primaries based upon their race.[27]

The leadership of the NAACP immediately grasped the significance of the *Elmore* decision. There was something groundbreaking about the tone and language of Waring's decision, clearly reflecting that the iron wall of segregation had come down in a federal courthouse in the Deep South. Walter White wrote President Truman a private note on July 14, 1947, two days after the decision, providing him with a copy of Waring's order and describing it as "an extraordinary decision by a southern judge in a primary case." White noted Waring's reference to Truman's NAACP speech, stating, "I thought you would be interested in seeing this admirable use of an admirable statement so soon after it was made." Several days later, Governor Hastie wrote a private handwritten note to Thurgood Marshall, stating, "I have read the South Carolina opinion three times and I still don't believe it. In many respects, I think it is your greatest legal achievement."[28]

Waring's decision hit the state's political class like a "bombshell" and produced a "storm of protest," primarily directed at Waring. The *News and Courier* warned that the decision could cause an "upheaval" that could threaten white control of nineteen counties and three of the state's six congressional districts. Senator Maybank denounced the decision as "clearly wrong" and promised that review would be immediately sought in the Fourth Circuit Court of Appeals. He argued that the decision "cuts down the fundamental rights of all Americans under the guise of helping the few." Some claimed deep offense at Waring's suggestion that it was time for South Carolina to "rejoin the Union," and others viewed Waring as a "traitor to his class."[29]

The Charleston Evening Post, which was edited by his nephew Thomas R. Waring Jr., denounced the judge's decision in a front-page editorial on July 14, 1947, arguing that the order "arbitrarily" interfered with "the rights of private citizens" and "arrogated" to the courts "the power to amend the Constitution by judicial fiat." The paper urged the Democratic Party to appeal the Waring order but acknowledged that "there is only a slim likelihood that the Supreme Court of the United States will upset Judge Waring's decision." This was because Waring's order "conforms snugly to the policy which the Supreme Court . . . has pursued in such matters." "In spite of all this," the editors concluded, "the case should be fought to the end."[30]

The denunciation of Waring by white South Carolinians was not universal. To the judge's pleasant surprise, he received several private notes praising his actions and personal courage. Waring responded to one supportive note from a woman living in the small rural community of Estill by asserting that "there is a substantial stratum of sanity, decency and liberality in our state." Notably, not one South Carolina attorney, public official, or other prominent white citizen publicly endorsed the *Elmore* decision. One newspaper editor, Tom Rogers of the *Florence Morning News*, sent a private note to Elizabeth Waring predicting that "your husband's court decision will be viewed as the signal turning point in South Carolina history."[31]

The black press and community leaders were not so reticent. *The Pittsburgh Courier* published a series of articles on Waring and his decision, including one that compiled words of praise from black citizens from across the country. In another article, titled "The Last of the White Primary," the paper wrote that "thus does a southern federal judge in a southern state carve an appropriate epitaph on the tomb of the white primary." Dr. Benjamin Mays, the president of Morehouse College, wrote Waring that his white primary decision was authored by "a great soul" and would go down in history "as one of the great documents of our time."[32]

Waring was initially somewhat philosophical about the public criticism he received. He wrote to a Florence, South Carolina, attorney, Stephen Nettles, that he had suffered "a great storm of condemnation because one dared to raise the iron curtain that has surrounded this state for many years." He observed that it was not pleasant to bring in a little light "for those that live in the dark." Waring declared, "It is time that we South Carolinians who have been fortunate enough to get our heads a little above the fog do what we can to bring our people out of it."[33]

The impact of the public denunciations of Waring was lessened to some extent by the fact that he and his wife had already faced a degree of public criticism and social isolation from elite Charleston social circles since their controversial 1945 marriage. As Elizabeth Waring's close friend Isabella Finnie astutely observed, "It is a strange turn of fate that Waties' ostracism on account of his marriage has really strengthened him for public service because there is nothing more public opinion can do to him—all the bricks have already been thrown."[34]

South Carolina Democratic Party leaders promised an appeal of the *Elmore* decision to the Fourth Circuit and appeared confident that the state's white primary would be restored. The Fourth Circuit was then made up of three judges, the most prominent being its chief judge, John J. Parker. Remembering the controversy over Parker's racial views during his unsuccessful 1930 nomination for the Supreme Court, party officials were confident that he appreciated the southern way of life and would overturn Judge Waring's order.[35]

But these assumptions about Judge Parker and his views on race were widely off the mark. Parker had always asserted that his racial views had been distorted by his opponents in the 1930 Senate vote on his nomination to the U.S. Supreme Court, and he welcomed the opportunity to prove his critics wrong. His racial views were also likely influenced by his recent service on an international tribunal in Nuremberg, Germany, where he presided over trials of Nazi war criminals. Additionally, apparently unknown to those advocating an immediate and aggressive appeal, Parker was a friend of Waring's and admired his skill and integrity as a trial judge. When a prominent Virginia banker and close friend of the Virginia governor's was indicted on federal bank fraud charges and all of the Virginia-based federal judges declared a conflict, Parker sent Waring to Richmond in the spring of 1947 to try the case. After Virginia newspapers praised Waring's handling of this controversial case, Parker sent him the clippings and told Waring that he had "measured up" to the task just as he had expected.[36]

Parker was aware of the vilification Waring was experiencing in South Carolina and was determined to address the state Democratic Party's appeal as quickly as possible. Oral argument was set for November 18, 1947, shortly after the appellate briefs were filed, and a unanimous decision, authored by Parker, was issued less than six weeks later, on December 30, 1947. The Fourth Circuit found the party's defense that it was "a mere private aggregation of individuals, like a country club," to be a "fundamental error" and concluded that modern political parties in the one-party South were more akin to state institutions. Parker observed that "an essential feature of our form of government is the right of the citizen to participate in the governmental process" and "the disenfranchised can never speak with the same force as those who are able to vote." He concluded that "there can be no question . . . as to the jurisdiction of the court to grant injunctive relief" and "no error" in the decision of the lower court.[37]

The resounding affirmance of Judge Waring's order sent an unmistakable message that the Fourth Circuit intended to uphold the letter and spirit of *Smith v. Allwright* and that John J. Parker had Waties Waring's back. *The New York Times* observed that the decision, if not overturned by the Supreme Court, "may have far reaching effects on the political and economic structure of the southern states." The Democratic Party petitioned for review of the Fourth Circuit's order to the U.S. Supreme Court, which was swiftly denied in an unsigned order dated April 19, 1948. Chief Justice Fred Vinson later confided to Waring that some of his colleagues had regretted the quick rejection of the petition, feeling it would have been more effective to have granted review and affirmed the *Elmore* decision by unanimous vote.[38]

———

Waring's evolving views on race were soon evident in other actions he took as judge. In December 1947, a Darlington County, South Carolina, farmer, John Wilhelm, pleaded guilty to peonage before Waring. Peonage, which involved the forced uncompensated labor of another, was made a federal crime in 1867 in conjunction with the abolition of slavery. Peonage cases were the most common form of criminal civil rights cases brought by the U.S. Department of Justice in the 1930s and 1940s, and tended to stir little public controversy. These cases usually involved allegations that a farmer attempted to collect debts owed by a sharecropper by requiring him to work without pay until the debt was satisfied. Commonly referred to as debt peonage, most of these cases were disposed of by a guilty plea with a sentence of probation.

In *United States v. Wilhelm*, the defendant was indicted for peonage and kidnapping, the latter charge arising from Wilhelm's taking his black victim across state lines to Georgia to work on his father's farm to pay off his debt. Wilhelm agreed to plead guilty to peonage, with the expectation of a sentence of probation. The government made no recommendation for jail time.

During Wilhelm's sentencing hearing, Waring heard distressing details of abuse and harsh treatment of the African American victim, which seemed to Waring to represent a lingering legacy of slavery. He resolved to put an end to this practice by sentencing the very surprised farmer to a year and a day in federal prison. Waring was later informed by a local sheriff that his sentence had gotten the attention of the local farmers and had put an end to the practice of debt peonage. This experience demonstrated to Waring that the determined and consistent enforcement of federal civil rights statutes was effective in obtaining compliance with the law and deterring future violations.[39]

Waring also began changing long-standing racial practices around the Charleston Federal Courthouse. As a result of the white primary litigation, black voter registration increased. This generated greater representation of black jurors in the federal court's jury pool. Prospective black jurors in Charleston were identified on official juror lists with the letter c, for "colored." Waring directed the clerk to remove all racial designations. He also directed his bailiff to end segregated seating in his courtroom. Waring noted that black jurors invariably took the back seats in the jury box farthest from their fellow white jurors. Drawing upon the practice he observed in courts in New York, Waring began assigning jurors to a designated seat, eliminating voluntary segregation in the jury box. One day an African American juror, Samuel Fleming, an owner of a small business, complained when a deliberating jury was sent out to lunch under the supervision of a white marshal and the black juror was told to take his lunch in the kitchen. The purpose of the marshal's directive was apparently to remain in compliance with local segregation laws. Fleming protested to Waring, stating, "I don't eat in the kitchen in my own home, and there's no reason I should eat in the kitchen when I'm serving on the jury." Waring agreed and directed a stunned restaurant owner to seat the black juror with other members of the jury. In taking these steps, Waring explained that he was attempting to introduce "the American Creed" into his courthouse, "even sitting in segregated South Carolina."[40]

12.

THERE WILL BE
NO FINES

DESPITE THE SOUTH CAROLINA DEMOCRATIC PARTY'S singular lack of success in the *Elmore* case, party leaders persisted in their efforts to prevent African Americans from voting in the Democratic primary. The party adopted new rules that acknowledged the right of blacks to vote in the primary but required African Americans to sign an oath attesting to their opposition to racial integration and President Truman's proposed fair employment practices legislation. This new party oath predictably led to the filing of a new lawsuit, *Brown v. Baskin*, in early July 1948. The plaintiff, David Brown of Beaufort County, alleged that his name was struck from party election rolls because he had not signed the newly adopted party oath. The lawsuit named eighty-seven Democratic county chairmen, executive committeemen, and other party officials as defendants.

Brown's attorney, Thurgood Marshall, argued that the party oath made it impossible for blacks to vote in the primary because "no self-respecting Negro could ... swear that he did not believe in his own equality." The case was filed in the Charleston Federal Courthouse and assigned to Waring.

Marshall requested a temporary injunction and an immediate hearing on the matter. On July 8, 1948, Judge Waring set an injunction hearing for July 16 and issued a temporary restraining order, directing party officers not to interfere with the enrollment of African Americans in the upcoming August 10 Democratic primary or to deny them "full and equal participation." He also directed that all named defendants be present at the July 16 hearing and had the U.S. marshal personally serve the order compelling their attendance. Waring's initial actions certainly suggested that the party's new oath was skating on thin ice.[1]

The federal injunction hearing was scheduled in the midst of very tumultuous times in South Carolina politics. Southern Democrats were threatening to walk out of the Democratic National Convention over President Truman's civil rights program and to support a third-party candidate for president. This controversy was reaching a fever pitch as state party officials traveled to Philadelphia for the national convention, set for July 12–14.

On July 10, Judge Waring received a telegram from Philadelphia sent by the state party chairman, Baskin, requesting a one-week continuance in the scheduled July 16 hearing. Baskin explained that he and twenty other named defendants were delegates to the national convention and had already arrived in Philadelphia. Baskin stated that they would have to leave Philadelphia before the start of the convention if there was no continuance because of the need to meet with counsel and prepare for the hearing. Judge Waring responded by telegram the following day, July 11, ruling, "Request for continuance in Brown versus Baskin refused. Case will be heard July 16." Judge Waring scribbled on instructions to his secretary that his reply telegram should be sent to Baskin "collect." In fact, many of the South Carolina delegates in Philadelphia had no intention of participating in the full national convention activities, because they planned to walk out and reconvene in Birmingham, Alabama, on July 17 to nominate Governor Strom Thurmond as the Dixiecrat candidate for president. Attendance at Waring's July 16 injunction hearing in Charleston would obviously disrupt those plans.[2]

As if all of this were not enough drama, the Democrats were in the midst of a brawling U.S. Senate campaign, in which Burnet Maybank was seeking reelection. Maybank faced four challengers, all of whom were attacking him for his role in nominating Waring to the federal bench. One of those opponents, the Newberry attorney Alan Johnstone, sensed a political opportunity in appearing at the injunction hearing and publicly challenging Waring.

Dozens of lawyers, parties, reporters, and curious citizens crammed into Waring's elegant, mahogany-paneled courtroom in Charleston for the July 16 hearing. The atmosphere was "highly charged," with many seething with anger about their abrupt summoning to federal court and Waring's obvious resolve to destroy the white primary. Every seat in the courtroom was taken, even those in the jury box.[3]

As the hearing opened, Johnstone rose to request that he be allowed to make an appearance in the case. Waring did not seem to know who he was and asked whether he was a party or had a client in the case. Johnstone replied that he was a candidate for the U.S. Senate and demanded to be heard. Waring cut him off, telling him that the proceeding was "called for a judicial determination and not for campaign speeches." He told Johnstone that his request for an appearance was denied and directed the U.S. marshal to "put the gentleman in his seat. If he creates a disorder, put him out. You've got your soap boxes on the street; not in the courtroom." Johnstone took his seat. Later in the hearing, apparently unable to resist the big stage the courtroom provided, Johnstone rose again. Waring summarily cut him off, telling the candidate, "I don't care to sit here while you make a speech." The *News and Courier* reported Johnstone continued to talk in defiance of Waring's order until "three husky deputies moved in on him and Judge Waring told them to 'put him out.'" As Waring later recalled, "The last time I saw Johnstone he was going out the courtroom door . . . backwards."[4]

The forced removal of a candidate for the U.S. Senate was not the most remarkable moment of that day. Thurgood Marshall put two

witnesses on the stand to create a factual record for his request for tempo-
rary injunctive relief and rested. The Democratic Party's counsel, Sidney
Tison, then announced he would offer no witnesses and make no argu-
ment in defense of the party oath. Judge Waring was not pleased. He told
Tison, "It would interest me immensely if the authors [of the oath] could
explain to me the process by which they evolved this." Tison responded,
"I don't think I could explain to Your Honor satisfactorily." Waring stated,
"No, sir; I don't think so."[5]

Waring admonished the party leaders, telling them, "It's a disgrace
and a shame you've got to come into court and ask one judge to tell you
that you are American citizens and going to obey the law." Waring stated
that he recognized the party leaders were putting the burden on him to
end the white primary and that this was an unpopular decision. He told
them, "I'm going to do my duty . . . and I don't care whether there are any
people who agree with me. The law of the land is going to be obeyed." Waring advised the parties that he was entering an order enjoining the Democratic Party from enforcing its loyalty oath and any other practices that
interfered with the right of black citizens to vote in the Democratic primary.

But Judge Waring was not finished. He advised those assembled,
some of the most powerful public officials in South Carolina, that he
would not tolerate any further violations of his orders. He explained that a
federal judge confronted with contempt had the power to punish "by fine
or imprisonment." Because, in Waring's view, any future violations would
be deliberate, he warned those assembled that if there were any further
acts of contempt, there would be no fines.[6]

A sullen crowd exited Waring's courtroom stunned by the judge's
threat to jail white men to protect the voting rights of black citizens.
Charleston's *News and Courier* recommended in a front-page editorial
that the Democratic Party defy Waring's order by simply closing its local
offices, thereby preventing blacks from enrolling as members. The editors further lamented that Waring's order was "un-American" because it
prevented "white men in South Carolina" from being free to assemble
and "speak their mind" by conducting a white primary.[7]

Within days, public attacks were unleashed against Waring unlike anything a sitting federal judge had ever experienced. The Warings were bombarded with hostile and threatening letters, and they received obscene telephone calls at all hours of the day and night. Elizabeth Waring was accosted as she walked down the sidewalk, with people intentionally bumping into her or blocking her path. By this point, the white community in Charleston had almost completely ostracized the Warings, with former friends refusing to speak to them or to acknowledge their presence. Judge Waring later observed, "There was this complete hatred and complete blot-out of all friendly associations . . . We were strangers in a foreign land." He explained, "Day after day, I met dozens of people whom I had known intimately and who talked my language and knew my way of thought excepting on one point. And that point completely separated me from the entire . . . white community."[8]

Following Waring's issuance of the temporary injunction on July 16, 1948, the vitriol in the U.S. Senate race escalated. Two of Maybank's opponents, Congressman Bryan Dorn and Alan Johnstone, declared Maybank disqualified for reelection because of his role in Waring's nomination. In turn, Maybank denounced Waring's civil rights decisions as "deplorable" and contended that the late senator Cotton Ed Smith had been Waring's chief proponent for his judgeship, not him. This led to a series of news articles in which Cotton Ed's son publicly denied that his father supported Waring's nomination. Correspondence from Cotton Ed to the Justice Department was then released by the Maybank campaign, which revealed that Waring had been one of Cotton Ed's top three choices for the nomination. Waring later observed that at the time of his confirmation as a federal judge both senators took credit for his nomination and "later refuse[d] to take the blame."[9]

Dorn, using his position as a sitting congressman, introduced a resolution in the U.S. House of Representatives to investigate Waring, which he explained was preliminary to filing an impeachment resolution. In fact, Dorn initially attempted to file an impeachment resolution with the House Judiciary Committee, which had jurisdiction over the impeachment of federal judges. The committee's chairman, Representative Earl Michener of Michigan, refused to accept the resolution, explaining that his committee "was not going to be used as a vehicle for getting back at a judge simply because [Dorn] was mad at him." The Rules Committee chair, Representative Leo Allen of Illinois, also declared that his committee would allow no House action on the Dorn resolution.[10]

Despite being rebuffed in Congress, Dorn sensed he was getting political mileage in his U.S. Senate campaign. He purchased statewide radio time to make a major address on his efforts to impeach the judge. Dorn told his radio audience that Waring was "overstepping his authority" and his rulings reflected "arrogance and insolence." He implausibly contended that his efforts to impeach Waring had nothing to do with "the race issue." Dorn also referenced Waring's divorce and remarriage and service of legal papers by the U.S. Marshals Service in the injunction case "in the dead hours of the night" as additional grounds for Waring's removal from office.[11]

The public attacks on Waring were not limited to those by U.S. Senate candidates. On August 4, 1948, Congressman Mendel Rivers of Charleston went onto the floor of the House of Representatives and denounced Waring for his "unjudicial, ungentlemanly, outrageous and deplorable conduct." Rivers described Waring as "cold as a dead Eskimo in an abandoned igloo" and claimed "lemon juice flows in his rigid and calculating veins." He declared that if Waring was not removed from office, "I prophesize bloodshed because he is now in the process of exacting a pound of flesh from the white people of South Carolina." Rivers denied that his comments related to Waring's voting rights decisions, because anyone "could see that the federal courts were going to permit Negroes to vote in South Carolina primaries."

Congressman Rivers announced the following day that he would soon be filing his own documents in order to initiate formal impeachment proceedings against Waring. The *News and Courier* reported, relying on a confidential source, that Rivers had first approached Chief Justice Fred Vinson seeking an investigation of Waring but was told that any action must be taken by Congress, not by the Supreme Court. Within days, however, Rivers announced the abandonment of his impeachment efforts after "legal advisors skilled in impeachment" told him that his resolution was too indefinite to advance. These hyperbolic public attacks on Waring became a national story, with *Time* running an article titled "The Man They Love to Hate."[12]

Waring wrote a private note to Judge Parker on July 20, 1948, informing him that he had issued a preliminary injunction after "the Democratic Party here had flaunted the Elmore vs. Rice decisions by both of our courts." Sensing that perhaps the worst was behind him, he told Parker that he believed the resistance by the party had ended and "apparently [the injunction] is being obeyed." He wrote to Parker again on August 5, following the floor speech by Congressman Rivers, candidly telling him "it is pretty lonely here" and that it had gotten more difficult since the Rivers attack. Waring lamented the "miserable newspaper articles" but observed that "when one has a duty to perform he has to have with it a strong stomach to stand poison of this kind."[13]

Parker responded sympathetically, observing that "it is most unfortunate that a member of Congress should so far forget himself as to make this sort of attack on a member of the judiciary." He urged restraint on Waring's part, because "a judge cannot enter into a name calling contest." He recognized that "it is hard for a man to restrain himself from utterance when this sort of attack is made upon him; but that is the only thing to do . . . Every brave man resents an attack on one who is not in the position to strike back."[14]

Waring let it be known that he would be in the federal courthouse on primary day, August 10, prepared to issue contempt citations and jail any person who disrupted the election process. The voting was orderly, even festive, with thousands of well-dressed African American voters patiently waiting in line to vote for the first time in their lives. Thurgood Marshall issued a press release, announcing that "35,000 Negroes participated in the primary" without "any friction" and "the skies did not fall." South Carolina's experience in the 1948 Democratic primary was markedly different from the experience of Mississippi, where officials had dropped its prohibition against black participation but widespread violence and Election Day intimidation limited black voting to only three thousand hardy souls.

Waring later recounted the story of a Charleston County executive committeeman who heard that some of his fellow Democrats, who were not named parties in the white primary lawsuit, intended to undertake actions to prevent blacks from voting. The executive committeeman denounced such activities, explaining that their names were not on Judge Waring's order but his was. As Waring observed, the political leadership of the state was "staggered" by his resolve to enforce the order opening the Democratic primary to black voters, but when he "laid down the law" and held party officials personally responsible, people obeyed it. As *The Pittsburgh Courier* noted, "With the threat of jail staring them in the face, the white Democrats bowed to Judge Waring's ruling."[15]

Waring reported to Parker the morning after the primary that "the election went off smoothly yesterday and they didn't shoot me." He thanked Parker for his "thoughtfulness and friendship" through the ordeal. Parker responded that he was pleased that the primary had gone smoothly and anticipated things might settle down now for Waring. Senator Maybank won his primary without a runoff, further suggesting that the public attacks on Waring might subside.[16]

As things calmed down, Waring scheduled a final hearing in *Brown v. Baskin* to bring the case to a close and to make the injunction permanent. On the morning of the hearing, he received, by special delivery to his chambers, an unsigned letter from the Ku Klux Klan, in "the name of the white citizens of South Carolina." The letter urged Waring to reconsider his preliminary injunction because the ending of the white primary would "tend to break all segregation laws and customs in our state." The letter went on to warn about "the fearful racial hatred that will follow any adverse decision that you may render in the present case under your consideration against the white people of your State."[17]

Waring interpreted the letter as an effort to intimidate him and released it to the press to let the public know of the "attempt to threaten and influence a United States Judge in his judicial decisions." Parker wrote to Waring following news articles about the KKK letter, urging him not to respond publicly to the attacks. Parker stated that he "understood your lot has been made unpleasant by the attacks which have occurred" and hoped that things would improve once the election was held on November 2.[18]

Waring did not heed Judge Parker's advice. He traveled to New York on October 11 and delivered an address to the New York chapter of the National Lawyers Guild, a progressive advocacy organization. Waring directly addressed southern racial controversies, stating, "My people have an outstanding fault—the terrible fault of prejudice. They have been born and educated to feel that the Negro is some kind of animal that ought to be well-treated and given kindness, but as a matter of favor, not right." Waring referenced the mounting public criticism of his voting rights decisions, observing that "not one man in public life has dared to support these decisions based on the fact that the Negro is entitled to vote as an American citizen." He urged the activist lawyers to continue their efforts advancing civil rights in the South and to deal with the region's opposition "firmly."[19]

Waring's address was reported extensively the following day by *The New York Times*, and the article was reprinted in the Columbia *State* on October 17, 1948. Two days later, defendants in *Brown v. Baskin* filed a motion to disqualify Waring, citing both his Lawyers Guild speech and statements in open court. Eighty defendants filed affidavits supporting the motion, arguing that Waring had a personal bias against them and in favor of the African American plaintiff. This was a very unusual motion at a time when few attorneys would dare challenge the conduct of a sitting federal judge.[20]

Waring denied the disqualification motion on October 22, 1948, observing that it was based on "public statements that I believed in the enforcement of the Constitution and laws of the United States relative to the equal protection of the rights of citizens to vote regardless of race or religion." He summarily dismissed this argument, stating that the motion "is entirely without merit and I refuse to disqualify myself." Several weeks later, on November 26, Waring entered a final order granting a permanent injunction in *Brown v. Baskin*. He found that the "proposed oath cannot be said to have any purpose other than the exclusion of Negro voters." He went on to find that it was "quite apparent that the defendants and those working with them deliberately set out to continue a form of racial discrimination in the conduct of primary elections in this state. This is illegal and must be stopped." Waring then permanently enjoined the use of the party oath or any other device to prevent blacks from participating in the Democratic Party primary.[21]

The defendants appealed Waring's order to the Fourth Circuit, arguing that the court should revisit its earlier affirmance of Waring's decision in *Elmore* and disqualify Waring as the presiding judge because of personal bias. Judge Parker, again writing for a unanimous court, affirmed Waring's permanent injunction by an order dated May 17, 1949. The Fourth Circuit declined to reconsider its order in *Elmore* because "the decision in that case was entirely correct." In response to the defendants' motion to disqualify Waring, Parker wrote that the record showed "no personal bias on the part of the judge . . . but, at most, zeal for upholding the rights of Negroes under the Constitution and indignation that attempt should be made to deny them their rights." Parker noted that "a judge cannot be disqualified merely because he believes in upholding the law." With the Fourth Circuit's affirmance of Waring's order, the days of the white primary came to an end in South Carolina.[22]

———

While Waring was being pilloried by elected officials and newspaper editors in South Carolina, he emerged as a respected national figure on civil rights. *Time* referred to him as "a man of cool courage," and civil rights advocates viewed him as the "conscience of the South." Attorney General Tom Clark consulted with Waring on reforms recommended by the President's Committee on Civil Rights.[23]

As a measure of Waring's growing national prominence, private meetings were arranged for him during a Washington visit by Attorney General Clark with Chief Justice Vinson and President Truman. Waring had a long, private discussion with Vinson on civil rights issues and followed this with a confidential note to Thurgood Marshall, assuring him that the civil rights community had a friend in the chief justice. The unanimous decisions of the Vinson Court in *Shelley v. Kraemer, Sweatt v.*

Painter, and other civil rights cases in 1949 and 1950 confirmed the accuracy of Waring's assessment.[24]

The highlight of Waring's Washington trip was a meeting at the White House with President Truman. The meeting occurred on December 2, 1948, less than a month after Truman's stunning election victory. Truman opened the meeting by sharing with Waring the story of the blinded sergeant from South Carolina, repeating an account of the Isaac Woodard incident he had told and retold to many others when discussing civil rights issues. The president was astonished to learn that Waring had presided over the criminal prosecution of the police officer who had blinded Woodard. Waring candidly shared with Truman the shortcomings in the Justice Department's prosecution of Lynwood Shull and his distress about the inability of the judicial system to produce a just result in the case. After discussing Woodard's beating and blinding, an incident that had troubled and inspired both men, Truman and Waring proceeded to discuss the president's civil rights program and his administration's plans for the next term.[25]

Following their meeting, Waring wrote to Truman and provided him with further insights into the situation in South Carolina. He explained to the president that white South Carolinians "will not voluntarily do anything along the lines suggested by you" and that it was "necessary for the federal government to firmly and constantly keep up the pressure." He observed that there were South Carolinians "ripe and ready for your program, but they do not include any of our so called political leaders." "The whole trouble," Waring continued, "is *fear* and it is only when the good people (who, however, unfortunately are timid people) see that strength and force is behind your program that they will feel it safe to join you." Truman responded to Waring's letter, telling him that he had greatly enjoyed their time together and was "hoping to make real progress along the lines you and I are interested." Truman then concluded by telling the embattled Waring, "I wish we had more federal judges like you on the bench."[26]

13.

FIGHTING THE
"BATTLE ROYAL"

A S THE DOOR slammed shut on their personal relationships in the white community of Charleston, Waties and Elizabeth Waring began to develop a new set of friends and confidants. Some came from a small cadre of white southern-born liberals who reached out to the judge after his voting rights decisions and embraced him as a model for the New South. Others were from New York, where Judge Waring began an annual practice of spending several weeks assisting colleagues in the Southern District of New York with their chronic backlog of cases. He described these New York visits as coming up "for air." But the most surprising and unconventional of the Warings' new friends were African Americans, both in Charleston and around the country, who shared their growing passion for civil rights. These new friends provided the Warings with critical support and comfort in the face of unremitting vilification from South Carolina elected officials and other proponents of white supremacy.

Dr. Benjamin Mays, a South Carolina native and president of Morehouse College in Atlanta, became a friend and admirer of Judge Waring's. Mays praised Waring in a May 1949 column in *The Pittsburgh Courier* for his personal courage in telling difficult truths to his native city and state. He noted that Supreme Court justices can do this from Washington, but to do it, as Waring had, in his own hometown was "a great accomplishment." Mays astutely observed that while some had ostracized the judge and sought to impeach him, he was not too concerned about the well-being of the Warings, because "I am convinced that this man and his charming wife have achieved moral and spiritual freedom."[1]

The Warings' new friendships with southern-born civil rights activists connected them with kindred spirits in various regional and national progressive organizations. These new activist friends were generally a decade or more younger than the Warings, and many were veterans of the New Deal. They had made the decision, after working and studying outside the South, to return home in the hope of orchestrating a Second Reconstruction.

James Dombrowski, a Florida native and Methodist minister who studied under the renowned theologian Reinhold Niebuhr at Union Theological Seminary in New York, reached out to Judge Waring soon after his white primary decision. Dombrowski headed two civil rights organizations, the Southern Conference Educational Fund and the Southern Conference for Human Welfare. He was also a co-founder of the Highlander Folk School, a Tennessee-based civil rights training program whose students included Martin Luther King Jr. and Rosa Parks. Dombrowski was a close friend and confidant of Eleanor Roosevelt's and helped connect the Warings to a network of civil rights activists inside and outside the South.

Dombrowski worked closely with another southern-born activist, Aubrey Williams. An Alabama native, Williams was intimately involved in the establishment of several New Deal programs, including the Works

Progress Administration and the National Youth Administration, which he directed. Williams appointed a then-unknown twenty-six-year-old Texan, Lyndon Johnson, to run the Texas NYA program, and the two developed a lifelong friendship. He was also a close friend of Eleanor Roosevelt's. Williams moved to Montgomery in 1945 and purchased a newspaper, *Southern Farmer*, which became a leading voice for civil rights in the South.[2]

Waring also connected with another Alabama-based activist, Clifford Durr. A graduate of the University of Alabama, Durr was awarded a Rhodes Scholarship and earned his law degree at Oxford University. He returned home to Montgomery and established a lucrative corporate law practice. He was a close friend and brother-in-law of Supreme Court justice Hugo Black. Durr was appointed a commissioner of the Federal Communications Commission during the New Deal, and he and his wife, Virginia, lived in Washington and developed close friendships with a network of southern progressives. These included Aubrey Williams and Lyndon and Lady Bird Johnson. The Durrs returned to Alabama and became actively engaged in the early civil rights movement. Clifford Durr's corporate clients faded away as he became one of the South's premier civil rights attorneys. Durr would be the lawyer who bailed Rosa Parks out of jail after she refused to relinquish her seat on a Montgomery bus.

Durr connected Waring to a network of activist attorneys associated with the National Lawyers Guild, which Durr served as president. In February 1949, the group awarded Waring its highest honor, the Franklin Delano Roosevelt Award for public service. In presenting the FDR Award to Waring at the group's national meeting in Detroit, Durr discussed the importance of courage in the fight for justice:

> A courage of a greater and rarer kind is required to face the
> disapproval of society in defense of a basic democratic principle.
> It hurts to be shut off from one's own people. It hurts even more
> when they are good people—friendly, basically decent and
> kindly, and the only barrier is an idea. Loneliness can be more

painful than the wounds of battle, and few are willing to risk it. It takes real courage for a judge, in opposition to the deep seated folkways of those with whom he lives and will continue to live to say, "This is the law. It is my duty to enforce it and I will do my duty."[3]

To the shock and chagrin of many of their South of Broad neighbors, the Warings' new friends included prominent members of Charleston's black community. Neighbors would observe black visitors regularly arriving and leaving through the Warings' front door, violating the well-established custom that blacks would enter the homes of whites as maids and deliverymen and only through the back door. Septima Clark, a fiery civil rights activist and teacher, was a frequent visitor to the Waring home. She would later be discharged from her teaching position in Charleston for her advocacy work and became an early member of the staff of the Southern Christian Leadership Conference, where Dr. King dubbed her the "queen mother of the civil rights movement." The Warings frequently exchanged home visits with Dr. Aylwood Cornwell, a black dentist, and his wife, Ruby, a tireless advocate in Charleston's small civil rights community. *Collier's*, a prominent national magazine, published in April 1950 a multipage story on the Warings and their social ostracism in Charleston, titled "Lonesomest Man in Town." Most local talk centered on a picture from the article of a Waring dinner party in which Elizabeth and Waties Waring were the only white people seated at the table. The group included Clark, the Cornwells, and John Fleming, Judge Waring's bailiff. The *News and Courier* characterized the Warings' interracial socializing as "an extraordinary and all but unique development in Charleston."[4]

In early 1951, the Warings had a visit from Carl Rowan, a young African American reporter for *The Minneapolis Tribune* who would later become a prominent public official and nationally syndicated columnist. Rowan noted that he rang the doorbell and was invited into the Waring home through the front door, the first time he had ever entered a white southerner's home in that manner. Rowan expected to meet "two lonely old people, bent under the terrible weight of social ostracism." Instead, he observed "little loneliness" and heard "words I never expected to hear from a native southerner." The judge dismissed his ostracism in Charleston as unimportant because "I have met southern negroes and northerners of both races whom I would not have known but for this." After eating dinner with the Warings and leaving, as he came, through the front door, Rowan rode to the Battery several blocks away and "gazed at the lights in the Charleston harbor." "Thank God," he murmured to himself, "after these tens of years, Charleston has a new and brighter beacon."[5]

Perhaps the most influential of the Warings' new relationships was their close friendship with the NAACP's executive secretary, Walter White, and his wife, Poppy Cannon White. The Warings and the Whites obviously shared a passion for civil rights. But they also shared the experience of being ostracized from longtime friends and associates when they left their spouses to marry their lovers. Walter White left his wife of many years to marry Poppy Cannon, his longtime mistress. The breakup of the White marriage was highly controversial within the upper echelons of the NAACP and left White and his new wife socially isolated. The fact that Poppy Cannon, a prominent cookbook author and food editor of *Ladies' Home Journal*, was white only added to the controversy. Apparently finding kindred spirits, the Whites and the Warings socialized together frequently, particularly when the judge was in New York holding court. The two couples were so close that when Walter White and Poppy Cannon traveled to England to marry, the first person to whom the new Mrs. White wrote to announce the marriage was Elizabeth Waring. The Warings kept a picture of the Whites in their living room, at a time when interracial marriage was unlawful in South Carolina. Walter White was fiercely loyal to Judge Waring and was his confidant during some of the judge's most difficult moments.[6]

———

As Waties Waring continued his studies and reflection on race and justice, he was becoming increasingly impatient with the pace and manner of change in the South's racial practices. He recognized that African Americans were experiencing some measure of progress, noting that they "generally have better homes, a little better education, a little kindlier treatment, a few cents more in wages, and, occasionally, equality in our courts." But this was not good enough. In a keynote address to the national meeting of the National Lawyers Guild in February 1949, upon the occasion of receiving the organization's Franklin Delano Roosevelt Award, Waring argued that receipt of the full benefits of American citizenship was not an act of charity but a right protected by "a living, vital" Constitution. He asserted that blacks were entitled to enjoy the full measure of American citizenship, including the right "to live as a decent citizen; ... to eat dinner in a dining car on a railroad train; ... and to get a fair wage, and if you are good enough to qualify for a job, to get the job and keep it." He stated, "I am not a pessimist on the subject but I am impatient," declaring that promising "truth and justice and beauty and sweetness and light a thousand years from now" simply would not do.[7]

Waring desired to play a contributing role in advancing these changes but recognized that time was not on his side. Then approaching his sixtyninth birthday, he was invited to speak in June 1949 to a group of wealthy New York civil rights activists that included Eleanor Roosevelt. James Dombrowski arranged the speaking engagement and a follow-up private meeting with Roosevelt. Waring's talk to the group impressed Roosevelt, who described the judge's speech in her nationally syndicated "My Day" column of June 3, 1949, as "courageous" and "inspiring."

The Warings were themselves deeply moved by their private meeting with Roosevelt, which the judge later described to Dombrowski as "important and thrilling." Waring's excitement about meeting with Roosevelt reflected much about the journey he had traveled in recent years. In private correspondence with a fellow southern gradualist just four years earlier, Waring had referred dismissively to Roosevelt's "radical methods" and contrasted those with "liberal minded southerners" who could address the region's race problems "by moderate, gradual and understanding action." Now, four years into the fight, Waring had lost his patience with gradualism and publicly called for aggressive federal action to make real progress.[8]

In their private meeting with Roosevelt, the Warings described their personal challenges in Charleston. Roosevelt observed that "Charleston, being what it was," may be the last place to see any improvement in race relations. Elizabeth responded that "while it was true, perhaps this would be the best place to strike a brave blow." Roosevelt agreed, and the Warings returned home with a plan for Elizabeth to deliver what they hoped would be an inspiring and aggressive speech on racial justice to a local African American audience.[9]

The plan that ultimately took shape was a speech to be delivered by Elizabeth to the black affiliate of the Charleston YWCA. When white officers of the local YWCA chapter learned about Elizabeth's scheduled talk, they sought to persuade the officers of the black affiliate to rescind the invitation. The Y's African American leadership, led by Septima Clark, refused to withdraw the invitation and stood by the decision to host Elizabeth. The primarily African American audience that gathered at the Y on the evening of January 16, 1950, was likely unprepared for the tone and substance of Elizabeth Waring's address.

Elizabeth delivered a blistering attack on white supremacy. After initially referring to the efforts to cancel her speech, she denounced the white YWCA leaders "for their stupidity" and their "selfish and savage white supremacy way of life." She effusively praised her husband's "wonderful opinions" as a "clear call of the Liberty Bell" and observed that it was the "guilty consciences" of white southerners that made them fear civil rights advocates. She told her audience that "white supremacist southerners have done everything to break your spirit but your spirits are forged in the furnace of persecution and shame and have risen triumphant." Declaring African Americans "spiritually . . . way ahead of the white people," she described white southerners as "sick, confused and decadent people. Like all decadent people, they are full of pride and complacency, introverted, morally weak and low."[10]

Elizabeth's stunned audience had never heard such talk in Charleston. Septima Clark's elderly mother was so shocked and frightened that she had to be carried from the room. Many present, while deeply admiring the courage of Judge Waring and his wife, simply did not share Elizabeth's condemnation of all southern whites. Hodding Carter, a prominent Mississippi journalist who advocated gradual reform of southern racial practices, denounced the speech as "Bilboism in reverse," referencing the late notorious racist senator from Mississippi.[11]

Elizabeth's speech received widespread coverage in the local and national media and generated great debate. While some, including Walter White and Eleanor Roosevelt, praised the speech, the local denunciations were almost deafening. Governor Strom Thurmond called Elizabeth's remarks "beneath comment," and excerpts from her speech were read on the floor of the South Carolina House of Representatives. Critical letters to the editor flooded South Carolina newspapers, and the dormant Waring impeachment movement stirred once again.[12]

Elizabeth's controversial public pronouncements, which were made with the full support of her husband, resulted in an invitation to appear as the main guest on *Meet the Press* on February 11, 1950. Elizabeth defended her earlier statement describing white southerners as "morally weak and low" as necessary "shock treatment" for the South and stated that she spoke out only after no one else would do so. She denounced Hodding Carter as a "parlor liberal" and the Deep South press as "below the level of the people." In response to repeated questions about her views on social relations with African Americans, she indicated she and her husband had no problem with interracial marriage and proudly confirmed that she had a picture of Walter and Poppy Cannon White in her living room. She dismissed the talk of impeachment as unimportant because "our cause is bigger than ourselves."[13]

Undoubtedly, Elizabeth Waring's public comments escalated the attacks on the judge. The South Carolina state representative Charles Garrett proposed a resolution to pay for one-way tickets for Waring and his wife to leave the state. The resolution was quickly adopted by the South Carolina House and sent to the South Carolina State Senate. More ominously, a group of "adult, white voting citizens," headed by J. C. Phillips of Aiken County, began widely distributing a petition for Waring's impeachment. The petition accused Judge Waring of calling for "revolution on the part of the negro against white . . . South Carolina," which made him "unfit to adjudicate any case in which ANY white person is involved." The petition also referenced the "public utterances and agitations and Un-American harangues of Mrs. Waring." The petition concluded by asking the South Carolina congressional delegation and the U.S. House of Representatives to impeach Judge Waring as a federal district judge.[14]

Waring publicly denounced the impeachment effort, declaring that there was a "campaign of prejudice" to remove him from office. He noted that the petitions circulating accused him of opposing white supremacy, which he acknowledged was true. In fact, Waring asserted, "any judge . . . who attempts to pass upon the rights of American citizens blinded by color prejudice is an unfit public servant."[15]

The Waring impeachment group, working in close concert with the South Carolina congressman Mendel Rivers, arranged a meeting with the entire South Carolina congressional delegation on March 8, 1950, and submitted more than twenty thousand signatures on their Waring impeachment petitions. Reportedly, Charleston County was the hotbed of petition activity, with nearly ten thousand signatures. Despite the enthusiasm of Rivers and a few other delegation members for the effort, it was clear that the U.S. House leadership was unsupportive. One confidential source told the *News and Courier*, "We don't have the evidence to impeach him . . . We certainly can't impeach him for making pro-negro statements. If we try to base it on the white supremacy issue, we couldn't muster a handful of votes." It was also reported that "high ranking members of the House Judiciary Committee" had been consulted by South Carolina delegation members and indicated that "there is now no evidence at hand which would serve as the basis for a successful action against Waring." The South Carolina delegation's chairman, James Richards, also voiced skepticism about the Waring impeachment effort, asking when "the legal proof for impeachment" would be forthcoming. Richards opposed any action on the impeachment resolution until a "sound legal basis" was set forth by the proponents, adding, "I do not think anybody should go off half-cocked."[16]

Despite the underwhelming response for the Waring impeachment resolution in the U.S. Congress, local efforts to oust him persisted. The South Carolina House voted on March 14, 1950, to appropriate $10,000 in state funds to finance a Waring impeachment campaign. This effort was led by the state representative John Long of Union County, long a stronghold of Klan activity, who explained that impeachment was necessary because Waring and "his northern-born wife have advocated a negro revolution against white supremacy." The state appropriation to fund the impeachment campaign against Judge Waring backfired, with members of the U.S. House denouncing it as an "unwarranted invasion of the rights of the federal government by a state." One unidentified U.S. House leader told the *News and Courier* that "if the [South Carolina] legislature wants to keep Judge Waring on the bench forever all it has to do is to appropriate that money. I do not believe a successful effort to impeach him could ever be brought before the House after that." The bill to appropriate state funds to support Waring's impeachment quietly died in the state senate.[17]

On April 6, 1950, Congressman Rivers went onto the floor of the U.S. House of Representatives to state the case for Waring's impeachment. In a talk he titled "Some Facts on Judge J. Waties Waring," Rivers claimed that Waring advocated the "use of force by a minority group to obtain its objectives," which Rivers described as a "high crime and misdemeanor." He further charged Waring with such offenses as opposing gradualism, being a hypocrite by not opposing white supremacy while an active member of the Democratic Party, and being "insincere" in his advocacy of equal rights. Rivers contended that Waring was "soiling the robes of his office and the dignity of the federal bench." Representative John Rankin of Mississippi, perhaps the House's most outspoken segregationist, responded, "Of course I will vote for your resolution," but urged

Rivers to add a "charge of insanity." Following Rivers's floor speech, the Waring impeachment effort seemingly evaporated with little further public comment.[18]

Years later, an aging Thurgood Marshall, then serving as an associate justice of the U.S. Supreme Court, shared with a historian the backstory of the demise of the Waring impeachment resolution. In attempting to explain the extraordinary power of Speaker of the House Sam Rayburn, Marshall recounted being summoned to Charleston by Judge Waring and being asked to "take care" of the Rivers resolution. Marshall told the judge not to worry about the impeachment effort, that "those things just sit there and die." Waring was not satisfied and told Marshall he wanted the resolution defeated. Marshall traveled to Washington and met with Peyton Ford, deputy attorney general and longtime liaison between the Department of Justice and Congress. Ford assured Marshall that the Rivers resolution was going nowhere, but Marshall explained that the "judge wants assurances." Ford then called Speaker Rayburn and told him of Marshall's inquiry. Marshall was put on the phone with the Speaker, who told him that he could give Waring "my word, personally, that nothing will happen to that bill." Marshall then replied, "Mr. Sam, does that mean it's not going to get out of committee?" Rayburn responded, "Get out of committee? It's not in committee, it's in my safe."[19]

———

On March 11, 1950, in the midst of the impeachment petition campaign, a cross was burned in the backyard of the Waring residence. At the time, the Warings were in New York, where the judge was holding court. A neighbor described the scene as a "tremendous blaze," and reporters received an anonymous tip before the cross was lit. The Warings' backdoor neighbor observed two middle-aged men wrapping the crudely made cross with burlap before lighting it. When local officials arrived on the scene, they found the charred remains of a cross with the initials "KKK" etched into it.[20]

The story of the cross burning at the Waring residence spread across the national media, with Waring accusing the Klan of trying to intimidate him. The *News and Courier*, forever obsessed with Charleston's national image, sought to minimize the incident, describing the cross as "small" and "constructed of old wood." The paper reported that perhaps the incident was a "prank," because, quoting a local police detective, "we have nothing to prove it was put there by the KKK." Waring rejected the claim that the cross burning was merely the work of "pranksters," asserting that the Klan was actively functioning in Charleston with four hundred to five hundred members. The perpetrators of the cross burning were never identified.[21]

This would not be the last attack on the Waring home. Months later, on October 9, 1950, the Warings were engaged in an evening game of canasta in their living room when they heard what they perceived to be gunshots. Suddenly a concrete block and other objects crashed through their living room window, falling near where they sat. They raced to the adjacent dining room and crouched behind a protective wall, believing that their lives were in jeopardy. The FBI and the U.S. Marshals Service were summoned to the scene. Later that evening, Elizabeth called Walter and Poppy Cannon White, telling them, "I had to call you—just to reassure myself there is a civilized world . . . outside this jungle."

The FBI took charge of the investigation and carried off pieces of brick and concrete that were found inside the home, as well as shattered glass from the broken living room window. It appeared the attackers had thrown the objects from an automobile. The agents were unable to find evidence of bullets inside the home but were actively investigating whether shots had been fired into the air. The FBI thereafter announced that a full investigation would be conducted because it was an attack on a federal official.[22]

Walter White wrote to Attorney General Howard McGrath on October 12, 1950, to express his alarm over the attack on Judge Waring's home. White recommended the immediate assignment of bodyguards to protect the Warings. Deputy Attorney General Ford responded for the attorney general, informing White that the U.S. Marshals Service was now providing the judge with twenty-four-hour protection and had done so since October 10. Ford further stated that the investigation was ongoing and the "Attorney General and this Department . . . were greatly concerned about the injury to Judge Waring's property. I can assure you that we will do all we can to see that it is not repeated." For the balance of Judge Waring's service on the bench, he had twenty-four-hour security provided by the U.S. Marshals Service.[23]

The *News and Courier* condemned the attack on the Waring home as "harmful to South Carolina's reputation" but speculated, as it did with the cross burning, that the attack had likely been the work of "pranksters," not Klansmen. Several weeks later, the *News and Courier* criticized the decision of the Justice Department to conduct a full FBI investigation into the incident and to provide around-the-clock marshal protection to Waring, claiming that these decisions were Attorney General McGrath's craven response to Walter White's control of the "negro bloc vote." The *News and Courier* editorial ended with this question: "Is [McGrath] the yes-man for Walter White and the NAACP?"[24]

Congressman Rivers, continuing his personal crusade against Waring, leaped into the controversy over U.S. Marshals Service protection for Judge Waring by writing to McGrath on October 19, 1950, and demanding to know the attorney general's legal authority for providing such protection to a federal judge. Rivers asserted that Judge Waring had become "the most expensive luxury on the federal payroll." He further observed that it was "a particular twist of irony to note that the man who has run up and down the landscape of the United States advocating force, now cries for help when the practical application of his theories is brought to bear on him." Several weeks later, Rivers reported that the U.S. Marshals Service had already expended more than $1,000 providing additional protection for Waring, which he characterized as both unlawful and "totally unnecessary." He also promised to "tell the world" in "a very few days" the real reasons Waring was ostracized in South Carolina, contending they were unrelated to his court decisions. Rivers's report was never delivered.[25]

While controversies swirled around Elizabeth's public statements, the Waring impeachment effort, and attacks on the Waring home, Judge Waring began to quietly formulate a plan for overturning *Plessy v. Ferguson*. Initially, he focused on three important civil rights cases that were on the Supreme Court's 1950 docket. Two of the cases involved claims of unequal treatment in graduate programs in public universities in Texas and Oklahoma. The Texas case, *Sweatt v. Painter*, asserted that the recently established "black" law school was markedly inferior to the nationally renowned all-white University of Texas Law School, denying aspiring black attorneys in the state equal protection of the laws. In *McLaurin v. Oklahoma State Regents*, black graduate students, who attended the University of Oklahoma graduate school of education but were required to sit physically separate from their white classmates, asserted that the segregation denied them the equal right to interact with and learn from their fellow students. In the third case, *Henderson v. United States*, African American passengers traveling in interstate railcars challenged a government practice requiring segregation in dining cars.[26]

The Supreme Court's acceptance of these three cases involving government-mandated racial segregation suggested to Waring that the Court might be prepared to overturn *Plessy v. Ferguson*. He sought to help that process along by persuading national religious organizations and others to file amicus briefs, to demonstrate growing public support for ending racial segregation in public facilities. Waring privately consulted with James Dombrowski, who had close relationships with national religious organizations. He suggested that Dombrowski approach the Federal Council of Churches, an umbrella organization that included the National Baptist Convention, the Methodist Church, and the United Presbyterian Church, to see if it would consider filing an amicus brief. He also recommended that Dombrowski approach Jewish and Catholic organizations with the same idea. The Federal Council of Churches, the American Jewish Committee, and B'nai B'rith filed amicus briefs in

Sweatt v. Painter. Waring also recommended to Aubrey Williams that a group of prominent white southerners file an amicus brief and suggested names of those who might sign on. He explained to Williams how critical these pending civil rights cases were, saying there was "a battle royal, and either we are going to take a horrible licking or move forward to a new atmosphere."[27]

The Supreme Court handed down its decisions in *Henderson, Sweatt,* and *McLaurin* on the same day, June 5, 1950. The plaintiffs won unanimously in all three cases, but the Court made no direct reference or citation to *Plessy* in any of the cases. There was debate about what the Court's silence meant. Many read the plaintiffs' victories as a further incremental whittling away of the *Plessy* doctrine, with these new decisions establishing that the specific practices and policies challenged by the plaintiffs would now no longer be tolerated. But Waties Waring read much more into these decisions. He viewed the cases collectively as reflecting a fundamental shift in the Court's thinking: there was now no practical way that segregated facilities could meet the justices' exacting standards for equality. He was convinced that if the Supreme Court was presented squarely with the question of whether *Plessy v. Ferguson* was still good law, the separate but equal doctrine would be overturned. Whether the justices had come at this point as far as Waring perceived is certainly debatable, but his confidence that a majority of the Supreme Court was now ready to reject the *Plessy* doctrine propelled him forward. Waring decided to look for a case on his docket in which the plaintiffs could openly challenge the continued viability of *Plessy.*

Waring publicly discussed his views about the far-reaching implications of the Supreme Court's three recent civil rights decisions in a speech to the Council for Civic Unity in San Francisco on August 3, 1950. He acknowledged that the Supreme Court in both *Sweatt* and *McLaurin* did not directly address the *Plessy* question, but observed that the decisions, "when carefully read, show a distinct conflict in the reasoning in the *Plessy* case" and "throw grave doubts upon the *Plessy* holding." What was clear, he argued, was that the "separate but equal doctrine as to postgraduate education has been completely destroyed."[28]

Waring was not the only Supreme Court observer who saw the potentially groundbreaking implications of the civil rights decisions of the Court's 1950 term. Thurgood Marshall read his office's unanimous victories in *Sweatt* and *McLaurin* as a significant development and convened a meeting of forty NAACP attorneys from around the country in July 1950 to discuss the Legal Defense Fund's plans going forward. At the completion of the two-day conference, the group adopted a policy that the NAACP would no longer pursue cases for equalization under the *Plessy* doctrine and established as a goal the end of segregation in all educational facilities. This policy was adopted that same year by both the NAACP's annual convention and its board.[29]

This new policy did not establish a specific schedule for the filing of lawsuits to challenge public school segregation. This was not an oversight. The long-standing and successful practice of the NAACP Legal Defense Fund under its first chief counsel, Charles Hamilton Houston, and now Thurgood Marshall, was to carefully build one legal precedent on top of another and avoid pushing the Supreme Court further than it was ready to go.

This incrementalist, lawyerly approach did not sit well with Marshall's boss, Walter White, and certain activist members of the NAACP board and staff. These included the board members Hubert Delany, a New York domestic relations judge, and John Hammond, a renowned music producer who promoted such great talents as Benny Goodman, Count Basie, and Billie Holiday. This group also included Franklin Williams, Isaac Woodard's attorney and a member of Marshall's legal staff, who was suspected by Marshall of being a closet ally of Walter White's in an ongoing internal battle between White and Marshall over control of the NAACP's legal strategy.

The activists wanted Marshall and his team to pull the trigger now with a frontal challenge to public school segregation. Marshall resisted, believing the approach unnecessarily risky. Walter White and the NAACP board members Delany and Hammond had developed close personal relationships with Judge and Mrs. Waring and shared their view that Marshall was being excessively cautious in challenging the *Plessy* doctrine. Waring agreed with White and the other activists that the time to directly challenge *Plessy* had arrived.[30]

Beyond the question of when the first public school cases might be brought, there remained the issue of selecting the right cases in the right communities to mount a challenge. Marshall envisioned a process by which the first challenges would arise in communities outside the South, where local resistance and intimidation of plaintiffs would be a lesser concern. Once those cases were won, the Legal Defense Fund would focus on major school districts in the urban South, and then finally turn to rural school districts. Thus, under this strategy, rural Deep South school districts would likely be the last battleground over public school segregation. In light of the remarkable run of successes the NAACP Legal Defense Fund had enjoyed with Houston's and Marshall's careful and deliberate approach, it is hard to argue that such a strategy was not among the legitimate and reasonable options available.

Marshall's strategy and pace clearly did not suit Waties Waring. Now approaching seventy years old, Waring wanted the NAACP to move forward immediately with a frontal challenge to public school segregation, and he intended to be part of that challenge. In the summer and early fall of 1950, he carefully formulated a plan to place the *Plessy* question on the docket of the U.S. Supreme Court. Under his plan, South Carolina plaintiffs would challenge the constitutionality of the state statute mandating public school segregation under the equal protection clause of the Fourteenth Amendment. A challenge in federal court to the constitutionality of a state statute required the convening of a three-judge panel. Waring knew that if the suit was initially filed in his court, he would almost certainly be one of the three judges appointed to the panel. He fully appreciated the plaintiffs would lose 2 to 1 before the three-judge panel, because he knew that no other judge in the South would declare the separate but equal doctrine overruled. But even in defeat, he would have the opportunity to file a dissenting opinion, which would be the first judicial dissent from *Plessy* since Justice Harlan's legendary dissent in the case fifty-five years earlier. Waring further understood that under court rules the appeal from a three-judge panel decision would skip over the court of appeals and be placed automatically onto the docket of the U.S. Supreme Court. Thus, under his plan, the Supreme Court could not easily dodge the *Plessy* question and would effectively be forced to decide once and for all whether the separate but equal doctrine was dead or alive. From Waring's analysis of the Court's recent decisions, he was confident he knew the answer. There was, in Waring's plan, the mark of real strategic genius.[31]

But there was one rather significant problem in the Waring plan. He had no case pending on his docket that raised the constitutionality of public school segregation. In fact, no such suit had ever been filed by the NAACP or any other group. Waring carefully reviewed his pending cases and eyed an NAACP case from the rural community of Summerton, South Carolina, *Briggs v. Elliott*, as a potential vehicle to raise a frontal challenge to *Plessy*. *Briggs* was a rather straightforward *Plessy* case in which the plaintiffs alleged that white children in this predominantly rural school district were provided with school bus transportation and superior facilities and textbooks denied to black children.

Briggs had an involved procedural history that went back several years. A local schoolteacher and AME minister, the Reverend Joseph A. DeLaine, had first organized a group of black parents in 1947 to petition their county board of education for equal bus transportation, noting that some black children were required to walk nine miles to school. A clearer violation of the separate but equal doctrine would be hard to find. Despite the obvious merit of the request, on both legal and fundamental fairness grounds, the citizen group's petition was ignored by the county board of education. The group retained Harold Boulware, the Columbia attorney and local NAACP counsel, to file a lawsuit in U.S. district court requiring the Clarendon County Board of Education provide equal bus transportation services to the district's black children. The case was filed in the name of a single plaintiff, Levi Pearson, a local farmer. The school district discovered that although Pearson's children attended the Summerton schools, his residence lay just outside the school district's boundary. The case was dismissed because the sole plaintiff did not have legal standing to bring the suit. One local white politician ridiculed the failed lawsuit, telling his friends, "Our niggers don't even know where they live." DeLaine and other community leaders were disheartened and embarrassed by this technical defect in their suit and resolved not to give up their fight.[32]

Thurgood Marshall personally took charge of this new effort and insisted on twenty district residents agreeing to serve as plaintiffs before the case would be refiled. DeLaine, who did not personally reside in the district and thus could not be a plaintiff, actively recruited understandably fearful school district parents to join the suit. Eventually, twenty-one district residents agreed to serve as plaintiffs, led by the gas station attendant and navy veteran Harry Briggs and his wife, Eliza Briggs, a maid at a local motel. The case advanced on the Charleston federal court docket and was set for trial for Monday, November 20, 1950. Judge Waring scheduled a pretrial conference for Friday, November 17, presumably to address final details related to the trial.[33]

When Marshall arrived at the courthouse, he was advised by court personnel that Waring wished to see him in chambers. In a private closed-door meeting, Waring informed Marshall he had bigger plans for the *Briggs* case. He told Marshall, "I don't want to hear another separate but equal case. Bring me a frontal attack on segregation." Marshall resisted, telling him, "This is on our agenda but it's not tonight. We don't think this is the case. We don't think this is the time." Waring was unpersuaded, telling Marshall, "This is the case and this is the time." Marshall continued to push back, telling Waring that under his plan the plaintiffs would win before him but lose in the Fourth Circuit. Waring explained that he planned to recommend the convening of a three-judge panel. Marshall responded that the plaintiffs would lose before the panel. Waring agreed, telling him, "You're going to lose in the three judge court. You'll get two votes against one . . . Then you're automatically in the Supreme Court. That's where you want to be."[34]

Marshall left his private meeting with Waring "very upset" and shared with his associates the dramatic encounter with the judge. Moments later, Waring convened the pretrial hearing in open court with all

counsel present and raised the question of the scope of the present litigation. Still resisting the three-judge-panel plan, Marshall argued that the
issue of the constitutionality of segregated public schools was implicitly
already before Waring and could be addressed in the course of the trial
set for the following week. Waring responded that the pleadings did not
raise the school segregation question. Marshall asked to be allowed to
amend his pleadings. Waring suggested an alternative, the voluntary dismissal of the present suit and the bringing of a new suit that clearly asserted the constitutional question. Waring informed Marshall that if he
did this, he would ask Judge Parker to convene a three-judge panel.

Marshall, whipsawed by Judge Waring and the leadership of the
NAACP to adopt a more aggressive (and risky) strategy than he was
comfortable with, reluctantly agreed to Waring's plan, later telling colleagues that he felt he had no other choice. Waring then stated, "Very
good. I'll sign an order, dismissing without prejudice, and I'll expect you
to file a suit bringing that issue clearly before the Court." As the former
NAACP general counsel and Sixth Circuit Court of Appeals Judge Nathaniel Jones later observed, "Waring's reasoning encouraged the NAACP
legal team to shift its strategy from pushing for equalization of facilities
to total elimination of segregation, root and branch."[35]

Although Marshall had agreed to dismiss his action and refile a new
case, he still required the consent of his clients. Fearing that they could
face severe retaliation if they joined this new suit, Marshall sent Robert
Carter to Summerton to candidly share with their clients the potential
risks they might face as plaintiffs in this newly filed lawsuit. Carter reviewed with the plaintiffs the language of the new pleadings and warned
that those who agreed to participate could be exposed to violence and
other forms of retaliation. Carter explained that the NAACP felt the time
had come to challenge segregation head-on but needed their consent to
proceed. An elderly gentleman rose to his feet and stated, "We wondered
how long it would take you lawyers to reach that conclusion," and the
audience erupted in thunderous applause. Few of the original plaintiffs
withdrew, and as predicted, all suffered severe retaliation for their participation as litigants in *Briggs*.[36]

Shortly after Carter's visit to Summerton, Marshall dismissed the former suit and on December 22, 1950, filed the first challenge to public school racial segregation in modern American history. Waring formally requested the appointment of a three-judge panel in the newly filed *Briggs v. Elliott* on January 12, 1951. Three days later, Judge John J. Parker granted the request and appointed himself, Waring, and Judge George Bell Timmerman to the panel. Waties Waring now had in place his three-judge panel and was staring down his barrel with a clean shot at *Plessy v. Ferguson*.[37]

14.

——

DRIVING THE
"LAST NAIL IN THE COFFIN
OF SEGREGATION"

CLARENDON SCHOOL DISTRICT NUMBER 22 was a poster child for the failures of the separate but equal doctrine. Centered on the rural and impoverished community of Summerton, South Carolina, the district was ruled by an all-white school board, even though the community was 75 percent African American. All political power and virtually all of the community's wealth were held by the white minority. The buildings and grounds of the white schools were relatively modern and attractive, with indoor restrooms and running water. The black schools were ramshackle structures with outdoor privies and a community well for water. A credible claim of equality of facilities simply could not be made.

The school district was represented by a local attorney, Joseph Rogers, who had long been concerned that the obvious inequalities in the

district's black and white schools could not withstand even the most minimal judicial scrutiny. As early as 1947, Rogers consulted with Robert
Figg, a Charlestonian regarded by many as the state's keenest legal mind,
when a group of black parents petitioned the county board of education
seeking school bus transportation for their children. Figg had previously served as the solicitor, or chief prosecutor, in Charleston County,
and he and Judge Waring knew each other well. Waring suspected that
Figg was the primary strategist behind the Democratic Party's white primary defense, including the adoption of the party oath he had enjoined
in *Brown v. Baskin*. Waring had little use for Bob Figg, and the feeling was
mutual.[1]

As soon as Thurgood Marshall filed his new suit challenging the constitutionality of South Carolina's segregated public school system, Rogers
arranged for the school district to retain Bob Figg as lead counsel. Figg initially assessed the members of the three-judge panel and realized his case
must focus on capturing the vote of John J. Parker, who was undoubtedly
the swing vote. Judge Timmerman, an ardent segregationist, was a sure
vote for the defense. Waties Waring was a guaranteed vote for the plaintiffs. Figg appreciated that while Parker was no civil rights activist, he had
twice written strong decisions affirming Waring's orders in the white primary and party oath cases. Under the right set of circumstances, Parker
might side with Waring, particularly if the state offered a weak defense.

After touring the Clarendon School District, Figg had no doubt that
an equal facilities defense would not fly with Judge Parker. The likely consequence of mounting such a defense, the approach in virtually every
separate but equal case, would be to drive Parker into the embrace of
Waring. But if the schools were not equal, what then was the school district's defense under the *Plessy* doctrine? Applying all of his reputed skills
as a cagey strategist, Figg proposed an out-of-the-box defense: the adoption by the State of South Carolina of a massive school bond issue to fund
a new generation of black public schools in South Carolina. The price tag
was a whopping $75 million, equivalent today to more than $700 million.
This was to be funded by a new $.03 sales tax, the first sales tax in South

Carolina history. In Figg's view, this was the price that South Carolinians must pay for the maintenance of racial segregation.

Figg pitched his idea to the state's newly elected governor, James F. Byrnes. No living South Carolinian had the governmental experience of Byrnes or the ability to appreciate the need to undertake a grand strategy to address a great challenge. Byrnes had served in all three branches of the federal government, including stints as secretary of state, justice on the Supreme Court, and member of both the House and the Senate. He had also held key positions in the Roosevelt administration during World War II and, due to his close relationship with FDR, was often referred to as the "assistant president." Despite his broad worldly experience, he remained an unreconstructed segregationist.[2]

Figg explained to the governor the sad state of affairs in the segregated schools of Summerton. He shared the example of a well-equipped home economics class at the white high school and the presence of a single broken sewing machine in the home economics class at the black high school. As Figg later recalled, Byrnes "saw the point" and agreed to endorse Figg's school bond strategy.[3]

The proposed $75 million bond issue was not an easy sell to the profoundly conservative South Carolina General Assembly, which viewed public school funding as primarily a local responsibility. Byrnes initially laid out his ambitious plan in a private meeting with state legislative leaders at his beach home near Charleston. The powerful and fiscally conservative Speaker of the House, Solomon Blatt, voiced concerns about the governor's proposal. The Speaker wondered whether this was just an expensive, futile gesture by the state, speculating that the Supreme Court might still order the integration of the public schools after South Carolina spent all that money building new black schools. Byrnes responded that he had served on the Supreme Court, and he could guarantee Blatt that the justices would never order the integration of the public schools.[4]

Byrnes featured the school bond plan in his inaugural address on January 16, 1951. He explained that the state had a duty to provide education for all children, "white or colored," and "we must have a state building program." He went on to assert that there must be "substantial equality in school facilities," both to meet any legal challenges and "because it is right."

The size and scope of the undertaking produced considerable legislative resistance, and time was not on the state's side. The *Briggs* trial was scheduled to begin on May 28, 1951, and Figg needed an adopted plan ready to present to the court when the trial opened. Byrnes put his high standing and prestige behind the bond issue, winning legislative approval just weeks before the trial opened. School officials from the Summerton school district, with Figg's guidance, conferred with the state's newly created bonding agency, the State Educational Finance Commission, on a plan to construct new schools in the district for its black students. Blueprints were produced for the proposed new black schools.[5]

With the funding plan in place, Figg had another trick up his sleeve. He proposed to Byrnes that the state open the trial with an admission of liability. Figg knew that the NAACP planned to bring in numerous witnesses from across the country to prove the glaring inequalities in the school district and this would be the focus of their case. No state had ever admitted a violation of the Fourteenth Amendment in a civil rights case and thrown itself at the mercy of a federal court. Under Figg's plan, he would admit liability, provide the three-judge panel with evidence of the newly adopted bond issue, and ask the court for time to allow South Carolina to equalize its schools. To heighten the anticipated impact of this admission of liability, Figg proposed to keep it secret until the trial opened. He hoped to catch Thurgood Marshall flat-footed and expected that the panel would immediately accept the proposal and adjourn the planned multiweek trial.[6]

The NAACP's trial team members, consisting of Marshall, Robert Carter, Spottswood Robinson, and Harold Boulware, were engaged in their own intense preparations, mindful of what was at stake in their decision to challenge the *Plessy* doctrine and its application to segregated public schools. If they succeeded, they would have the legal tools to dismantle Jim Crow and change the face of the segregated South. If they ultimately lost before the U.S. Supreme Court, they would experience a personal and professional disaster and throw decades of painstaking legal work onto the trash heap of history.

There was little thought by the NAACP counsel that they would win before the South Carolina three-judge panel. Their plan was to build a strong factual record for their Supreme Court appeal, hoping to follow a familiar pattern of losing in the lower court, only to prevail on appeal. They were optimistic about their chances. Since their win in 1944 in the Texas white primary case, *Smith v. Allwright*, with an 8–1 vote, the NAACP had been on an unprecedented winning streak, prevailing unanimously in every civil rights case before the Supreme Court. Surely, they believed, there were at least five votes among the justices to overrule *Plessy*.

In the months preceding the *Briggs* trial, the NAACP litigation team gathered evidence to demonstrate the profound inequalities in the Clarendon district. They arranged, as part of pretrial discovery, to obtain access for one of their expert witnesses, Dr. Matthew Whitehead of Howard University, to the school district's facilities. Whitehead visited and photographed each school within the district. His findings were simply devastating.[7]

Recognizing that the eyes of history were on them, the NAACP trial team explored innovative ways they might prove their case, particularly the issue of the effect of racial segregation on black children. This was a critical issue, because if racial segregation itself injured children, even where equal facilities were provided, then the doctrine of separate but equal could no longer stand. Robert Carter devoted considerable personal time to developing the testimony of a young and unheralded psychology professor at City College of New York, Dr. Kenneth Clark, who had conducted cutting-edge psychological studies on the impact of racial segregation on black children.

Clark and his wife and research partner, Dr. Mamie Clark, utilized otherwise identical black and white dolls in interviews with grammar-school-aged black children, asking them which doll represented positive traits and which one represented negative traits. The black children consistently picked the white dolls for positive attributes and the black dolls for negative ones. From these findings, the Clarks concluded that children living in segregated communities developed a sense of inferiority that retarded their personal development and resulted in lifelong psychological injury.

Although Kenneth Clark's research had been published in more than two dozen professional journals and presented at the White House Conference on Children and Youth the prior year, few outside academic circles had ever heard of him. Some of the NAACP's senior legal advisers feared that the Clark testimony would be seen as a cheap trial gimmick. Robert Carter argued passionately for using the Clark testimony, and Thurgood Marshall finally came down on his side, observing that every plaintiff must prove his injuries. Marshall proposed one additional step to heighten the credibility of Clark's testimony. He wanted Clark to travel to Summerton the week before the trial and conduct sessions with a random sample of black children from Clarendon School District Number 22 to demonstrate that he could obtain the same responses as reported in his earlier published studies. Clark's testimony would be the first instance in which social science evidence of this type had ever been offered in an American courtroom.[8]

A week prior to trial, Marshall, Carter, and Clark traveled by train from New York to Charleston, with Clark carrying his dolls in a special case. They ate dinner together in the train's dining car, with Marshall casually mentioning to Clark that they were able to dine there because of the NAACP's court victories banning segregation in interstate travel. When they arrived in Charleston, the NAACP legal team set up at the home of Reginald and Eva Boone, two stalwarts of the Charleston NAACP. The Boones had a large ground-level basement and an attached garage at their home at 184 Smith Street, which they handed over to the ever-growing group preparing for the *Briggs* trial. The Boones brought in a cook to feed the hungry lawyers, reporters, expert witnesses, and hangers-on who gathered in preparation for what they believed might be the most important trial in American history.

After their arrival in Charleston, Clark asked Marshall whether he or another one of the attorneys would be traveling to Summerton with him to conduct the new round of doll studies. Marshall replied, "We're here to prepare for a trial and—well, you know, it's dangerous over there." Clark thought Marshall was kidding and would join him the next morning for the trip to Summerton. Instead, a young man appeared to drive Clark to Clarendon County. Before he departed, Marshall pulled Clark aside and gave him a $50 bill. "Look, if you get into trouble over there, you might try showing them this . . . It might help." With that, Clark left the NAACP legal team in Charleston to face he did not know what in Summerton. In fact, Clark's new round of doll studies was conducted without incident and produced the same results as he had obtained in his earlier field studies.[9]

Although Clark's visit to Summerton was uneventful, the *Briggs* plaintiffs and their leader, the Reverend Joseph A. DeLaine, were being subjected to a merciless and methodical campaign of retaliation and intimidation. The school district fired DeLaine, his wife, two of his sisters, and a niece from their teaching positions. A year earlier, in the midst of the legal fight, the DeLaine family home burned to the ground while the local volunteer fire department stood by and refused to provide assistance. In what DeLaine described as a "sly reign of terror," school officials, reportedly "on the advice of the school attorney," had "called the white folks of the town and advised them how to punish the concerned parents and children." Each plaintiff was reported individually targeted. Credit was denied at the beginning of planting season, outstanding notes were called, and "threats and intimidations were made." The lead plaintiffs, Harry and Eliza Briggs, were fired from their respective longtime jobs as a gas station attendant and motel maid, and other named plaintiffs suffered similar fates. Despite these retaliatory actions, not one of the named *Briggs* plaintiffs asked that his or her name be withdrawn from the suit.[10]

———

The trial of *Briggs v. Elliott* was scheduled to convene in Judge Waring's courtroom in the Charleston Federal Courthouse on May 28, 1951. Civil rights trials of that era were often conducted in half-empty courtrooms because many African Americans feared retaliation should their attendance at such a trial be interpreted by the white power structure as an affiliation with the NAACP or support for racial integration. Black schoolteachers and other black public employees had been fired for less.

But as the sun rose in Charleston on the first day of the *Briggs* trial, African Americans arrived by the carload from Summerton and across the state, and hundreds lined up outside the historic courthouse and down Broad Street as far as the eye could see. Thurgood Marshall, arriving at the courthouse that morning, was deeply moved by the massive crowd of humble but proud people lining up at the federal courthouse door. He turned to Robert Carter as they entered the building and said, "Bob, it's all over." A perplexed Carter asked Marshall what he meant. Marshall replied, "They're not scared anymore."[11]

Judge Waring also arrived at the courthouse early and observed this "rather interesting and dramatic situation. These people entering, they were people in from the country. They had come there on a pilgrimage. There were battered looking automobiles parked all around the courthouse." Waring observed that the African American citizens lining up to enter his courtroom "had never known before that anybody would stand up for them, and they came there because they believed the United States district court was a free court, and believed in freedom and liberty." Waring described the scene as "a little breath of freedom."[12]

When the court was called into session at 10:00 a.m., the courtroom was packed, with hundreds still standing outside the room, down the stairs, and onto the street below. Those standing in line waited patiently, grabbing a seat whenever someone stepped out of the courtroom. Reports would be given to individuals in the line about what was going on inside the courtroom, and it would be whispered to others like a telephone chain. Some were never able to get into the courtroom but were satisfied simply to be there at this historic moment. One Summerton farmer, James Gibson, remembered, "I never got tired standing that day. The fact that Judge Waring was there meant that we were going to get a hearing."

The courtroom spectators were largely African American and were allowed to sit anywhere they desired, because Judge Waring had abolished segregated seating in his courtroom years earlier. Ruby Cornwell had arrived at 7:00 a.m. and was a notable presence in the front row. Joseph DeLaine and the named plaintiffs were in attendance and guaranteed a seat. Local and national reporters squeezed into the courtroom, including representatives from *The New York Times*, the *New York Post*, the Associated Press, *The Pittsburgh Courier*, and *The Chicago Defender*. In the back row and little noticed was a recent graduate of the South Carolina State Law School, Matthew Perry, who had awakened in his hometown of Columbia hours before and was in line when the sun rose in Charleston. Within a decade, Perry would launch a civil rights litigation crusade in South Carolina, winning dozens of suits challenging every aspect of Jim Crow. In 1979, he would be appointed South Carolina's first African American federal judge.[13]

Notably absent that morning was Elizabeth Waring, normally a constant presence in her husband's courtroom. Elizabeth confided to her diary, "The day [I] dreamed and prayed would arrive has come." She lamented, "I can't go to the trial," fearing that she would be a distraction and "might cause a riot." She received frequent reports from the judge's secretary and friends in attendance and followed trial developments with great interest.[14]

The trial opened with the three judges being announced by Judge Waring's African American bailiff, John Fleming. Marshall and the other members of the NAACP trial team were ready, with a planned strong opening statement to be followed by a litany of witnesses to prove the plaintiffs' claims. Judge Parker, serving as the presiding judge, called the proceeding to order and prepared to ask Marshall to deliver his opening statement. Before he could do so, Figg rose and asked Parker for the opportunity to address the court. Parker suggested that it would be more appropriate for him to wait until his opening statement to do this. But Figg persisted, telling the court that his statement might simplify the proceedings and "eliminate the necessity of taking a great deal of testimony." Parker told him to go ahead. Figg informed the court that his investigation into

the "educational facilities, equipment, curricula, and opportunities afforded in School District No. 22 for colored pupils" revealed that they
"are not substantially equal to those afforded in the District for white
children." He then explained that the South Carolina General Assembly
had recently adopted a $75 million state bond issue, funded by a $.03
state sales tax. The governor was prepared to seek further legislation to
ensure equal educational opportunities for all children. Consequently, Figg
told the stunned courtroom, the defendants were admitting liability. They
would not oppose the entry of an order for the plaintiffs finding inequality in the educational opportunities for black children within the school
district and an injunction prohibiting future violations of the plaintiffs'
constitutional rights. Figg only asked that the school district be afforded
"a reasonable time to formulate a plan for ending such inequalities" and
for the court to retain jurisdiction to confirm compliance with the granted
injunctive relief.[15]

Figg's admission of liability initially had its intended effect, surprising the judges and the NAACP's litigation team. But Marshall quickly
recovered, arguing that the "statement just made has no bearing on this
litigation" because the plaintiffs were asserting that "segregation in and of
itself is unlawful." He urged the court to allow him to build his record to
demonstrate both the presence of the inequality and the "effect of segregation in the county under discussion." The panel conferred privately
among themselves while sitting on the bench, with Waring noting to his
colleagues that Figg's admission did not address the issue of whether segregation was per se unlawful, even if the facilities were equal. Waring
stated that the plaintiffs were entitled to make a record on that question.
Parker concurred, and Marshall was told to proceed. Now it was Figg's
turn to be surprised. He had been so confident of the success of his strategy and the court's willingness to adjourn the trial that he had not prepared any witnesses to testify.[16]

Until Figg's admission of liability, the defendants had maintained
that the district's facilities and programs were equal and met constitutional requirements. Most of the plaintiffs' witnesses were directed at

proving the district's profound inequalities, which Marshall planned to argue could not be remediated in a segregated school system. Now the state was attempting to sweep this powerful evidence aside and force the NAACP to offer evidence only on the narrower issue of whether racial segregation caused injury to black children if the facilities were actually equal. After spending months preparing for an evidentiary battle over unequal facilities, the NAACP legal team had difficulty suddenly changing the trial plan. This was, of course, exactly the type of confusion Figg was hoping to produce.

Marshall's initial difficulty in making this adjustment was evident when he called as his first witness the Clarendon County superintendent of education, L. B. McCord. Marshall's plan had been to question McCord as a hostile witness to obtain grudging admissions regarding the inequality of resources and facilities for the black and white schools. An impatient Parker cut Marshall off as he questioned the county superintendent, asking Marshall was he not asking the witness "questions about which there is no dispute in the world . . . Let's come to the disputed matter." When Marshall next called the local school board chairman, R. W. Elliott, Parker became impatient again with counsel for both sides because they continued to address issues regarding the inequality of facilities that Parker felt had already been admitted by the school district.[17]

The plaintiffs proceeded to call their first expert witness, Dr. Matthew Whitehead, who had visited each of the district schools and methodically cataloged the inequities present. Plaintiffs sought to demonstrate through Whitehead's testimony that the disparities were systemic and irremediable in a racially segregated school system. Further, Marshall believed that the glaring inequities in the black and white schools made a mockery of the school district's present claim of a good-faith intention to equalize the schools. Figg raised no objection to this testimony, and the very evidence he had hoped to keep out of the record by his admission of liability, regarding the profound inequality in the school district's facilities and programs, was presented in full by Whitehead.

Whitehead first compared the grounds of the schools, noting that the white schools were landscaped and had perimeter fences for student safety. The grounds of black schools were "exceptionally poor" and unfenced. The white schools, Whitehead testified, were constructed of stone or red brick, while the black schools were, for the most part, deteriorating wooden structures. Many of the black schools had no desks or an inadequate number, while the white schools were well equipped. The cost of the furnishings and fixtures at the white schools was $12,000, compared with $1,800 for the black schools. The white schools had a lower teacher-student ratio, while a number of the black schools had different grades lumped together under a single teacher. The white schools had auditoriums, gyms, and lunchrooms; the black schools did not. When Whitehead described the presence of indoor facilities and running water in the white schools and the absence of these in the black schools, Waring had him confirm that the black schools had no functioning indoor toilets. Whitehead offered photographs that corroborated his testimony regarding the dismal state of affairs within the school district.[18]

Figg attempted to cross-examine Whitehead but found himself digging a deeper hole just about every time he asked the well-prepared witness a question. When Figg attempted to make the point that the black children irregularly attended school, Whitehead noted that during his travels he observed school-aged children plowing the fields, suggesting that the local white farmers were contributing to the absenteeism problem. Figg questioned Whitehead's findings about the absence of desks in many of the black schools, contending that the modern trend was to use tables and chairs rather than desks. Whitehead disagreed, responding that the tables provided in the black schools were largely unfit for any purpose. When Figg attempted to ask Whitehead an esoteric question about the use of blackboards, which were mostly absent from the black schools, Whitehead launched into a detailed discussion about the limited presence of visual aids at the black schools. Parker asked Figg whether this had already been covered in the witness's direct testimony, and Figg responded, rather helplessly, "I didn't ask the witness to list it all, Your Honor." Finally recognizing that every question to Whitehead produced an avalanche of information about the district's inequalities, Figg sat down.

Dr. Kenneth Clark was called to the stand to testify after the court's luncheon recess. With the district's admission of inequality, his testimony took on a heightened importance, because it directly challenged the premise of *Plessy* that racially segregated schools could be equal. Clark described his innovative research methods utilizing black and white dolls and his conclusion that segregation has "detrimental effects on the personality development of the Negro child." These injuries included "confusion in the child's concept of his own self-esteem" and "basic feelings of inferiority." Clark then revealed that he had traveled to Summerton the week before the trial and administered his doll tests to twenty-six students in the defendant school district. He testified that "the conclusion which I was forced to reach was that these children of Clarendon County, like other human beings subjected to an obviously inferior status in society in which they live, have been definitely harmed in the development of their personalities" and that such injuries were "enduring."[19]

Figg was unaware of Clark's visit to Summerton and appeared unfamiliar with his methods, research history, and findings. He expressed surprise that Clark had been given direct access to district students by one of the elementary school principals and appeared perturbed that no one from the district had bothered to share that with him. He attempted to question Clark about his research instrument and was given detailed responses regarding how the instrument was developed and how it had been applied in the field in more than four hundred interviews in Arkansas, New York, and South Carolina. Recognizing that he was unprepared to effectively cross-examine Clark, Figg abruptly terminated the examination, likely anticipating that no reasonable judge would give any weight to such cutting-edge social science research. It was a decision that would come back to haunt him and his clients.

As the day progressed, Marshall's trial team began to appreciate the practical impact of Figg's admission of liability and how it had dramatically narrowed the scope of the trial. A number of the plaintiffs' anticipated witnesses were no longer needed. Robert Carter conducted the direct examinations of two experts, Dr. Harold McNally, a professor at Teachers College at Columbia University, and Dr. Ellis Knox, a professor at Howard, both of whom testified briefly that black children could not obtain an equal education in a segregated school. On cross-examination, Figg had the witnesses acknowledge that they had never worked in South Carolina schools and let them go. Suddenly an anticipated two-week trial looked more like a two-day event. By the afternoon of the first day, Marshall found himself running out of witnesses. He suggested that because the case was being tried to the court, rather than a jury, the defendants could begin putting up their witnesses that afternoon. This would allow Marshall time to get additional experts in town to testify the following morning.[20]

Judge Parker was receptive to Marshall's suggestion, pointing out that the defendants' surprising admission of liability that morning had "curtailed the length of the case," and it was "nothing but fair that they go ahead with their testimony." Now it was time for Figg to admit he was not ready either, stating, "I haven't conferred with our witnesses present preparatory to examining them." Parker then gave Figg fifteen minutes to prepare his witnesses to testify.[21]

After the brief recess, Figg called E. R. Crow, the newly appointed director of the State Education Finance Commission. Crow had recently assumed his duties over the new state agency responsible for distributing funds from the state educational bonds, after serving as a superintendent in Sumter County. He initially testified in a businesslike fashion about the school construction program, detailing the financing components of the plan. This demonstrated that the state's financial commitments were serious. But Figg could not let well enough alone, and asked Crow his opinions concerning whether integrated schools could work in South Carolina. Crow was more than willing to weigh in on the subject. He testified that "it would be impossible to have peaceable association" between black and white students and that there would likely be violent emotional reactions in the community if the court ordered the schools to desegregate. He further testified that if the court ordered public school integration, it was his opinion that most communities would simply abolish their public schools. He also claimed that black school administrators had privately told him they preferred segregated schools.[22]

As soon as Figg tendered his witness, Thurgood Marshall pounced. He asked Crow whether he was suggesting that local communities would defy an order of the court directing the desegregation of the schools. Crow quickly disavowed such an idea, and Parker sternly interjected that "any injunction issued by this Court would be obeyed." Marshall then questioned Crow's testimony that segregated schools were the preference of black school administrators. He asked Crow for the names of the black administrators who told him that. Crow admitted he could not remember their names. Marshall asked Crow incredulously whether the white people of South Carolina would deprive their own children of an education to avoid integration. Crow responded that he did not think the South Carolina General Assembly would appropriate funds for integrated schools. Marshall wound up his spirited cross-examination by having Crow admit that his opinions were based "at least in part" on a lifelong belief in the separation of the races.[23]

Marshall's public flailing of Crow thrilled the mostly African American audience. Many were humored by the witness's last name, associating it with the Jim Crow practices they were challenging. One spectator observed that Marshall "sure loves to eat crow." Another attendee observed that "Mr. Figg got his law degree when he finished school but he just got his baccalaureate address from Thurgood Marshall."[24]

Figg then called to the stand District Number 22's superintendent, H. B. Betchman. He questioned Betchman about the high rate of absenteeism among black students and then turned to the superintendent's impression of the physical condition of the various schools. Parker complained that Figg was attempting "to bring up equality" when he already admitted that "the conditions are not equal." Figg agreed, telling Parker, "I was attempting to explain something that did not count. I will turn the witness over to the other side." Figg sat down, and Marshall tore into his witness. Marshall asked Betchman whether high student absenteeism might be related to the "bad condition" of the black schools. Betchman admitted that "sometimes the condition of the school gives no encouragement to the child to come back."[25]

As the district superintendent left the stand, the court adjourned for the evening, with counsel for both parties promising to streamline the balance of their testimony the next day. The following morning, plaintiffs offered the testimony of two expert witnesses, Dr. David Krech, a widely published psychologist at the University of California who testified that segregated schools damaged black children, and Helen Trager, a lecturer at Vassar College and author of studies on integrated public schools. Figg's cross-examination of Krech and Trager was brief and focused on the fact that neither was from the South nor had lived in a segregated society. The judges were informed that the plaintiffs' one remaining witness, the renowned anthropologist Dr. Robert Redfield, was en route from Chicago but would not arrive in Charleston until late that afternoon. After some discussion among counsel, it was agreed that the court would include in the record Redfield's testimony offered in *Sweatt v. Painter*, in which he testified that racial segregation in educational facilities injured the students, the school, and the community. With the stipulated admission of Redfield's testimony, the plaintiffs rested. Figg indicated that he had no more witnesses and rested as well.[26]

The panel then heard two and a half hours of closing argument. Predictably, Marshall and Figg took fundamentally different views regarding the federal court's role and authority concerning public school segregation. Marshall argued that the segregated school system in Clarendon County created "psychological roadblocks" to the personal development of black students, thereby violating the rights of the district's children to equal protection of the laws. He argued that the district violated the rights of those children "every single day" and they were entitled to rights "that must be given now," not at some undetermined time in the future. Figg argued that racial segregation of the schools was the "normal" consequence of the region's history. He dismissed plaintiffs' evidence, arguing that the state had no obligation to accept the scientific opinions of out-of-state experts or to adapt its educational programs for the "personality development" of any students. Figg noted that the same Congress that had adopted the Fourteenth Amendment maintained segregated schools in the District of Columbia. Figg finished by asking the court for a "reasonable time" to address the district's inequities, which would be performed under the panel's continuing supervision.[27]

The three judges adjourned to Waring's chambers to discuss their decision in the case. The judges were essentially a microcosm of the debate roiling the courts and the public on the role and responsibility of the federal courts to address government-mandated racial segregation in the nation's public schools. Judge Timmerman voiced the widely held view in the South that the State of South Carolina had every right to segregate its schoolchildren by race "and the United States Constitution had nothing to do with it." Waring asserted that racial segregation under the order and direction of a state government violated the Fourteenth Amendment's guarantee of equal protection of the laws. He further argued that the Supreme Court's decisions of the prior summer in *Sweatt* and *McLaurin* "pointed the way" to the unavoidable conclusion that "segregation in education was unconstitutional." Parker took the middle ground, insisting that the separate but equal doctrine be enforced. He urged his colleagues to give Byrnes time to fix the inequalities in the district, expressing confidence in the governor's capacity to equalize school facilities. Clearly, Figg had read Parker correctly, and his costly defense of public school segregation won him the one vote he absolutely had to have to prevail before the *Briggs* panel.

After protracted discussions, Parker proposed that he prepare an order finding that the facilities and resources provided to the district's black children were not substantially equal to those provided to white children, violating the plaintiffs' rights under the Fourteenth Amendment. He further proposed that the order recognize that *Plessy v. Ferguson* remained the law of the land and that the school district be given a reasonable time to equalize the presently unequal schools through the state's new school bonds. Timmerman agreed to join Parker's proposed order. Parker attempted to persuade Waring to join the order as well, but Waring made it clear he was not willing to travel that path. The judges then adjourned, with Parker and Waring planning to prepare orders setting forth their respective positions.[28]

Waring returned home that evening exhausted and dejected. Despite his anticipation of this very result, a 2–1 split in the panel, he had privately held out some small hope that he could move Parker to his position. But Parker and Waring's formerly close relationship had been strained in recent months, likely caused by Waring's outspoken advocacy on the speaker's circuit and Elizabeth's public pronouncements. Further, it was clear from the judges' discussion in conference that Parker would not abandon the separate but equal doctrine until the Supreme Court explicitly overruled *Plessy*.[29]

The panel issued its majority opinion and Judge Waring's dissent on June 23, 1951. Parker, writing for the majority, found that Clarendon School District Number 22 had violated the constitutional rights of its black students by providing them with inferior educational services and opportunities and directed the district to remediate these constitutional violations. The majority's decision rejected the plaintiffs' argument that the Fourteenth Amendment prohibited government-mandated segregated school systems, noting that *Plessy* continued to control the question and the decision to maintain racially segregated schools was a matter reserved to state policy makers, with "which the federal courts are powerless to interfere."[30]

Waring appreciated the significance of his dissent, which he had thought about, researched, and brooded over for years. He knew this was his moment. The dissent opened with his declaring that the time had now arrived for the federal judiciary to "face, without evasion or equivocation, the question as to whether segregation in education in our schools is legal." He praised the "unexampled courage" of the plaintiffs in bringing the suit and recognized the right of their children to relief now, not at some unstated time in the future. He turned to the "real rock" on which the defendants rested, *Plessy v. Ferguson*. He analyzed the expert testimony offered at trial, particularly Clark's studies demonstrating that segregation "had a deleterious and warping effect upon the minds of children." Waring stated that Clark's studies clearly showed that "the humiliation and disgrace of being set aside and segregated as unfit to associate with others of a different color had an evil . . . effect upon the mental processes of our young." Based on this evidence, Waring concluded it was "clearly apparent . . . that segregation in education can never produce equality and it is an evil that must be eradicated . . . The system of segregation in education adopted and practiced in the state of South Carolina must go and must go now. Segregation is per se inequality." Noting that his colleagues viewed the matter otherwise, Waring concluded that he could not join their opinion and, therefore, "this opinion is filed as a dissent."[31]

Waring's dissent presented a new and far different equal protection analysis. In prior separate but equal cases, the Supreme Court and lower courts carefully analyzed the facilities or services provided to African American citizens and then compared them with those provided to white citizens. If the comparison demonstrated inequality, then the disparity was unconstitutional. This approach invited protracted and costly litigation, allowing any change in southern racial practices through litigation to be slow and incremental. Waring's dissent reasoned that the separate but equal analysis was fundamentally flawed, burdensome, and wholly unnecessary because "segregation is per se inequality." Under Waring's per se analysis, the day of tedious comparisons by the courts of black and white services and facilities would be a thing of the past, because racial segregation, standing alone, would be unlawful. Some variety of Waring's per se approach had been presented to the Supreme Court from time to time by the NAACP and in amicus briefs, but his dissent in *Briggs* was the first instance where the per se analysis was fully developed in a decision issued by a federal judge. Moreover, Waring had encapsulated this new approach with his own memorable phrase, "Segregation is per se inequality." His per se analysis would appear once again and be the defining holding of the most important case in American history, *Brown v. Board of Education.*[32]

The news of Waring's historic dissent spread rapidly through the civil rights community, and he received tributes from across the country.

Judge Hubert Delany, then one of the nation's few sitting African American judges, wrote to Waring on June 26, 1951, stating that his dissent "will go down in the history of jurisprudence . . . as a document comparable to nothing that has heretofore been said with such clarity, wisdom and courage." The Charleston NAACP president, A. J. Clement, wrote to Waring the same day, declaring, "Your dissent today will be the assent in an early tomorrow." He went on to state, "The people of my group have thanked God for you in the past. America will thank God for you in the future and at some later date the South will raise a monument to you." Aubrey Williams wrote to Waring on June 29, 1951, stating that he had "done an enduring and permanent chapter in the history of man's long struggle for justice."[33]

Waring responded to these tributes with candor about his purpose in filing the dissent. He told Judge Delany that the Supreme Court cases of the prior summer "almost cross the threshold but do not quite do so. I have great hopes that the Briggs case may shove them across." To Aubrey Williams, he wrote, "I can only hope that I have spoken sufficiently clear and strong enough to force the Supreme Court of the United States to . . . make a full declaration of the meaning of the American Constitution . . . I hardly dare to hope that I may have had a small part in bringing these vital issues to the attention of the top court." Responding to a telegram from James Dombrowski, Waring shared his disappointment in not getting "a majority of the court to see the light but after all perhaps it is better. It gave me an opportunity to show the two pictures of the South."[34]

But the clearest statement of Waring's intent can be found in an enthusiastic entry in Elizabeth's diary on the date the dissent was filed: "I feel now that it is done that this is our last act, that we have driven the last nail in the coffin of segregation . . . We may rest assured we have done all we can do." The importance of Elizabeth's partnership was encapsulated in the copy of the dissent the judge inscribed and gave to her: "To my precious Elizabeth. This could not have been done without her love and encouragement and support."[35]

Despite the widespread enthusiasm in the civil rights community over Waring's dissent, there was an undercurrent of criticism among some activists about Marshall's decision to bring a direct challenge to public school segregation at this time, rather than proceed more cautiously. The most notable of these criticisms was published in *The Pittsburgh Courier* in a column by Margaret McKenzie, a prominent African American attorney. McKenzie accused the "NAACP high command" of injecting "new vigor in the moribund *Plessy v. Ferguson* doctrine" by directly challenging the precedent in *Briggs*, arguing that it would have been "wiser simply to let the ancient *Plessy* doctrine fade away." Other black publications ran their own articles second-guessing the NAACP's litigation strategy. Marshall and his team organized a vigorous counteroffensive, accusing their critics of supporting a gradualist approach and proposing a legal strategy based on fear and timidity. These criticisms never really disappeared until the Supreme Court's decision in *Brown*.[36]

Charleston's *News and Courier* addressed the Waring dissent in a hyperbolic editorial titled "Contention for Miscegenation." The editors argued that the establishment of "mixed race schools," as supported by Waring, would lead to the "extermination of the white race in the United States and supplant it with a mixed race, Negro and Caucasian," through the "forced association in school of little boys and girls, white and colored." South Carolina would not tolerate such a result, the editors insisted, and would give up "public or tax supported schools" rather than allow black and white children to be "educated together." The paper published in full Waring's dissent and urged its readers to "examine with care the dissenting opinion of Federal Judge J. W. Waring in the Clarendon case."[37]

———

On January 26, 1952, some six months after issuing the *Briggs* dissent, Judge Waring, now seventy-one years old, advised President Truman that he intended to retire. Truman addressed Waring's retirement a few days later at a presidential press conference, calling him "a very great judge."

Friends and allies from around the nation wrote to Waring to thank him for his service and to praise his courage and vision. Waring announced that he and Elizabeth had sold their Charleston home and would be moving to New York City.[38]

Among his many well-wishers was the *Minneapolis Tribune* reporter Carl Rowan. In a private note, Rowan informed Waring that he received the news of his retirement with "a great deal of sadness" because "I . . . think of you there, eternally, on Meeting Street, a symbol of a man who dared to stand for justice." Waring responded, telling Rowan, "I have done all the judicial work that has been brought before me and cannot see where anything more important will come in the future." He explained that the Clarendon County case was then in the hands of the U.S. Supreme Court and should the plaintiffs not succeed, "I would not be interested . . . in passing upon separate but equal issues."[39]

Waring explained his retirement to a disappointed Dr. Benjamin Mays: "I feel there is nothing more in South Carolina for me to do. I have raised the constitutionality of segregation . . . It is now up to the Supreme Court to declare the law." He stated that he believed "there is a wider field of endeavor for me [in New York] living as a retired judge and no longer muzzled by cases pending or expected to be brought before me."[40]

The New York Times, in an editorial titled "A Judge Worthy of Honor," praised Waring's service on the bench as reflecting "courage, integrity and intelligence" and observed that his alienation from the white citizens of Charleston was the consequence of his devotion to two documents, the Declaration of Independence and the U.S. Constitution. Even his old nemesis, the editorial page of the *News and Courier*, acknowledged that but for his "crusading on the Negro question," Waring had achieved "an excellent record on the bench," showing "judicial dignity, intelligence and ability as a lawyer."[41]

The Warings left Charleston and moved into a small Upper East Side apartment in New York. Judge Waring became actively involved with various civil rights and civil liberties organizations, serving on the national boards of the ACLU and the National Urban League. In retirement, he reviewed drafts of the briefs submitted by the Legal Defense Fund in the various *Brown*-related cases before the Supreme Court and gave Thurgood Marshall editorial suggestions. He was honored by numerous religious, service, and legal organizations and was treated in his adopted city as an icon of the civil rights movement.[42]

Waring closely monitored the Supreme Court's handling of *Briggs v. Elliott*, as well as other cases raising the constitutionality of public school segregation from Delaware, Virginia, the District of Columbia, and Kansas. The first school segregation case filed after *Briggs* was from Topeka, Kansas, *Brown v. Board of Education*, and was presided over by a three-judge federal panel. That panel ruled unanimously a few months after the *Briggs* decision that *Plessy* remained good law and that the facilities and educational resources provided to black children within the district were substantially equal to those provided to white students.[43]

Another suit arose out of Prince Edward County, Virginia, where students protested that the county's segregated school system deprived them of equal educational opportunities. The Virginia case, *Davis v. County School Board of Prince Edward County*, was also assigned to a three-judge panel. That panel, following the *Briggs* decision, found that the separate schools in the county were unequal and gave the State of Virginia time to equalize the facilities.[44]

Plaintiffs in Delaware brought a state court suit challenging school segregation, arguing that *Plessy*'s separate but equal doctrine was no longer good law. The Delaware Supreme Court, in *Gebhart v. Belton*, rejected the plaintiffs' argument that *Plessy* had been overruled, but found that educational facilities within the state were not equal. Rather than allow the state time to correct this inequality, as was permitted in the South Carolina and Virginia cases, the Delaware Supreme Court ordered the immediate integration of state's public schools. The Delaware Supreme Court held that if the state's educational inequality problems were resolved, the defendants could petition the court to modify its integration order and, presumably, return to a segregated school system.[45]

The final school segregation case pending before the U.S. Supreme

Court, *Bolling v. Sharpe*, challenged segregation in the District of Columbia public schools. Because the District of Columbia is not part of any
state and not subject to the Fourteenth Amendment, *Bolling* presented
the issue of whether segregation was lawful under the Fifth Amendment's
due process clause.[46]

Eventually, all of the school segregation cases, except the one from
the District of Columbia, were consolidated by the U.S. Supreme Court
under the name *Brown v. Board of Education*. Some have observed that
because *Briggs* was the first case filed, tried, and appealed to the Supreme
Court, it should have been the lead case, rather than the Topeka, Kansas,
case. The original appeal in *Briggs* was remanded to the three-judge panel
to make updated findings regarding the new school construction funding, and it could perhaps be argued that the Kansas case then became the
most senior case. A more plausible explanation for the consolidation of
the cases under the *Brown v. Board of Education* name was that with a
Kansas case as the lead, the South could not claim that the Supreme
Court had unfairly targeted the region.[47]

When the dust finally settled on the various school segregation appeals that were docketed by the Supreme Court, Judge Waring's dissent
was the clear outlier. In all of the other cases, involving at some level the
participation of fourteen different judges, only Waring had ruled that
public school segregation violated the Fourteenth Amendment, regardless of whether the facilities and educational resources were equal. In this,
Waties Waring stood alone.

———

A definitive decision on the U.S. Supreme Court's pending school segregation cases encountered a series of delays. Chief Justice Vinson died
unexpectedly in September 1953. President Eisenhower nominated California's governor, Earl Warren, as chief justice, and he assumed his duties
on October 1, 1953, in a recess appointment. For the benefit of Warren,
reargument was scheduled on the pending school segregation cases in
December 1953. Warren was formally nominated by Eisenhower as chief

justice in January 1954 and confirmed by the U.S. Senate on March 1, 1954. Even after reargument and Warren's confirmation, months passed as the justices exchanged drafts of the proposed order. Warren, relying on considerable political skills and personal charm, persuaded one justice after another to support his simple and eloquent draft order. Eventually, all eight of his colleagues agreed to join the single decision of the chief justice.[48]

As winter turned to spring in 1954, speculation abounded regarding the likely outcome of the school cases. Supreme Court decisions for the current term are announced no later than the end of the term, which routinely ends in late June. Many close Court observers, allegedly "in the know," forecast a 6–3 or 7–2 victory for the plaintiffs. On Monday morning, May 17, 1954, Waties Waring awoke with a hunch that the decision would come down that day. He readied a few notes for possible press calls and waited. Shortly after noon, an excited staff member from the NAACP called to inform him that the association had been alerted that the decision would be announced within minutes but the outcome was not yet known.[49]

After several routine matters were addressed by the Court, Chief Justice Warren announced at 12:52 p.m. that he would read the Court's decision in the school segregation cases, which he had authored. This was his first major order since becoming chief justice. The initial portion of the decision traced the history of Plessy and the Court's recent civil rights decisions, providing no hint regarding how the Court would rule. Warren then stated that the critical question before the Court was, "Does segregation of children in public schools solely on the basis of race . . . deprive the children of the minority group of equal educational opportunities? We believe that it does." He continued to read on to the audience, made up mostly of the Supreme Court press corps. "We conclude"—Warren paused momentarily for emphasis—"unanimously, that in the field of public education the doctrine of 'separate but equal' has no place." A "sound of muffled astonishment" spread around the Supreme Court's chamber with the announcement of a unanimous decision for the plaintiffs. All the decisions in the school segregation cases pending before the Court, including *Briggs v. Elliott*, were reversed and remanded to lower courts for further action consistent with the Supreme Court's order. The Court further announced in *Bolling v. Sharpe* that its ruling extended to the District of Columbia public schools as well.[50]

A critical portion of the Supreme Court's decision in *Brown* addressed the emerging scholarship on the psychological damage inflicted on children involuntarily segregated on the basis of race. The Court noted that this research was not available to the justices at the time of the *Plessy* decision. In support of this important new development, the Court cited, in its now famous footnote 11, the research of Dr. Kenneth Clark presented at the 1950 White House Conference on Children and Youth as its first authority on this issue. The footnote referenced other scholarly works as well and ended with a reference to Gunnar Myrdal's *An American Dilemma*.[51]

The Supreme Court concluded its historic decision by adopting Waring's per se analysis, finding that "the doctrine of 'separate but equal' has no place. Separate educational facilities are inherently unequal." In an apparent recognition that Waring was a deeply polarizing figure in the South, no explicit reference was made to his dissent. The Court announced no date to implement its order, indicating that the justices desired additional briefing on remedy.[52]

On the evening of the *Brown* decision, May 17, 1954, a celebratory crowd gathered in the Warings' East Side apartment to toast the judge who had played such an important role in this historic day. Walter White and Poppy Cannon White were in attendance, as were the *Briggs* co-counsel Robert Carter (who had personally argued the *Brown* case before the Supreme Court), the author Alan Paton (*Cry, the Beloved Country*), and the *New York Post* reporter Ted Poston. In recognition of the historic moment, someone turned on a tape recorder and captured Walter White's remarks, which Paton later described as "the unforgettable part of this unforgettable occasion."[53]

White stated that when he heard of the decision, "I thought of Waties. I thought of the pounding he took when he wrote the dissenting opinion in South Carolina." Then, implicitly referencing Waring's insistence that Thurgood Marshall file the first school segregation case before him, White stated, "Waties, I pay tribute to you that, in so short a time . . . , you have been proven right." White praised the courage of Judge Waring and Elizabeth, recalling "the night they stoned your house." He also remembered the bravery of the plaintiffs from Clarendon County, South Carolina, who "took a stand even though to take such a stand might have meant death at almost any time. They had the courage to stand up . . . in this struggle. Without them neither the NAACP nor Waties Waring nor the Supreme Court could have taken the stand which they have taken today."[54]

Waring's courage and persistence did not go unnoticed by the justices. In a private discussion with Chief Justice Warren after the *Brown* decision, Waring told him how much he admired the Court's "clear cut" order and made a humorous aside, "I felt greatly relieved when you decided that Clarendon school case. I'd been very lonely up to that time." The chief justice responded to Waring, then living in exile in New York City, "Well, you had to do it the hard way."[55]

CONCLUSION:
UNEXAMPLED COURAGE

WORLD WAR II left much of Europe and Asia devastated. A fear of widespread economic dislocation and political instability threatened the postwar recovery, with the great powers of the United States and the Soviet Union competing for the hearts and minds of a war-ravaged world. Gunnar Myrdal observed that at this critical moment in human history "mankind . . . needs the youthful moralistic optimism of America." But America's promotion of democracy as the path for peace and prosperity was undermined by the glaring injustices inflicted on this nation's African American citizens residing in the Jim Crow South, and the best minds in American government and public life could not solve this great American dilemma.

There was, in short, no easy fix to American apartheid. Disenfranchisement denied minority citizens a voice in the state and local governments in the South, where three out of every four African American citizens lived. A calcified system of seniority rules and filibuster practices allowed an intransient minority of segregationists to choke off any efforts in the U.S. Congress to address the most glaring injustices and racial mob violence. The federal courts, charged with upholding the Constitution and the rule of law, sanctioned Jim Crow practices under the benign slogan of "separate but equal." The Democratic Party, which had carried the hopes and aspirations of black voters during the Roosevelt era, was hopelessly compromised by its alliance with southern segregationists.

In the midst of what seemed to be an unsolvable crisis in American government and character, courageous citizens, recognizing the demands of the times, stepped forward to challenge the racial status quo. Most had little to gain and much to lose. These remarkable citizens willingly took a stand for a more just and inclusive society against the tide of public opinion. Such courageous citizenship is indispensable to the maintenance of democratic institutions and practices. Although to the modern observer the collapse of the Jim Crow world may be viewed as the inevitable consequence of a growing and prosperous postwar nation, the truth was that in 1946 America's racial future was uncertain. This band of diverse, courageous citizens, some prominent and others from humble backgrounds, altered the course of American history, displaying what Judge Waring ascribed to the *Briggs* plaintiffs, "unexampled courage."[1]

When Sergeant Isaac Woodard stepped onto the Greyhound bus in Augusta, Georgia, on the evening of February 12, 1946, he did not set out to be a hero or martyr for the cause of civil rights. Like hundreds of thousands of other returning black veterans, he was unwilling to acquiesce to the Jim Crow practices of his prewar life. When a white bus driver cursed him in response to his request to step off the bus to relieve himself, Woodard demanded to be treated with respect, boldly declaring, "I am a man just like you." Although he was still wearing his nation's uniform, adorned with sergeant stripes and battlefield honors, Woodard had crossed the line for acceptable conduct by a black man. The response to this transgression was unforgiving: removal from the bus, arrest, and a severe beating on the way to the jail. This over-the-top reaction left Woodard blinded, and he became a symbol of the nation's failure to honor the service of its black veterans and of the brutality of Jim Crow.[2]

It would have been far easier for Isaac Woodard to have simply nodded obsequiously in response to the bus driver's discourtesy and shuffled back to his seat. Surely the tragedy of that night would have been avoided. But having unloaded American ships in the face of enemy fire, the sergeant knew something about courage and service. He refused to back down or accept his lot at the bottom of American society. Woodard voiced the resolve of an entire generation of young black veterans that enough was enough, displaying "unexampled courage."

When Harry Truman met with civil rights leaders on September 19, 1946, he planned to repeat the advice of his staff that while he was sympathetic to the cause of civil rights, there was nothing he could do as president to address the wave of racial violence that was sweeping across the South. This was certainly the politically safe approach. But when Walter White shared the story of Isaac Woodard's blinding, Truman realized that the calculated, politically correct response was no longer acceptable. Having served in wartime and commanded troops under fire, he knew something about courage and service to his nation. Casting aside the myopic vision of the political insiders, Truman resolved to do something that mattered on civil rights.

Truman wrote to his attorney general, Tom Clark, the day following his meeting with civil rights leaders and let him know that the conventional way of doing things was no longer acceptable. Something new and different had to be done to confront this wave of racial violence. Pressed by Truman, a slumbering Justice Department suddenly sprang into action. Criminal civil rights charges were filed against Lynwood Shull for the blinding of Woodard, and documents were prepared that would create the first presidential committee on civil rights. A little more than a year later, Truman's civil rights committee produced its groundbreaking report, candidly detailing America's serious deficiencies in justice and equality and providing a visionary set of recommendations. Truman embraced the committee's recommendations and issued landmark executive orders ending segregation in the armed services and in federal agencies.

Truman's civil rights program produced open rebellion from southern legislators of his own party and triggered a third-party challenge that threatened his election. Even his most loyal supporters urged him to back down, to reach an accommodation with the segregationist South. But Truman was unwilling to step back, declaring, "I shall fight to end evil like this." In a private letter to his former army buddy Ernie Roberts, Truman shared the story of the blinding of Woodard and the abuse of other black veterans. He told Roberts, "I am going to try to remedy it and if that ends up in my failure to be reelected, that failure will be in a good cause." Literally putting his presidency on the line, Truman displayed "unexampled courage."[3]

Waties Waring was the presiding federal judge in Charleston, South Carolina, a position of prominence and prestige in a town his family had resided in for generations. Every instinct of political and personal survival must have counseled him against taking the side of civil rights plaintiffs in litigation against his native city and state. But Waring recognized his choices were that "you were going to be entirely governed by the doctrine of white supremacy and just shut your eyes and bowl this thing through, or you were going to be a federal judge and decide the law." Waring, standing alone among his southern judicial peers, resolved to uphold the rule of law, demonstrating "unexampled courage."[4]

The *Briggs* plaintiffs understood that their decision to join the groundbreaking lawsuit would not go unnoticed by the white establishment. They were plainly warned of the practical consequences of their decision, yet they did not flinch or back down. They sought nothing for themselves, only hoped that their children and grandchildren might have a better life. They were on the receiving end of what the Reverend Joseph DeLaine described as a "sly reign of terror and fear," which included termination from longtime employment, loss of essential credit to finance their modest farming operations, and random acts of terror and violence. No *Briggs* plaintiff escaped this withering, targeted retaliation. In Judge Waring's great dissent, he noted the plaintiffs' "unexampled courage in bringing and presenting this cause" challenging "the long established and age-old pattern of the way of life which the state of South Carolina has adopted and practiced and lived in since and as a result of the institution of human slavery."[5]

What finally broke the hold of the segregationists on American life and government was the willingness of these courageous citizens, and many others like them, to stand up for the highest and noblest traditions of this nation. Many suffered mightily for their courageous actions, but they undermined and ultimately destroyed the seemingly impregnable world of Jim Crow.

———

A defining characteristic of the segregationist South was an intolerance of any dissent. Judge Waring described the South of that era as akin to living behind the Iron Curtain. Segregationists believed that any crack in white solidarity constituted an existential threat to white supremacy. Retaliation for any dissent was usually swift and decisive, sending a clear message to others of the consequences of any defiance of the racial status quo. A white minister who preached respect for the rule of law or equal justice to his congregation might find himself packing before the next Sunday's sermon. A newspaper editor who urged his readers to consider a more just and inclusive future for the South could expect cancelations of subscriptions and threats of an advertising boycott. A college professor who proposed open discussion of current racial practices faced the prospect of being told it was time for him to move on. Any outspoken southern-based white civil rights activist could expect allegations of disloyalty or other forms of official and unofficial harassment.

Judge Waring was the nightmare opponent of the segregationists. He had a lifetime appointment as a federal judge, making him immune from economic retaliation. Although there were definite efforts to physically intimidate him, the effectiveness of these methods of coercion and fear was lessened by the presence of U.S. marshals guarding the judge twenty-four hours a day. Even with the protections afforded by his position and prominence, Waring lived with the realization that he was an inviting target for assassination. Frequent death threats, both written and communicated by harassing telephone calls, reminded him of that. Waring wrote the Fourth Circuit's chief judge, John J. Parker, the morning after the 1948 Democratic primary that "the primary election went off smoothly yesterday and they didn't shoot me." He mentioned in a speech to out-of-state lawyers in February 1949 that "you see here someone who has not been lynched—yet. Why it has not happened I do not know." While there was always an element of jest in these comments, Waring accepted the fact that he might one day give his life for upholding the rule of law.[6]

This intolerance of dissent was extremely effective, keeping generations of fair-minded white southerners from challenging the racial orthodoxies of the day. Despite these efforts to suppress dissent, however, Judge Waring received numerous private letters from white southerners who praised his decisions and courage (while making it clear that they could not publicly voice their views). Waring always believed there was a great silent South out there, and the loudest voices were not the South's best voices on race and justice.

———

It was argued by many Truman opponents in the South that his advocacy of civil rights was nothing but a cynical appeal to black voters. Political considerations undoubtedly played a role in his civil rights efforts. But Truman could have embraced issues less controversial than desegregating the armed forces and likely still received strong black support. Harry Truman wanted to make a difference, and he had the authority as commander in chief to end segregation in the military, then arguably the most revered American institution. In the face of reasonable political advice to the contrary, he told a largely unsympathetic nation that a decent, God-fearing people did not deny their fellow citizens the right to vote and to enjoy equal opportunity and equal justice. As a result of his resolve to end segregation in the armed forces, against the vigorous opposition of the army brass, Truman helped create the first genuinely multiracial institution in America, a model that would mark the beginning of the end of Jim Crow.

Truman's responsiveness to African American calls for assistance and justice was not evidence of an illicit motive or improper purpose. The genius of democracy is that elected officials are held accountable at the ballot box. Black voters in the North and the Midwest were not voiceless, because they were not disenfranchised. Truman heard their pleas for help and knew that black voters could reward or punish him based on his response. This was the normal work of a functioning democracy. What was broken was the southern political system, which rendered disenfranchised black citizens politically impotent.

———

Without question, Waties Waring exerted considerable effort to place a case challenging the viability of the *Plessy* doctrine on the docket of the U.S. Supreme Court. He persuaded Thurgood Marshall to dismiss his unequal facilities case in *Briggs v. Elliott* and refile it as the first frontal challenge to public school segregation in American history. Waring then facilitated the appointment of a three-judge panel and issued a brilliant dissent that articulated a simple per se rule for equal protection analysis that became the Supreme Court's unanimous holding in *Brown v. Board of Education*.

A natural question raised by these events is whether Waring should have been disqualified to sit on the *Briggs* three-judge panel. A little historical perspective is necessary. In late 1949, when Waring was first developing his plan to attack the *Plessy* doctrine, judicial standards of conduct were far different in practice from what they are today. A good example of this occurred in the criminal prosecution of Lynwood Shull, when the U.S. attorney Claud Sapp met privately with Judge Waring in an effort to persuade the judge to continue the case. No such ex parte communication between a litigant and a judge would be tolerated today. At the

Supreme Court level, it was not uncommon for a justice to play poker with the president when important matters involving executive power were pending before the Court. Notably, no one moved to disqualify Chief Justice Fred Vinson from participating in the critical racially restrictive covenants case, *Shelley v. Kraemer*, which was pending before the Supreme Court when Vinson sat on the rostrum at the NAACP's annual meeting in June 1947 during President Truman's historic civil rights speech. A year later, Chief Justice Vinson authored the Supreme Court's landmark decision in *Shelley*. During the Supreme Court's deliberations in *Brown v. Board of Education*, Justice Frankfurter regularly communicated with his former law clerk Philip Elman concerning drafts of the Court's decision, even though Elman had authored and signed the solicitor general's amicus brief urging the justices to overrule *Plessy*. Elman would later defend these ex parte contacts with Justice Felix Frankfurter by explaining that *Brown* "transcended ordinary notions about propriety in litigation" and "went to the heart of what kind of country we are."[7]

Under today's standards of judicial ethics, a strong argument could be made that none of the members of the *Briggs* panel, including Judge Waring, would be qualified to sit. Judge Timmerman was an outspoken segregationist, and his son was the sitting lieutenant governor of South Carolina and aspired to seek the office of governor on a segregationist platform. Judge Parker made statements as a political candidate years before on matters of segregation and voting rights that had led the U.S. Senate to reject his nomination to the Supreme Court. Indeed, a careful assessment of the racial views of all of the sitting federal judges in the South in 1951 would have likely revealed disqualifying bias related to support for racial segregation if present-day standards of judicial ethics were applied.

Further, the issue of Waring's personal bias was thoroughly addressed in the Fourth Circuit's decision in *Brown v. Baskin*. The defendants submitted news reports of public statements by Waring in a speech delivered in New York City that were highly critical of southern racial practices and included additional statements he made in open court that reflected strong negative feelings against the South Carolina Democratic Party's effort to preserve the white primary. The Fourth Circuit rejected the bias argument, finding that the evidence reflected, "at most, zeal for upholding the rights of Negroes under the Constitution and indignation that attempt should be made to deny them their rights." The Court went on to state that "a judge cannot be disqualified merely because he believes in upholding the law." In light of this strong defense of Waring by the Fourth Circuit, it is hardly surprising that the defendants in *Briggs* did not seek to disqualify him from sitting on the panel. In hindsight, a persuasive argument can be made that the judge's public comments and those of his wife were ill-advised. But reviewing the entire story of Waties Waring's determination to uphold the American Constitution and the rule of law, one might say, using a baseball metaphor, that although he did not throw a perfect game, he pitched a winning masterpiece.[8]

———

While the Supreme Court in *Brown v. Board of Education* embraced Waring's equal protection standard that all government-mandated segregation was per se unconstitutional, it did not adopt his dissent's approach regarding remedy. Waring, who had tamed strong public resistance to his white primary decision by drawing a clear line and announcing that anyone who crossed it would face incarceration, stated in his *Briggs* dissent that "segregation . . . must go and must go now." He envisioned a prompt implementation of a school desegregation order, before popular resistance could form. Waring believed that a firm ruling by the federal court, immediately implemented, would result in compliance by the public, because "when people are told to conform and they realize that the people who tell them mean business, they'll conform." The Supreme Court, however, took a different approach, directing the lower courts in a second decision in 1955, known as *Brown II*, to implement desegregation orders "with all deliberate speed."

Waring commented to a historian in 1957 that the Supreme Court's "all deliberate speed" decision was a mistake because this "gave an opportunity to gather together a group of people to pass these so called interposition resolutions and to get up their manifestos, and do things of those kind." In fact, it would take another nearly fifteen years for courts to finally fully implement school desegregation orders across the South. In a 2011 conference, Professor Charles Ogletree of Harvard Law School argued that Waring's great dissent in *Briggs* provided the clearest and most effective approach for remedy. Ogletree lamented the years lost and the protracted legal battles that resulted from the Supreme Court's failure to follow Waring's lead by ordering a full and immediate remedy.[9]

———

At the height of Isaac Woodard's notoriety, when he was among the most recognizable names within the black community in America, an NAACP staff member astutely observed that "right now he is riding the crest of a wave of popularity but ten years from now no one will remember Woodard." Following Shull's acquittal, Woodard was again briefly in the news when, with the assistance of the NAACP, he filed a $50,000 civil suit against the Atlantic Greyhound Corporation. He alleged in the suit that the bus company had improperly removed him from the bus in Batesburg, South Carolina, and was thus responsible for his beating and blinding. The suit was brought in state court in Charleston, West Virginia, Greyhound's principal place of business.[10]

The civil case certainly had its challenges. Suing a major company in its hometown is never easy, and Greyhound had a strong argument that Lynwood Shull, not its bus driver, was responsible for the brutal assault on Woodard. The more logical suit, a direct action against Shull for the use of excessive force, was not a realistic option for Woodard at the time. Moreover, West Virginia had a reputation as a more open and tolerant racial environment than the Deep South, and the state had a respectable level of black voter registration and black jury service.

Woodard was represented by the NAACP's local counsel, Gillis Nutter, a skilled litigator who had served two terms in the West Virginia Legislature, from 1918 to 1922, as a Republican. In agreeing to assume responsibility for the civil case, Nutter was under no illusions about his chances for success. He felt it was important, however, to undertake the lawsuit, because "it would be nothing less than a crime if Isaac Woodard is denied his day in court for the want of a fair forum." Greyhound took the case seriously, sending lawyers as far as the Philippines to take the deposition of two passengers on the bus. The NAACP also expended considerable time and resources supporting the suit. The case was tried over two days in November 1947. The jury of eleven white men and one black man, after deliberating for four hours, returned a verdict for Greyhound. No appeal was taken from the lower court decision.[11]

After the civil trial, Isaac Woodard faded into obscurity. He initially struggled to support himself financially, receiving only a partial disability payment because his blindness was classified as non-service-related. In 1952, he wrote a desperate letter to his VA counselor, stating, "I am in great need for financial aid." He explained that he was living on a pension of $60 per month and "it is not enough to feed a man and [clothe] him." He noted that his means were so limited that "here is winter and I don't own an overcoat." Soon thereafter, his VA benefits more than doubled, to $135 per month, equivalent to approximately $14,000 per year today.[12]

Woodard's home, purchased with proceeds from the *Amsterdam News* benefit concert, was taken by eminent domain by the New York Housing Authority to build a housing project. Woodard then moved into public housing. He took the proceeds from the sale of his home to purchase a commercial building in the Bronx that had multiple tenants, including a funeral home, a small factory, and several apartments. With the assistance of family members, he collected rent from his tenants and began to earn a more livable wage. For a while, he operated a newsstand at Thirtieth Street and Seventh Avenue in Manhattan, but the harsh New York winters and the long commute from his home in the Bronx eventually forced him to give that up. In addition to his parents, the Isaac Woodard household included a son, Isaac III, born from a relationship with a partner, Mildred Lovejoy, and an adopted son, George.[13]

In 1956, ten years after his blinding, *Jet* magazine published an article titled "Isaac Woodard: America's Forgotten Man," which described Woodard's quiet life in his Bronx neighborhood, where he greeted housewives, children, and local merchants as he took a daily stroll down his street. Woodard was pictured caring for his toddler son and elderly parents. It was noted that his neighbors were unaware of his former notoriety, making the point that the nation had long ago moved past the tragic story of this blinded veteran. Woodard was upbeat, stating, "I make out all right, but I just can't see."[14]

His VA benefits substantially increased in the early 1960s, when Congress passed legislation awarding full disability benefits to any serviceman injured between the time of his discharge and his arrival home, equivalent in today's dollars to over $45,000 per year. As his parents aged, Woodard relied on a nephew, Robert Young, a New York City transit employee, to assist him in his trips to the bank, physician appointments, and meetings with the VA and other governmental agencies. Young remembered his uncle as a contented and religious man who enjoyed listening to Sunday-morning church services on his radio. Family members jokingly referred to Woodard as an "arm chair Christian."[15]

Woodard was evaluated by a VA social worker in April 1964, when he was forty-five years old. The social worker documented his capable management of his household, which then included his eighty-year-old father with cancer, his sixty-nine-year-old mother with varicose veins, and two minor children. The family lived together in a five-room third-floor walk-up apartment in the Bronx. The social worker noted that Woodard drew great satisfaction from caring for his extended family, who depended on him, and observed that he "seemed shrewd in many respects." The social worker questioned Woodard about the circumstances of his blindness and found that he still had "intense emotional reaction" to those events.[16]

Woodard utilized a VA loan program in 1978 to purchase a home, a two-story semi-attached residence with three bedrooms at 3728 Dyre Avenue in the Bronx. He resided in the home with his two sons. In the late 1980s, he began to experience a variety of health problems, the most serious being prostate cancer. He died at age seventy-three on September 23, 1992, and was buried at Calverton National Cemetery in Calverton, New York.[17]

Woodard shared with his family members the story of his blinding and his brief moment in the national limelight. His adopted son, George, made efforts to promote his father's story, sharing the details with a teacher at a school where he worked as a custodian. The teacher, Christopher Roberts, was so moved that he wrote a play inspired by the Woodard story, titled *Reflections of a Heart*, which had a limited run in a community theater in New York in 2010. By all accounts, Isaac Woodard was never aware of the impact of his blinding on President Truman or Judge Waring. Ironically, the story of Walter White's sharing the details of the Woodard incident with President Truman was included in Poppy Cannon White's 1956 biography of her husband and in a 1965 column she authored for the *Amsterdam News*. In a world before Google and the Internet, the word simply never got to Isaac Woodard.[18]

Lynwood Shull left his position as police chief of Batesburg, South Carolina, in 1952 and thereafter served in various appointed and elected positions in Lexington County, South Carolina. His criminal prosecution and role in the blinding of Isaac Woodard were not referenced in subsequent news reports regarding his public service. Shull died in December 1997 at age ninety-two and was remembered as a kindly and faithful elderly usher at the local Methodist church. Until recently, few Batesburg residents were aware of Woodard's blinding or of Shull's prosecution in federal district court.[19]

Franklin Williams, the NAACP attorney at Woodard's side during the Shull criminal trial, moved in 1950 to Los Angeles to head the association's West Coast operations. He emerged as an important civil rights and political leader in California and was appointed to a number of positions in the Kennedy and Johnson administrations, including three years as ambassador to Ghana. He later taught at Columbia University and served as president of the Phelps-Stokes Fund, a philanthropic organization devoted to improving educational opportunities for minorities. He died in 1990 at age seventy-two.[20]

Claud Sapp, the U.S. attorney for South Carolina, who participated in the prosecution of Shull in November 1946, died months after the trial, in February 1947, at age sixty. His co-counsel, Fred S. Rogers, continued to work at the Department of Justice until he was appointed a few years later to the U.S. Parole Commission. In 1953, Rogers returned to his native Texas, where he practiced law until his death in 1968.[21]

Orson Welles, whose promotion of the Woodard story on ABC Radio brought the incident to national prominence, lost the Lear Corporation's sponsorship of his radio program shortly thereafter, reportedly because of the controversy surrounding the Woodard segments. He never returned to radio but continued to work in Europe and the United States as a director and actor. Welles made references to the Woodard story in his later work, discussing it in a May 1955 BBC television program titled *Orson Welles' Sketch Book* and by infusing his experiences with the Woodard story into his classic 1958 movie *Touch of Evil*. Welles died in October 1985 at age seventy.[22]

———

George Elmore, the plaintiff in the South Carolina white primary case, faced severe retaliation for his participation in the litigation. Wholesalers refused to stock his Columbia, South Carolina–based grocery and liquor stores, which led to the closing of his businesses and the loss of his home. His wife had a nervous breakdown associated with the stress of the family's business reverses, and his children were sent north to live with an aunt. Elmore died penniless on February 25, 1959, at age fifty-three. A historic marker was placed at the former site of Elmore's grocery store, the Waverly Five and Dime, in 2012 by the Historic Columbia Foundation and the City of Columbia, noting his courageous role in *Elmore v. Rice*.[23]

———

The plaintiffs in *Briggs* mostly left Summerton, South Carolina, after their Supreme Court victory, driven away by local hostility and the lack of economic opportunity. Harry and Eliza Briggs moved to New York and raised three children in the Bronx. The Reverend Joseph A. DeLaine fled South Carolina after dubious criminal charges were brought against him when he returned fire against unknown men attacking his home. He pastored for years at an AME church in Buffalo, New York. Judge Waring developed a personal relationship with DeLaine shortly before his retirement from the bench, and they stayed in contact after both moved to New York. Waring assisted DeLaine's wife in finding employment in New York and in arranging a full academic scholarship for their son, Joseph DeLaine, to attend Lincoln University. DeLaine's Buffalo church was later renamed the DeLaine Waring African Methodist Episcopal Church. The church remains active today. Joseph A. DeLaine longed to return to his native South Carolina after he retired but feared he would face criminal prosecution for the decades-old arrest warrant. He moved instead to Charlotte, North Carolina, where he died in 1974 at age seventy-six.

DeLaine's reputation as one of the heroes of the civil rights movement began to emerge with Richard Kluger's 1975 classic history, *Simple Justice*, which opened with an extraordinary telling of the abuses and injustices inflicted on him because he was "black and brave." In September 2004, DeLaine was posthumously awarded the Congressional Gold Medal in a ceremony in the Capitol Rotunda attended by his family members. Harry and Eliza Briggs and Levi Pearson were honored posthumously in the same ceremony.[24]

Walter White suffered from chronic heart failure in the later portion of his life and died on March 21, 1955, less than one year after the NAACP's triumphant win in *Brown v. Board of Education*. During much of his adult life, White was the preeminent civil rights leader in America and had personal access to and influence with President Truman that was unparalleled in that era. His historic stature has faded over the years, but the Woodard story makes clear that in his day Walter White was an effective and influential voice for racial justice.

Poppy Cannon White survived her husband and was a devoted proponent of his historic legacy, authoring a biography, *A Gentle Knight*, a year after his death and writing a regular column for the *Amsterdam News*, which frequently recounted her husband's contributions to the civil rights movement. She also remained an intimate friend of the Warings' and became, as their health faded, a caregiver for both of them. She also featured periodic tributes to the Warings in her columns, extolling their courage and contributions in the face of intense opposition in Charleston. Poppy Cannon White died in New York City on April 1, 1975.[25]

The *Briggs* legal team went on to storied careers. In October 1961, on the nomination of President Kennedy, Thurgood Marshall was appointed to the Second Circuit Court of Appeals, where he served until he was appointed solicitor general of the United States in August 1965. In October 1967, on the nomination of President Johnson, Marshall became the first African American to serve on the U.S. Supreme Court. He retired from the Court in October 1991 and died at age eighty-four on January 24, 1993.[26]

Robert Carter, Marshall's co-counsel in *Briggs*, was appointed a U.S. district judge for the Southern District of New York in July 1972 on the nomination of President Nixon and served as an active judge until December 1986. He continued as a senior judge until his death at age ninety-four in January 2012.[27] The NAACP's local counsel Harold Boulware was appointed the first African American family court judge in South Carolina in 1974 and served until his retirement in 1982. He died on January 27, 1983, at age sixty-nine.[28]

Dr. Kenneth Clark continued his pioneering work in child psychology as a professor at the City College of New York and the Northside Center for Child Development in Harlem. He was the first African American president of the American Psychological Association and became one of America's preeminent social science researchers. Clark and Waring developed a close personal relationship after the Warings relocated to New York, with the judge frequently reading Clark's publications in draft for editorial comment. Clark published a tribute to Waring after his death, titled "Reflections on the Loss of a Friend," in which he stated that Waring "demonstrated that life could not be lived without courage . . . He lived what he believed. He risked, and therefore, lived." Clark died on May 1, 2005, at age ninety.[29]

Gunnar Myrdal continued his renowned scholarship on race and economics and was active in early United Nations work promoting economic justice and racial equality on the world stage. The U.S. Supreme Court cited his pioneering work, *An American Dilemma*, in its famous footnote 11 in *Brown v. Board of Education*. In 1974, Myrdal was awarded the Nobel Prize in Economics, and his wife and academic partner, Alva Myrdal, was awarded the Nobel Peace Prize in 1982. He died on May 17, 1987, at age eighty-eight.[30]

Robert Figg, lead counsel for the defendants in *Briggs*, was appointed dean of the University of South Carolina School of Law in 1959, a position he held until his retirement in 1970. He died in 1991. Figg's co-counsel, Joseph Rogers, continued to practice law in Clarendon County until he was appointed U.S. attorney for the District of South Carolina in August 1969. He was thereafter nominated by President Nixon to the U.S. district court. His nomination was vigorously opposed by the NAACP because of his role in the *Briggs* case. Rogers's judgeship nomination stalled, and he resigned his U.S. attorney position in protest, returning to his hometown of Manning, South Carolina, to practice law. He died in April 1999 at age seventy-seven.[31]

John J. Parker served in his position as chief judge of the Fourth Circuit Court of Appeals until March 17, 1958, when he died in office at age seventy-two after more than three decades on the court. George Bell Timmerman Sr. continued his active service on the district court until 1962 and assumed senior judge status until his death on April 22, 1966. He remained a vocal opponent of civil rights litigation. In one long-running case, *Sarah Mae Flemming v. South Carolina Electric and Gas*, the Fourth Circuit twice reversed his dismissal of the suit. Timmerman informed the jury in the third proceeding before him that he did not agree with the civil rights decisions of the Fourth Circuit and the U.S. Supreme Court. He also reportedly played an active role in the dismissal of his minister at the First Baptist Church of Batesburg after the minister privately expressed support for racial integration. Judge Timmerman's son, George Bell Timmerman Jr., was elected governor of South Carolina in 1954 and was the state's last segregationist governor.[32]

Mendel Rivers continued to represent Charlestonians in Congress until his death on December 28, 1970, at age sixty-five, after nearly thirty years in office. He became chairman of the House Armed Services Committee in 1965 and was, at the time of his death, one of the most powerful members of the House. After Judge Waring's retirement in 1952, Rivers actively campaigned for appointment as Waring's successor. The NAACP vigorously opposed his appointment to the federal bench, with Walter White personally communicating with President Truman on the subject. By all accounts, the Rivers nomination was never seriously considered by Truman.[33]

Aubrey Williams, Clifford Durr, and James Dombrowski continued their passionate advocacy for civil rights. All came under vigorous attack by segregationists after the Supreme Court's decision in *Brown v. Board of Education*, with claims that they were communist sympathizers. Mississippi's senator James Eastland scheduled Senate hearings in New Orleans in 1954 and subpoenaed Clifford and Virginia Durr and Aubrey Williams to testify. Senator Lyndon Johnson, a longtime friend of the Durrs and Williams and then the minority leader in the Senate, let his colleagues know that he took Eastland's attacks personally. No other senator dared to appear at the New Orleans hearing, and Eastland's campaign against the Durrs and Williams soon abated. Dombrowski found himself repeatedly under investigation and threatened with prosecution by state officials in Louisiana, who raided and seized the records of his New Orleans–based organization, the Southern Conference Educational Fund. When state officials would not return his papers, he sued them in federal court. The U.S. Supreme Court, in *Dombrowski v. Pfister* (1965), reversed a lower court's dismissal of Dombrowski's suit, finding ample support for his allegations that state officials were harassing him for his advocacy of civil rights. The Supreme Court directed the lower court to issue an injunction to protect Dombrowski's right to freedom of speech and expression if the evidence showed his allegations were true.[34]

———

Harry Truman left the presidency in January 1953 and returned to his home in Independence, Missouri. He left office with low public approval, mostly due to the quagmire of the Korean War. Truman damaged his reputation as an advocate for civil rights during the early 1960s when he claimed the civil rights movement was under communist influence. He also angered national Democrats in 1960 when he was slow to endorse the party's nominee, John F. Kennedy. Some suggested that perhaps the former president was showing his age. Truman's standing began to improve during the Johnson administration, when LBJ, a great admirer of Truman's, publicly praised his role as an early advocate for federal health programs for the elderly. Johnson traveled to Independence on July 30, 1965, to sign the Medicare bill into law and to provide Harry and Bess Truman with the first two Medicare cards. Truman died on December 26, 1972, at age eighty-eight. In recent years, there has been a reconsideration of his civil rights record, recognizing his critical role in integrating the armed forces and his advocacy of the ambitious agenda of his civil rights committee.[35]

———

Waties Waring lived out his life in New York City and never lost his passion for civil rights. On February 10, 1957, Waring, then seventy-six years old, was on a national public television show with a young African American minister fifty years his junior, Martin Luther King, who had just successfully completed a bus boycott in Montgomery, Alabama. King was clearly an admirer of Waring's, and the judge praised King's tactics and passion. A few years later, King paid public tribute to Waring at an event in New York, noting that "the name of Judge Waring and his wife will long be remembered, for his minority opinion has now become a majority opinion. And I guess when he cast the dissenting vote in [that] decision

some years ago, there were those who said he was an impractical idealist."
King went on to say that "history has proven that the impractical idealists
of yesterday become the practical realists of today, and we are all indebted
to him for what he has done in this nation."[36]

Waring was always philosophical about what he called the "unpleasant repercussions" of his civil rights decisions and his exile to New York
after his retirement. In an oral history interview late in life, he observed
that "taking the whole thing in balance, I think I'm enormously fortunate,
because you don't often in life have an opportunity to do something that
you really think is good . . . I think a great stroke of fortune came down
my alley . . . The other penalties don't amount to anything. They're off-
set by what I think is really an important contribution to the history of
our country."[37]

Waring returned to Charleston only once before his death, when he
was honored by the South Carolina NAACP in November 1954 for his
contributions to *Brown v. Board of Education*. Local and national civil
rights figures attended the dinner. Waring stayed at the home of the
Cornwells during his Charleston visit, refusing to patronize a segregated
hotel. He spent most of his last years caring for his bedridden wife in their
apartment in New York.

Judge Waring died at age eighty-seven on January 11, 1968. He was
buried in Magnolia Cemetery in Charleston after a funeral that was attended primarily by members of Charleston's African American community. Elizabeth died later that same year and was buried next to her
husband in Charleston. The Warings' grave site is set off to the side, away
from family and former friends.[38]

Waties Waring was a largely forgotten figure in his native city when
the South Carolina Supreme Court Historical Society sponsored a widely
attended two-day conference in 2011 titled "J. Waties Waring and the
Dissent That Changed America." Local members of the Charleston Bar
thereafter established a committee to honor Waring and to erect a life-
size statue on the federal courthouse grounds. The Waring statue committee found widespread support in the bar and the community for its

effort, and the Post and Courier Foundation was a major contributor, fulfilling the prediction of Charleston's NAACP president, A. J. Clement, in 1951 that one day "the South will raise a monument to you." U.S. Attorney General Eric Holder was the keynote speaker at the 2014 statue dedication ceremony. Holder stated that he was born in the year of Waring's great dissent, 1951, and owed many of the opportunities he had enjoyed to the courage and vision of Waties Waring. Charleston's longtime mayor, Joseph Riley, declared that the Waring statue symbolized the fact that the great judge had now finally come home.[39]

A year later, the retired senator Ernest F. "Fritz" Hollings, for whom the Charleston Federal Courthouse had been named, made the unprecedented request that his name be removed from the courthouse and that it be renamed for Judge Waring. As Hollings explained it, he had simply gotten the money for the courthouse, but Judge Waring "made history in it." The South Carolina congressional delegation honored Hollings's request, and the U.S. House and Senate unanimously adopted legislation renaming the courthouse. President Obama signed the bill into law on August 7, 2015, and the courthouse was formally rededicated as the J. Waties Waring Judicial Center on October 2, 2015.[40]

Recently I visited the town of Batesburg-Leesville and retraced the fateful path of Isaac Woodard, from the bus stop where he was removed from the Greyhound bus and arrested, to the storefront around the corner where he was beaten and blinded, and then to the location up the street where the town jail and court once stood. Joining me on this solemn walk was the town mayor, Lancer Shull (no relation to Police Chief Lynwood Shull), and the town attorney, Christian G. Spradley, both of whom had only recently learned of the Woodard incident. On June 1, 2018, Spradley, acting on behalf of the town, filed a motion in town court to reopen the case of Isaac Woodard and to overturn the sergeant's criminal conviction. The motion was granted, expunging Woodard's conviction and bringing a final closure to the tragic events of February 12, 1946.

APPENDIX:
A FORENSIC ANALYSIS
OF THE BLINDING OF
ISAAC WOODARD

The historical record regarding the cause of Isaac Woodard's blinding is conflicted. Woodard asserted that his blinding followed a severe beating he received from Lynwood Shull with the officer's blackjack, culminating in Shull's jamming the end of the blackjack into each of his eyes. Shull maintained that he struck Woodard only once in the head with his blackjack and this was done only in self-defense.

As a former litigator and trial judge, I was aware that law enforcement, the military, and trial attorneys frequently call upon forensic pathologists to analyze physical evidence to reconstruct how a particular injury occurred. I wondered whether forensic science might assist in better understanding the nature and cause of Woodard's injuries.

I had the good fortune that my dear friend and colleague U.S. district judge David Norton is married to Dr. Kim Collins, an internationally renowned forensic pathologist and the 2018–2019 president of the National Association of Medical Examiners. I asked Collins to review the available medical evidence to see if she could offer any opinions and insights into the nature and manner of Woodard's injuries. She agreed to help and asked that I do my best to gather all available medical records from the 1946 incident.

I began my search for Woodard's medical records by communicating with Robert Young Sr., Woodard's nephew and caregiver in the final years of his life. As Woodard's closest living relative, he had the authority to sign release forms authorizing my access to his late uncle's medical records. Young was a supportive and invaluable ally in my work and agreed to sign any necessary forms. Because Woodard obtained his initial medical treatment following his injuries at the VA Hospital in Columbia, I first focused on the Veterans Administration as a potential source for contemporaneous medical records.

As any veteran relying on VA medical care can attest, locating medical records in the VA system can often be quite challenging. Aware that a routine application for Woodard's medical records would likely be unproductive, I requested the assistance of the then U.S. attorney for the District of South Carolina, William Nettles, to determine whether Woodard's medical records from his 1946 hospitalization could be located. Nettles had recently heard a talk I had given to a national meeting of U.S. attorneys on Woodard's blinding and was enthusiastic about joining the hunt for his medical records.

At Nettles's request, the Department of Veterans Affairs Office of General Counsel undertook a diligent and thorough search of all available records. I was soon advised that there was bad news and good news. The bad news was that the full VA Hospital record from Woodard's 1946 admission had long ago been destroyed under the agency's normal records retention policy. However, Woodard's regular VA file, which included information related to his application for disability benefits, was still in existence and contained a number of relevant records from his 1946 hospital admission. These records included his "Final Hospital Report," of April 17, and the "Final Progress Note" of his treating physician, Arthur Clancy, of April 11. These reports detailed the diagnostic findings of plain film X-rays of the skull performed on February 15 and March 15, 1946.[1]

I was also able to locate in the files of the NAACP, now preserved at the Library of Congress, a May 7, 1946, medical report of an ophthalmologist from New York, Chester Chinn, who performed a comprehensive eye examination of Woodard. Chinn was the first eye specialist to evaluate Woodard and diagnosed ruptures to the globes of both of his eyes. Further, from the FBI's investigative files at the National Archives, I found detailed interviews with two of Woodard's treating physicians who performed the initial evaluations on his arrival at the VA Hospital in Columbia. I provided these various medical records, as well as sworn statements and FBI witness interviews of Woodard and Shull describing the circumstances of the evening of February 12, 1946, to Collins. I also provided her with two blackjacks that fit the general description of the device used by Shull on the night of his encounter with Woodard.[2]

Collins provided me with a formal expert report dated August 20, 2015. She first explained the physiology of the eyes. She stated that the eyes are located within an elaborate set of structures that protect their globes. These include "a pear shaped bony cavity," which involves the orbits of the eyes and adjacent bony structures. Collins stated that "the globe does not protrude from this bony cavity but sits slightly posterior" within it. In addition to this bony protective cavity, Collins explained, the eyelids, the cornea, surrounding fat, the cheekbones, and the nasal bones protect the globes.

Because of these structural protections for the eyes, Collins stated, "it is unusual for the globe to be damaged by trauma except by sharp force, penetrating injuries or direct blunt force trauma." A sharp force or penetrating injury that ruptures the globe would bypass the bony protections of the eye and would necessarily involve an object smaller than the bony orbit. Because the average adult bony orbit is 4 cm long and 3.5 cm wide, the penetrating object would need to be smaller than those dimensions to avoid the bony protections of the eyes.

The other method by which a globe of the eye can be ruptured is by blunt force trauma that would necessarily involve "significant force to the eye." Before rupturing the globe, the implement of blunt force trauma would need to strike and fracture the bony orbits of the eye. If a single blunt force trauma ruptured the globes in both eyes, it would, in addition to fracturing the orbits, fracture the nasal bones. Thus, Collins explained, the presence or absence of fractures to the orbits and nasal bones would enable her to rule in or out a single blunt force trauma, such as a blackjack strike to the face, as the cause of Woodard's bilateral blindness.

After explaining the types of trauma that can cause the rupture of one or both globes of the eyes, Collins turned to the available medical evidence. The "Final Hospital Report" and "Final Progress Note" both confirmed that the plain film X-rays of the skull taken in February and March 1946 demonstrated no fractures of the skull or facial bones. This same finding was reported by one of the VA treating physicians, Mortimer Burger, to the investigating FBI agents.

Because of the absence of fractures to the facial bones, Collins stated that she could rule out a single broadly inflicted blunt force trauma as the cause of the bilateral rupture of Woodard's globes. After ruling out blunt force trauma, Collins concluded that Woodard's blindness was the result of at least two separate penetrating injuries, one to each eye, from an object no larger than 4 cm long and 3.5 cm wide. She measured the size of the handles of the exemplar blackjacks and determined that they were small enough to penetrate the eyes without fracturing the protective orbits.

Based upon the available evidence, Collins concluded that a single defensive strike allegedly made by Shull could not have and did not cause the rupture of the globes of either of Woodard's eyes. She further concluded that Woodard's claim that Shull drove the end of a blackjack into each of his eyes is consistent with the available medical evidence and is the most probable cause of the rupture of the globes of both eyes and his resulting blindness. In sum, Collins concluded to a reasonable degree of medical certainty that Woodard's account of the mechanism of his eye injuries and blindness was true and Shull's account was not.[3]

NOTES

INTRODUCTION: A COLLISION OF TWO WORLDS

1. Gunnar Myrdal, *An American Dilemma: The Negro Problem and Modern Democracy* (Harper & Brothers, 1944), xix, xlvii.

2. Julian Bond had me promise him an early copy of my book, a commitment I was regretfully unable to keep because of his death on August 15, 2015.

1. A TRAGIC DETOUR

1. President's Press Conference, Aug. 14, 1945, Truman Library; David McCullough, *Truman* (Simon & Schuster, 2009), 461–63.

2. C. Vann Woodward, *The Strange Career of Jim Crow* (Oxford University Press, 1955); Stephen Kantrowitz, *Ben Tillman and the Reconstruction of White Supremacy* (University of North Carolina Press, 2000); *Plessy v. Ferguson*, 163 U.S. 537 (1896); *Williams v. Mississippi*, 170 U.S. 213 (1898). "Grandfather clauses" provided that no citizen could vote unless his grandfather was a registered voter, which eliminated most African Americans because their grandfathers had been enslaved.

"Understanding clauses" allowed voter registrars to administer tests of knowledge before a citizen would be allowed to vote. These tests were often used abusively to prevent even well-educated African Americans from registering. All-white primaries were utilized by the Democratic Party in the southern states and were justified on the basis that a political party was a private club and could establish rules for its membership. Because the Democratic primary was the only election that mattered in the South, a denial of the right to vote in the primary effectively disenfranchised the few African Americans able to register to vote.

3. Carol Anderson, "Clutching at Civil Rights Straws: A Reappraisal of the Truman Years and the Struggle for African American Leadership," in *The Civil Rights Legacy of Harry S. Truman*, ed. Raymond H. Geselbracht (Truman State University Press, 2007), 31–33; Rawn James Jr., *The Double V: How Wars, Protest, and Harry Truman Desegregated America's Military* (Bloomsbury Press, 2013), 141–43; Patricia Sullivan, *Lift Every Voice: The NAACP and the Making of the Civil Rights Movement* (New Press, 2009), 287–88; John Egerton, *Speak Now Against the Day: The Generation Before the Civil Rights Movement in the South* (New Press, 2009), 352–58. See generally *To Secure These Rights: The Report of the Presidential Committee on Civil Rights* (Government Printing Office, 1947); Myrdal, *American Dilemma*.

4. *Durham Sun*, July 11, 1946; *Chicago Defender*, Oct. 14, 1944; "Jim Crow, Meet Lieutenant Robinson: A 1944 Court-Martial," *Prologue* 40, no. 1 (Spring 2008); Andrew Myers, *Black, White, and Olive Drab: Racial Integration at Fort Jackson, South Carolina, and the Civil Rights Movement* (University of Virginia Press, 2006), 58–59; Andrew Myers, "The Blinding of Isaac Woodard," *Proceedings of the South Carolina Historical Association* (2004): 63–73; Andrew Myers, "Resonant Ripples in a Global Pond: The Blinding of Isaac Woodard," faculty.uscupstate.edu/amyers/conference .html. Professor Myers deserves commendation not just for his first-rate scholarship but also for his posting of important original documents on the aforementioned website.

5. VA Social Survey, Isaac Woodard Jr., April 1, 1964, and Woodard Separation Qualification Record, Isaac Woodard Veteran Administration Records (hereafter cited as VA Records), in possession of author; *Amsterdam News*, Aug. 3 and 17, 1946; Robert Young, interview by author; Christopher Roberts, interview by author.

6. Woodard VA Separation Qualification and Honorable Discharge Record, Woodard VA Records; *Chicago Defender*, July 27, 1946; Transcript in *Isaac Woodard Jr. v. Atlantic Greyhound Bus Company*, Circuit Court, Kanawha County, W.V., at 47–50 (hereafter cited as Civil Trial Transcript), Isaac Woodard Files, NAACP Papers, Library of Congress (hereafter cited as Woodard Files). The author has been unable, despite considerable efforts, to locate a transcript of the November 1946 criminal trial held in the U.S. District Court in Columbia, South Carolina. The author has access to and has cited notes and reports of observers of the criminal trial, including the NAACP's counsel Franklin Williams, the supervising FBI agent in the case, the Department of Justice special counsel, and various reporters who covered the trial. Subsequent to the criminal trial in South Carolina, the NAACP brought

a civil suit against Greyhound Bus Company in West Virginia, which resulted in a defense verdict. The testimony in both the civil and the criminal trials was substantially the same, and the civil trial transcript has been relied upon to confirm information from other sources.

7. Civil Trial Transcript, 50; Isaac Woodard Jr. Affidavit, April 23, 1946, FBI Field Report, Aug. 5, 1946, and Savannah Supervising Agent in Charge (SAC) to J. Edgar Hoover, FBI memorandum, Nov. 13, 1946, FBI Field Investigation File, *United States v. Lynwood Shull*, Civil Rights Division, Class 44, Litigation Case Files, Case No. 144-67-12, box 1414, 230/22/23/6, National Archives (hereafter cited as FBI Files); *State*, Nov. 6, 1946; *Columbia Record*, Nov. 5, 1946; *Daily Worker*, July 13, 1946; *PM*, July 17, 1946.

8. Alton Blackwell Affidavit, Aug. 1, 1946, FBI Files; Civil Trial Transcript, 160–70; *Columbia Record*, Nov. 5, 1946.

9. Lincoln Miller Affidavit, Aug. 8, 1946, and Jennings Stroud Affidavit, Sept. 25, 1946, FBI Files; McQuilla Hudson Affidavit, and Civil Trial Transcript, 216–26, 343, 364, 388.

10. "The Isaac Woodard Story," n.d., "Batesburg SC Police System," Aug. 22, 1946, and "Memorandum to Orson Welles Program," Sept. 19, 1946, Woodard Files; John McCray Papers, South Caroliniana Library, University of South Carolina; FBI Field Report, Aug. 1946, FBI Files; *Chicago Defender*, Sept. 7, 1946.

11. Jennings Stroud Affidavit, July 26, 1946, Lincoln Miller Affidavit, Aug. 31, 1946, Woodard Affidavit, April 23 and July 29, 1946, FBI Field Report, Aug. 26, 1946, and SAC to Hoover, memorandum, Nov. 13, 1946, FBI Files; *Daily Worker*, July 13, 1946.

12. Lynwood Shull Affidavit, July 30, 1946, FBI Field Report, Aug. 5, 1946, 15–17, and SAC to Hoover, memorandum, Nov. 13, 1946, FBI Files; Civil Trial Transcript, 290–93, 298, 300, 323–34; *State*, Nov. 6, 1946; *Columbia Record*, Nov. 6, 1946.

13. Civil Trial Transcript, 279, 298; Robert M. Stewart (retired South Carolina law-enforcement chief), interview by author; *Kopf v. Skyrm*, 993 F.2d 374, 378 (4th Cir. 1993). Blackjacks are considered such dangerous weapons that South Carolina state law prohibits a civilian to possess one. S.C. Code Section 16-23-430(A).

14. Woodard Affidavit, April 23 and July 29, 1946, FBI Field Report, Aug. 26, 1946, 2–5, and SAC to Hoover, memorandum, Nov. 13, 1946, FBI Files; Civil Trial Transcript, 52; *State*, Nov. 6, 1946; *Columbia Record*, Nov. 6, 1946; House to SAC Brown, memorandum, Sept. 29, 1946, and Steiner to SAC Brown, memorandum, Sept. 28, 1946, FBI Files.

15. *New York Times*, Aug. 17, 1946; Lynwood Shull Affidavit, July 30, 1946, FBI Files; Civil Trial Transcript, 295–97, 323–34.

16. Shull Affidavit, July 30, 1946, FBI Files; Civil Trial Transcript, 299–300.

17. Woodard Affidavit, April 23, 1946, FBI Files; Civil Trial Transcript, 54–55; Batesburg, South Carolina, Town Court Records, Feb. 13, 1946, Batesburg-Leesville Town Hall.

18. Shull Affidavit, July 30, 1946, FBI Files; Civil Trial Transcript, 276–78, 302–305; Woodard Eye Examination Report of Dr. Chester Chinn, May 7, 1946 (hereafter cited as Chinn Report), Woodard Files.

19. Civil Trial Transcript, 56–57, 307–309; FBI Field Report, Aug. 5, 1946, 17–18, FBI Files; *Chicago Defender*, Sept. 7, 1946; Orson Welles Broadcast, "The Place Was Batesburg," www.youtube.com/watch?v=Jg4YbRxZpfl.

20. Civil Trial Transcript, 144; Woodard VA Hospital Discharge Record, April 17, 1946, VA Records; FBI Field Report, Aug. 5, 1946, 7, FBI Files.

21. Woodard Discharge Record, VA Records; Civil Trial Transcript, 108–109; FBI Field Report, July 30, 1946, 8, FBI Files.

22. FBI Field Report, Aug. 5, 1946, 8–9, FBI Files; Woodard Discharge Record, VA Records.

23. Woodard Discharge Record, VA Records; *Daily Worker*, July 13, 1946.

24. The American Legion communicated with the VA on Woodard's behalf on November 18, 1963, concerning his eligibility for full disability benefits because of congressional action in 1961 allowing a soldier's active service status to continue for a discharged soldier until he arrived at home, codified at 38 U.S.C. Section 101(21)(E), Pub. L. No. 87–102. The VA responded four days later, on November 22, granting Woodard full disability benefits retroactively to July 21, 1961, the effective date of the congressional action. Woodard Rating Decision, Nov. 22, 1963, William McDermott (director of the New York Department of the American Legion) to L. M. Hylton (VA adjudication officer), Nov. 18, 1963, VA Records.

25. *New York Post*, July 17, 1946; *Amsterdam News*, Aug. 17, 1946; Robert Young, interview by author.

26. *Amsterdam News*, Aug. 3, 1946; *Chicago Defender*, July 27, 1946.

27. *Amsterdam News*, Aug. 3, 1946; Chinn Report.

2. A WAVE OF TERROR

1. *To Secure These Rights*, 146, 147. See generally Mary L. Dudziak, "Desegregation as a Cold War Imperative," 41 *Stanford Law Review* 61 (Nov. 1988).

2. *Pittsburgh Courier*, Feb. 14, March 7, April 18, 1942; James, *Double V*, 77–79, 141–43.

3. Walter White, *A Man Called White* (Viking Press, 1948), 262–64; Michael R. Gardner, *Harry Truman and Civil Rights* (Southern Illinois University Press, 2002), 12, 58–59; Sullivan, *Lift Every Voice*, 193, 196–97, 204, 226, 229, 255, 311; William E. Leuchtenburg, *The White House Looks South* (Louisiana State University Press, 2005), 70. Civil rights leaders were surprised and impressed by Roosevelt's calling out the U.S. Army in Philadelphia in 1944 to break a transit strike over white worker protests concerning orders of the FEPC to open employment opportunities for black workers.

4. Leuchtenburg, *White House Looks South*, 158.

5. Sullivan, *Lift Every Voice*, 73–75, 196–97; Gardner, *Harry Truman and Civil Rights*, 12; McCullough, *Truman*, 234, 247, 323; *New York Times*, March 22, 1955; Leuchtenburg, *White House Looks South*, 157.

6. Richard M. Yon and Tom Lansford, "Political Pragmatism and Civil Rights Policy: Truman and Integration of the Military," in Geselbracht, *Civil Rights Legacy of Harry Truman*, 108–109; Clark M. Clifford, Oral History Interview, Oct. 4, 1973, 263–69, Harry W. Truman Library.

7. Sullivan, *Lift Every Voice*, 229–34, 249–50; *New York Times*, Jan. 25, 1993; Gilbert King, *Devil in the Grove: Thurgood Marshall, the Groveland Boys, and the Dawn of a New America* (Harper Perennial, 2012), 49–50; Nathaniel Jones, *Answering the Call: An Autobiography of the Modern Struggle to End Discrimination in America* (New Press, 2016), 127–31; Nathaniel Jones, interview by author.

8. Sullivan, *Lift Every Voice*, 282–83, 296–97; *Smith v. Allwright*, 321 U.S. 649 (1944); *King v. Chapman*, 62 F. Supp. 639 (D. Ga. 1945), *aff'd*, 154 F.2d 460 (5th Cir. 1946); Egerton, *Speak Now Against the Day*, 380–81, 406–407; White, *Man Called White*, 89.

9. James, *Double V*, 134–35; White, *Man Called White*, 301; Sullivan, *Lift Every Voice*, 267; Egerton, *Speak Now Against the Day*, 325–26.

10. Sullivan, *Lift Every Voice*, 311–14; Egerton, *Speak Now Against the Day*, 363–65; King, *Devil in the Grove*, 7–14; Eleanor Bontecou Oral History, 20–28, Truman Library.

11. Woodard Affidavit, April 23, 1946, FBI Files; "The Isaac Woodard Story," McCray Papers.

12. Hinton to Carter, May 5, 1946, Marshall to Hinton, April 30 and May 8, 1946, Woodard Files.

13. White to Patterson, May 6, 1946, Patterson to White, June 17, 1946, Woodard Files.

14. NAACP press release, July 17, 1946, Woodard Files; *PM*, July 17, 1947; *Chicago Defender*, July 20, 1946.

15. R. R. Wright Sr. to Truman, July 18, 1946, Truman Library; Alexander Coffield et al. to President NAACP, July 20, 1946, Woodard Files; *Washington Post*, July 23, 1946.

16. Franklin Williams to Walter White, memorandum, July 31, 1946, Woodard Files; *Amsterdam News*, July 27, 1946; *New York Times*, July 25, 1946.

17. "The Case of Mr. Isaac Woodard," July 24, 1946, and White to Branch Presidents, memorandum, July 25, 1946, Woodard Files.

18. Sullivan, *Lift Every Voice*, 318–19; Egerton, *Speak Now Against the Day*, 365–67; *New York Times*, March 18, 2007; *Washington Post*, Feb. 13, 2007; Representative Sanford D. Bishop Jr. (Ga.), "In Honor of Maceo Snipes," Cong. Record, vol. 153, no. 119, E1604 (July 24, 2007).

19. Egerton, *Speak Now Against the Day*, 366–69; Anderson, "Clutching at Civil Rights Straws," 42–43; Sullivan, *Lift Every Voice*, 318–19; *New York Times*, July 26, 1946; *To Secure These Rights*, 22.

20. Egerton, *Speak Now Against the Day*, 369–71; *To Secure These Rights*, 22–23.

3. "THE PLACE WAS BATESBURG"

1. Sullivan, *Lift Every Voice*, 313, 320; Harrington to White, memorandum, July 17, 1946, NAACP press release, July 17, 1946, Franklin Williams to Harrington,

memorandums, Aug. 2 and 26, 1946, "Mr. Current" to Publicity Department, memorandum, Oct. 7, 1946, and "Suggestion for Isaac Woodard Meeting," n.d., Woodard Files; Brian Dolinar, *The Black Cultural Front: Black Writers and Artists of the Depression Generation* (University Press of Mississippi, 2012), 171–223. Harrington drifted leftward after leaving the NAACP and had close associations with Ben Davis Jr., Paul Robeson, and other prominent black communists. Harrington left the United States for Paris in 1951 after coming under scrutiny by the FBI for his political affiliations and eventually moved to East Berlin, where he lived for the remainder of his life.

2. Simon Callow, *Orson Welles*, vol. 2, *Hello Americans* (Viking Press, 2009), 323–27; White to Welles, July 24, 1946, Woodard Files.

3. Callow, *Hello Americans*, 328–30; White, *Man Called White*, 326; Sullivan, *Lift Every Voice*, 320.

4. Callow, *Hello Americans*, 330–31. The full transcript of the July 28, 1946, broadcast of the "Affidavit of Isaac Woodard" can be found at www.italkyoubored .wordpress.com/2014/09/02/isaac-woodard-officer-x-and-orson-welles, note 2. An audio file of the broadcast can be found at www.youtube.com under the title "Orson Welles: Affidavit of Isaac Woodard."

5. Woodard Affidavit, April 23, 1946, FBI Files.

6. *State*, Aug. 2 and 10, 1946; *New York Times*, Aug. 9, 1946; *Augusta Chronicle*, Aug. 12, 1946.

7. Miller to Walter White, July 27, 1946, G. S. Ellington to White, Aug. 14, 1946, A. D. Smith to Roy Wilkins, Aug. 16, 1946, and Miller Affidavit, Aug. 8, 1946, Woodard Files.

8. Callow, *Hello Americans*, 334–36. The full transcript of the August 4, 1946, broadcast, "The Peacemakers," can be found in the www.italkyoubored website referenced in note 4 above, at note 3. The audio file containing the broadcast can be found at www.youtube.com under "Orson Welles: The Peacemakers."

9. Carter to Boulware, Aug. 15, 1946, Woodard Files.

10. Rankin to Hoover, Aug. 7, 1946; Hoover to Rankin, Aug. 12, 1946; and Hoover to Caudle, memorandum, Aug. 12, 1946, Department of Justice File, *United States v. Lynwood Shull*, Civil Rights Division, Class 44, Litigation Case Files, Case No. 144-67-12, box 1414, 230/22/23/6, National Archives (hereafter cited as DOJ Files).

11. *New York Times*, Aug. 18, 1946; *State*, Aug. 18, 1946; *Chicago Defender*, Aug. 24, 1946; Harrington to Welles, telegram, Aug. 14, 1946, Woodard Files. The full transcript of the August 18, 1946, broadcast, titled "Banned Film," can be found at the www.italkyoubored.com website referenced in note 4 above, at note 5. The audio file of the broadcast can be found on www.youtube.com under the title "Orson Welles: Banned Film."

12. Callow, *Hello Americans*, 339–41. The full transcript of the August 25, 1946, broadcast, titled "The Place Was Batesburg," can be found in the www.italkyoubored .com website referenced in note 4 above, at note 7. The audio file of the broadcast can be found at www.youtube.com under the title "Orson Welles: The Place Was Batesburg."

13. Callow, *Hello Americans*, 341.

14. *Amsterdam News*, Aug. 24, 1946 (multiple articles); *PM*, Aug. 20, 1946.

15. *Amsterdam News*, Aug. 24 and Sept. 7, 1946.

16. "National Organizations Meet to Join Joint Action on Wave of Terror in South," press release, Aug. 8, 1946, Woodard Files; Sullivan, *Lift Every Voice*, 322–23; White, *Man Called White*, 329–30.

4. THE BYSTANDER GOVERNMENT

1. U.S. Constitution art. I, sec. 2, art. IV, sec. 2; Richard Kluger, *Simple Justice* (Alfred A. Knopf, 1975), 31–32.

2. Kluger, *Simple Justice*, 35–38; Eric Foner, *The Fiery Trial: Abraham Lincoln and American Slavery* (W. W. Norton, 2010), 63–69, 91, 92.

3. The Emancipation Proclamation, Jan. 1, 1863, National Archives; Orville Vernon Burton, *The Age of Lincoln* (Hill and Wang, 2007), 160–64; Eric Foner, *Reconstruction: America's Unfinished Revolution* (Harper & Row, 1988), 4–10; Kluger, *Simple Justice*, 42–43. See generally Don H. Doyle, *The Cause of All Nations* (Basic Books, 2015).

4. Foner, *Reconstruction*, 228–81; Richard Zuczek, *State of Rebellion: Reconstruction in South Carolina* (University of South Carolina Press, 1996), 15–16.

5. Richard Gergel, "The Rise of One Party Racial Orthodoxy in South Carolina," *Proceedings of the South Carolina Historical Association* (1977): 5–16; Richard Gergel and Belinda Gergel, "'To Vindicate the Cause of the Downtrodden': Associate Justice Jonathan Jasper Wright and Reconstruction in South Carolina," in *At Freedom's Door: African American Founding Fathers and Lawyers in Reconstruction South Carolina*, ed. James Lowell Underwood and W. Lewis Burke (University of South Carolina Press, 2000), 51–64.

6. C. Vann Woodward, *Reunion and Reaction: The Compromise of 1877 and the End of Reconstruction* (Little, Brown, 1951), 7–8, 245.

7. *Williams v. Mississippi*, 170 U.S. 213 (1898); *Plessy v. Ferguson*, 163 U.S. 537 (1896); Woodward, *Strange Career of Jim Crow*, 70–72; Kantrowitz, *Ben Tillman and the Reconstruction of White Supremacy*, 53–54, 198–99, 221–28; Michael J. Klarman, *From Jim Crow to Civil Rights: The Supreme Court and the Struggle for Equality* (Oxford University Press, 2004), 34–36, 52–53, 69.

8. Sullivan, *Lift Every Voice*, 75–76, 105–109, 194–97, 203–204; McCullough, *Truman*, 234, 297; *To Secure These Rights*, 22–25.

9. 18 U.S.C. § 51, later recodified as 18 U.S.C. § 241; 18 U.S.C. § 52, later recodified as 18 U.S.C. § 242; Anderson, "Clutching at Civil Rights Straws," 35–36; *To Secure These Rights*, 114–19, 151; *Screws v. United States*, 325 U.S. 91 (1945).

10. Anderson, "Clutching at Civil Rights Straws," 35–36; *To Secure These Rights*, 119–22; Lynda G. Dodd, "Presidential Leadership and Civil Rights Lawyering in the Era Before *Brown*," 85 *University of Indiana Law Review* 1599, 1612, 1626–27 (2010).

11. Anderson, "Clutching at Civil Rights Straws," 34–35; Egerton, *Speak Now Against the Day*, 415, 452, 536.

12. Anderson, "Clutching at Civil Rights Straws," 34–36; *To Secure These Rights*, 120–23.

13. Caudle to Hoover, memorandum, July 17, 1946, DOJ Files.

14. Walter White to Clark, July 17, 1946, and Hoover to Caudle, memorandum, July 22, 1946, DOJ Files; R. R. Wright Sr. to Truman, July 18, 1946, and David Niles to Wright, July 25, 1946, Truman Library; Clark to White, July 25, 1946, and Civil Rights Conference to Clark, telegram, July 18, 1946, Woodard Files.

15. Brown to Hoover, telex, July 30, 1946, FBI Files.

16. FBI Field Report, Aug. 5, 1946, Statement of Lincoln Miller, Aug. 31, 1946, and Statement of Jennings Stroud, July 26, 1946, FBI Files; Hoover to Caudle, memorandum, July 30, 1946, DOJ Files.

17. Holloran to Smith, memorandum, Aug. 21, 1946, and Caudle to Hoover, memorandum, Aug. 21, 1946, DOJ Files.

18. Ladd to Hoover, memorandum, Sept. 3, 1946, FBI Files.

19. Ibid.

5. "MY GOD . . . WE HAVE GOT TO DO SOMETHING"

1. McCullough, *Truman*, 67–73, 104–109, 119, 120–23; Ken Hechler, "Truman Laid the Foundation for the Modern Civil Rights Movement," in Geselbracht, *Civil Rights Legacy of Harry S. Truman*, 51–52, 69.

2. McCullough, *Truman*, 143–56, 159–65, 172–78, 182, 195–98.

3. Ibid., 160, 197, 213, 240; James, *Double V*, 102.

4. McCullough, *Truman*, 203–11.

5. Ibid., 213–19, 225–27, 234–36, 239–52.

6. *Time*, March 8, 1943.

7. Ibid., 256–62, 285–86, 293–323; David Robertson, *Sly and Able: A Political Biography of James F. Byrnes* (W. W. Norton, 1994), 85–86, 283–84, 296; Leuchtenburg, *White House Looks South*, 161–62.

8. McCullough, *Truman*, 324–27, 333–36, 339, 341–42.

9. Ibid., 354–55, 376–79, 439–44, 454–63.

10. Leuchtenburg, *White House Looks South*, 162–64.

11. Hechler, "Truman Laid the Foundation for the Civil Rights Movement," 52; Gardner, *Harry Truman and Civil Rights*, 12; Anderson, "Clutching at Civil Rights Straws," 33; Kari Frederickson, "'The Slowest State' and 'Most Backward Community': Racial Violence in South Carolina and Federal Civil-Rights Legislation, 1946–1948," *South Carolina Historical Magazine* 98 (April 1997): 177–202; Clark Clifford, Oral History Interview, 53–54, Truman Library; Yon and Lansford, "Political Pragmatism and Civil Rights Policy," 108–109; Leuchtenburg, *White House Looks South*, 163–64.

12. Dodd, "Presidential Leadership and Civil Rights Lawyering," 1613–17; Frederickson, "'Slowest State' and 'Most Backward Community,'" 179–80; Sullivan, *Lift Every Voice*, 311–14, 318–19; Egerton, *Speak Now Against the Day*, 363–69; Anderson, "Clutching at Civil Rights Straws," 41–43.

13. Anderson, "Clutching at Civil Rights Straws," 34–36; Dodd, "Presidential Leadership and Civil Rights Lawyering," 1613–18.

14. White, *Man Called White*, 329–32; Dodd, "Presidential Leadership and Civil Rights Lawyering," 1619–21; Gardner, *Harry Truman and Civil Rights*, 17–18, 21; McCullough, *Truman*, 589; Leuchtenburg, *White House Looks South*, 166; "Statement to Be Presented to the President, September 19th," National Committee Against Mob Violence File, Woodard Files.

15. Truman to Clark, Sept. 20, 1946, and Truman to Niles, memorandum, Sept. 20, 1946, Truman Library.

16. The Civil Rights Section had, with much less fanfare, initiated a criminal civil rights case against the town marshal of Branford, Florida, Tom A. Crews, arising from the murder of a black resident of the town who had been feuding with the law-enforcement officer. The Department of Justice charged Crews only with a misdemeanor to avoid the necessity of presenting the case to a Florida federal grand jury for a felony indictment. Earlier, a Florida county grand jury had refused to indict Crews for murder. The defendant did not deny viciously beating the victim, whipping him until the cow whip broke, and forcing him to jump off a highway bridge after he told Crews he could not swim. Instead, Crews claimed this was an act of personal malice and not part of official action. Thus, Crews argued, the federal government could not convict him of depriving the victim of his civil rights, because the statute required a showing that the defendant was acting under color of state law. Both the federal district judge and the Fifth Circuit Court of Appeals rejected that curious defense. Crews was convicted by an all-white jury in Jacksonville, Florida, and sentenced to the maximum of one year in prison and a fine of $1,000. The case received little notoriety from the civil rights community because the facts were so egregious that the conviction of the law-enforcement officer under these extreme circumstances did not seem like such a great accomplishment. The Department of Justice prosecutor in the case, Fred S. Rogers, later appeared in South Carolina to try the federal government's case against Lynwood Shull in the blinding of Isaac Woodard. *Crews v. United States*, 160 F.2d 746 (5th Cir. 1947); *Daytona Beach Morning Journal*, Oct. 4, 1946; *Pittsburgh Courier*, Oct. 12, 1946.

17. Clark to Truman, Oct. 11, 1946, and Draft of "Executive Order Establishing the President's Committee on Civil Rights," Truman Library.

18. Caudle to Sapp, Sept. 25, 1946, DOJ Files; SAC Brown to Hoover, "Most Urgent" telex, Sept. 27, 1946, Ladd to Tamm, memorandum, Oct. 2, 1946, FBI Files; Federal Rules of Criminal Procedure 6(a), (f).

19. Ladd to Tamm, memorandum, Oct. 2, 1946, Ladd to Hoover, memorandum, Oct. 3, 1946, 8, FBI Files.

20. Jack Irby Hayes, *South Carolina in the New Deal* (University of South Carolina Press, 2001), 15; *State*, Feb. 3, 1947.

21. Tamm to Ladd, memorandum, Oct. 2, 1946, FBI Files; Department of Justice, press release, Sept. 26, 1946, Truman Library; "Information" in *United States v. Shull*, Sept. 26, 1946, Case No. 16,603, National Archives, Atlanta (hereafter cited as *United States v. Shull* Case File); *New York Times*, Sept. 27, 1946; *New York Post*, Sept. 27, 1946; *State*, Sept. 27, 1946; *PM*, Sept. 27, 1946.

22. SAC Brown to Hoover, "Most Urgent" telex, Sept. 27, 1946, Ladd to Hoover,

memorandum, Oct. 3, 1946, 8, and SAC Brown to Hoover, memorandum, Oct. 30, 1946, FBI Files.

23. *State*, Sept. 27, 1946; SAC Brown to Hoover, Sept. 29, 1946, FBI Files.

24. SAC Brown to Hoover, Sept. 29, 1946, Agent House to SAC Brown, memorandum, Sept. 29, 1946, and Agent Steiner to SAC Brown, memorandum, Sept. 28, 1946, FBI Files.

25. *State*, Oct. 16 and Nov. 1, 1946.

26. Hoover to McGregor, memorandum, Oct. 11, 1946, DOJ Files; *State*, Oct. 8, 1946.

27. J. K. Mumford to Ladd, memorandum, Sept. 30, 1946, FBI Files.

28. Caudle to Sapp, Oct. 23, 1946, DOJ Files; SAC Brown to Hoover, memorandum, Oct. 30, 1946, FBI Files; "The Reminiscences of J. Waties Waring" (hereafter cited as Waring Oral History), 215–18, J. Waties Waring Papers (hereafter cited as Waring Papers), Moorland Springarn Research Center, Howard University.

29. Tinsley Yarbrough, *A Passion for Justice: J. Waties Waring and Civil Rights* (Oxford University Press, 1987), 7–9, 13–21; Kluger, *Simple Justice*, 295–97.

30. Draft Order, *United States v. Shull*, n.d., Waring Papers, Howard University; Waring Oral History, 217–18; Caudle to Sapp, Oct. 23, 1946, DOJ Files.

31. Draft Order, *United States v. Shull*, n.d. A memorandum attached to the draft order, apparently prepared by Waring as an explanatory note to accompany his papers when delivered to Howard University, stated that U.S. Attorney Sapp wanted a continuance in the *Shull* case, which Waring refused. Judge Waring informed Sapp that if the government was not ready to proceed when the case was called in early November 1946, he would dismiss the case and issue an order explaining his actions. Waring's explanatory note concluded that because the government indicated it would be ready to proceed when the case was called, "this Order was never put in final form or filed." Waring Papers.

32. Waring Oral History, 215–18; SAC Brown to Hoover, memorandum, Oct. 30, 1946, FBI Files.

33. Rogers to Caudle, memorandum, Nov. 8, 1946, DOJ Files.

6. THE ISAAC WOODARD ROAD SHOW

1. Woodard Discharge Record, VA records; *Amsterdam News*, Aug. 3, 1946; *Chicago Defender*, July 27, 1946; *New York Post*, July 17, 1946; Chinn Report; Robert Young, interview by author.

2. Williams to White, memorandum, July 31, 1946, Agreement between Woodard and NAACP, July 24, 1946, White to Legal Department, memorandum, July 29, 1946, "Isaac Woodard Tour Instructions," NAACP press statement announcing exclusive relationship with Woodard, Aug. 1, 1946, White to Gloster Current, memorandum, Sept. 12, 1946, White to File, memorandum, Aug. 16, 1946, and White to Neil Scott, *Amsterdam News*, Aug. 5, 1946, Woodard Files.

3. Carter to White, memorandum, Aug. 22, 1946, Esquire Men's Club to Ella Baker, Aug. 11, 1946, White to Chicago Branch, telegram, Aug. 28, 1946, White to

Carter, memorandum, Aug. 29, 1946, Williams to Woodard, Sept. 23, 1946, and Madison Jones to Williams, memorandum, Aug. 14, 1946, Woodard Files.

4. White to Williams, memorandum, Aug. 26, 1946, White to Gloster Current, memorandum, Sept. 12, 1946, White to Committee on Administration, memorandum, Sept. 14, 1946, Gloster Current to Branches, memorandum, Oct. 15, 1946, White to Williams, memorandum, Aug. 28, 1946, and Williams to White, memorandum, Sept. 23, 1946, Woodard Files.

5. Hurley to White, memorandum, Aug. 30, 1946, Jones to White, memorandum, Sept. 5, 1946, and Williams to White, memorandum, Sept. 12, 1946, Woodard Files.

6. Gloster Current to Branches, memorandum, Oct. 15, 1946, "Suggestions for Isaac Woodard Meeting," Woodard Files; *Amsterdam News*, Aug. 24, 1946; *Washington, D.C., News*, Oct. 22, 1946.

7. Current to Publicity Department, memorandum with attached "Proposed Itinerary for Isaac Woodard," Oct. 7, 1946, Current to Branches, memorandum, Oct. 16, 1946, Woodard Files.

8. "Isaac Woodard Mass Meeting at Central Baptist Church" (Pittsburgh), "Gigantic Mass Meeting, Greater Zion Baptist Church" (Harrisburg, Pa.), "D.C. Branch Presents Isaac Woodard, the Vet Whose Reward Was Eye-Gouging and Blindness" (Washington, D.C.), "See and Hear Isaac Woodard, Oakhill Avenue AME Church" (Youngstown, Ohio), Woodard Files.

9. "Speaker's Information on Woodard," "Isaac Woodard Tour Instructions," Current to Branches, memorandum, Oct. 18, 1946, and "Suggestions for Isaac Woodard Meeting," Woodard Files.

10. Current to Branches, memorandum, Oct. 18, 1946, "Isaac Woodard Tour Instructions," Memorandum to Mr. White, Re: Isaac Woodard Tour, Oct. 16, 1946, "Proposed Train Schedule for Isaac Woodard Tour," "Blinded Veteran to Be Heard at Mass Meeting," unidentified and undated article, "Isaac Woodard Arrives in Columbus Saturday to Appear at Gigantic Sunday Afternoon Mass Meeting," unidentified source, Nov. 30, 1946, "Woodard and Marshall Move Large Audience in Bethel Mass Meeting," unidentified and undated article, and "Isaac Woodard Mass Meeting Program" (Grand Rapids, Mich.), Nov. 26, 1946, Isaac Woodard Program (Philadelphia), Dec. 8, 1946, Woodard Files.

11. "Blinded Veteran Tells His Story," unidentified and undated article, "Negro Vet Pleads for Equality," unidentified and undated article, "Overflow Crowd at Oak Hill Ave. AME Church for Woodard Meeting," *Youngstown Buckeye Review*, n.d., Woodard Files; *Amsterdam News*, Aug. 24, 1946; Nathaniel Jones, interview by author.

12. *Amsterdam News*, Aug. 24, Sept. 7, and Oct. 19, 1946, July 12 and Aug. 2, 1947; *Chicago Defender*, Feb. 22, 1947; Jones to White, memorandum, Sept. 19, 1946, Powell to White, Oct. 30, 1946, Marian Wynn Perry to White, memorandum, Aug. 26, 1946, White to Williams, memorandum, Oct. 16, 1946, Williams to White, memorandum, Dec. 14, 1946, White to Mrs. Waring, memorandum, Jan. 9, 1947, Roy Wilkins to White, memorandum, Jan. 14, 1947, Williams to Woodard,

Feb. 8, 1947, Williams to File, memorandum, Feb. 28, 1947, "Mama" to Woodard, telegram, Nov. 20, 1946, Woodard Files.

13. Carter to Marshall, handwritten memorandum, n.d., Woodard Files.

14. Marshall to Rev. J. M. Hinton, Nov. 1, 1946, and Williams to Marshall, memorandum, Nov. 12, 1946, Woodard Files.

7. THE GRADUALIST

1. Waring Oral History, 3; Yarbrough, *Passion for Justice*, 304; Ruby Cornwell Oral History, in possession of author; Caryl Phillips, *The Atlantic Sound* (Vintage Books, 2000), 233–34.

2. Waring Oral History, 2–6; Yarbrough, *Passion for Justice*, 3–4.

3. Waring Oral History, 18, 26–30.

4. Ibid., 31, 43, 48–49; Yarbrough, *Passion for Justice*, 5–7, 29–30; Annie Gammell to Waties Waring, Feb. 15, 2012, Nov. 7, 2012, April 5, 2013, and April 9, 2013, South Carolina Historical Society. Waties Waring's family connection to his first wife, Annie Gammell Waring, came through his father's sister, Jane Waring Ancrum. Jane Ancrum married Dr. John L. Ancrum, a prominent Charleston physician and the brother of Maria Ancrum Gammell, the mother of Annie Gammell Waring. Thus, Waties Waring and Annie Gammell Waring shared a common aunt Jane, who was related to Waties by blood and to Annie by marriage.

5. Kluger, *Simple Justice*, 297; Yarbrough, *Passion for Justice*, 15–17; Waring Oral History, 49–53, 130a–31a.

6. Waring Oral History, 50, 77, 79, 88, 93–96, 99–100, 106–107; Yarbrough, *Passion for Justice*, 9–11.

7. Waring Oral History, 129a–33a.

8. Yarbrough, *Passion for Justice*, 16–17.

9. Waring Oral History, 135a–36a.

10. Ibid., 136a–38a; Yarbrough, *Passion for Justice*, 19–21.

11. Waring Oral History, 143a–44a.

12. Ibid., 11–12.

13. *Smith v. Allwright*, 321 U.S. 649 (1944); *Alston v. School Board of City of Norfolk*, 112 F.2d 992 (4th Cir. 1940); Kluger, *Simple Justice*, 302–303; Waring Oral History, 215, 246–48, 358.

14. *Duvall v. Seignous*, C.A. No. 1082 (E.D.S.C.) Case File, National Archives, Atlanta.

15. James Felder, *Civil Rights in South Carolina: From Peaceful Protests to Groundbreaking Rulings* (History Press, 2012), 30–31; "Thanks to Henry Yaschik," McCray Papers; Miles S. Richards, "Osceola E. McKaine and the Struggle for Black Civil Rights" (Ph.D. diss., University of South Carolina, 1994), 142–46. The Maryland case referenced by Waring was *Mills v. Lowndes*, 26 F. Supp. 209 (D. Md. 1939).

16. *Duvall v. Seignous*, Judgment (E.D.S.C. Feb. 14, 1944), National Archives, Atlanta; Waring Oral History, 225–26; Peter F. Lau, *Democracy Rising: South Carolina and the Fight for Black Equality Since 1865* (University Press of Kentucky, 2006),

129-30. *Duvall* was tried without a jury because Marshall made no request on behalf of the plaintiff for common-law money damages and sought only equitable relief (a declaration that the school district's pay policy was unconstitutional and an injunction against the school district's continued use of the discriminatory pay scheme). In the absence of a request for common-law money damages, the defendant was not entitled to a jury trial.

17. Yarbrough, *Passion for Justice*, 43; *Amsterdam News*, June 9, 1951; "Thanks to Henry Yaschik"; Richards, "Osceola McKaine and the Struggle for Black Civil Rights," 146; W. Lewis Burke, *All for Civil Rights: African American Lawyers in South Carolina, 1868–1968* (University of Georgia Press, 2017), 171–72.

18. Edward Dudley to Harold Boulware, Feb. 18, 1944, Hinton to Marshall, March 17, 1944, and S. Morgan to Marshall, July 22, 1944, *Duvall* Case File, NAACP Papers; *State*, March 16, 1944; *Thompson v. Gibbes*, 60 F. Supp. 872, 874–75 (E.D.S.C. 1945).

19. *Thompson*, 60 F. Supp. at 876–78; Waring Oral History, 226–29, *Thompson v. Gibbes* Transcript of Record, Sept. 25, 1944, *Thompson* Case File, NAACP Papers.

20. "A Statement on the Race Problem in South Carolina," March 16, 1944, Dr. J. Heyward Gibbes Papers, South Caroliniana Library.

21. *Thompson*, 60 F. Supp. at 874, 876; Waring Oral History, 229–32. Shortly after the state implemented the new pay and certification system that required all present teachers to take the NTE, a testing scandal arose in which numerous black teachers were prosecuted for distributing or using an illicit answer key for the test. Later commenting on the test key debacle, Waring viewed this as an unfortunate and unintended consequence of moving the state to a racially neutral pay system. Waring Oral History, 231–32.

22. *Thompson*, 60 F. Supp. at 878–89; Waring Oral History, 229, 234–35.

23. *Thompson*, 60 F. Supp. at 878–89.

24. Waring to Gibbes, June 12, 1945, Gibbes Papers.

25. *Columbia Record*, May 27, 1945; Waring to Brown, June 12, 1945, Waring Papers.

26. Waring Oral History, 235–36.

27. Cornwell Oral History.

28. Yarbrough, *Passion for Justice*, 32–33; Phillips, *Atlantic Sound*, 240–41.

29. Yarbrough, *Passion for Justice*, 33–35.

30. Jessica Letizia Lancia, "Giving the South the Shock Treatment: Elizabeth Waring and the Civil Rights Movement" (master's thesis, Graduate School of the College of Charleston, 2007), 7–19, 31; Cornwell Oral History; Samuel Grafton, "Lonesomest Man in Town," *Collier's*, April 29, 1950, 21; *New York World-Telegram*, Feb. 20, 1950.

31. Yarbrough, *Passion for Justice*, 31–35; Waring Oral History, 402–403.

32. Waring Oral History, 215–18; Draft Order, *United States v. Shull*, Waring Papers; Yarbrough, *Passion for Justice*, 49–50; *United States v. Shull* Case File, No. 16,603, National Archives, Atlanta.

8. A "BAPTISM IN RACIAL PREJUDICE"

1. *Pittsburgh Courier*, Nov. 2 and 16, 1946; *New York Times*, Oct. 29, 1946; Dolinar, *Black Cultural Front*, 209–10.

2. Marshall to Harrington, memorandum, Nov. 4, 1946, Woodard Files.

3. Williams to Marshall, memorandum, Nov. 12, 1946, and Williams handwritten trial notes, Woodard Files; SAC to Hoover, memorandums, Oct. 30 and Nov. 13, 1946, FBI Files.

4. SAC to Hoover, memorandum, Nov. 13, 1946, FBI Files; Rogers to Caudle, memorandum, Nov. 21, 1946, DOJ Files; Williams handwritten trial notes, Woodard Files.

5. Williams to Marshall, memorandum, Nov. 12, 1946, Woodard Files.

6. SAC to Hoover, memorandum, Nov. 13, 1946, FBI Files.

7. Williams handwritten trial notes, and Williams to Marshall, memorandum, Nov. 12, 1946, Woodard Files; Rogers to Caudle, memorandum, Nov. 8 and 21, 1946, DOJ Files.

8. Williams to Marshall, memorandum, Nov. 12, 1946, Woodard Files; Lynwood Shull, sworn statement, July 30, 1946, and Jennings Stroud, sworn statement, Sept. 25, 1946, FBI Files.

9. FBI Field Report, Aug. 5, 1946, 7, FBI File; *United States v. Shull* Court File, National Archives, Atlanta.

10. SAC to Hoover, memorandum, Nov. 13, 1946, FBI Files; *State*, Nov. 4 and 5, 1946.

11. The African American population of South Carolina was 42.9 percent in 1940 and 38.8 percent in 1950. 1940 and 1950 U.S. Censuses.

12. Williams to Marshall, memorandum, Nov. 12, 1946, Woodard Files; Marshall to Tom Clark, Nov. 14, 1946, DOJ Files; "Jefferson Davis Griffith," Memory Hold the Door, University of South Carolina Law School.

13. Williams to Marshall, memorandum, Nov. 12, 1946, Williams handwritten trial notes, and Williams to S. Ralph Harlow, Jan. 16, 1947, Woodard Files; Rogers to Caudle, memorandum, Nov. 21, 1946, DOJ Files.

14. Williams to Marshall, memorandum, Nov. 12, 1946, Williams handwritten trial notes, and Williams undated trial memorandum, Woodard Files.

15. *Columbia Record*, Nov. 5, 1946; *State*, Nov. 6, 1946; SAC to Hoover, memorandum, Nov. 12, 1946, and Isaac Woodard Affidavit, July 29, 1946, reprinted in Field Report, Aug. 26, 1946, FBI Files; Waring Oral History, 218–23.

16. *Columbia Record*, Nov. 5, 1946; *State*, Nov. 6, 1946; Woodard Affidavit, July 29, 1946, Woodard Files.

17. *Columbia Record*, Nov. 5, 1946; *State*, Nov. 6, 1946; Williams to Marshall, memorandum, Nov. 12, 1946, Woodard Files; Waring Oral History, 245–46.

18. *Columbia Record*, Nov. 5, 1946; *State*, Nov. 6, 1946; Williams to Marshall, memorandum, Nov. 12, 1946, and Williams handwritten trial notes, Woodard Files. In modern jurisprudence, dating perhaps from the 1980s forward, a physician can offer an expert opinion regarding the cause of an injury only if he or she can state that

opinion with a "reasonable degree of medical certainty," which simply means that some factor or condition is the "most probable" cause. Thus, Dr. King's trial testimony that a single blow of the blackjack "could have" caused Woodard's bilateral blindness would not today be admissible evidence, because it would be deemed too speculative and uncertain.

19. *State*, Nov. 6, 1946; *Columbia Record*, Nov. 5, 1946; Williams to Marshall, memorandum, Nov. 12, 1946, and Williams handwritten trial notes, Woodard Files; FBI Field Notes, Aug. 5, 1946, 8–9, FBI Files.

20. *United States v. Shull* Court File, National Archives; Williams to Marshall, memorandum, Nov. 12, 1946, and Williams handwritten trial notes, Woodard Files.

21. *State*, Nov. 6, 1946; *Columbia Record*, Nov. 5, 1946; SAC to Hoover, Nov. 13, 1946, FBI Files; Williams to Marshall, memorandum, Nov. 12, 1946, Woodard Files.

22. Williams to Marshall, memorandum, Nov. 12, 1946, and Williams handwritten trial notes, Woodard Files; SAC to Hoover, memorandum, Nov. 13, 1946, FBI Files.

23. *United States v. Shull* Court File, National Archives; Williams to Marshall, memorandum, Nov. 12, 1946, Woodard Files; SAC to Hoover, memorandum, Nov. 13, 1946, FBI Files.

24. *State*, Nov. 6, 1946; *Columbia Record*, Nov. 6, 1946; Williams to Marshall, memorandum, Nov. 12, 1946, and Williams handwritten trial notes, Woodard Files.

25. SAC to Hoover, memorandum, Nov. 13, 1946, FBI Files. Under present practice, a prosecutor must provide a criminal defendant with a copy of any prior written statements before the trial. Federal Rules of Criminal Procedure 16(a)(1).

26. Lynwood Shull sworn statement, July 30, 1946, and SAC to Hoover, Nov. 13, 1946, FBI Files; *State*, Nov. 6, 1946; Williams to Marshall, memorandum, Nov. 12, 1946, Woodard Files; *Columbia Record*, Nov. 6, 1946; *Amsterdam News*, Nov. 9, 1946.

27. *United States v. Shull* Court File, National Archives; Williams to Marshall, memorandum, Nov. 12, 1946, and Williams handwritten trial notes, Woodard Files; *State*, Nov. 6, 1946.

28. SAC to Hoover, memorandum, Nov. 13, 1946, FBI Files; Williams to Marshall, memorandum, Nov. 12, 1946, Woodard Files; *United States v. Shull* Court File, National Archives; *State*, Nov. 6, 1946.

29. SAC to Hoover, memorandum, Nov. 13, 1946, FBI Files; Williams to Marshall, memorandum, Nov. 12, 1946, Woodard Files; *Amsterdam News*, Nov. 9, 1946; *United States v. Shull* Court File, National Archives.

30. Williams handwritten trial notes, and Williams to Marshall, memorandum, Nov. 12, 1946, Woodard Files; SAC to Hoover, memorandum, Nov. 13, 1946, FBI Files; *Amsterdam News*, Nov. 9, 1946; Waring Oral History, 221.

31. Williams to Marshall, memorandum, Nov. 12, 1946, Woodard Files; SAC to Hoover, memorandum, Nov. 13, 1946, FBI Files.

32. Williams to Marshall, memorandum, Nov. 12, 1946, Woodard Files; SAC to Hoover, memorandum, Nov. 13, 1946, FBI Files.

33. Waring Oral History, 221–23; Williams handwritten trial notes, and Williams to Marshall, memorandum, Nov. 12, 1946, Woodard Files; SAC to Hoover, memorandum, Nov. 13, 1946, FBI Files; *United States v. Shull* Court File, National Archives.

34. *Pittsburgh Courier*, Nov. 16, 1946; Marshall to Clark, Nov. 14 and Dec. 27, 1946, Randolph to Clark, Nov. 9, 1946, and Clark to Marshall, Jan. 13, 1947, DOJ Files.

35. *State*, Nov. 1946.

36. A detailed forensic analysis of Woodard's injuries, based on the medical records and X-ray findings of his treating physicians, can be found in the appendix of this book. Dr. Kim Collins, one of the nation's premier forensic pathologists, concluded that Woodard could not have suffered the crushing of the globes of both eyes with a single strike of a blackjack to the head. Collins concluded that to crush the globes in both eyes of an adult required a penetrating injury into each eye, consistent with Woodard's claim that Shull drove the handle end of his blackjack into each eye.

37. Waring Oral History, 218–24.

38. Ibid., 223–24; Cornwell Oral History.

39. Waring Oral History, 223–24; Cornwell Oral History; Phillips, *Atlantic Sound*, 245.

9. "I SHALL FIGHT TO END EVIL LIKE THIS"

1. Clark Clifford to Truman, memorandum, Nov. 19, 1947, 45–47, Truman Library; McCullough, *Truman*, 523.

2. Yon and Lansford, "Political Pragmatism and Civil Rights Policy," 108–10; Clark Clifford Oral History, April 13, 1971, 55, Truman Library; Clifford to Truman, memorandum, Nov. 19, 1947, 11–12.

3. Clifford Oral History, 269; Truman Gibson Oral History, July 27, 2001, 14, Truman Library; Richard M. Dalfiume, *Desegregation of the U.S. Armed Forces: Fighting on Two Fronts, 1939–1953* (University of Missouri Press, 1969), 136; Harry S. Truman, *Memoirs of Harry S. Truman* (Doubleday, 1956), 180, 182; Yon and Lansford, "Political Pragmatism and Civil Rights Policy," 107; Harry S. Truman, Speech to Howard University, June 13, 1952, 2, Truman Library; Philleo Nash Oral History, Feb. 21, 1947, 623, Truman Library.

4. Hechler, "Truman Laid the Foundation for the Civil Rights Movement," 53; Truman, Speech to Howard University, 2; Nash Oral History, 624–26.

5. White to Niles, Sept. 26, 1946, Truman Library; Attorney General's Recommendations for President's Committee, Oct. 14, 1946, Truman Library.

6. Dodd, "Presidential Leadership and Civil Rights Lawyering," 1623–24; Nash Oral History, 629–37.

7. Leuchtenburg, *White House Looks South*, 167.

8. Executive Order 9808, Dec. 5, 1946, Truman Library. When Truman ultimately sent his special civil rights message to Congress in February 1948, only

6 percent of the voters supported his civil rights program. Raymond Frey, "Truman's Speech to the NAACP," in Geselbracht, *Civil Rights Legacy of Harry S. Truman,* 99.

9. Remarks of Harry S. Truman to the President's Committee on Civil Rights, Jan. 15, 1947, Truman Library.

10. *To Secure These Rights,* x, 26.

11. Ibid., 23.

12. Frey, "Truman's Speech to the NAACP," 96–97; Dodd, "Presidential Leadership and Civil Rights Lawyering," 1631; Harry S. Truman to Mary Jane Truman, June 28, 1947, Truman Library; White, *Man Called White,* 348–49.

13. Harry S. Truman, Speech to the NAACP, June 29, 1947, Truman Library; Frey, "Truman's Speech to the NAACP," 97–98; Gardner, *Harry Truman and Civil Rights,* 29.

14. White, *Man Called White,* 348–49; Frey, "Truman's Speech to the NAACP," 98.

15. Clifford to Truman, memorandum, Nov. 19, 1947, 3, 11–12, 40–41.

16. Clifford Oral History, 51–55.

17. *To Secure These Rights,* 7–9, 20–25.

18. Ibid., 25–27.

19. Ibid., 35–40.

20. Ibid., 40–47.

21. Ibid., 81–87.

22. Ibid., 17–19.

23. Ibid., 151–73.

24. Ibid., 126–33, 166–67; Morton Sosna, *In Search of the Silent South* (Columbia University Press, 1977), 151–52.

25. *To Secure These Rights,* 152; Dodd, "Presidential Leadership and Civil Rights Lawyering," 1637–39.

26. Dodd, "Presidential Leadership and Civil Rights Lawyering," 1639; Egerton, *Speak Now Against the Day,* 416; White, *Man Called White,* 333; Tom Clark Oral History, Oct. 17, 1972, 97–98, Truman Library.

27. President's Annual Message to Congress, Jan. 7, 1948, Truman Library.

28. President's Special Message to Congress on Civil Rights, Feb. 2, 1948, Truman Library.

29. Dodd, "Presidential Leadership and Civil Rights Lawyering," 1644; Frey, "Truman's Speech to the NAACP," 99; Gardner, *Harry Truman and Civil Rights,* 78–80; Frederickson, "'Slowest State' and 'Most Backward Community,'" 199.

30. McCullough, *Truman,* 588; Michael Gardner, "A President Who Regarded Civil Rights as a Moral Imperative," in Geselbracht, *Civil Rights Legacy of Harry S. Truman,* 22.

31. Hechler, "Truman Laid the Foundation for the Civil Rights Movement," 57; Frey, "Truman's Speech to the NAACP," 100; Margaret Truman, *Harry S. Truman* (William Morrow, 1973), 392; Leuchtenburg, *White House Looks South,* 366.

32. Clifford Oral History, 232–33, 267–68.

292 NOTES TO PAGES 152–159

33. McCullough, *Truman*, 656–57; 1948 Republican Party Platform, Truman Library.

34. McCullough, *Truman*, 638–40; Hechler, "Truman Laid the Foundation for the Civil Rights Movement," 57; Dodd, "Presidential Leadership and Civil Rights Lawyering," 1645; Clifford Oral History, 265–67.

35. Truman Speech Accepting Democratic Party Nomination, July 15, 1948, Truman Library; McCullough, *Truman*, 642–44; Hechler, "Truman Laid the Foundation for the Civil Rights Movement," 57–58.

36. McCullough, *Truman*, 644; Hechler, "Truman Laid the Foundation for the Civil Rights Movement," 58.

37. Truman, *Memoirs of Harry S. Truman*, 2:183; Leuchtenburg, *White House Looks South*, 197.

38. McCullough, *Truman*, 645; Patricia Sullivan, *Days of Hope: Race and Democracy in the New Deal Era* (University of North Carolina Press, 1996).

39. Executive Orders 9980, July 26, 1948, and 9981, July 26, 1948, Truman Library. During the period Truman was considering his response to the report of his Civil Rights Committee, A. Philip Randolph, a prominent civil rights leader, announced that unless segregation was ended in the armed forces, he would recommend that young black recruits refuse to report for military service. The Randolph announcement appears to have been an effort to create pressure from the Left for integration of the armed forces as a countervailing force against the efforts of the military brass and southern congressmen to maintain a segregated military. There is little evidence that Randolph's efforts influenced Truman, who appears to have been sold on the need for the executive order ending segregation in the military as soon as the report of the Civil Rights Committee was received. Indeed, Truman announced his intention to issue an executive order regarding segregation in the military in his State of the Union speech on January 7, 1948, and the executive order was not issued until six months later, on July 26, 1948. Hechler, "Truman Laid the Foundation for the Civil Rights Movement," 59.

40. Hechler, "Truman Laid the Foundation for the Civil Rights Movement," 58; McCullough, *Truman*, 651; Harry S. Truman to Bess Truman, July 23, 1948, Truman Library.

41. Roberts to Truman, Aug. 8, 1948, and Truman to Roberts, Aug. 18, 1948, Truman Library; Gardner, *Harry Truman and Civil Rights*, 130–33.

42. McCullough, *Truman*, 653–67, 674–82, 688–97; Clifford Oral History, 242–46.

43. McCullough, *Truman*, 668–74, 697, 703; Clifford Oral History, 243–44.

44. Harry S. Truman, Speech in Harlem, Oct. 29, 1948, Truman Library; McCullough, *Truman*, 702.

45. McCullough, *Truman*, 704–10.

46. Leuchtenburg, *White House Looks South*, 210–11.

47. McCullough, *Truman*, 711; Clifford Oral History, 54–55. Truman carried Illinois by thirty-three thousand votes, Ohio by seven thousand, and California by seventeen thousand. The African American voters in those three states were over-

293

whelmingly supportive of Truman and provided far more votes than Truman's margin of victory in each of those states.

10. "WE KNOW THE WAY. WE NEED ONLY THE WILL."

1. Hechler, "Truman Laid the Foundation for the Civil Rights Movement," 59–61; Dodd, "Presidential Leadership and Civil Rights Lawyering," 1647–50.

2. Dalfiume, *Desegregation of the U.S. Armed Forces*, 171–72; Yon and Lansford, "Political Pragmatism and Civil Rights Policy," 111; President's News Conference, July 29, 1948, and Executive Order 9981, Truman Library; *New York Times*, July 27 and 30, 1948.

3. Dalfiume, *Desegregation of the U.S. Armed Forces*, 176; Leuchtenburg, *White House Looks South*, 206. Other members of the committee included Dwight R. G. Palmer, a business executive and active member of the board of the National Urban League, and William Stevenson, the president of Oberlin College. Truman anticipated a seven-member committee, but ultimately only five of the appointed members actively served.

4. Truman, Address to Fahy Committee, Jan. 12, 1949, Truman Library; Yon and Lansford, "Political Pragmatism and Civil Rights Policy," 104–105; Dalfiume, *Desegregation of the U.S. Armed Forces*, 178–79.

5. Dalfiume, *Desegregation of the U.S. Armed Forces*, 175–200; Yon and Lansford, "Political Pragmatism and Civil Rights Policy," 113; Truman, Speech to Howard University.

6. Dalfiume, *Desegregation of the U.S. Armed Forces*, 4, 220; Yon and Lansford, "Political Pragmatism and Civil Rights Policy," 105, 113.

7. Harry S. Truman, Memorandum of Disapproval of Bill Requiring Segregation in Certain Schools on Federal Property, Nov. 2, 1951, Truman Library; Hechler, "Truman Laid the Foundation for the Civil Rights Movement," 61; Public Law 83–248, Aug. 8, 1953.

8. Kluger, *Simple Justice*, 558; Dodd, "Presidential Leadership and Civil Rights Lawyering," 1651; *Shelley v. Kraemer*, 334 U.S. 1 (1948); Brief of the United States as Amicus Curiae, *Shelley v. Kraemer*, Dec. 5, 1947, 1947, WL 44159.

9. *Henderson v. United States*, 338 U.S. 816 (1950); Brief of the United States, *Henderson v. United States*, Oct. 5, 1949, 1949, WL 50329; *Sweatt v. Painter*, 339 U.S. 629 (1950); *McLaurin v. Oklahoma State Regents*, 339 U.S. 637 (1950); Memorandum of the United States as Amicus Curiae, *Sweatt v. Painter* and *McLaurin v. Oklahoma State Regents* (Feb. 1950), Archives of the U.S. Supreme Court, 9–14.

10. *Brown v. Board of Education*, 347 U.S. 483 (1954); Brief of the United States as Amicus Curiae, *Brown v. Board of Education*, Dec. 2, 1952, 1952, WL 82045 (1952).

11. Dodd, "Presidential Leadership and Civil Rights Lawyering," 1638–39; Philip Elman and Norman Silber, "The Solicitor General's Office, Justice Frankfurter, and Civil Rights Litigation, 1946–1960: An Oral History," 100 *Harvard Law Review* 817 (1987); Randall Kennedy, "A Reply to Philip Elman," 100 *Harvard Law Review* 1938 (1987).

12. Executive Orders 10210, Feb. 2, 1951, 10216, Feb. 23, 1951, 10227, March 24, 1951, 10231, April 5, 1951, 10243, May 11, 1951, 10298, Oct. 31, 1951, and 10308, Dec. 3, 1951, Truman Library; Hechler "Truman Laid the Foundation for the Civil Rights Movement," 60–61.

13. William Hastie Oral History, Jan. 5, 1972, 3–4, 67–68, Truman Library; Egerton, *Speak Now Against the Day*, 507; Gardner, *Harry Truman and Civil Rights*, 135–36, 152–53. Hastie had served for two years in the 1930s as a district judge for the Virgin Islands, which was then an Article I (executive branch) appointment with a fixed term of office. Thus, when Truman appointed Hastie to the Third Circuit, he was the first black Article III (judicial branch) judge appointed in American history.

14. Anderson, "Clutching at Civil Rights Straws," 34–41; Tom Clark Oral History, 124, 129–30; Dalfiume, *Desegregation of the U.S. Armed Forces*, 223.

15. Kluger, *Simple Justice*, 249–50; John Lewis, "A President Who Got in Trouble—Good Trouble, Necessary Trouble," in Geselbracht, *Civil Rights Legacy of Harry S. Truman*, 9; Leuchtenburg, *White House Looks South*, 417.

16. Gibson Oral History, 14; Truman to Tom Clark, Sept. 20, 1946; Truman to Ernest Roberts, Aug. 23, 1948; McCullough, *Truman*, 589; Clark Clifford, *Counsel to the President* (Random House, 1991), 208; Waring Oral History, 223.

11. CONFRONTING THE AMERICAN DILEMMA

1. *Crisis*, April 1952, 233–34; Waring Oral History, 223–34; *San Francisco Sun Times*, Aug. 5, 1950; Cornwell Oral History; Phillips, *Atlantic Sound*, 245.

2. Waring to William Paul Miller, April 21, 1950; Waring to Arthur J. Clement, June 10, 1952, Waring Papers; *New York Times*, Feb. 24, 1952.

3. Grafton, "Lonesomest Man in Town," 20–21, 49–50; Sue Bailey Thurman, "A Portrait of Two Americans," *Sun Reporter*, n.d., Waring Papers; "Disowned in Dixie," *Christian Science Monitor*, Jan. 10, 1951.

4. W. J. Cash, *The Mind of the South* (Vintage Books, 1941), 31, 91, 245, 247, 336, 414, 428.

5. Ibid., 82–83, 115, 117.

6. J. Waties Waring, "The Struggle for Negro Rights," *Lawyers Guild Review*, Feb. 20, 1949.

7. Myrdal, *American Dilemma*, ix, xi, xviii.

8. Ibid., 60–61, 448–51, 529–30, 534–35, 547–52, 606–34, 640.

9. Ibid., xli, xlviii, 4–5, 1021–22.

10. Ibid., 470–72.

11. Waring, "Struggle for Negro Rights," 9–10; Grafton, "Lonesomest Man in Town," 49.

12. Thurman, "A Portrait of Two Americans"; *Christian Science Monitor*, Jan. 10, 1951.

13. *Slaughter-House Cases*, 83 U.S. 36 (1873); *United States v. Reese*, 92 U.S. 214 (1876); *United States v. Cruikshank*, 92 U.S. 542 (1876); *Civil Rights Cases*, 109 U.S.

3 (1883); *Hall v. DeCuir*, 92 U.S. 485 (1877); *Louisville, New Orleans & Texas Ry. Co. v. Mississippi*, 133 U.S. 587 (1890); *Plessy v. Ferguson*, 163 U.S. 537 (1896); *Williams v. Mississippi*, 170 U.S. 213 (1898). Woodward, *Strange Career of Jim Crow*, 71; C. Vann Woodward, "The New Reconstruction in the South: Desegregation in Historical Perspective," *Commentary*, June 1, 1956.

14. *Gaines v. Canada*, 305 U.S. 337, 352–53 (1938).

15. *Smith v. Allwright*, 321 U.S. 649, 661–62 (1944).

16. *King v. Chapman*, 62 F. Supp. 639, 650 (M.D. Ga. 1945), *aff'd*, 154 F.2d 460 (5th Cir. 1946), *cert. denied*, 327 U.S. 800 (1946); "The Reminiscences of Thurgood Marshall," Columbia University Oral History Project, reprinted in *Thurgood Marshall: His Speeches, Writings, Arguments, Opinions, and Reminiscences*, ed. Mark V. Tushnet (Lawrence Hill Books, 2001).

17. *Alston v. School Board of City of Norfolk*, 112 F.2d 992, 996 (4th Cir. 1940); *King v. Chapman*, 154 F.2d 460 (5th Cir. 1950).

18. Waring Oral History, 247–48.

19. *Wrighten v. Board of Trustees of the University of South Carolina*, 72 F. Supp. 948 (E.D.S.C. 1947); Waring Oral History, 248, 258.

20. *Wrighten*, 72 F. Supp. at 953; W. Lewis Burke and William C. Hine, "The South Carolina State College Law School: Its Roots, Creation, and Legacy," in *Matthew J. Perry: The Man, His Times, and His Legacy*, ed. W. Lewis Burke and Belinda F. Gergel (University of South Carolina Press, 2004), 17–60; Waring Oral History, 258.

21. Waring Oral History, 261–62; *New York Times*, Nov. 19, 1947; *State*, July 31, 2012.

22. *Elmore v. Rice*, 72 F. Supp. 516, 520–21 (E.D.S.C. 1947); Waring Oral History, 249–54.

23. Hastie to Marshall, Feb. 27, 1947, *Elmore* Litigation File, NAACP Papers.

24. Waring Oral History, 256–58, 324.

25. *Elmore* at 520–21, 525–26, 527; Waring Oral History, 262–64; *Elmore v. Rice* Case File, National Archives, Atlanta.

26. *Elmore* at 525–27.

27. Ibid. at 527–28.

28. White to Truman, July 14, 1947, and Hastie to Marshall, July 17, 1948, *Elmore* Litigation File, NAACP Papers; Klarman, *From Jim Crow to Civil Rights*, 201.

29. *News and Courier*, July 13, 1947; *Charleston Evening Post*, July 12 and 14, 1947; *Greenville News*, July 13, 1947; *Columbia Record*, July 14, 1947; Yarbrough, *Passion for Justice*, 64–65; Waring Oral History, 267, 271; *New York Post*, Nov. 2, 1948.

30. *Charleston Evening Post*, July 14, 1947.

31. Luelle Clark to Waring, July 14, 1947, Waring to Mrs. George Howe, July 15, 1947, Waring to Mrs. S. B. Alexander, July 15, 1947, Waring to Father Jos. McElroy, July 17, 1947, and Rogers to Waring, June 9, 1948, Waring Papers.

32. *Pittsburgh Courier*, July 19 and 26 and Aug. 2, 1947; Mays to Waring, July 29, 1947, Waring Papers.

33. Waring to Stephen Nettles, Oct. 10, 1947, Waring Papers.

34. Finnie to Elizabeth Waring, July 7, 1947, Waring Papers; Waring Oral History, 403–404.

35. *Greenville News,* July 13, 1947; *State,* n.d., Waring Papers.

36. Waring to Parker, Oct. 10, 1946, and Parker to Waring, Oct. 10, April 29, and May 5, 1947, Waring Papers. Subsequently, a motion for a new trial was made in the Virginia bank fraud case when it was revealed that a juror had advised Waring that he had been approached by persons on behalf of the defendants to hang the jury. Waring did not remove the juror or reveal the communication to defendants. Waring disqualified himself from hearing this post-trial motion, and a newly assigned district judge granted the motion for a new trial. This error by Waring would later be referenced by advocates of his impeachment to support his removal from office. *Washington Post,* Oct. 31, 1947.

37. *New York Times,* Nov. 19 and Dec. 31, 1947; *Rice v. Elmore,* 165 F.2d 387, 392n1 (4th Cir. 1947).

38. *Rice v. Elmore,* 333 U.S. 875 (1948); Waring Oral History, 272; *New York Times,* Dec. 31, 1947.

39. Waring Oral History, 197–205; *New York Times,* Dec. 4, 1947.

40. Waring Oral History, 236–45; Yarbrough, *Passion for Justice,* 53–54. Waring later appointed Samuel Fleming's son, John Fleming, as his bailiff.

12. THERE WILL BE NO FINES

1. Temporary Restraining Order and Rule to Show Cause for Preliminary Injunction, *Brown v. Baskin,* Civil Action No. 1964 (July 8, 1948), National Archives, Atlanta; *Brown v. Baskin* (Final Order), 80 F. Supp. 1017, 1018 (E.D.S.C. 1948); "Tribute to J. Waties Waring by Thurgood Marshall," Feb. 20, 1949, J. Waties Waring File, NAACP Papers, 5–6.

2. Baskin to Waring, telegram, July 10, 1948, and Waring to Baskin, telegram draft, July 11, 1948, Waring Papers.

3. Waring Oral History, 289, 294–96.

4. Ibid., 289–93; Yarbrough, *Passion for Justice,* 82; Preliminary Injunction Transcript, July 16, 1948, 2–3, 59–60, Waring Papers; *Brown v. Baskin* Case File, National Archives, Atlanta; *News and Courier,* July 17, 1948.

5. Preliminary Injunction Transcript, 50.

6. Ibid., 55; "Tribute to J. Waties Waring by Thurgood Marshall," 9.

7. *News and Courier,* July 17, 21, and 22, 1948.

8. Waring Oral History, 303–306, 309–10, 324, 331.

9. *News and Courier,* July 15, 22, 24, 25, and 30, Aug. 3 and 5, 1948; Waring Oral History, 138a.

10. *News and Courier,* July 28, 1948; Leslie Perry to Thurgood Marshall, Aug. 6, 1948, NAACP Papers.

11. *News and Courier,* July 29 and 30, 1948; *New York Times,* July 28, 1948.

12. *News and Courier,* Aug. 5, 6, and 8, 1948; House Resolution 704, Waring Papers; Cong. Record 94: A4654–55, 9752–53; Yarbrough, *Passion for Justice,*

81–86, 89–91; "The Man They Love to Hate," *Time*, Aug. 23, 1948; Waring Oral History, 296–97, 301–302; *Washington Post*, Aug. 5, 1948.

13. Waring to Parker, July 20 and Aug. 5, 1948, Waring Papers.

14. Parker to Waring, Aug. 6, 1948, Waring Papers.

15. Waring Oral History, 294–97, 302; J. Waties Waring, "Does White Supremacy Menace America?," *Recorder*, Aug. 8, 1950, Waring Papers; Grafton, "Lonesomest Man in Town," 50; *Pittsburgh Courier*, Aug. 21, 1948; "Press Release from Thurgood Marshall," Aug. 12, 1948, *Brown v. Baskin* Litigation File, NAACP Papers; Sullivan, *Lift Every Voice*, 318; *Pittsburgh Courier*, July 24, 1948.

16. Waring to Parker, Aug. 11, 1948, and Parker to Waring, Aug. 18, 1948, Waring Papers.

17. Unsigned letter from Knights of the Ku Klux Klan to Waring, n.d., Waring Papers; Waring Oral History, 303.

18. Parker to Waring, Oct. 30, 1948, and Waring to Parker, Oct. 29, 1948, Waring Papers; *Amsterdam News*, Oct. 30, 1948.

19. *New York Times*, Oct. 12, 1948.

20. Motion to Disqualify, *Brown v. Baskin* Litigation File, NAACP Papers; *Amsterdam News*, Oct. 30, 1948.

21. *Amsterdam News*, Oct. 30, 1948; *Brown v. Baskin*, 80 F. Supp. 1017, 1019–21 (E.D.S.C. 1948); *Brown v. Baskin* Litigation File, NAACP Papers.

22. *Baskin v. Brown*, 174 F.2d 391, 393, 394 (4th Cir. 1949).

23. Waring to Clark, Dec. 12, 1947, Waring Papers.

24. Waring to Clark, Nov. 11, 1948, and Waring to Marshall, Dec. 4, 1948, Waring Papers; *Time*, Aug. 23, 1948; *New York Times*, Aug. 20, 1947.

25. Waring Oral History, 223; Truman Presidential Calendar, Dec. 2, 1948, Truman Library; Waring to Marshall, Dec. 4, 1948, Waring Papers.

26. Waring to Truman, Dec. 6, 1948; Truman to Waring, Dec. 9, 1948, Waring Papers.

13. FIGHTING THE "BATTLE ROYAL"

1. *Pittsburgh Courier*, May 21, 1949; Waring Oral History, 337–38.

2. Egerton, *Speak Now Against the Day*, 99–102, 160, 299–300, 565–66; *Amsterdam News*, Dec. 9, 1950; Waring to Dombrowski, Nov. 7, 1950, Waring Papers; "Aubrey W. Williams," in *Encyclopedia of Alabama*, www.encyclopediaofalabama.org.

3. Clifford J. Durr, "Tribute to Judge J. Waties Waring," 9 *Lawyers Guild Review* 5–6 (Winter 1949).

4. *News and Courier*, Jan. 30, 1952; *Collier's*, April 23, 1952, 20–21.

5. Rowan to Waties and Elizabeth Waring, Jan. 22, 1951, and Carl Rowan, "Hatred Seethes for Defender of the Negro," *Minneapolis Tribune*, n.d., Waring Papers.

6. Poppy Cannon, *The Gentle Knight* (Popular Library, 1956), 129.

7. Waring, "Struggle for Negro Rights," 9–12.

8. Waring to Dombrowski, June 6, 1949, Waring Papers; Eleanor Roosevelt, "My Day," June 3, 1949; Waring to Dr. Heyward Gibbes, June 12, 1945, Gibbes Papers.

9. Waring to Aubrey Williams, Jan. 25, 1950, Waring Papers.

10. Elizabeth Waring, YWCA Speech, Jan. 16, 1950, Waring File, NAACP Papers; *News and Courier,* Jan. 17, 1950; Septima Poinsette Clark, *Echo in My Soul* (E. F. Dutton, 1962), 95–100.

11. Yarbrough, *Passion for Justice,* 131; *Washington Post,* Feb. 5, 1950.

12. Roosevelt to Elizabeth Waring, Feb. 6, 1950, Waring Papers; White to Elizabeth Waring, Jan. 17, 1950, Waring File, NAACP Papers; *News and Courier,* Jan. 17, 18, 20, and 21, 1950; *Washington Post,* Jan. 18 and Feb. 6, 1950; *New York Post,* Feb. 7, 1950; *Pittsburgh Courier,* Jan. 18 and Feb. 4, 1950.

13. Transcript of *Meet the Press,* Feb. 11, 1950, Waring File, NAACP Papers; *News and Courier,* Feb. 12, 1950.

14. *News and Courier,* Feb. 15, 16, and 17, 1950; "Petition of White Voting Citizens of South Carolina," Waring Papers.

15. *Washington Post,* Feb. 8, 1950.

16. *News and Courier,* Feb. 21 and March 6, 9, and 15, 1950.

17. *News and Courier,* March 15 and 24, 1950.

18. Cong. Record, April 6, 1950, A2790; *Washington Post,* April 7, 1950; *New York Times,* April 7, 1950.

19. "Reminiscences of Thurgood Marshall," 491.

20. *News and Courier,* March 12, 1950; Rutledge Young, interview by author.

21. *New York Post,* March 13, 1950; *New York Mirror,* March 13, 1950; *New York Herald Tribune,* March 13, 1950; *News and Courier,* March 13, 1950.

22. Cannon, *Gentle Knight,* 130; Waring to the Agent in Charge of the Charleston Office of the FBI, Oct. 12, 1950, and Statement of Judge J. Waties Waring, n.d., Waring Papers; *News and Courier,* Oct. 10, 11, 14, and 22, 1950; *Pittsburgh Courier,* Oct. 21, 1950; *Amsterdam News,* Oct. 14, 1950; *Washington Post,* Oct. 10, 1950; Paul Sann to Frank Gilbreath, Oct. 26, 1950, Waring Papers; Yarbrough, *Passion for Justice,* 157–58.

23. White to McGrath, Oct. 11, 1950, and Ford to White, Oct. 23, 1950, Waring File, NAACP Papers.

24. *News and Courier,* Oct. 14 and Nov. 4, 1950.

25. Rivers to McGrath, Oct. 19, 1950, Waring File, NAACP Papers; *News and Courier,* Oct. 18 and Nov. 13, 1950.

26. *Sweatt v. Painter,* 339 U.S. 629 (1950); *McLaurin v. Oklahoma State Regents,* 339 U.S. 637 (1950); *Henderson v. United States,* 339 U.S. 816 (1950).

27. Waring to Williams, Jan. 25, 1950, Waring to Dombrowski, Dec. 15, 1949, Jan. 3, 6, and 25, 1950, and Waring to White, Jan. 6, 1950, Waring Papers; Brief of the American Jewish Committee and B'nai B'rith in *Sweatt v. Painter,* 1950 WL 78684 (April 1, 1950); Brief of the Federal Council of Churches in *Sweatt v. Painter,* 1949 WL 50366 (Sept. 23, 1949).

28. Waring, Speech to the Council for Civic Unity, Aug. 3, 1950, Waring Papers.

29. Sullivan, *Lift Every Voice,* 381–82; Memorandum to Henry Lee Moon, May 15, 1951, and attached Background Information on Clarendon School District Suit, *Briggs v. Elliott* File, NAACP Papers.

30. Kluger, *Simple Justice*, 303–304; Waring Oral History, 338–40; Jack Greenberg, *Crusaders in the Courts* (Basic Books, 1994), 121–22; Elizabeth Waring Diary, 1, and J. Waties Waring to Delany, Oct. 12, 1950, Waring Papers.

31. Waring Oral History, 343–46; Alexander Rivera Oral History, Southern Oral History Collection, University of North Carolina at Chapel Hill, Nov. 30, 2001, 30–31; Kluger, *Simple Justice*, 304.

32. Kluger, *Simple Justice*, 15–23.

33. Ibid., 23–25.

34. Rivera Oral History, UNC–Chapel Hill, 30–31; Alexander Rivera Oral History, Interview about Life in the Jim Crow South, Duke University Libraries, June 2, 1995, 47–48; Waring Oral History, 343–46; Kluger, *Simple Justice*, 303–305. Rivera was a longtime photojournalist for *The Pittsburgh Courier* and a close friend and fraternity brother of Thurgood Marshall's. According to Rivera's account, shared with historians from the University of North Carolina and Duke University, he was present in the Charleston Federal Courthouse when Marshall left Judge Waring's chambers and heard Marshall's account of his meeting with the judge. Rivera observed with admiration the accuracy of Judge Waring's predictions of the outcome of the case before the three-judge panel and the U.S. Supreme Court under the Waring plan. Rivera stated that "I don't know why nobody seems to want to tell that story" or give Judge Waring credit for pushing Marshall further than he was prepared to go at the time. Rivera Oral History, UNC–Chapel Hill, 30–31.

35. Waring Oral History, 343–45; Rivera Oral History, UNC–Chapel Hill, 30–31; *New York Times*, Nov. 18, 1950; Kluger, *Simple Justice*, 304–305; Ophelia De Laine Gona, *Dawn of Desegregation: J. A. De Laine and Briggs v. Elliott* (University of South Carolina Press, 2011), 136; Jones, *Answering the Call*, 130, 182. In his classic work, *Simple Justice*, Richard Kluger observed that Marshall's confrontation with Waring made him look "either incompetent or craven. He was neither. He had simply tried to maneuver through very difficult terrain." Robert Carter, Marshall's co-counsel in *Briggs*, told Kluger, "Thurgood was not dragging his feet in this. We were struggling to find the right way." Kluger, *Simple Justice*, 304–305.

36. Sullivan, *Lift Every Voice*, 402–403, Robert Carter, *A Matter of Law: A Memoir of Struggle in the Cause of Equal Rights* (New Press, 2005), 97–98.

37. *Briggs v. Elliott* Case File, National Archives, Atlanta; Waring to Parker, Jan. 12, 1951, and Parker to Waring, Jan. 15, 1951, Waring Papers.

14. DRIVING THE "LAST NAIL IN THE COFFIN OF SEGREGATION"

1. Kluger, *Simple Justice*, 340–42; Yarbrough, *Passion for Justice*, 173; Peter F. Lau, "From Periphery to the Center: Clarendon County, South Carolina, *Brown*, and the Struggle for Democracy and Equality in America," in *From the Grassroots to the Supreme Court: Brown v. Board of Education and American Democracy*, ed. Peter F. Lau (Duke University Press, 2004), 105–22.

2. Sullivan, *Lift Every Voice*, 402; Egerton, *Speak Now Against the Day*, 521–22; Kluger, *Simple Justice*, 344; Elizabeth Waring Diary, 9.

3. Kluger, *Simple Justice*, 345; Carter, *Matter of Law*, 96, 99.

4. Judge Solomon Blatt Jr., interview by author.

5. Kluger, *Simple Justice*, 334–35, 344–45; Robertson, *Sly and Able*, 505–508; Waring Oral History, 350–51.

6. Kluger, *Simple Justice*, 345.

7. Ibid., 330–33.

8. Ibid., 313–31; Sullivan, *Lift Every Voice*, 404.

9. Kluger, *Simple Justice*, 328–31.

10. J. A. DeLaine to Elizabeth Waring, Sept. 23, 1950, Waring Papers; Kluger, *Simple Justice*, 3; *News and Courier*, Dec. 17, 1950.

11. Kluger, *Simple Justice*, 346–47; Sullivan, *Lift Every Voice*, 404–405; Marshall, letter to the editor, *Afro-American*, June 16, 1951; Carter, interview by author; Egerton, *Speak Now Against the Day*, 595.

12. Waring Oral History, 358.

13. Sullivan, *Lift Every Voice*, 404–405; Egerton, *Speak Now Against the Day*, 595; Kluger, *Simple Justice*, 346–47; Perry, interview by author.

14. Elizabeth Waring Diary, 1–3.

15. *Briggs v. Elliott* Transcript of Record, U.S. Supreme Court, 35.

16. Ibid., 36, 105; Waring Oral History, 353.

17. *Briggs v. Elliott* Transcript of Record, 39, 45–46.

18. Ibid., 47–58.

19. Ibid., 83–90.

20. Ibid., 104–5.

21. Ibid., 105.

22. Ibid., 105–13.

23. Ibid., 116–20.

24. Yarbrough, *Passion for Justice*, 184–85; Waring Oral History, 354; Carter, *Matter of Law*, 104.

25. *Briggs v. Elliott* Transcript, 129–30.

26. Ibid., 131–48, 156–75.

27. *New York Times*, May 30 and June 3, 1951.

28. Waring Oral History, 358–59; Elizabeth Waring Diary, 3, 9.

29. Elizabeth Waring Diary, 9; Waring Oral History, 358–59.

30. *Briggs v. Elliott*, 98 F. Supp. 529, 530–38 (E.D.S.C. 1950), *rev'd*, *Brown v. Board of Education*, 347 U.S. 483 (1954).

31. *Briggs*, 98 F. Supp. at 538–48.

32. Ibid. at 548; Kennedy, "Reply to Philip Elman," 1940–41; Amicus Brief of the American Jewish Committee and B'nai B'rith in *Sweatt v. Painter*, 1950 WL 786694 at *29–39 (April 1, 1950); Amicus Brief of the National Lawyers Guild in *Henderson v. United States*, 1949 WL 50669 at *19–23 (Nov. 14, 1949); Amicus Brief of the American Federation of Teachers in *McLaurin v. Oklahoma State Regents*, 1949 WL 50349 at *10–12 (Dec. 8, 1949); Amicus Brief of the Federal Council of Churches in *Sweatt v. Painter*, 1949 WL 50366 at *7–9 (Sept. 23, 1949); Brief of the United States in *Henderson v. United States*, 1949 WL 50329 at *24–27 (Oct. 4, 1949). See also Christopher W. Schmidt, "J. Waties Waring and

the Making of Liberal Jurisprudence in Postwar America," in Lau, *From the Grassroots to the Supreme Court*, 173–97; David Southern, "Beyond Jim Crow Liberalism: Judge Waring's Fight Against Segregation in South Carolina, 1942–1952," *Journal of Negro History* 66, no. 3 (Fall 1981): 209–27; Marguerite Cartwright, "J. Waties Waring: Latter Day Emancipation," *Negro History Bulletin* (Dec. 1955): 61–63.

33. Delany to Waring, June 26, 1951, Clement to Waring, June 26, 1951, and Williams to Waring, June 29, 1951, Waring Papers.

34. Waring to Delany, June 28, 1951, Waring to Williams, July 2, 1951, Waring to Dombrowski, June 26, 1951, Waring Papers.

35. Elizabeth Waring Diary, 15, and Copy of Waring's Dissent with personal inscription to Elizabeth Waring, Waring Papers.

36. *Pittsburgh Courier*, July 9, 1951; *Lighthouse and Informer*, July 1, 1951; *Chicago Defender*, July 2, 1951; Carl John, letter to the editor, *Pittsburgh Courier*, July 9, 1951; Marshall to NAACP state leaders, draft telegram, July 6, 1951; and draft letter to *Pittsburgh Courier*, July 5, 1951, *Briggs v. Elliott* File, NAACP Papers.

37. *News and Courier*, June 30, 1951.

38. Waring to Truman, Jan. 26, 1952, Waring Papers; Transcript of Presidential Press Conference, Jan. 31, 1952, Truman Library; *News and Courier*, Jan. 29 and Feb. 3, 1952.

39. Rowan to Waring, Feb. 4, 1952, and Waring to Rowan, Feb. 7, 1952, Waring Papers.

40. Waring to Mays, March 29, 1952, Waring Papers.

41. *New York Times*, Feb. 4, 1952; *News and Courier*, Feb. 5, 1952.

42. Waring to Marshall, July 26, 1951, and Jan. 27 and Dec. 26, 1953, Waring Papers; *New York Times*, April 17 and May 11, 1952, Nov. 21, 1954; *Amsterdam News*, April 21 and May 10, 1952, Jan. 3, 1953, Oct. 16, 1954, April 27, 1957, Nov. 11, 1959; *News and Courier*, April 22 and June 14, 1952, July 19, 1956, Dec. 18, 1957, Nov. 22, 1959.

43. *Brown v. Board of Education of Topeka, Kansas*, 78 F. Supp. 797, 798 (D. Kan. 1951).

44. *Davis v. County School Board of Prince Edward County*, 103 F. Supp. 337340–41 (W.D. Va. 1952).

45. *Gebhart v. Belton*, 91 A. 2d 137, 149–73 (Del. 1952).

46. *Bolling v. Sharpe*, 344 U.S. 873 (1952).

47. Waring Oral History, 363.

48. Kluger, *Simple Justice*, 696–99.

49. Waring Oral History, 369.

50. Kluger, *Simple Justice*, 702–707; *Bolling v. Sharpe*, 347 U.S. 497 (1954).

51. *Brown v. Board of Education*, 347 U.S. 483, 494–95 (1954).

52. Ibid. at 495.

53. Cannon, *Gentle Knight*, 191–92; Waring Oral History, 370–71.

54. Cannon, *Gentle Knight*, 193–95.

55. Waring Oral History, 364–65, 367, 377–78.

CONCLUSION: UNEXAMPLED COURAGE

1. *Briggs v. Elliott*, 98 F. Supp. 529, 540 (E.D.S.C. 1950).

2. Isaac Woodard Affidavit, April 23, 1946, FBI Field Report, Aug. 5, 1946, FBI Files.

3. Truman to Clark, Sept. 20, 1946, Truman to Roberts, Aug. 18, 1948, Truman Library; *To Secure These Rights*, 7–9, 20–25; Margaret Truman, *Harry S. Truman*, 392.

4. Waring Oral History, 2–6, 256.

5. *Briggs v. Elliott*, 98 F. Supp. at 540.

6. Waring to Parker, Aug. 8, 1948, Waring Papers; Waring, "Struggle for Negro Rights," 10.

7. McCullough, *Truman*, 887; Frey, "Truman's Speech to the NAACP," 96; *Shelley v. Kraemer*, 334 U.S. 1 (1948); Elman and Silber, "Solicitor General's Office, Justice Frankfurter, and Civil Rights Litigation," 843–44.

8. *Brown v. Baskin*, 174 F.2d 391, 393–94 (4th Cir. 1949).

9. *Brown v. Board of Education* (*Brown II*), 349 U.S. 294, 301 (1955); Waring Oral History, 296–97, 319, 371, 385–88; Charles Ogletree, Keynote Address, South Carolina Supreme Court Historical Society 2011 Colloquium, "J. Waties Waring and the Dissent That Changed America," May 19, 2011.

10. Madison Jones to Walter White, memorandum, Sept. 19, 1946, Woodard Files. Woodard had the right as a citizen of another state to bring his lawsuit in the federal district court in West Virginia. NAACP counsel, after considering the potential benefits and challenges of state and federal venues, elected to bring the action in state court.

11. Nutter to Franklin Williams, Jan. 29, 1947, Transcript of Record, *Isaac Woodard v. Atlantic Greyhound Corporation*, Woodard Files; *Pittsburgh Courier*, Feb. 15 and Nov. 22, 1947; *New York Times*, Nov. 14, 1947; *State*, Nov. 12 and 13, 1947.

12. Woodard to Mr. Hylton, Jan. 3, 1952, Woodard VA File.

13. Robert Young, interview by author; Property Records of 1075 Forest Avenue and 973 Tinton Avenue, Bronx City Register Office, Bronx, New York; VA Pension Statement, Oct. 8, 1954, Woodard VA File.

14. "Isaac Woodard: America's Forgotten Man," *Jet*, March 1, 1956, 12–14.

15. Young, interview by author; VA Pension Statement, Oct. 31, 1962, Woodard VA File.

16. Woodard Social Survey, April 1, 1964, Woodard VA File.

17. Property Records, 3728 Dyre Avenue, Bronx City Register Office, Bronx, New York; Isaac Woodard Estate File, File No. 783, Surrogate's Court, Bronx, New York; Isaac Woodard Death Certificate, Woodard VA File.

18. Robert Young, interview by author; Christopher G. Roberts, interview by author; Cannon, *Gentle Knight*, 30–31; *Amsterdam News*, April 24, 1965; Roberts, *Reflections of a Heart* (2006), manuscript in possession of author; "Steppingstone Theatre Co. Presents 'Reflections of a Heart,'" www.broadwayworld.com/off-broadway, June 11, 2010.

19. *State*, Dec. 17, 1951, April 24, 1952, March 20 and June 13, 1956, March 17,

1964, Aug. 23, 1968, March 23 and June 6 and 9, 1976, Dec. 28, 1997; Michele Norris, *The Grace of Silence* (Pantheon Books, 2010), 126–29; Andy Duncan, interview by author.

20. *New York Times*, May 22, 1990.

21. Fred Stanley Rogers Death Certificate, April 14, 1968, Texas Department of State Health Services; Obituary of Neilson Rogers (son of Fred S. Rogers), *Herald (Tex.) Democrat*, Aug. 11, 2009; Obituary of Claud Sapp, *State*, Feb. 3, 1947.

22. Callow, *Hello Americans*; Walter White to David Niles, Sept. 26, 1946, Truman Library.

23. *State*, July 31, 2012.

24. Kluger, *Simple Justice*, 3–4, 611, 778; Egerton, *Speak Now Against the Day*, 611; James Clyburn, "South Carolina Desegregation Heroes Receive Congressional Gold Medal," Sept. 8, 2004; Joseph DeLaine Jr., interview by author.

25. Cannon, *Gentle Knight*; *Amsterdam News*, March 9, 1964, April 24 and Dec. 25, 1965, Jan. 27, 1968; *New York Times*, April 2, 1975.

26. *New York Times*, Jan. 25, 1993; Wil Haygood, *Showdown: Thurgood Marshall and the Supreme Court Nomination That Changed America* (Alfred A. Knopf, 2015); Thurgood Marshall, Biographical Directory of Federal Judges, Federal Judicial Center.

27. *New York Times*, Jan. 3, 2012; Robert Carter, Biographical Directory of Federal Judges, Federal Judicial Center.

28. *New York Times*, Jan. 30, 1983.

29. *New York Times*, May 2, 2005; Clark to Waties and Elizabeth Waring, Jan. 27, 1954, Kenneth Clark inscription to the Warings on cover of *Journal of Social Issues*, March 24, 1954, Clark to Waties and Elizabeth Waring, May 28, 1958, and "Reflections on the Loss of a Friend," Jan. 17, 1968, Waring Papers.

30. Kluger, *Simple Justice*, 706; *Brown v. Board of Education*, 347 U.S. 483, 692n11 (1954); entries on Gunnar Myrdal and Alva Myrdal, www.nobelprize.org.

31. *State*, Feb. 1, 1991; Biographical Notes, Joseph O. Rogers Jr., South Carolina Political Collections, University of South Carolina; "Joseph O. Rogers Jr.," Memory Hold the Door; Biographical Note, Joseph O. Rogers Papers, South Carolina Political Collections, University of South Carolina.

32. John Johnston Parker, Biographical Directory of Federal Judges, Federal Judicial Center; Cameron McGowan Currie, "Before Rosa Parks: The Case of Sarah Mae Flemming," in Burke and Gergel, *Matthew J. Perry*, 81–95; *Flemming v. South Carolina Electric and Gas*, 128 F. Supp. 469 (E.D.S.C. 1955), rev'd, 224 F.2d 752 (4th Cir. 1955) and 239 F.2d 277 (4th Cir. 1956); George Bell Timmerman Sr., Biographical Directory of Federal Judges, Federal Judicial Center; Yarbrough, *Passion for Justice*, 229. An all-white jury ruled for the bus company in the third proceeding before Judge Timmerman, and Ms. Flemming, exhausted from her legal battles, abandoned the case.

33. "Mendel Lucius Rivers," in Walter Edgar, ed., *The South Carolina Encyclopedia* (University of South Carolina Press, 2006), 807–808; White to Truman, telegram, March 28, 1952, and NAACP Board Minutes, March 1952 (White described Rivers

as "one of the most vindictive opponents of constitutional rights for minorities" and reported that the president's assistant had assured him that the NAACP's views regarding Rivers's nomination to the district court would be "carefully considered"), Waring File, NAACP Papers.

34. Maarten Zwiers, *Senator James Eastland: Mississippi's Jim Crow Democrat* (Louisiana State University Press, 2015), 117; Clifford Durr Oral History, Southern Historical Collection, UNC–Chapel Hill; David L. Chappell, *Inside Agitators: White Southerners in the Civil Rights Movement* (Johns Hopkins University Press, 1996), 54; *Dombrowski v. Pfister*, 380 U.S. 479 (1965).

35. McCullough, *Truman*, 970–74; Raymond H. Geselbracht, "The Truman Library and Truman's Civil Rights Legacy," in Geselbracht, *Civil Rights Legacy of Harry S. Truman*, 143–48.

36. "The New Negro," *The Open Mind*, PBS, Feb. 10, 1957; Martin Luther King Jr., "Desegregation and the Future," Address to the Annual Luncheon of the National Committee for Rural Schools, Dec. 15, 1956, Martin Luther King Library, Atlanta.

37. Waring Oral History, 268–69.

38. A. J. Clement to Waring, Oct. 26, 1954, Waring to Clement, Oct. 28, 1954, and NAACP press release, "Judge Waring Honored at Charleston Testimonial," Oct. 10, 1954, Waring Papers; *New York Times*, Jan. 18, 1968; *Washington Post*, Jan. 18, 1954.

39. *Post and Courier*, April 12, 2014; Remarks of Attorney General Eric Holder at Dedication Ceremony Honoring Judge J. Waties Waring, April 11, 2014, U.S. Department of Justice.

40. *Post and Courier*, March 15, 2015; Andy Brack, "In Renaming Courthouse, Hollings Is Still Teaching Us," *Huffington Post*, Oct. 6, 2015; Public Law 114–48, 114th Cong. (Aug. 7, 2015).

APPENDIX: A FORENSIC ANALYSIS OF THE BLINDING OF ISAAC WOODARD

1. Woodard Final Hospital Report, April 17, 1946; Woodard Final Progress Note, April 11, 1946, VA Records.

2. FBI Field Report, Aug. 5, 1946, 8–9, FBI Files; Report of Chester W. Chinn, M.D., May 7, 1946, Woodard Files.

3. Report of Kim A. Collins, M.D., "Re: Isaac Woodard Jr.," Aug. 20, 2015, in possession of author.

ACKNOWLEDGMENTS

The research and writing of this book has been possible only with the selfless assistance of family, friends, and new friends I have made along the way. First and foremost, my dear wife, Belinda Friedman Gergel, a highly skilled historian, who has been with me at every library and archive, helping dig out seeming needles in haystacks that helped tell this remarkable story. She also has patiently tolerated the devotion of almost all of our family vacations in recent years to what one of my law clerks dubbed "writing holidays." This book would not have happened without Belinda's support and assistance.

I have leaned on my historian friends for advice and insight, recognizing that my background in law rather than history required extra work to close gaps in my knowledge. Patricia Sullivan, Marjorie Spruill, Don Doyle, and John White have endured extended discussions and early-morning phone calls to help me sort out this complicated story. I am indebted to the readers of my

306 ACKNOWLEDGMENTS

manuscript—Belinda Gergel, Patricia Sullivan, Don Doyle, David Norton, Adair Boroughs, Leon Friedman, and Deena Smith McRackan—all of whom offered valuable suggestions.

I cannot thank enough Dr. Kim Collins, one of the nation's premier forensic pathologists, who volunteered to study and reconstruct the blinding of Isaac Woodard. She enthusiastically undertook this task, carefully studying medical records and other relevant documents, and has now definitively informed all of us how Isaac Woodard was blinded.

Family members of many of the participants in this book have generously shared their stories and photographs. These have included Robert Young, the nephew and caregiver of Isaac Woodard; Joseph DeLaine, the son of the Reverend J. A. DeLaine; Angela Martin, the niece of Viola Duvall; Hemphill Pride, the nephew of Ruby Cornwell; and Tom and Brad Waring, family members of Judge Waring.

No meaningful piece of history is possible without the assistance of archivists and research librarians, and I have received the generous help of countless individuals. These have included the staffs at the Library of Congress, the Moorland-Spingarn Research Center at Howard University, the Harry S. Truman Presidential Library, the South Caroliniana Library and South Carolina Political Collections at the University of South Carolina, and the Avery Institute of the College of Charleston. Special thanks to Bill Nettles, former United States attorney for South Carolina, and the staff in the legal counsel's office of the Veterans Administration, who were able to track down the VA record of Isaac Woodard, which included critical medical records and other important materials. I am also indebted to the staff of the National Archives, who were able to locate the FBI and Department of Justice files related to the prosecution of Lynwood Shull. These previously undisclosed documents filled in many of the gaps regarding the blinding of Isaac Woodard and the flawed investigation and prosecution of Lynwood Shull. I also appreciate the generous assistance of Cecil Williams, South Carolina's premier photographer of the civil rights movement, who has allowed me to use his iconic photograph, and Andre Vann, North Carolina Central University's archivist, who has allowed me access to and use of the newly obtained historical photographs of Alexander Rivera.

One of the occupational hazards of a judge is a tendency to write in wooden and legalistic prose, something my gifted editor, Sarah Crichton, has attempted to beat out of me. Sarah and her highly talented team at Farrar, Straus and Giroux have shared my passion for this story and helped make the manuscript more readable and approachable.

Finally, I wish to acknowledge those participants in this remarkable moment in American history who displayed unexampled courage and helped this great country to live up to its highest ideals. They have much to teach the rest of us.

RICHARD GERGEL

INDEX

Acheson, Dean, 25
African Americans:
  children of, 225–27, 233–36, 238,
    245–46, 252
  churches for, 88–89
  as citizens, 41, 47, 126, 141–42, 145,
    166–67, 192, 204, 228, 249–50
  communities of, 30, 37, 45–46,
    87–88, 107
  employment of, 13, 101, 102, 149,
    152, 160, 189, 278n3
  equal rights of, 54, 110, 162, 165,
    167, 177, 184, 197; see also civil
    rights movement
  as freedmen, 50–51
  as judges, 168, 179, 239–40, 294n13
  on juries, 188, 258
  in law schools, 25, 176–77, 179–80,
    213–14
  as military veterans, 11–12, 71,
    146–47, 169–70
  murder of, 35–36, 57, 71, 157, 172,
    283n16

  newspapers for, 25, 39, 90, 184–85
  oaths required of, 189, 192, 197–98,
    222
  political influence of, 27–29, 118,
    136–37, 143–45, 250
  as sharecroppers, 12–13, 187–88
  as teachers, 102–10, 177–78,
    287nn16, 21
  voting rights of, 3–4, 25, 26, 27–29,
    34–35, 51–53, 54, 101, 103, 113,
    140, 145–46, 150, 152, 173, 174,
    175, 176, 177, 179–87, 188,
    189–99, 249–50, 275n2
  as witnesses, 224, 229, 230–31, 234,
    238
Aiken, S.C., 14, 31–32, 41, 42, 56
Alexander, Sadie, 138
"all deliberate speed," 257–58
Allen, Leo, 194
Alston v. School Board of City of Norfolk,
  102, 103, 104, 177–78
American Civil Liberties Union
  (ACLU), 46, 242

American Communist Party, 85
"American Creed," 174–75, 182–83, 188
American Dilemma, An: The Negro Problem and Modern Democracy (Myrdal), 173–75, 246, 265
American Federation of Labor (AFL), 46, 138
American Jewish Committee, 213–14
American Jewish Congress, 46
American Legion, 278*n*24
American Psychological Association, 264
amicus briefs, 148–49, 161, 165, 166–67, 213–14
Amsterdam News, 45, 46, 85, 259, 261, 264
Ancrum, Jane Waring, 286*n*4
Ancrum, John L., 286*n*4
Appomattox, surrender at (1865), 50–51
Armed Forces Institute of Pathology, 131
Arnall, Ellis, 34, 35
Associated Press (AP), 18, 43, 78, 229
Association for the Protection of the Colored Race, 118–19
Atlantic Greyhound Corporation, 258–59
Augusta, Ga., 32, 250

Baltimore, Md., 87, 89
Barkley, Alben, 160
baseball, 12, 147–48, 175
Basie, Count, 215
Baskin, William P., 181–82, 190–91
Beechem, Archie, 126
Bernhardt, Sarah, 96
Betchman, H. B., 235
Birmingham, Ala., 154
Black, Hugo, 202
Black Codes, 52
Blackwell, Alton, 14–15, 123
Blatt, Solomon, 223

"Blinding of Isaac Woodard, The" (Guthrie), 45
B'nai B'rith, 213–14
Bolling v. Sharpe, 243–44, 246
Bond, Julian, 5–6
Boone, Reginald and Eva, 226
Booth, John Wilkes, 64
Bootsie (Harrington), 39
Boulware, Harold, 42, 217, 224–25, 264
Bradley, Omar, 161
Breakthrough on the Color Front, 164
Brice, Carol, 45
Briggs, Harry and Eliza, 211, 218, 227, 262–63
Briggs v. Elliott, 5, 217–20, 224–46, 250, 252–53, 255–58, 262–63, 264, 265, 299*nn*34, 35
Brockington, D. A., 97
Brooklyn Dodgers, 147–48, 175
Brown, David, 189–90
Brown, D. K., 57, 77, 79, 82
Brown II, 257–58
Brown v. Baskin, 189–99, 222, 256–57
Brown v. Board of Education, 5, 28, 164, 166–67, 177, 239, 241, 243–47, 255–58, 263, 265, 266, 268
Buckeye Review, 90
Bunche, Ralph, 173
Burger, Mortimer, 21–22, 57, 121–22, 274
Byrd, Harry F., 150
Byrnes, James F., 68–69, 96, 98, 223–24, 237

Callow, Simon, 44
Calloway, Cab, 45
Campbell, Lyle, 79
Camp Gordon, 14, 22, 31–32
Carey, James, 138
Carr, Robert K., 138, 141
Carter, Hodding, 207
Carter, Jimmy, 90, 179

Carter, Robert:
  Briggs v. Elliott and, 219–20, 224–25, 226, 228, 233–34
  Brown v. Board of Education and, 246
  district court, appointment to, 264
  doll studies of, 225–26
  Woodard blinding and, 32, 42, 92
Cash, W. J., 172–73, 175
Caudle, Theron Lamar, 43, 56, 58, 80
Caughman, Henry, 78–79, 126
Chamberlain, Daniel, 52
Charleston, W.Va., 258–59
Charleston County, S.C., 98–99, 170, 196, 208, 222, 226
Charleston Evening Post, 184, 227–28
Charleston Federal Courthouse, 98, 188, 190, 268–69, 299n34
Charleston News and Courier, 172, 183–84, 191, 192, 194, 203, 208, 209, 211, 212, 241, 242, 269
Charleston School District, 102–106
Chicago Defender, 162, 229
Chinn, Chester, 23, 272–73
Christian Science Monitor, 175
Churchill, Winston S., 70, 136
Citizen Kane, 40
Civilian Conservation Corps (CCC), 13
Civil Rights Cases, 176
civil rights movement:
  criminal investigations in, 15, 30–31, 54–56, 150, 168–69, 211, 212
  federal support for, 52–53, 71–72, 109, 136, 139–42, 147, 150, 155, 164, 199, 283n16
  leadership of, 25–26, 54, 68, 85–91, 105, 137–38, 144, 201–202, 215–16, 239–40, 251, 263–64, 278n3, 292n39
  legislation for, 38–39, 44, 152, 187–88
  organizations in, 26–29, 39–46; *see also specific organizations*
  political aspect of, 55–56, 103, 150, 159

  public support for, 72, 149, 152, 157, 158
  southern opposition to, *see* South, U.S.
  "unexampled courage" in, 250, 252
Civil Rights Section (Justice Department), 54–56, 59, 74, 75, 80, 82, 168, 283n16
Civil War, U.S., 50–52, 95
Civil War Amendments, 53, 169
Clancy, Arthur, 21, 57, 121–22, 272
Clarendon County Board of Education (School District No. 22), 217–18, 222, 229–30, 247
Clark, Bennett, 67
Clark, Kenneth, 173, 225–27, 233, 238, 246, 264–65
Clark, Mamie, 225–27
Clark, Mark, 163
Clark, Septima, 203, 206–207
Clark, Tom, 28, 35, 36, 47, 56–57, 71, 73, 74, 75, 77, 114, 129, 141, 198, 251
Clement, A. J., 240, 269
Clifford, Clark, 136, 143–45, 153, 159, 170
Cole, Nat King, 45
College of Charleston, 95–96
Collier's, 203
Collins, Kim, 271–74, 290n36
Columbia, S.C., 5, 12, 15, 80, 82, 87, 91–92, 100, 115, 117, 135, 171, 262
Columbia, Tenn., riot (1946), 30–31, 71, 72, 79–80
Columbia Division of the Eastern District of South Carolina, 80, 99–100, 102, 178, 276n6
Columbia Record, 109
Columbia *State*, 130, 197
Committee on Equality of Treatment and Opportunity in the Armed Services (Fahy Committee), 162–65, 168

Committee on Government Contract
    Compliance, U.S., 167–68
Committee on Un-American Activities
    (HUAC), 43
communism, 85, 150, 155, 175, 266, 267
Compromise of 1877, 52–53
Congress, U.S., 22, 28, 38–39, 50, 53,
    70–75, 102, 135–37, 149–50, 164,
    176, 194, 236, 250, 260
    see also House of Representatives,
    U.S.; Senate, U.S.
Congress of Industrial Organizations
    (CIO), 46, 138
Constitution, U.S., 4, 49, 108, 110, 139,
    142, 165, 167, 177, 181, 184, 197,
    204, 237, 242, 257
    see also specific amendments
Constitutional Convention (1787), 49
"Contention for Miscegenation," 241
Cornwell, Aylwood, 203, 268
Cornwell, Ruby, 110, 203, 229, 268
Council for Civic Unity, 214
Crews, Tom A., 283n16
Criminal Division (Justice
    Department), 54, 56
Crisis, 143
Crow, E. R., 234–35
Cry, the Beloved Country (Paton), 246

Darlington County, S.C., 187–88
Davis, T. Hoyt, 177, 178
Davis v. County School Board of Prince
    Edward County, 243
Declaration of Independence, 142, 242
Defense Department, U.S., 167
DeLaine, Joseph A., 217–18, 227, 229,
    252–53, 263
DeLaine Waring AME Church, 263
Delany, Hubert, 215, 239–40
Delaware Supreme Court, 243
Democratic National Conventions:
    of 1932, 76
    of 1938, 99

of 1944, 68–69, 152
    of 1948, 152, 190
Democratic Party:
    all-white primaries for, 11, 27–29,
        72, 102, 146, 177, 179–87, 188,
        189–99, 201, 222, 256–57, 262,
        276n2
    black support for, 27–29, 136–37,
        143–45, 250
    civil rights platform of, 135, 136–37,
        152–55
    congressional majority of, 74–75,
        135–36, 158, 160
    southern influence in, 27–29, 48,
        70–71, 76, 135, 141, 143–45,
        150–53, 159, 179–85, 190–91,
        209, 254, 256–57
Democratic Party Platform Committee,
    152
Des Moines Register, 157
Dewey, Thomas E., 28, 143–44, 154,
    157, 158–59
Dickey, John, 138
District of Columbia, 147, 236, 243–44,
    246
dolls (racial) study, 225–27, 233
Dombrowski, James, 201, 204, 213,
    240, 266–67
Dombrowski v. Pfister, 266–67
Doolittle's Lumber, 13
Dorn, Bryan, 193, 194
Dorsey, George, 35
"Double V" campaign, 25
Durr, Clifford, 202–203, 266
Durr, Virginia, 202
Duvall, Viola, 102–106
Duvall v. Seignous, 102–106, 109–10,
    287n16

Eaddy, Albert, 21
Eastland, James, 266
Egerton, John, 149
Eisenhower, Dwight D., 163, 244

elections, U.S.:
  of 1860, 50
  of 1866, 51
  of 1876, 52–53
  of 1920, 103
  of 1922, 63, 65, 139
  of 1926, 65
  of 1930, 97–98
  of 1932, 74, 76
  of 1934, 65–66
  of 1938, 98–102
  of 1940, 63, 66
  of 1944, 67–69, 146, 182
  of 1946, 29, 34–35, 74–75, 81,
    135–36, 144, 182
  of 1948, 27, 63–64, 139–40, 143–59,
    160, 190, 195, 252, 254, 292n37
  of 1960, 267
Electoral College, 49, 52, 154, 157–58
"Eliminating Discrimination," 109
Elliott, R. W., 231
Elman, Philip, 165, 256
Elmore, George, 179–81, 262
Elmore v. Rice, 179–87, 189–99, 262
Emancipation Proclamation (1862), 50
Estill, S.C., 184
Executive Order 9980, 155
Executive Order 9981, 155

Fahy, Charles, 162
Fahy Committee, 162–65, 168
Fair Employment Practices Committee
  (FEPC), 26, 70, 278n3
Fairfield County, S.C., 12–13, 32
Federal Bureau of Investigation (FBI),
  15, 30–31, 55, 56, 168–69, 211,
  212, 280n1
Federal Communications Commission
  (FCC), 202
Federal Council of Churches, 46, 213
Federal Housing Administration
  (FHA), 169
Fifteenth Amendment, 11, 51, 53, 145

Fifth Amendment, 244
Fifth Circuit Court of Appeals, U.S.,
  177, 178, 283n16
Figg, Robert, 222–23, 224, 229–30,
  232, 234–37, 265
filibusters, 26, 38–39, 53, 160, 250
Finney, Ernest, 179
Finnie, Isabella, 185
Fleming, John, 229
Fleming, Samuel, 188
Flora, A. C., 107, 108, 109
Florence Morning News, 184
Florida, 111, 283n16
Ford, Peyton, 210, 211–12
Fort Jackson, 12, 13
429th Port Battalion, U.S., 13–14
Fourteenth Amendment, 53, 105, 145,
  165, 166, 167, 176, 216, 224, 236,
  237, 238, 244
Fourth Circuit Court of Appeals, U.S.,
  97, 218–19, 265
  *Alston v. School Board of City of
    Norfolk* (1940), 102–103, 177–78
  Brown v. Baskin (1948), 198, 256–57
  Elmore v. Rice (1947), 184–87
Frankfurter, Felix, 165, 256
Fugitive Slave Act (1850), 50

Gaines v. Canada, 176–77
Gammell, Maria Ancrum, 286n4
Garrett, Charles, 207
Gebhart v. Belton, 243
General Services Administration,
  U.S., 167
Gentle Knight, A (White), 263–64
Georgia, 14, 34–36, 74, 145, 177, 178,
  187–88
Georgia Democratic Party, 29, 71
Germany, Nazi, 3, 24, 186
Gettysburg Address (1863), 143
Gibbes, J. Heyward, 107, 108–109
Gibson, James, 228
Gibson, Truman, 137

Goodman, Benny, 215
Graham, Frank Porter, 138, 148
"grandfather clauses," 11, 275n2
grand juries, 31, 36, 55, 71, 72, 75, 129, 283n16
Granger, Lester, 162
Great Depression, 98, 136
Great Society, 169
Greyhound Bus Co., 12, 14–15, 31, 56–57, 99, 115, 117, 127, 250–51, 258–59, 269, 276n6
Griffith, Jefferson Davis, 118, 127
Guthrie, Woody, 45

Hall, Jack D., 118, 127
Hall v. DeCuir, 176
Hammond, John, 215
Handy, W. C., 45
Harlan, John Marshall, 216
Harrington, Oliver "Ollie," 39, 40, 43, 114, 280n1
Harris, Albert, 36
Harvard Law Review, 168
Harvey, Wilson G., 97
Hastie, William, 168, 181, 183, 294n13
Hayes, Rutherford B., 52
Henderson v. United States, 166, 213, 214
Hinton, James, 32, 105–106, 130
Hiroshima bombing (1945), 70
Hoffman, Henry, 110–11
Holder, Eric, 269
Holiday, Billie, 215
Hollings, Ernest F. "Fritz," 269
Holloran, William J., 58
Holocaust, 41
Hoover, Herbert, 135, 168
Hoover, J. Edgar, 43, 55, 56–59, 77–78, 79, 82, 146
House, Ralph, 77–78, 116
House of Representatives, U.S., 70, 135, 154, 158, 182, 193–94, 208–10, 223, 266, 269
    Armed Services Committee of, 266

Judiciary Committee of, 193–94, 208–10
    Rules Committee of, 70
Houston, Charles Hamilton, 28, 215, 216
Howard University Law School, 28, 168
Hudson, McQuilla, 115, 117, 122–23
Humphrey, Hubert, 153

interracial marriage, 174, 207
Interstate Commerce Commission (ICC), 166
Iron Curtain, 172, 185, 253
"Isaac Woodard: America's Forgotten Man," 259–60
"Isaac Woodard Day," 88–89

Jackson County, Mo., 63, 64–65, 66, 67, 139
Jacobson, Eddie, 64
Japan, 3, 9–10, 69–70
Jensen, H. H., 79
Jet, 259–60
Johnson, Andrew, 50–51
Johnson, James Weldon, 27
Johnson, Lady Bird, 202
Johnson, Lyndon B., 169, 202, 261, 264, 266, 267
Johnston, Olin, 78, 99, 180–81
Johnstone, Alan, 191, 193
Jones, John C., 36
Jones, Madison, 87, 91
Jones, Nathaniel, 90, 219
judges, 168, 179, 239–40, 294n13
"Judge Worthy of Honor, A," 242
juries, 31, 36, 55, 71, 72, 75, 83, 118–19, 129, 140, 148, 171, 188, 234, 258, 283n16, 296n36
Justice Department, U.S.:
    amicus program of, 164–67
    civil rights enforcement and, 29, 54–56, 148–49, 251
    Civil Rights Section of, 54–56, 59, 74, 75, 80, 82, 168, 283n16

Columbia, Tenn., incident and, 30–31
and Marshal Service protection of Waring, 212
peonage cases brought by, 187
Waring impeachment effort and, 210
and Waring nomination to district court, 100, 193
Woodard and, 4, 5, 33, 48, 87, 114, 129, 131, 199, 251

Kansas City, Mo., 26, 64–65
Kansas-Nebraska Act (1854), 50
Kennedy, John F., 261, 264, 267
King, Martin Luther, Jr., 201, 203, 267–68
King, W. W., 20–21, 117–18, 125, 288n18
Kluger, Richard, 169, 263
Knox, Ellis, 233–34
Korean War, 267
Krech, David, 236
Ku Klux Klan (KKK), 30–31, 36, 97, 119, 129, 138, 196–97, 209, 210–12

labor unions, 67, 68, 136, 144, 147
Ladd, D. M., 59
Ladies' Home Journal, 204
"Last of the White Primary, The," 185
law schools, 25, 176–77, 179–80, 213–14
Lear Corporation, 262
Lee, Robert E., 50
Leesville, S.C., 16, 269
legal system:
appeals in, 103, 106, 168, 177–78, 186, 216–17, 225
case law in, 176
common law in, 287n16
equal protection in, 105, 140, 145, 197, 237, 239, 257
federal, 168, 176, 180, 194, 250
injunctions in, 148, 190, 191–98, 235
precedent in, 103, 167, 215

state, 51, 108, 111, 176, 180–82, 283n16
trials in, 55, 83, 100, 118–19, 140, 148, 171, 234, 296n6
Lewis, John, 169
Lexington County, S.C., 78–79, 119, 261
liability admissions, 224–25, 229–30, 231, 233
Lighthouse and Informer, 31, 103–104
Lincoln, Abraham, 50, 64, 140, 143, 144, 169
literacy tests, 11, 176
"Lonesomest Man in Town," 203
Long, Elliot, 16, 18, 19, 123–24
Long, John, 209
Louis, Joe, 45, 46–47
Louisiana, 6, 36, 145, 266
Louisville, New Orleans & Texas Ry. Co. v. Mississippi, 176
Lovejoy, Mildred, 259
Luckman, Charles, 138

Mabry, Willie, 87, 89
Malcolm, Roger, 34–35
Marshall, George, 163
Marshall, Thurgood:
in *Briggs v. Elliott*, 215–20, 222–36, 241, 299nn34, 35
in *Brown v. Baskin*, 189–92, 195
in *Duvall v. Seignous*, 103–106, 287n16
in *Elmore v. Rice* and, 180–81
as General Counsel of NAACP, 28, 165
in *Smith v. Allwright*, 28, 177
Supreme Court, appointment to, 264
To Secure These Rights, response to, 149
Truman and, 169
Waring and, 105, 198, 210, 218–19, 243, 247, 255, 299nn34, 35
Woodard incident and, 32, 42, 89, 92
Martin, Joe, 154

Maybank, Burnet, 81, 97–100, 184, 191, 193, 196

Mays, Benjamin, 185, 201, 242

McCord, L. B., 231

McCray, John, 31, 103–104, 105

McCullough, David, 170

McGrath, Howard, 211

McGregor, Douglas, 79

McKenzie, Margaret, 241

McLaurin v. Oklahoma State Regents, 166, 213, 214, 215, 237

McNally, Harold, 233–34

Meet the Press, 207

Michener, Earl, 194

Miller, Lincoln, 17, 42, 57–58, 115–16, 117, 127, 129–30

Mind of the South, The (Cash), 172–73

Minneapolis Tribune, 203

Mississippi, 51, 52, 71, 118, 153, 180, 195

Missouri, 26–27, 64, 176–77

Missouri, University of, Law School of, 176–77

Missouri Compromise (1820), 50

"Missouri Compromise" (1944), 69

Monroe, Ga., 35, 72

Montgomery bus boycott, 202, 267

Moore's Ford lynchings (1946), 35–36, 57, 71, 157

"My Day" (E. Roosevelt), 205

Myers, Frank K., 98

Myrdal, Alva, 265

Myrdal, Gunnar, 4, 49, 173–75, 182–83, 246, 249, 265

NAACP Legal Defense Fund, 28, 165, 167, 215, 216, 242–43

Nagasaki bombing (1945), 70

National Association for the Advancement of Colored People (NAACP):

and amicus program of Justice Department, 165, 167

public school segregation challenged by, 215–16, 243–44

Smith v. Allwright and, 27–29

Truman and, 27, 71, 72–73

To Secure These Rights, reaction to, 149

Woodard incident and, 16, 32–34, 38–46

National Association of Colored Women's Clubs, 72

National Baptist Convention, 213

National Emergency Committee Against Mob Violence, 46–47, 72–73

National Guard, U.S., 64, 146, 169

National Lawyers Guild, 197, 202, 204

National League, 148

National Teachers Exam (NTE), 106, 108, 287n21

National Urban League, 46, 162, 242

National Youth Administration (NYA), 201–202

Nettles, Stephen, 185

Nettles, William, 272

New Deal, 4, 25–26, 48, 65, 99, 136, 152, 201–202

Newsweek, 158

New York Post, 229, 246

New York State, 144, 147, 159, 188

New York Times, 154, 187, 197, 229, 242

Nicholson, Marguerite, 12

Niebuhr, Reinhold, 201

Niles, David, 73, 74, 138

Nixon, Richard M., 264, 265

North Carolina, 13, 103

Norton, David, 271

Nuremberg war crimes trials, 186

Nutter, Gillis, 258–59

Oak Hill Avenue AME Church, 90

Obama, Barack, 269

O'Daniel, W. Lee "Pappy," 150

O'Dwyer, William, 45

Ogletree, Charles, 258
Orson Welles Commentary, 39–44
Orson Welles' Sketch Book, 262

Palmer, Dwight R. G., 293*n*3
Parker, John J.:
    *Alston v. School Board of City of
    Norfolk* and, 103
    Briggs v. Elliott and, 220, 222, 229–38
    Brown v. Baskin and, 198
    death of, 265
    Elmore v. Rice and, 185–87
    racial issues, early statements on,
        103, 256
    Supreme Court, nomination to, 103
    Waring and, 185–86, 195, 196–98,
        254
Parks, Rosa, 201, 202
Parole Commission, U.S., 262
Paton, Alan, 246
Patterson, Robert, 32–33
Pearson, Drew, 89
Pearson, Levi, 217–18, 263
Pendergast, Jimmy, 64
Pendergast, Tom, 26, 64–66, 67
peonage, 187–88
Perry, Matthew J., 179–80, 229
Philadelphia, 190, 278*n*3
Philadelphia transit strike (1944), 278*n*3
Phillips, J. C., 208
Pittsburgh Courier, 25, 39, 129, 184–85,
    196, 201, 229, 241, 299*n*34
Plessy v. Ferguson, 10, 53, 101, 103, 108,
    147, 166, 167, 176, 178–79, 213–17,
    220, 222, 224–25, 233, 237–38,
    241, 243, 245, 246, 255, 256
poll taxes, 11, 26, 146, 150, 152, 176
Poston, Ted, 246
Potsdam Conference (1945), 70
Powell, C. B., 45, 46, 85, 90–91
President's Committee on Civil Rights,
    4–5, 73–74, 137–41, 143, 145–50,
    165, 168, 198, 251–52, 292*n*39

Progressive Party, 155
public opinion polls, 152, 157, 158

Quarles, H. E., 19–20, 126

Randolph, A. Philip, 26, 129, 292*n*39
Rankin, John E., 43, 209–10
Rayburn, Sam, 69, 159, 210
Reconstruction, 50–53, 176, 201
Reconstruction Acts, 51
Redfield, Robert, 236
Reflections of a Heart (Roberts), 261
"Reflections on the Loss of a Friend"
    (Clark), 264–65
Republican Party, 28, 50, 65, 135–37,
    144, 152, 153
restrictive covenants, 147, 165–66,
    169
Richards, James, 208–209
Richland County School District One,
    106–10
Riley, Joseph, 269
Rivera, Alexander, 299*n*34
Rivers, Mendel, 150, 194–95, 208,
    209–10, 212, 266, 303*n*33
Roberts, Christopher, 261
Roberts, Ernest W., 156–57, 252
Robeson, Paul, 280*n*1
Robinson, Jack Roosevelt "Jackie,"
    11–12, 147–48, 175
Robinson, Spottswood, 224–25
Rogers, Fred S., 82, 115, 116–17,
    122–23, 127, 129, 130, 262,
    283*n*16
Rogers, Joseph, 221–22, 265
Rogers, Tom, 184
Roosevelt, Eleanor, 109, 141, 201,
    202
    civil rights advocacy of, 25–26, 156
    Truman informed of FDR's death
        by, 69
    Waring, J. Waties and Elizabeth, and,
        205–206, 207

Roosevelt, Franklin D., 76, 136
  civil rights and, 25–26, 48, 144, 152,
    250, 278n3
  Truman selected as vice president by,
    67–69
Roosevelt, Franklin D., Jr., 138
Rowan, Carl, 203–204
Royall, Kenneth, 162, 163
Rule XXII, of U.S. Senate, 160

Sapp, Claud, 75–78, 80, 82, 91–92, 113,
    115, 116, 117, 118, 120, 124, 125,
    127–28, 129, 255–56, 261–62,
    284n31
Sarah Mae Flemming v. South Carolina
    Electric and Gas, 265
Second Circuit Court of Appeals, U.S.,
    264
segregation:
  of armed forces, 5, 146–47, 150,
    161–64, 169, 254–55, 292n39
  in bus transportation, 11, 12,
    14–15, 31, 56–57, 80, 99, 115,
    117, 127, 250–51, 258–59, 269,
    276n6
  in employment, 13, 67, 101, 102,
    149, 152, 160, 189, 278n3
  in housing, 148, 152, 165–66, 169
  in public accommodation, 3–4, 174,
    179, 180, 188, 214
  in public schools, 101, 104–10, 147,
    149, 152, 164, 179–80, 214, 217,
    222–23, 244, 255–58, 287n16
  in railroad transportation, 12, 166,
    204, 213, 226
  "separate but equal" doctrine for, 10,
    53, 101, 103, 108, 147, 166, 167,
    176, 178–79, 213–17, 220, 222,
    224–25, 233, 237–38, 241, 243,
    245, 246, 255, 256
  social science analysis of, 147,
    173–75, 225–27, 233–36, 238,
    245–46, 264

  southern support for, 4–5, 16, 25,
    38–39, 67, 80, 93–94, 101, 107,
    128–30, 136, 139–50, 180–84,
    200–201, 206–209
"Segregation Reconsidered: The
    'Separate but Equal' Failure," 147
Senate, U.S., 26, 56, 93–94, 99–100,
    135, 158, 160, 168, 191, 193–94,
    223, 245, 256, 266, 269
  Special Committee to Investigate the
    National Defense Program of, 67
Sengstacke, Robert, 162
Shealy, G. C., 126
Shelley v. Kraemer, 165–66, 198–99, 256
Shishkin, Boris, 138
Shull, Lancer, 269
Shull, Lynwood Lanier:
  blackjack used by, 17–21, 22, 31, 42,
    43, 56, 57–58, 78, 117, 120, 121,
    124, 125–26, 130, 146, 271–74,
    288n18, 290n36
  civil rights violations by, 56–59,
    82–83, 87, 113, 127–30
  culpability of, 58–59, 127–28
  FBI investigation of, 56–59, 75–80,
    82, 83, 115–16, 117, 122, 123,
    124, 125–26, 130, 131
  final years of, 261
  identification of, 39–44, 48–49, 56
  NAACP and prosecution of, 118–19,
    127, 130
  as "Officer X," 40–41
  popular support for, 119
  press coverage of, 43, 76, 77, 81, 82,
    90, 115, 118, 128, 129, 130
  prosecution of, 5, 82–83, 87, 113,
    114–32, 261–62, 269
  Woodard arrested by, 16–18, 42, 57,
    59 120–21, 124, 269
Shull, Lynwood Lanier, trial of, 75–85,
    87, 91–132, 135, 251, 255–56,
    258, 261, 284n31
  acquittal in, 127–28, 135

closing statements in, 127–28, 129
continuance issue in, 80, 81–82, 113, 190–91, 255–56, 284n31
cross-examinations in, 121, 122–23, 125
evidence in, 116–17, 122–23, 128, 130–31, 288n18
jury in, 118–19, 127–28, 131
Marshall and, 115, 119, 129
rebuttals in, 122–23
self-defense claim in, 129–30
Shull's testimony in, 125–26
Waring and, 5, 80–85, 91–92, 113–32, 171–72, 190–91, 199, 255–56, 284n31
witnesses in, 82, 115–16, 117, 121–26, 129
Woodard's testimony in, 120–21
Simkins, Modjeska, 25
Simple Justice (Kluger), 169, 263
Slaughter-House Cases, 176
slavery, 49–50, 94, 145, 173, 187–88, 253, 275
Smith, Ellison "Cotton Ed," 81, 97, 98–102, 193
Smith, Turner L., 58, 75–76, 77
Smith v. Allwright, 27, 71, 102, 177, 178, 181, 186–87
Snipes, Maceo, 34, 71
Solicitor General, U.S., 161, 164–67, 168, 256, 264
"Some Facts on Judge J. Waties Waring" (Rivers), 209–10
South, U.S.:
as Confederate states, 10, 50–51, 64, 94, 95, 142–43
Deep, 29, 82–83, 136, 140, 207, 216, 258
Jim Crow laws in, 4–5, 10–11, 25, 37, 54, 101, 132, 138, 145, 148, 171, 174, 175, 179–80, 224–25, 229, 235, 249–51, 253, 255

liberalism in, 101, 174–75, 200, 204–205, 207
lynchings in, 24–25, 26, 27, 30, 34–36, 46–47, 53, 57, 68, 71, 101, 114, 140, 145–46, 148, 150, 152, 157, 172, 254
mob violence in, 29–31, 32, 34–37, 46–47, 53, 54, 56, 57, 88–89, 136–37, 139, 140, 142, 145–46, 173
New, 200
political influence of, 10–11, 26–29, 48, 70–71, 76, 135–36, 141, 143–45, 150–53, 159, 179–85, 190–91, 209, 254, 256–57
racial violence in, 24–25, 29, 34–37, 48, 51–52, 114, 136, 171–72, 195–96, 219–20, 227–28, 251, 252–53
segregation supported by, 4–5, 16, 25, 38–39, 67, 80, 93–94, 101, 107, 128–30, 136, 139–50, 180–84, 200–201, 206–209
white supremacy in, 107, 180–84, 200–201, 206–209
see also specific cities and states
South Carolina, 29, 31, 33, 50, 51, 52, 75, 78–80, 109, 118–19, 127, 131, 134, 138, 156–57, 170, 177, 179–80, 187–88, 194, 199, 200–201, 212, 222–23, 229, 234–35, 239, 241, 243, 247, 253, 264, 268
South Carolina, University of, Law School of, 179–80
South Carolina Democratic Party, 76, 179–85, 256–57
South Carolina General Assembly, 105–106, 109, 180–81, 223, 230, 235
South Carolina House of Representatives, 207, 209

South Carolina Law Enforcement
Officers' Association, 79
South Carolina State College, 179
South Carolina Supreme Court
Historical Society, 268
Southern Christian Leadership
Conference (SCLC), 203
Southern Conference Educational
Fund, 201, 266
Southern Conference for Human
Welfare, 201
Southern Farmer, 202
Soviet Union, 23, 155, 175–76, 249
Speak Now Against the Day (Egerton),
149
Spicely, Booker T., 11
Spradley, Christian G., 269
Sprawls, J. M., 41
Stalin, Joseph, 70
Stark, Lloyd, 66, 67
State Educational Finance Commission,
224, 234
"Statement on the Race Problem in
South Carolina, A," 107
states' rights, 52, 150, 176
States' Rights Democratic Party
("Dixiecrats"), 150–53, 159,
190–91
Steiner, Leroy, 78
Stephenson, James, 30
Stevenson, William, 293n3
Stroud, Jennings, 57–58, 117, 122–23,
126–27, 129–30
"Suffrage in the Poll Tax States," 146
Summerton, S.C., 217–28, 233,
262
Supreme Court, U.S., 27–29, 53, 66, 68,
71, 99, 102, 103, 147, 164, 165,
166, 167, 176–77, 180, 186, 187,
194, 201, 210, 213–14, 223–25,
237–47, 255, 256, 264, 265,
266–67, 299n34; *see also specific
decisions*

Sweatt v. Painter, 166, 198–99, 213–14,
215, 236, 237
Symington, Stuart, 162

Talmadge, Eugene, 34, 36, 71, 118
taxation, 101, 222–23, 230, 241
Taylor County, Ga., 34, 71
Tennessee, 30–31, 74
Tennessee Valley Authority (TVA), 167
Texas, 157–58, 159, 213, 225
Texas Democratic Party, 27–28, 102,
177, 180
Third Circuit Court of Appeals, U.S.,
168, 294n13
Thirteenth Amendment, 53, 145
Thompson, Albert, 106–10
Thompson v. Gibbes, 106–10
Three-Fifths Compromise, 49
Thurmond, Strom, 154–55, 159,
190–91
Tilden, Samuel, 52
Tilly, Dorothy, 138, 148
Time, 67, 195, 198
Timmerman, George Bell, Jr., 266
Timmerman, George Bell, Sr., 80, 94,
100, 102, 106, 220, 222, 237, 256,
265–66
Tison, Sidney, 192
Tobias, Channing, 138
To Secure These Rights (1947), 145–49
Trager, Helen, 236
Truman, Bess, 65, 69, 156, 157
Truman, Harry S.:
armed forces desegregated by, 5, 150,
161–64, 169, 254–55, 292n39
black support for, 26–27, 64, 67,
143–44, 159, 168, 254–55,
292n47
civil rights supported by, 4–5, 26–27,
35–36, 39, 47, 48, 54, 67, 70–74,
81, 135–59, 165, 168, 189, 198,
199, 251–55, 266, 267, 292n39
Clifford memorandum to, 143–45

as Democratic leader, 65, 71,
143–44, 150–53, 267
executive orders of, 139, 150, 155,
161, 164, 167–68, 292n39
FBI investigations ordered by, 35–36
FDR supported by, 65, 66, 67–69,
154–55
first term of, 39, 69–71, 161
Missouri background of, 63, 64, 66,
142–43, 154
NAACP address of (1947), 140–43,
165–66, 183, 256
in Pendergast political machine, 26,
64–66, 67
personality of, 135–36
presidential campaign of (1948),
63–64, 138–39, 143–44, 190, 252,
292n47
as presiding judge, 64–65
press coverage of, 67, 141–43, 147
Republican opposition to, 152,
153–54, 160
second term of, 160–61
Senate campaign of (1934), 65–66,
156
Senate campaign of (1940), 66, 156
as senator, 63, 65–68, 69
southern opposition to, 150–53, 156,
159, 254
special civil rights messages of, 150,
153, 160–61
speeches of, 141–43, 149–50,
156–57, 160
State of the Union addresses of,
149–50, 160
Turnip Day ("do-nothing") Congress
opposed by, 152–56, 157
vice presidency, nomination to, 68–69
as vice president, 67–69, 152
as war veteran, 63, 64
"Whistle Stop Tour" of, 156–57
Woodard case as viewed by, 34, 73,
137, 156–57, 170, 199, 261

Truman, Margaret, 157
Truman, Martha Ellen "Mattie," 64
Truman, Mary Jane, 141

"understanding clauses," 11, 146, 276n2
United Nations, 70, 142, 265
United Nations Charter (1945), 70
United Nations International Bill of
Rights, 142
United States:
"American dilemma" in, 49, 173–75,
246, 265
democratic system of, 10, 49, 143,
149–50, 167, 173–76, 249–50, 255
federal government of, 52–53, 67,
109, 136, 139–42, 147, 150, 155,
164, 167–68, 199, 283n16
international reputation of, 24, 164,
174–76, 182–83, 185, 253
legal system of, see legal system
national security of, 103, 150, 155,
166–67
political vs. social equality in, 26, 107
United States v. Lynwood Lanier Shull,
see Shull, Lynwood Lanier, trial of
United States v. Wilhelm, 187–88
U.S. Attorney's Office, 55–56, 75–77,
97, 115, 117, 118
U.S. Marshals Service, 119, 190, 191,
194, 211–12

Veterans Administration, U.S., 169,
259, 260
Veterans Administration (VA) Hospital
(Columbia, S.C.), 21–23, 31,
56–57, 58, 59, 84–85, 121–22,
125, 130, 131, 271–74, 278n24
Vinson, Fred, 141, 166, 187, 194, 198,
244, 256
Virginia, 186, 243, 296n36

Wallace, Henry, 67–68, 69, 152, 155, 159
War Department, U.S., 32–33

Waring, Anna Waties, 95
Waring, Anne, 96
Waring, Annie Gammell, 96, 110–11,
112, 286n4
Waring, Benjamin, 94
Waring, Edward Perry, 95, 96
Waring, Elizabeth Avery Mills
Hoffman, 238, 242
and attack on Waring home, 211–12,
247
Briggs v. Elliott and, 229, 240
civil rights advocates, relationships
with, 200–204
criticism of, 207–208
divorce from Henry Hoffman, 110–12
illness and death of, 268
marriage to J. Waties Waring, 110–12,
185
Meet the Press appearance of, 207
praised by Benjamin Mays, 201
praised by Martin Luther King Jr.,
267
ostracism in Charleston of, 112, 185,
193
racial awakening of, 172–76, 181
Roosevelt, Eleanor, and, 205–206, 207
White, Walter and Poppy Cannon,
and, 204, 211, 247, 264
Woodard incident, impact of, 128,
131–32, 171
YWCA speech of, 206–208
Waring, J. Waties:
as assistant U.S. attorney, 113
in *Brown v. Baskin*, 189–99
black associates and friends of,
200–203
bodyguards for, 211–12, 253–54
in *Briggs v. Elliott*, 5, 217–20, 224–28,
237, 239–46, 250, 252–53,
255–58, 262–63, 264, 265,
299nn34, 35
as Charleston resident, 80–81,
94–100, 102, 110–12, 170, 185,

191, 200, 203–208, 226–27,
241–42, 252, 268–69
as city attorney, 97–98
civil rights views of, 93–102, 108–10,
113, 127, 131–32, 171–83, 199,
200–220, 241, 252–53, 264
cross burning to scare, 210–12
death of, 264–65, 268
as Democrat, 96, 97–99
disqualification motion against,
196–98
dissenting opinion of, 216–17,
238–41, 244, 246, 253, 255, 258,
267, 268, 269
divorce of, 110–12, 113
docket of, 100, 102
in *Duvall v. Seignous*, 102–106, 109–10
in *Elmore v. Rice*, 179–87, 189–99
FDR supported by, 98, 99, 100
as federal judge, 80–81, 93–94,
99–100, 110, 112, 184–85, 192,
194–95, 198–99, 211–12, 238,
253–58
first marriage of, 110–11
Franklin Delano Roosevelt Award
given to, 202, 204
as gradualist, 93–94, 108–109, 113,
175, 204–205, 215–20, 241
grave site of, 268
impeachment movement against,
193–95, 201, 207–10, 211, 212,
296n36
injunctions issued by, 190, 191–98,
235
"J. Waties Waring and the Dissent
That Changed America"
conference (2011), 268
J. Waties Waring Judicial Center,
269
later years of, 263, 264, 267–69
law practice of, 95–96
marriage of, 96, 110–12, 113,
171–72, 185

Marshall and, 104–106, 198, 210, 215–30, 243, 247, 255, 299nn34, 35
NAACP and, 94, 102, 110, 183, 204, 215–30, 239–40, 245, 258–59, 268, 269
in New York City, 200, 204, 210, 241–42, 247, 256–57, 264, 267–68
press coverage of, 183–84, 187, 191, 192, 193–97, 198, 201, 203–204, 207, 210–11, 229, 241, 242, 299n34
racism as viewed by, 113, 131–32
reputation of, 193–95, 197, 198–99, 241–42, 256–58, 267–69, 296n36
retirement of, 241–43, 247, 266, 267–68
second marriage of, 110–12, 113
social ostracism of, 111–12, 185, 191, 192, 203–12, 213, 241–42
southern background of, 94–95, 104, 112, 171–72, 200–204, 244, 253–54, 286n4
speeches of, 206, 214, 254, 256–57
statue of, 268–69
in *Thompson* case, 106–10
on three-judge panel, 216–20, 222, 224, 225, 229, 236–37, 243–44, 255, 257, 299n34
Truman and, 199, 241–42
in *United States v. Lynwood Shull*, 5, 80–85, 91–92, 113–32, 171–72, 190–91, 199, 255–56, 284n31
in *United States v. Wilhelm*, 187–88
white opposition to, 100–101, 109–10, 127, 181, 183–84, 192–97, 253–57
Woodard case and, 170, 171, 199, 261
in *Wrighten v. Board of Trustees of the University of South Carolina*, 178–79
Waring, Thomas, Sr., 95, 97

Waring, Thomas R., Jr., 184
Warren, Earl, 244–45, 247
Washington Post, 33
Waties, Thomas, 94–95
Weeks, Odell, 41
Welles, Orson, 39–44, 46, 81, 85, 89, 137–38, 262
Wells, H. G., 39–40
Weston, Francis H., 97
White, Poppy Cannon, 204, 207, 211, 246, 261
White, Walter:
    Columbia, Tenn., incident and, 31, 71
    death of, 263
    as NAACP executive secretary, 27, 39, 68
    Moore's Ford incident and, 36
    presidential committee on civil rights and, 73, 137–38
    Truman and, 27, 70, 73, 137–38, 141–42, 144, 149, 183, 251, 261, 266, 303n33
    Waring, J. Waties and Elizabeth, and, 204, 207, 211–12, 215–16, 246–47
    Welles and, 39–40
    Woodard and, 32–34, 39–41, 73, 86, 89, 90–91
Whitehead, Matthew, 225, 231–32, 246
White House Conference on Children and Youth, 226
"white riots," 30–31, 71, 72, 79–80
Wilhelm, John, 187–88
Williams, Aubrey, 201–202, 214, 240, 266
Williams, Franklin, 31–32, 89, 90, 92, 115, 116–17, 119, 122–23, 126, 128, 215, 261, 276n6
Williams v. Mississippi, 11, 53, 176
Willkie, Wendell, 109
Wilson, Charles E., 137, 138
Woodard, George, 259, 261
Woodard, Isaac, III, 259

Woodard, Isaac, Jr.:
   affidavit of, 31–33, 40–42
   arrest of, 15–18, 29–30, 42, 57, 59
      120–21, 124, 269
   in Batesburg, S.C., 4–5, 14–22, 32,
      41–44, 57–59, 77, 78, 80, 88,
      117–18, 123, 126, 258, 261, 269
   beating and blinding of, 4–5, 9–23,
      31–34, 56–59, 72, 73, 84–85, 86,
      88, 90–91, 115–18, 120, 121–25,
      129–30, 137, 170, 250–51, 252,
      258–61, 269, 271–74, 288n18,
      290n36
   bilateral phthisis bulbi diagnosis for,
      22, 23, 57, 130
   blackjack used against, 17–21, 22,
      31, 42, 43, 56, 57–58, 78, 117,
      120, 121, 124, 125–26, 130, 146,
      271–74, 288n18, 290n36
   Bronx residence of, 23, 31, 56, 85,
      91, 260
   in bus incident, 57–59, 88, 115–16,
      117, 120–21, 123, 127, 250–51,
      269
   celebrity of, 44–46, 85, 91, 258–61
   civil rights of, 56–59, 82–83, 87, 113,
      127–30
   death of, 260
   disability benefits for, 169, 259, 260,
      272–73, 278n24
   disorderly conduct charge against,
      15, 58, 59, 116, 117, 120, 123,
      124–25, 130
   family of, 12–13, 22–23, 34
   FBI field reports on, 15, 17, 18–19,
      42–44, 56–59, 116, 273, 274
   finances of, 22–23, 85–91, 258–59
   fine paid by, 19–20, 120, 121, 125
   forensic analysis of, 23, 131, 271–74,
      290n36
   fund-raising benefit concert for,
      44–46, 85, 91, 259
   grave site of, 260
   guilty verdict for, 20, 124–25, 126
   in jail, 18–20, 120, 123–25, 269
   later years of, 258–61
   medical evaluations of, 20–21, 23,
      56–57, 58, 59, 84–85, 117–18,
      121–26, 130–31, 271–74, 288n18,
      290n36
   NAACP representation of, 29–34,
      39–44, 72, 79, 81, 85–91, 215,
      258–59, 261, 272–73, 276n6,
      302n10
   pension benefits of, 22, 34, 84, 85,
      86, 91
   press and radio coverage of, 18, 30,
      32, 44, 81 85, 138, 259–60, 262,
      276n6
   public support for, 33–34, 44–49, 58,
      85–91
   speaking tour of, 46, 85–92
   testimony of, 113, 120–21
   Truman's interest in, 34, 73, 137,
      156–57, 170, 199, 261
   as veteran, 4–5, 13–17, 56–57, 73,
      84, 85, 116, 120, 131, 250–51,
      278n24
   witnesses for, 42, 57–58
   X-rays taken of, 22, 272, 273–74,
      290n36
Woodard, Isaac, Sr., 12–13
Woodard, Rosa Scruggs, 14, 22–23, 85
Woodard, Sarah, 12–13
Woodward, C. Vann, 169
Works Progress Administration
   (WPA), 201–202
World War I, 25, 63, 64, 137, 156
World War II, 3, 9–14, 16, 23, 25, 39,
   53, 54, 63, 69–70, 175, 223, 249
Wright, Fielding, 150, 154
Wrighten v. Board of Trustees of the
   University of South Carolina, 178–79
Wyche, Charles Cecil, 102

Young, Robert, 260, 272